STATISTICS

To Judy, a never-ending source of inspiration and patience.

Richard M. Jaeger

STATISTICS
A Spectator Sport
Second Edition

SAGE PUBLICATIONS
The International Professional Publishers
Newbury Park   London   New Delhi

For information address:

SAGE Publications, Inc.
2455 Teller Road
Newbury Park, California 91320

SAGE Publications Ltd.
6 Bonhill Street
London EC2A 4PU
United Kingdom

SAGE Publications India Pvt. Ltd.
M-32 Market
Greater Kailash I
New Delhi 110 048 India

Printed in the United States of America

Library of Congress Cataloging-in-Publication Data

Jaeger, Richard M.
    Statistics: a spectator sport / Richard M. Jaeger. — 2nd ed.
        p.   cm.
    Includes bibliographical references (p. 364) and index.
    ISBN 0-8039-3420-3. — ISBN 0-8039-3421-1 (pbk.)
    1. Statistics.   I. Title.
QA276.12.J33   1990.
001.4'22 — dc20   90-8580
                                                                        CIP

FOURTH PRINTING, 1991

Sage Production Editor: Susan McElroy

Contents

Preface

Like its progenitor, this edition of *Statistics: A Spectator Sport* is grounded in two premises: First, that statistics abound in the lives of researchers, educators, sports fans, managers, political analysts, business persons, poll watchers, and citizens to the degree that they should be *understood* by almost every educated adult. Second, that it is unnecessary to compute statistics in order to understand them. In keeping with these premises, we have emphasized the illustration and description of statistical procedures and applications, and scrupulously avoided the use of symbols and equations. Statistical concepts are described fully; statistical computations are avoided just as assiduously. By reading this book you will learn the concepts underlying the content of a full year of graduate statistics courses as taught in departments of psychology, schools of education, departments of sociology, and departments of political science throughout the United States. The knowledge you gain will equip you to be a more astute reader of research papers and evaluation reports in a wide variety of social and behavioral science fields, including education. If you want to learn to produce statistics, you will have to turn elsewhere, although you will find that beginning with this book will help you immeasurably in understanding what you're doing before you become mired in the z's, μ's, Σ's, y's, and π's of more conventional statistics books.

This edition of *Statistics: A Spectator Sport* contains new content, and several new features. Some fundamental procedures from John Tukey's exploratory data analysis have been added to the chapter on tabulation and portrayal of data. The chapter on measurement has been brought up to date, consistent with the latest edition of the *Standards for Educational and Psychological Testing*. An entirely new chapter containing a discussion of threats to the internal and external validity of conclusions that derive from flaws and limitations of research designs will enable readers to examine critically the research and evaluation studies they encounter. As its name suggests, the content of this particular chapter is essential to those who want an answer to the fundamental question, "Can you trust the conclusions?" New, updated examples of research applications can be

ix

found in every chapter of the book. As in the earlier edition, examples of research applications have been gleaned from the files of the Educational Resources Information Centers (ERIC). The examples illustrate use of the statistical procedures described in each chapter of the book in actual research studies. The glossary of statistical terms that follows Chapter 15 has been expanded substantially. Finally, an unfortunate omission in the first edition of *Statistics:A Spectator Sport* has been rectified: this edition contains a complete index.

It is a pleasure to acknowledge the diligence and inspiration of several important contributors to this book. Gingerlee Ingels, Sandra Drury, and Virginia Kelly, graduate students at the University of North Carolina at Greensboro, spent countless hours in the university library, poring through ERIC files in search of just the right illustrations of the two-sample *t*-test, one-factor analysis of variance, and the balance of the statistical procedures described in this edition. Theirs was a labor of love that somehow survived the finicky demands of a taskmaster who sometimes understood what he *didn't* want more clearly than he knew what he wanted. As always, Judy M. Jaeger contributed to this book in far more ways than can be told—from sustaining the author to soothing the text. My debt to her is joyfully acknowledged, although it will never be paid. I would also like to recognize the contributions of RaVonda Dalton-Rann, a graduate student at the University of North Carolina at Greensboro who provided an insightful critical reading of all new material in this edition, and of my wonderful editor C. Deborah Laughton of Sage Publications, who provided just the right mixture of encouragement, cajoling, and friendly demands to keep me within reasonable sight of my production deadline.

Richard M. Jaeger
Greensboro, North Carolina
November, 1989

Preface to the
First Edition

It is virtually impossible to avoid statistics as a spectator sport. Statistics are everywhere—in baseball and football scores, in weather reports, in reports on stock and bond markets, and in descriptions of election prospects and outcomes. In addition, statistics form the bedrock of empirical research and evaluation in fields as diverse as education, the social sciences, and quantum physics. Certainly, if you hope to be an intelligent consumer of research in any of these fields, you must *understand* some statistics.

This book is designed for those who simply want to understand statistics, as they appear in the research and evaluation reports of educators, social and behavioral scientists, business and governmental reports, and so on. Those who want to learn how to *compute* statistics should seek some other text because, unlike most other books on statistics, this one has *absolutely no equations*. We have eliminated equations so as to avoid the frequent tendency of symbols to *obscure* the understanding of what is generally a very logical and straightforward subject area, especially for those with little mathematical expertise. By reading this book you will learn what statistics are, what they mean, and how they are used and interpreted. If you want to become an expert producer of statistics, you might start with this book, but you'll then have to move on to other texts that abound with x's, y's, and a lot of Greek. We think you'll find those books easier to handle once you've been through this one.

The first four chapters of the book are concerned with topics that fall under the general heading of *descriptive statistics*. These include methods for organizing, tabulating, and graphing data; statistics that indicate the center of a distribution of scores (measures of central tendency); statistics that indicate the spread of a distribution of scores (measures of variability); and statistics that indicate the degree of relationship between two or more variables (measures of correlation). The fifth chapter is devoted to the basic measurement concepts of validity, reliability, and transformed score scales. Chapters 6 through 8 [7 through 9 in this edition] introduce the fundamental concepts of inferential statistics: estimation and hypothesis testing, and provide a conceptual framework for the remainder of the book. Chapters 9 through 14 [10 through 15 in this edition] describe applications of inferential statistics to a wide range of research and evaluation problems, beginning with inferences concerning a single population average, and ending with problems involving the prediction of one variable from a number of other variables (multiple regression analysis). The analysis of covariance and factor analysis are also described and illustrated in the final chapter.

To aid understanding and interpretation of statistics in the context of research and evaluation, we have provided detailed illustrations of each of the inferential statistical procedures discussed in Chapters 9 through 14 [10 through 15 in this edition]. As illustrative material, since everyone has been through and continues to have a stake in the educational system, we have used excerpts from educational research and evaluation studies contained in the computerized files of the Educational Resources Information Centers (ERIC). The reader will therefore encounter real research results in this text, and will learn how those results can be interpreted and used.

Although the title page bears the name of a single author, this book reflects the contributions of a great many people. It was first conceived as a joint work with Dr. Alexander Law of the California Department of Education. Dr. Law provided initial drafts of a number of chapters on descriptive statistics, and helped to shape the final text through many helpful and enjoyable conversations. Ms. Judy M. Jaeger and Dr. Donata Renfrow of Georgia State University edited major portions of the text, and made countless excellent suggestions on substance as well as editorial style. They deserve credit for resulting clarity, but certainly, none of the blame for remaining opacity. I am truly grateful for their help. Ms. Emily Barnes spent countless hours in the university library, digging for appropriate examples in the ERIC files. Her work was truly heroic. Participants in Nova University's National Ed.D. Program in Educational Leadership proofread major portions of an early draft of the book, and provided a number of helpful suggestions on layout and substance. Their assistance is gratefully acknowledged. It is unlikely that this book would have been written without the encouragement and helpful prodding of Dr. Michael Scriven of the University of San Francisco. The title and typesetting are his, and a detailed editing job in between.

Richard M. Jaeger
Greensboro, North Carolina
August, 1983

1.

Making Numbers Make Sense

Introduction and Overview

There are hundreds of statistics books in libraries and bookstores. When they were written, the author of every one thought his or hers was unique, and probably better than all the others, at least for some purposes. This book is different from the others in one obvious way, and that difference makes it better for some purposes.

Our statistics book doesn't have any equations in it. We don't know of any other statistics book that can meet that claim. If you want to know how to *compute* statistics, not having any equations is a serious limitation, and we recommend that you go to your bookstore or library and get someone else's book. We're particularly fond of Glass and Hopkins's treatise on statistics for those working in the fields of education and psychology (1984). It is clear, almost always correct, and contains a wealth of information. But if you just want to know how to *understand* statistics, as you will find them in research reports, journal articles, and evaluation reports, stick with us. Through diligent study of this book, paying particular attention to our real-life excerpts from research and evaluation reports, you'll learn a great deal about what statistics say and what they mean. And you can leave the computing to people who have the time, the need, and the inclination.

Many people find serious statistics scary or complicated. Actually, statistics are just the same friendly sort of numbers you've been dealing with all your life. They're things like baseball

1

players' batting averages, the chances of rain tomorrow (when it's expressed as a number), the odds on a Kentucky Derby favorite, the total rainfall during the month of May, and the Dow Jones stock average, to name just a few. The word *statistics* comes from the Latin root "status," which suggests that statistics should be useful in describing how things are.

Every discipline has its own set of concepts, terms and specialized language, and the field of statistics is no exception. Necessarily then, much of the early part of this book will consist of introducing concepts and giving their definitions in the context of problems and practical examples. We begin with four chapters on statistical concepts that are used to *describe*—the heart of **descriptive statistics**. We then spend a chapter on important things to know about **tests and measurements**. This is particularly important for people who work in education, psychology, or other social or behavioral sciences; measurement is especially tricky when people are being measured. The resulting numbers don't always mean what the measurer expects. It's useful to know where the pitfalls are, and in fact there are special statistics that describe the quality of measurement. Our sixth chapter will help you figure out whether you can trust the results and conclusions of a research or evaluation study. You'll find that an appropriate level of trust depends on how the study was designed and how well it was conducted. Finally, if you stick with this book to the end, you'll find chapters on **inferential statistics**—a set of statistical procedures that allows a researcher to go beyond a group that's been measured and make statements about the characteristics of a much larger group, just as the Gallup poll does.

You've probably noticed that we've printed some words in **boldface** type, and you've speculated that we think those are important terms. You're right. In fact, we think they're so important that we've included them in a glossary. Whenever you encounter a **boldface** term, throughout the remainder of the book, just look in the Glossary to find out what it means.

In the remainder of this chapter we begin our presentation of descriptive statistics. We start with a discussion of tabular arrangements of numbers (these numbers describe some facts about the world, so they are called **data**; one such fact is a "datum" and the plural is "data"), and we end by considering the pictorial display of data in **graphs**. In all of these procedures, as will be true

TABLE 1.1: Achievement Test Scores for a Class of Ninth-Grade Students

42	78	63	37	42	45	52	52
60	26	35	35	83	61	49	58
70	39	61	63	65	65	39	79
46	57	33	72	46	71	58	40
57	29	72	65	49	52	57	60

throughout the book, we'll devote far more attention to what the tables and graphs *mean* than to the way they were *created*. Statisticians *create* them—you have to *understand* them.

Interpreting Data Tables

Table 1.1 contains the test scores earned by 40 students who completed an 85-item mathematics achievement test at the end of their ninth-grade school year. Their scores are not arranged in any particular order. We've listed the scores in eight different columns only so the table will fit nicely on the page. These data present just the kind of problem that descriptive statistics is designed to handle—how do you say something enlightening about a mass of numbers; how do you "boil it down"? (Remember, there might be 4,000 or 4,000,000 scores instead of 40.)

What can you tell about the performance of this group of students from this arbitrarily arranged list of their scores? How easy is it to figure out what the highest score was? Can you readily find the lowest score? Did the scores tend to bunch up in a particular score interval (say, between 50 and 70)? Overall, were there more high scores or more low scores? With enough effort, you could answer all of these questions. But you'd have to spend a great deal of time going over the numbers, and errors would be quite likely.

We've used the data in Table 1.1 to construct a number of tables and graphs that make it far easier to understand how the 40 students performed on the test. These tables and graphs are typical of those you'll find in countless research and evaluation reports, and in dozens of journal articles and statistics books.

Making sense of the data in Table 1.1 is greatly assisted by creating a new table in which the scores are arranged in order, from highest to lowest. Table 1.2 contains the results of this simple

TABLE 1.2: Achievement Test Raw Scores and Corresponding Ranks for a Class of Ninth-Grade Students

Raw Score	Rank	Raw Score	Rank
83	1	57	20
79	2	52	23
78	3	52	23
72	4.5	52	23
72	4.5	49	25.5
71	6	49	25.5
70	7	46	27.5
65	9	46	27.5
65	9	45	29
65	9	42	30.5
63	11.5	42	30.5
63	11.5	40	32
61	13.5	39	33.5
61	13.5	39	33.5
60	15.5	37	35
60	15.5	35	36.5
58	17.5	35	36.5
58	17.5	33	38
57	20	29	39
57	20	26	40

procedure, together with a useful description of the original scores in terms of their **ranks**. A table that lists scores from highest to lowest is called an **ordered array**. Table 1.2 is an ordered array that also contains an associated listing of score ranks.

Table 1.2 contains two sets of columns, each headed "Raw Score" and "Rank." The right-hand set of columns is merely a continuation of the left-hand set. We've used two sets of columns instead of one, just to get the table to fit nicely on a page.

The Raw Score columns list each of the 40 scores shown in Table 1.1. These are called **raw scores** because the data have not been manipulated or changed in any way. Each number represents a score, just as it was originally measured. We'll get to the ranks in just a moment.

Looking at the ordered listing of raw scores in Table 1.2, it is very easy to answer several of the questions we posed above. First, the highest scoring student earned a score of 83. That's not bad on an 85-item test! Second, the score of the lowest scoring student was only 26. You can tell immediately that the scores of the 40 students are spread out over a wide range. It seems that most of the students scored in the 40s, 50s, and 60s, but it's not easy to tell whether the scores are bunched up within that range of values. Because each of the Raw Score columns lists 20 scores, and the score value 57 falls at the bottom of one and the top of the other, it appears that half the students earned scores above 57, while half scored below 57. Notice how much you can tell about the students' performance, just by looking at an ordered array!

The Rank columns are very useful for interpreting the performance of an individual student, compared to the performance of everyone else in the group. It should be obvious that the student who scored highest was assigned a rank of 1, the student who scored the next highest was assigned a rank of 2, and so on. That simple rule works well until we get to the two values of 4.5 in the left-hand Rank column. Notice that two students earned scores of 72 on the mathematics test. It wouldn't make sense to say that one of those students ranked above the other, since they both earned the same score. So what ranks do we give them? Informally, we'd say "they were both 4th"; but statisticians use a slight variation of this. They first figure out what their ranks would have been, had they earned different scores. Suppose one had earned a score of 72 and the other a score of 71.5. Then the student who earned the 72 would have been assigned a rank of 4 and the student who earned the 71.5 would have been assigned a rank of 5. But since they earned the same score (72), we assign them both the average of the ranks they would have received, had their scores been different. In this case, the average of 4 and 5 is $(4 + 5)/2 = 4.5$. Then the student who earned a score of 71 was assigned a rank of 6, since five students earned scores that were above that student's 71.

In assigning ranks to the three students who earned scores of 65, we applied the same logic we used for the two students who earned scores of 72. Had the three students with scores of 65 all earned scores that differed slightly from each other, the highest scoring student would have received a rank of 8, the next highest a rank of 9, and the lowest scoring a rank of 10. Since they all earned the same score, we give each of them the average of the ranks they would have received, had their scores been different. The average of 8, 9, and 10 is $(8 + 9 + 10)/3 = 27/3 = 9$. True, only seven students did better than any of these, so you would informally say they were "all 8th." But they each have fewer students *below* them than someone who came in 8th without being tied. So we split the difference and average the ranks of those who tie.

Ranks allow you to interpret a score **normatively**. That's a fancy way of saying that ranks tell you how high a person's score is, *compared to the others* in the group in which that person was tested or measured. Notice that the student who scored 40 on the test was assigned a rank of 32. Therefore, the student with a score of 40 (since no one else tied that student's score) is 32 students from the top; 31 of the 40 students in the group outscored that student. Compared to his or her classmates, the student with a score of 40 didn't make an impressive showing on the mathematics test.

When you look at a person's rank on a test or other measurement, you must be careful to remember that his or her rank is group-dependent. The same person might have a very different rank on the test, when compared with a different group. Compared to a group of 39 mathematics wizards, the student with a rank of 1 in Table 1.2 might have received a rank of 20 or 30. This would have happened if most of the mathematics wizards had earned perfect scores on the 85-item test.

Now let's change topics. Consider one of the important truisms of statistics: The more numbers a person has to think about at the same time, the more difficult it is to figure out what those numbers mean. This argues strongly for summarizing data as much as possible. The tables we'll consider next are motivated by the desire for summarization.

One way to summarize a group of scores is by eliminating those that are redundant. Table 1.3 is an example of something called a **frequency distribution**, in which this has been done.

Notice that Table 1.3 consists of two columns, one headed "Score" and the other headed "Frequency." The Score column contains a list of each of the score values that appeared in the original data in Table 1.1. Even though there were two scores of 72 in the original data, the score value 72 is listed only once. This is what we mean by eliminating redundant scores. To keep track of how many times each score value appeared in the original data, we show this number in the Frequency column. Since there was only one score of 83 in the original data, its frequency is 1. Likewise, since they appeared only once, scores of 79 and 78 receive

TABLE 1.3: Frequency Distribution of Achievement Test Scores for a Class of Ninth-Grade Students

Score	Frequency	Score	Frequency
83	1	52	3
79	1	49	2
78	1	46	2
72	2	45	1
71	1	42	2
70	1	40	1
65	3	39	2
63	2	37	1
61	2	35	2
60	2	33	1
58	2	29	1
57	3	26	1

frequency values of 1. The score value 72 receives a frequency of 2 because there were two 72s in the original data.

Instead of having 40 scores to consider, as was true in Table 1.2, in Table 1.3 we have only 24 unique score values and their associated frequencies. This kind of summarization has advantages beyond a mere reduction in the number of scores to be considered. From Table 1.3 you can get an impression of the "shape" of the distribution of students' scores. Notice that most of the scores with frequencies larger than 1 fall in the middle of the distribution. In contrast, almost all of the very high scores and very low scores have frequency values of 1. From this you can conclude that the students' scores tend to bunch up in the middle of the distribution. Looking at the data in Table 1.3, it is also easy to tell which score values occur most often; the values 65, 57, and 52 all have frequencies of 3. All of the other score values occur less frequently.

Additional summarization of the scores in Table 1.2 is provided by the **grouped frequency distribution** shown in Table 1.4. "Grouping" further reduces the number of separate lines on the table, as you can see; Table 1.3, by contrast, is an **ungrouped frequency distribution**.

To construct Table 1.4, we've grouped the original scores into categories of "Score Classes." We then counted the number of scores that fell into each score class, and listed these counts in the column headed "Frequency." Thus two score values (one 26 and

TABLE 1.4: Grouped Frequency Distribution of Achievement Test Scores for a Class of Ninth-Grade Students

Score Class	Frequency	Score Class	Frequency
80 – 84	1	50 – 54	3
75 – 79	2	45 – 49	5
70 – 74	4	40 – 44	3
65 – 69	3	35 – 39	5
60 – 64	6	30 – 34	1
55 – 59	5	25 – 29	2

one 29) fell into the score class 25-29; one score (the score of 33) fell into the score class 30-34; and so forth.

By constructing Table 1.4, we have further reduced the number of score values that must be considered when interpreting the test performances of the 40 students. Instead of the 40 scores of Table 1.2 or the 24 unique score values of Table 1.3, we need consider only 12 score classes and their associated frequencies. Our goal of summarization is well served by this reduction.

From Table 1.4 it is easy to get a picture of the overall test performance of the group of 40 students. For example, notice that five students earned scores between 55 and 59, and that an additional six students earned scores between 60 and 64. Adding these frequencies together, we can say that 11 of the 40 students (better than a fourth of them) earned test scores between 55 and 64. Doing more of the same kind of data sleuthing, we can add the frequencies 2, 1, and 5 associated with the lowest score classes 25-29, 30-34, and 35-39, respectively. From this total frequency of 8, we can say that 8 out of 40 (or 20%) of the students earned test scores that were below 39 on the 85-item test. Depending on our expectations for student performance, this might be a distressing finding.

Although grouped frequency distributions afford the advantage of summarization, they have an associated disadvantage. The price of summarization is losing the detailed information about the original data that is provided by an ungrouped frequency distribution. For example, had we begun with Table 1.4, and not had Tables 1.1 through 1.3 available, we could have concluded that two students earned test scores *somewhere* between 25 and 29, one student scored somewhere between 30 and 34, and so forth. However, we would not have known whether both of the students who scored between 25 and 29 earned scores of 25, or whether one scored 26 and the other 28, or whether both scored 29. Likewise, we would not have known whether the one student with a score in the 30-34 class scored at the top or the bottom of that class. This detailed information is sacrificed in order to summarize a set of data in a grouped frequency distribution. For some purposes the sacrifice is serious; for others, it is not.

Rules for constructing grouped frequency distributions are arbitrary, and vary from one statistics book to another. One author suggests that a grouped frequency distribution should have between 10 and 20 score classes. Another suggests that 12 to 15 score classes are appropriate. All of these rules are attempts to compromise between the desire to summarize data and the desire to retain as much detailed information as possible. The greater the number of score classes, the more detailed information about the original data is retained. The smaller the number of score classes, the more the data have been simplified. Our experience suggests that about 12 score classes often do the trick.

Two additional data displays that are used quite often in research and evaluation reports are illustrated in Table 1.5. This table combines the grouped frequency distribution of Table 1.4 together with a **cumulative frequency distribution** and a **cumulative percent frequency distribution**; long names, but easy to understand.

The cumulative frequency distribution part of this table consists of the columns headed "Score Class" and "Cumulative Frequency." Let's first consider where the numbers in the Cumulative Frequency column came from, and then we'll discuss the way they can be used.

Notice that the cumulative frequency associated with the *bottom* score class 25-29 is equal to the frequency of that score class, namely 2. The frequency of 2 means that two students scored somewhere between 25 and 29. The reason we say that the students scored in this interval is because, in scoring the mathematics achievement test, we count the number of items a student answered correctly. The only possible scores are, therefore, 0, 1, 2, and so on, up to a maximum score of 85.

Even if we were able to measure students' mathematics achievement more precisely than this, say as precisely as we wanted, we could still—for convenience—report a student's score

TABLE 1.5: Grouped Frequency Distribution, Cumulative Frequency Distribution and Cumulative Percent Frequency Distribution of Achievement Test Scores for a Class of Ninth-Grade Students

Score Class	Frequency	Cumulative Frequency	Cumulative Percent Frequency
80 – 84	1	40	100
75 – 79	2	39	97.5
70 – 74	4	37	92.5
65 – 69	3	33	82.5
60 – 64	6	30	75
55 – 59	5	24	60
50 – 54	3	19	47.5
45 – 49	5	16	40
40 – 44	3	11	27.5
35 – 39	5	8	20
30 – 34	1	3	7.5
25 – 29	2	2	5

to the nearest whole number, by "rounding" their actual scores in the traditional way. This means that any student who had a mathematics achievement level between 28.5 and 29.4999999 (for example) would have a reported whole-number score of 29. Any student who had a mathematics achievement level between 24.5 and 25.4999999 would have a reported whole-number score of 25. Normally, numbers ending in fractional values of 0.5 or above are rounded up, and numbers ending in fractional values below 0.5 are rounded down. Reasoning in this way, we could say that the score class 25-29 really represents mathematics achievement levels between 24.5 and 29.5. These values are called the **real limits** of the score class 25-29. The value 24.5 is called the **lower real limit**, and the value 29.5 is called the **upper real limit**.

Now we can give an exact definition of the numbers in the Cumulative Frequency column of Table 1.5. Beginning with the value 2 associated with the 25-29 score class, the numbers in this column correspond to the numbers of students who earned scores at or below the upper real limit of each score class. Using this explanation, we can see that the table says two students earned scores at or below 29.5, three students earned scores at or below 34.5, eight students earned scores at or below 39.5, 11 students earned scores at or below 44.5, and so on. Finally, the numbers in the Cumulative Frequency column indicate that all 40 students earned scores at or below 84.5, since the largest cumulative frequency is 40.

Where did the numbers in the Cumulative Frequency column come from? Let's illustrate. Looking at the previous table, you can see that two students scored in the 25-29 score class, and one student scored in the 30-34 score class; we merely add the 2 to the 1 to conclude that three students scored at or below the upper real limit of the 30-34 score class. The other numbers in the Cumulative Frequency column (called "cumulative frequencies") were found through similar logic.

The cumulative frequency distribution provides another useful way to depict the overall test performance of the group. Recall that the mathematics achievement test consisted of 85 items. Just by selecting a few values from the cumulative frequency distribution, we can get a pretty clear picture of the group's performance on this test. Notice that 11 of the 40 students earned scores of 44.5 or less. This means that more than a fourth of the students missed more than 40 of the items on the test. Three fourths of the students (30 out of 40) earned scores at or below 64.5. This means that three fourths of the students missed at least 20 of the 85 test items. Other cumulative frequencies could be interpreted similarly, but these two should give you an idea of the usefulness of the cumulative frequency distribution in summarizing a group of scores.

The right-most column in Table 1.5 lists "Cumulative Percent Frequency." Together with the Score Class column, the Cumulative Percent Frequency column forms a cumulative percent frequency distribution—another very useful data display. The cumulative percent frequencies were calculated simply by converting the cumulative frequencies to percentages of the total number of students in the group. For example, notice that the 60-64 score class has a cumulative frequency of 30 and a cumulative percent frequency of 75. The 75 was calculated as follows: The cumulative frequency of 30 was divided by the group size of 40: $30/40 = 0.75$. The resulting proportion (0.75) was then multiplied by 100 to convert it to a percentage (75%). From this figure we can see directly that 75% of the students in the group earned test scores at or below 64.5. Likewise, 20% of the group earned scores at or below 39.5; 40% of the group earned scores at or below 49.5; 60%

of the group earned scores at or below 59.5; and 92.5% of the group earned scores at or below 74.5. These statistics provide a very clear description of the test performance of the group of 40 students. In fact, you can probably get a better idea of the performance of the group from these five numbers than you could from the entire set of 40 scores shown in Tables 1.1 and 1.2. Typically, effective summarization of data enhances understanding.

In the late 1970s and early 1980s, John Tukey (1977) and others developed and popularized procedures for examining, representing, and summarizing data known as **exploratory data analysis** (EDA). EDA procedures emphasize visual display of a set of data, including the creation of tables that provide visual information. Among the most informative of these EDA methods is the **stem-and-leaf display**. Stem-and-leaf displays provide most of the advantages of grouped frequency distributions, since they allow a score distribution to be summarized, but they avoid the major disadvantage of a grouped frequency distribution, since all or almost all of the information in the original set of data is retained. Table 1.6 contains a stem-and-leaf display of the 40 achievement test scores that were introduced in Table 1.1.

In the stem-and-leaf display shown in Table 1.6, the numbers in the "Stem" column are values in the tens column of the original data. In other words, they represent the 20s through the 80s in the data. The numbers in the "Leaves" section of the table are values corresponding to the ones column of the original data. Taken together, the values in the Stem column and the Leaves represent every score in the original data. For example, the stem of 2 and the leaf of 6 form the data point 26, the stem of 2 and the leaf of 9 form the data point 29, the stem of 3 and the leaf of 3 form the data point 33, and so on, to the stem of 8 and the leaf of 3, which form the data point 83. So to find the value of an original data point, you merely take a stem value and place a leaf value to its immediate right. To let you know that the numbers in the Leaves portion of the display are values in the ones column, the information "Leaf Unit = 1" has been placed at the top of the table. Corresponding information should appear in every stem-and-leaf display you find in a research evaluation report. You can safely assume that the Stem values are ten times as large as the Leaf values; that is, if leaves have values from 0 through 9, then stems have values like 00, 10, 20, and so on.

TABLE 1.6: Stem-and-Leaf Display of Achievement Test Scores for a Class of Ninth-Grade Students

Stem	Leaves	(Leaf Unit = 1)
2	69	
3	355	
3	799	
4	022	
4	56699	
5	222	
5	77788	
6	001133555	
7	0122	
7	89	
8	3	

The shape of a distribution of scores is easily seen from a stem-and-leaf display. By looking at Table 1.6, we can see that the distribution tends to bunch up in the middle, and that most of the 40 students earned test scores between 45 and 65. In addition, it is easy to see that the lowest score was 26, the highest score was 83, and more students scored in the low 60s than in any other five-point interval. The data have been summarized, the shape of the score distribution has been portrayed visually, and no detailed information has been lost since we could list every score in the original distribution from the information given in Table 1.6.

If a stem-and-leaf display were to be constructed for a set of scores between 156 and 972, the scores might be rounded to the nearest tens digit. The stems then would be values in the hundreds column, and the Leaf Unit would equal ten. If this procedure were followed, 156 would be rounded to 160, and 972 would be rounded to 970. In the stem-and-leaf display, the original value of 156 would thus be represented by a stem of 1 and a leaf of 6; the original value of 972 would be represented by a stem of 9 and a leaf of 7. Although information in the ones column would be lost, the original data could be reproduced from the stem-and-leaf display, to the nearest value in the tens column.

Stem-and-leaf displays are becoming increasingly popular, and you will find them quite frequently in reports of applied research and evaluation studies in education and the social sciences. Although they're a bit mysterious to the uninitiated, they provide a wealth of succinct information to the literati (like you), who know how to read and interpret them.

A Picture Is Worth a Thousand Words— And at Least Ten Thousand Numbers

Tables are invaluable for communicating detailed information about a set of scores, but many people find it difficult to get the "big picture" from a table. To get an overall impression of the shape of a score distribution, or to get a quick idea of how several groups compare, there is no substitute for a **graph**. Graphs are irreplaceable tools in descriptive statistics. Personal computers and business computers are increasingly being used to display "graphics" (that is, graphs which summarize data) because graphs often are much easier to understand than even the best tables.

There are so many different types of graphs that it would be possible to devote an entire book to the subject. In fact, Mary Spear did essentially that in her 1952 volume entitled *Charting Statistics*, and Edward Tufte (1983) produced a brilliant volume on the power of visual display as a device for communicating quantitative information. We will confine our discussion to just a few of the more popular and useful types of graphs that you are likely to encounter in your study of research and evaluation reports. If you want more information, check with Spear and Tufte.

The **frequency polygon** shown in Figure 1.1 is a picture of the grouped frequency distribution in Table 1.4. When we drew the figure, we used the data in Table 1.4 as follows: First, we calculated the score value that would be right in the middle of each score class. For example, 27 is in the middle of the 25-29 score class, 32 is in the middle of the 30-34 score class, 37 is in the middle of the 35-39 score class, and so on. These middle score values are called the **midpoints** of the score classes. Next, we assumed that the score earned by every student who scored anywhere in a given score class fell at the midpoint of that score class. We then plotted the midpoints of each score class on the horizontal scale (called the *x*-axis or **abscissa**) of Figure 1.1, and the frequency values associated with each score class on the vertical scale (called the *y*-axis or ordinate) of Figure 1.1. Once we had constructed the horizontal and vertical scales, we plotted a point on the graph for each score class. Notice that there is a point just above the score value of 27 (the midpoint of the 25-29 score class) and just to the right of a frequency of 2. Similarly, there is a point just above the score value of 32 (the midpoint of the 30-34 score class) and to the right of a frequency of 1. Use the data in Table 1.4 to find each of the other points plotted in Figure 1.1.

Once the points were plotted, we connected adjacent points with straight lines, and then tied the resulting curve down at the ends by plotting one point at a score value of 22 and a frequency of zero, and another at a score value of 87 and a frequency of zero. The score values of these endpoints are equal to the midpoints of the score classes that would be just below, and just above, the lowest and highest score classes in Table 1.4. Since no students scored in these score classes, their frequencies would be zero.

Notice that the horizontal scale in Figure 1.1 is broken between 0 and 22. The figure contains two short diagonal lines to alert you to this fact. We broke the horizontal scale because the distance between 0 and 22 is not the same as the distance between 22 and 27, or the distance between any of the other plotted midpoints. In other words, the curve really doesn't start at zero. Since most of us expect the horizontal and vertical scales of a graph to cross at the zero-point, we must be warned so we won't be misled whenever a graph does not begin at zero.

Figure 1.1 does an excellent job of providing an overall impression of the test performance of the 40 ninth-grade students. We can see at a glance that their scores range from the low 20s to the high 80s. It is easy to see that more of them scored in a score class with a midpoint of 62 than in any other score class. The wide base of the peak that occurs at 62 tells us that many of the students scored in the 60s. The two smaller peaks below the highest one tell us that a number of the students scored in the high 30s and the high 40s as well. We can also see that the students' scores are spread out quite a bit across the middle of the distribution. No single score class has an extremely high frequency, compared to all of the others.

The **histogram** shown in Figure 1.2 is another popular way of graphing a grouped frequency distribution. To construct this graph we have again used the data in Table 1.4. Instead of plotting the midpoints of the score classes on the horizontal axis, we plot-

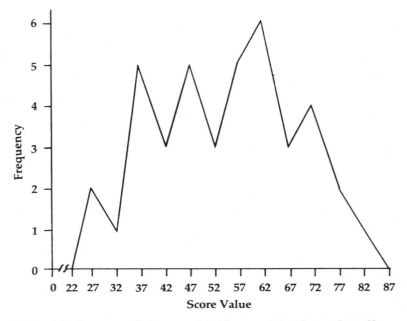

Figure 1.1 Frequency Polygram of Achievement Test Scores for a Class of Ninth-Grade Students

ted the lower real limit and upper real limit of each score class. We then drew a vertical bar for each score class, making the bar as wide as the real limits of the score class, and as tall as the frequency of the score class.

A frequency polygon and a histogram tell the same kind of story. Whether a writer uses one or the other to depict a grouped frequency distribution is strictly a matter of aesthetic taste. If a single graph is used to show two or more distributions (such as a distribution of scores for boys and the corresponding distribution for girls), a frequency polygon is often easier to read than a histogram. When one histogram is placed on top of another, the graph gets cluttered and confusing, though you can sometimes use color or shading or perspective to avoid confusion. (See Figure 1.1.)

Look at the histogram in Figure 1.2, and figure out how many students scored in the score class with real limits of 69.5 and 74.5. Did fewer students score in the interval with limits 39.5 and 44.5?

Figure 1.2 Histogram of Achievement Test Scores for a Class of Ninth-Grade Students

How many scored in the interval with limits 34.5 and 39.5? Your answers have been 4, yes, and 5.

Another exploratory data analysis procedure introduced by Tukey (1977) results in what he termed a **box-and-whisker chart**. Box-and-whisker charts provide a graphical summary of some of the most important characteristics of a distribution of scores, while providing useful and readily perceived information about the shape of a score distribution.

The box-and-whisker chart in Figure 1.3 illustrates the distribution of 40 achievement test scores listed in Table 1.3. The horizontal lines on the extreme left and the extreme right of the figure are the "whiskers," and the rectangle in the middle of the figure with a vertical line drawn inside it is the "box." The left-hand whisker begins with a point on the score scale that corresponds to the smallest score in the distribution (in this case, a score of 26), and extends to a point that separates the smallest 25% of the scores

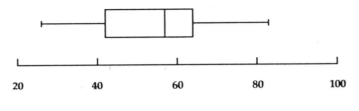

Score Value

Figure 1.3 Box-and-Whisker Chart of Achievement Test Scores for a Class of Ninth-Grade Students

from the rest of the scores (in this case a score of 42 appears to separate the smallest fourth of the distribution; i.e., the 10 scores that are smallest among the 40 scores in the distribution, from the other 30 scores). This point on the score scale is called the **25th percentile** or **first quartile** of the score distribution. The box in a box-and-whisker chart begins at the 25th percentile of a score distribution, and extends to a score value that separates the smallest three fourths of the scores from the 25% of the scores that are largest (in this case a score of 64 appears to separate the 10 scores that are largest among the 40 scores in the distribution from the 30 scores that are smaller). The upper end of the box thus falls at a value known as the **75th percentile** or **third quartile**, because 75% of the scores in a distribution fall below this point.

The right-hand whisker in Figure 1.3 begins at the 75th percentile, and extends to a point on the score scale that corresponds to the largest score in the distribution (in this case, a score of 83). We can therefore look at the box-and-whisker chart in Figure 1.3 and learn that the students who earned the top 25% of the scores on the ninth-grade achievement test scored roughly between 64 and 83.

Note the vertical line that appears inside the box in Figure 1.3. This line is drawn at a point on the score scale that corresponds to the **50th percentile**. The 50th percentile is a score value that divides a score distribution exactly in half, so that half the scores fall below this value and half fall above. In the distribution shown in Figure 3, the 50th percentile appears to be about 57. The 50th percentile is used so often in describing a score distribution that it has several aliases; it is sometimes called the **second quartile**, and most often it is called the **median**.

In describing the points in the score distribution that correspond to the 25th, 50th, and 75th percentiles, we have used the modifiers "about" and "roughly." This is because the score values that correspond to these percentiles cannot be determined precisely by inspecting a box-and-whisker chart. The values read here—42, 57, and 64—depend substantially on the eyesight of the reader. In fact, determining important points in a score distribution by reading a graph is known as "eyeballing" in the statistics trade, a procedure occasionally glorified with the label "interocular approximation." When exact values of the 25th, 50th, and 75th percentiles are needed, most standard statistics books provide formulas for determining them. Glass and Hopkins (1984) is one good source for these formulas.

The box-and-whisker chart shown in Figure 1.3 provides a good bit of information about the distribution of achievement test scores for the class of ninth-grade students. First, as already noted, it tells us that the scores ranged between the mid-20s and the low 80s. Second, it tells us that a fourth of the class scored below 41—thus missing more than half the test questions. Third, it tells us that half the class scored between 41 and 64, since 50% of a score distribution *always* falls between the 25th percentile and the 75th percentile. Fourth, it tells us that the highest-scoring fourth of the class earned scores between 64 and 83, thus missing no more than 21 of the 85 test items. Fifth, it tells us that half the students earned scores below 57 and half the students earned scores above that value; perhaps a disappointing result for the teacher of the class, since it means that half the students missed at least 28 of the 85 test items.

Notice that the vertical line corresponding to the 50th percentile of the score distribution does not fall right at the center of the box-and-whisker-chart's box; it falls distinctly to the right of the center. That fact tells us that the fourth of the students' scores between the 50th percentile and the 75th percentile tend to be "bunched up"—in this case, in the high 50s to mid-60s, while the fourth of the scores between the 25th percentile and the 50th percentile tend to be "stretched out"—in this case between the low 40s and the high 50s. Since the two whiskers in the chart are about equal in length, we know that the bottom fourth of the scores are about as spread out as the top fourth. Had one whisker been significantly longer than the other, we would have concluded otherwise.

In summary then, the box-and-whisker chart gives us approximate values of some important descriptors of a score distribution: the smallest score, the 25th percentile, the 50th percentile, the 75th percentile, and the largest value. In addition, it tells us a great deal about the shape of the score distribution. We will have more to say about the shapes of score distributions, and about percentiles, later in this section of the chapter. The median is such an important descriptor of a score distribution that we consider its properties at greater length in Chapter 2.

The **cumulative percent frequency polygon** shown in Figure 1.4 is a picture of the cumulative percent frequency distribution contained in Table 1.5. Although this graph doesn't give an immediate visual impression of the score distribution, it is among the most useful types of graphs in descriptive statistics. So what's it good for, you ask? Let's see.

Suppose you wanted to know the point on the score scale that would divide the 40 students exactly in half, in the sense that 20 of them earned scores above that point and 20 of them earned scores below. As noted earlier, that score value is called the **50th percentile**. Any conventional statistics book worth its salt will have a formula for calculating the 50th percentile. But for most practical purposes, you don't have to know the 50th percentile exactly; an approximation will do just fine. And you can use Figure 1.4 to get it, as we'll show you.

To find the 50th percentile, just read up the vertical scale of Figure 1.4 (the "Cumulative Percent Frequency" scale) to 50. At that point, draw a horizontal line, parallel to the x-axis, across to the curve. When you're finished with this step, your graph should look like Figure 1.5. Next, at the point your horizontal line crosses the curve, drop a vertical line, parallel to the y-axis, down to the horizontal scale. When you're finished with this step, your graph should look like Figure 1.6. The point where your vertical line crosses the x-axis is the 50th percentile. In this case, the 50th percentile is about 55.

You can find other percentiles just as readily from Figure 1.4. For example, to find the point on the score value that separates the lowest scoring 25% of the students from the highest scoring 75% (called the 25th percentile), just follow the steps for finding the

50th percentile, with one exception. Instead of reading up the Cumulative Percent Frequency scale to 50 in the first step, just go up to 25 (halfway between 20 and 30). Draw your horizontal line across to the curve at that point, and follow the rest of the steps in order. You should find that the 25th percentile is about 43. The 25th percentile is used so often in statistics that it has a special name. As noted earlier, it is called the **first quartile**, and is often denoted by Q_1.

To make sure you can use Figure 1.4 to find percentiles, try to determine the 75th percentile. This is another frequently used statistic that, as noted earlier, goes under the alias of the **third quartile** and is often denoted by Q_3. It is the point on the score scale that separates the lowest scoring 75% of the students from the highest scoring 25%. The 75th percentile is equal to 64.5.

If you wanted to describe the score distribution of the 40 students in very great detail, you could use Figure 1.4 to find 99 percentiles altogether. One percent of the students would have score values at or below the first percentile; 2% would have score values at or below the second percentile; and so on, up to the 99th percentile. It is rarely necessary to know all 99 of a distribution's percentiles, but it's nice to know they're around in case a complete description is needed.

Although you might be tired of Figure 1.4 by now, we've not yet exhausted its wonders. We can use it to generate yet another set of useful statistics. In an early part of this chapter, we described the use of ranks for interpreting a student's score in comparison with the scores of the other students. **Percentile ranks** are another set of statistics that perform a similar function, and we can determine approximate percentile ranks using Figure 1.4.

A student's percentile rank is equal to the percentage of students with scores that are less than or equal to his or her score. For example, a student who scored 54 on the mathematics achievement test would have a percentile rank of 47 (denoted "PR = 47"). This means that 47% of the 40 students earned scores of 54 or less.

We determined the percentile rank of the student who scored 54 by using Figure 1.4 as follows: First, we found the score value 54 on the horizontal axis of the figure. From that point, we drew a vertical line, parallel to the y-axis, up to the curve. At that point, we had a graph that looked like the one shown in Figure 1.7.

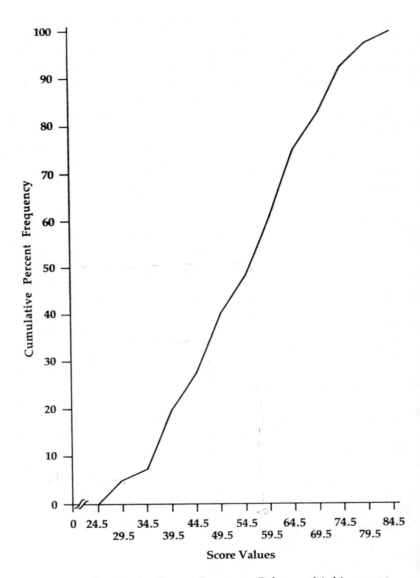

Figure 1.4 Cumulative Percent Frequency Polygon of Achievement Test Scores for a Class of Ninth-Grade Students

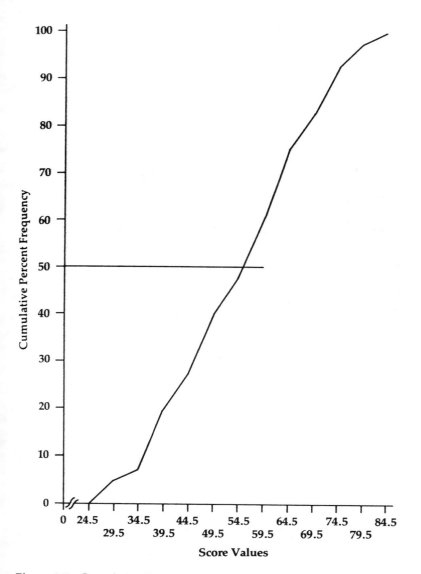

Figure 1.5 Cumulative Percent Frequency Polygon of Achievement Test Scores for a Class of Ninth-Grade Students

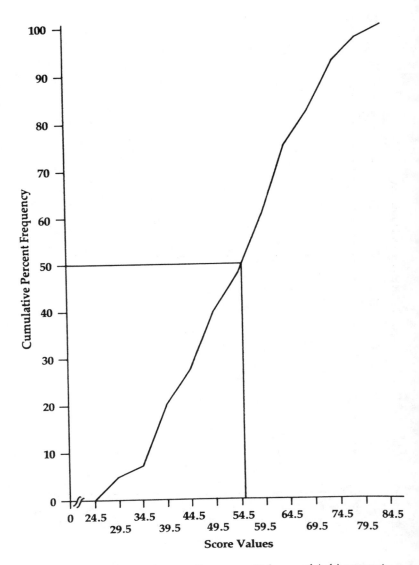

Figure 1.6 Cumulative Percent Frequency Polygon of Achievement Test Scores for a Class of Ninth-Grade Students

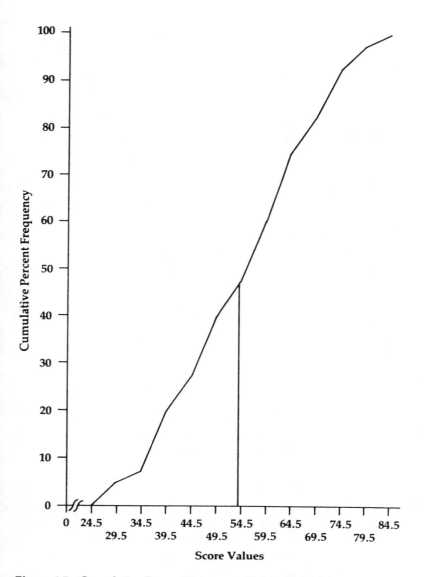

Figure 1.7 Cumulative Percent Frequency Polygon of Achievement Test Scores for a Class of Ninth-Grade Students

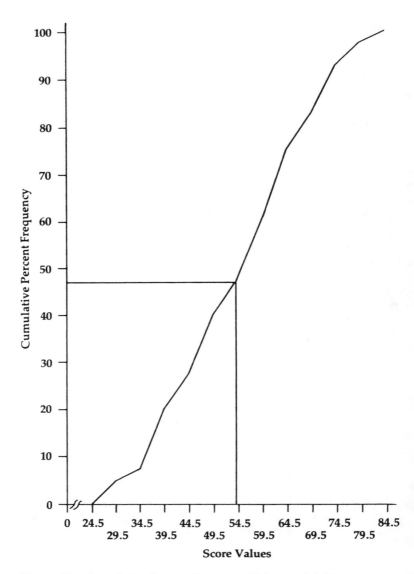

Figure 1.8 Cumulative Percent Frequency Polygon of Achievement
Test Scores for a Class of Ninth-Grade Students

Next, at the point where our vertical line crossed the curve, we drew a horizontal line, parallel to the *x*-axis, over to the Cumulative Percent Frequency scale. This gave us a graph like the one shown in Figure 1.8. Our horizontal line crossed the Cumulative Percent Frequency scale partway between 40 and 50, so we read the percentile rank of 54 to be 47.

You can find the percentile rank of other scores by following the same procedure we used. For practice, try to find the percentile rank of a student who scored 66 on the test. You should find that the PR of 66 is about 77.

Unlike most statistics, which describe the scores or other characteristics of a group of individuals, percentile ranks are used to interpret the performance of one individual. Percentile ranks provide the basis for a *normative* (i.e., comparative) interpretation of an individual's score, just like ranks. Percentile ranks have the added advantage of being on a 100-point scale.

Some Fancier Graphs. The types of graphs we've described so far are among the more common and most widely used in research and evaluation reports. But you'll find many other kinds of graphs in your wanderings through the research of your field, as well as variations on the themes we've discussed. For example, a **pie chart**, like the one shown in Figure 1.9, is often used to illustrate a

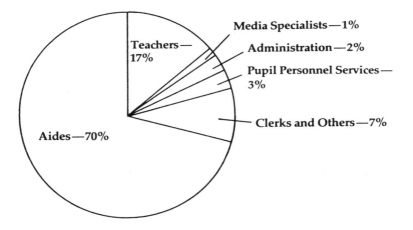

Figure 1.9 Types of Personnel Funded by ESEA Chapter I, by Grade Level, 1985-86

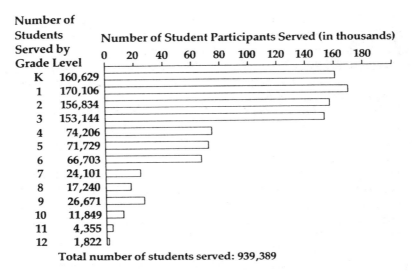

Number of Student Participants Served (in thousands)

Number of Students Served by Grade Level	
K	160,629
1	170,106
2	156,834
3	153,144
4	74,206
5	71,729
6	66,703
7	24,101
8	17,240
9	26,671
10	11,849
11	4,355
12	1,822

Total number of students served: 939,389

Figure 1.10 Number of Student Participants in ESEA Chapter I, by Grade Level, 1985-86

breakdown of some quantity—like income, expenditures, or personnel—across categories. A pie chart shows quite clearly which category is getting the largest slice. In the case of Figure 1.9, we can conclude without question that the vast majority of personnel funded by Chapter I of the Elementary and Secondary Education Act (ESEA) in 1985-86 were classified as Aides. The Aides slice is 70% of the entire pie!

Sometimes bar charts (a more common name for histograms) are presented horizontally instead of vertically. The graph in Figure 1.10 is an example of a **horizontal bar chart**. Notice that this histogram shows the distribution of students who participated in the ESEA Chapter I program in 1985-86 by grade level. Since the grade levels occur in discrete units (kindergarten, first grade, second grade, etc.), there really are no *score* classes and it is not necessary to plot real limits of score classes on one of the scales.

To show a graphical comparison of two score distributions, a graph similar to the **double-barred histogram** in Figure 1.11 is often useful. This graph shows the average scores earned by students in grades 1, 2, and 3 who participated in an early childhood

Figure 1.11 Pretest and Posttest Standard Scores in Mathematics Achievement, by Grade Level, for Schools Participating in Early Childhood Education Programs, 1986-87

education program during the 1986-87 school year. The average scores earned by these students at the beginning of the school year ("Pretest") and at the end of the school year ("Posttest") can be compared quite readily. It is also easy to see how the average scores compare to the national average of 50.

Describing the Shapes of Curves. Statisticians and researchers have developed a set of terms to describe the shapes of frequency polygons and other curves. Their specialized language is a form of jargon, but it saves many extraneous words once you know the language. Compare the following descriptions of the same frequency polygon: (1) The frequency distribution was very tall and skinny; it had one great big peak but the rest of it was much flatter toward the higher end of the score scale. (2) The frequency distribution was leptokurtic, unimodal, and positively skewed. These two descriptions are identical. Using a few technical terms, the second is far more concise and, once you know the language, more communicative.

Over the centuries, many frequency distributions describing real data have been found that have one particular shape. They have one peak in the middle of the distribution, and their frequencies get progressively smaller as one moves away from the middle of the distribution. Furthermore, the shape of these distributions

Figure 1.12 The Normal Curve

above their middle value is a mirror image of their shape *below* the middle.

In the early 1700s a mathematician named Abraham De Moivre developed the mathematical equation for a curve that approximates these distributions very well. This **normal distribution,** when graphed, produces a bell-shaped **normal curve** like the one shown in Figure 1.12. Through the years, statisticians have adopted the normal curve as a kind of benchmark, to be used as a reference when describing other frequency polygons.

The normal distribution is extremely useful, not only for approximating the shape of many frequency distributions, but for solving a variety of problems in inferential statistics as well. In fact, it is not an exaggeration to say that the field of statistics would still be in its infancy had the normal distribution never been derived. We will return to the wonders of the normal distribution repeatedly in later chapters. For the moment, just notice the friendly, familiar shape of the normal curve. It is neither too tall and skinny, nor too short and fat. In fact, it is regarded as a standard of moderation and middle-of-the-roadness in terms of the height and width of its peak. The normal curve is therefore labeled **mesokurtic**. That's a fancy Latin-root word that comes from "meso" meaning "middle," and "kurtic" meaning "peakedness." So the normal distribution is, as we say in the South, middling in its peakedness.

A frequency distribution that is taller and skinnier than the normal distribution, like the one shown in Figure 1.13, is called **leptokurtic**. To remember that label, just think of the distribution as "leaping up" in the middle. If you were to give an achievement test to a large sample of "C" students selected from a high school, their distribution of test scores would probably be leptokurtic, like the curve in Figure 1.13. Most of the students would score close to

Leptokurtic

Figure 1.13 A More-than-normally Peaked Curve

Platykurtic

Figure 1.14 A Flattened Curve

the middle of the distribution. There would be few, if any, students with very high or very low test scores.

A frequency polygon that is flatter, and more spread out, than a normal distribution is labeled **platykurtic**. If you were to select a 500-student sample from a high school, consisting of 100 "A" students, 100 "B" students, 100 "C" students, 100 "D" students, and 100 "F" students, a distribution of their achievement test scores would look like the platykurtic curve shown in Figure 1.14. You would expect the test scores of these students to cover a wide range of values, with approximately equal numbers of students scoring in the middle of the distribution and in the high and low score ranges.

To associate the term *platykurtic* with a relatively flat frequency polygon, just think of a duck-billed platypus. Agreed, you don't see many of those little critters wandering around the streets these days, but most people have heard of them, and they are wide and flat. If you can find a more familiar mnemonic device, by all means use it!

All of the frequency polygons we've described in this section share some important characteristics. Each of them has only one peak. And if we were to draw a vertical line right through the middle of any curve, its shape to the left of that vertical line would be a mirror image of its shape to the right of that vertical line. In other words, the left half of each curve would fall right on top of the right half, if the curves were folded around a vertical line in the middle. Both of these characteristics have statistical names. A frequency polygon that has only one peak is called **unimodal**. A

Figure 1.15   A Bimodal Distribution Curve.

frequency polygon that has mirror image shapes to the left and right of its middle is called **symmetric**. Although many frequency distributions are both symmetric and unimodal, there are exceptions.

The frequency polygon shown in Figure 1.15 has two peaks. It is therefore called **bimodal**. If you were to graph the frequency distribution of heights in inches for a sample consisting of 100 male basketball players and 100 male jockeys, you would probably have a bimodal curve like the one shown in Figure 1.15. If a frequency polygon has more than two peaks, it is called **multimodal**.

A frequency polygon that is shaped so that the curve to the left of its middle is *not* a mirror image of the curve to the right of its middle is called **skewed**. Many frequency distributions result in skewed frequency polygons. For example, suppose you were to collect data on annual salaries from people who happened to pass you on a downtown street corner in a randomly chosen American city. Most of the people who passed your corner would probably have low to moderate annual salaries. But there would be a few bank presidents and physicians, whose salaries would be well above those of the crowd. If you were to plot a frequency polygon of these salary data, it would probably look like the curve in Figure 1.16.

Figure 1.16   A Positively Skewed Curve

Figure 1.17   A Negatively Skewed Curve.

Notice that the salaries with high frequencies are in the left-hand end of the polygon (at the low end of the score scale) and that salaries at the high end of the scale have relatively low frequencies. This kind of frequency polygon is said to be **positively skewed** because the distribution is stretched out toward the high (or positive) end of the scale. (If you think of it as a diagram of a hand with one finger sticking out, the finger points in the direction of positive values on the x-axis.)

As you might expect, the converse of a positively skewed frequency polygon is called **negatively skewed**. A negatively skewed polygon is illustrated in Figure 1.17. If you were to sample 200 average adult males, and ask them each to run a timed 100-yard dash, and then plot a distribution of their running times, you'd probably find a negatively skewed curve like the one in Figure 1.17. Think of time needed to run 100 yards as being plotted on the x-axis and frequency being plotted on the y-axis. Relatively few men would be in superb physical shape, and would run the 100-yard dash in a short time (10 to 11 seconds). Most of the men would take a relatively long time to run 100 yards (20 to 25 seconds), so that the frequencies associated with these longer running times would be relatively high.

Well, enough of new terms for describing curves. Now when you read a research report that describes a distribution of scores as being unimodal, platykurtic, and symmetric, you can conjure up a mental image of the shape of its frequency polygon.

Problems — Chapter 1

1.1   A standardized achievement test in social studies was used in an evaluation of an innovative curriculum for sixth-graders. The 50-item test was administered to 100 participating students at the end of a one-year program, and the following cumulative frequency distribution was constructed using the resulting data:

Score Interval	Cumulative Frequency
46 – 50	100
41 – 45	96
36 – 40	91
31 – 35	75
26 – 30	42
21 – 25	21
16 – 20	10
11 – 15	5
6 – 10	2
1 – 5	0

Which of the following statements is supported by the data shown in the table?
   a. None of the students scored above 46 on the test.
   b. The majority of students scored below 36.
   c. The majority of students scored above 35.
   d. None of the students scored below 10.

1.2 Suppose that the distribution of employee salaries in your administrative unit looked like the curve shown below. If you were trying to describe this distribution to a fellow administrator in a phone conversation, would you say that it was:
   a. Symmetric and unimodal.
   b. Negatively skewed and bimodal.
   c. Positively skewed and bimodal.
   d. Positively skewed and unimodal.

1.3   The distribution of professional employees per school in the River Junction Unified School System is shown by the following histogram. What category of number of professional employees has the highest frequency of schools?_____ How many schools fall into this category?_____

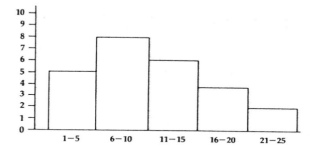

1.4   Look at the double-barred histogram shown in Figure 1.11. If you were interpreting the data reported in that figure, which of the following would be correct statements? (Circle the letter of *each* statement that is true.)

   a. More schools participated in the early childhood education program at the third-grade level than at the first-grade level.

   b. More schools participated in the early childhood education program at the first-grade level than at the second-grade level.

   c. The largest percentage of students with achievement above the national average on the posttest occurred at the first-grade level.

   d. The greatest apparent gain in achievement, from pretest to posttest, occurred at the first-grade level.

2.

Concepts of
Central Tendency

Where Is the Center?

As we noted in Chapter 1, one of the principal functions of descriptive statistics is summarization of data. We often use a set of data to compute other numbers, called **statistics**, that convey the essential information in the original scores.

One of the most elementary types of statistics indicates the location of the center of a score distribution. In many statistics texts, statistics that identify the center or middle of a set of scores are called **measures of central tendency**. In this chapter we'll define several measures of central tendency, examine their properties and assumptions, and try to give you a sense of when each of them should be used. With some sets of data, various measures of central tendency will give totally different indications of the center of a score distribution. It is important to learn when each measure of central tendency is appropriate, so you won't be misled by an author who has used the wrong one.

How to Define the Center

The center of a score distribution can be defined in many different ways. However, the most commonly used measures of central tendency are the **mode**, the **median**, and the **mean**.

When used with a simple listing of scores, an ordered array, or an ungrouped frequency distribution (see Tables 1.1, 1.2, and 1.3), the mode is defined as the most frequently occurring score. In a grouped frequency distribution, the score class that has the highest frequency (largest number of scores) associated with it is called the **modal interval**. The *mode* is the score value that is right in the middle (the midpoint) of the modal interval. Many statistics texts use the symbol "Mo." to define the mode. However, various authors use different symbols for the same statistics. A committee on statistical notation has existed within the American Statistical Association for over 30 years, and it's no closer to achieving totally consistent statistical notation than is the United Nations to bringing about world peace. We continue to hope fervently for both.

We described the *median* of a score distribution in Chapter 1. The median is another name for the 50th percentile. Recall that the 50th percentile is the score value that divides a distribution exactly in half, in the sense that 50% of the scores in the distribution fall at or below that value, and 50% of the scores fall above that value. Another name for the median is the **second quartile**. Just remember that the median, the 50th percentile, and the second quartile are all aliases for the same statistic.

Most statistics texts and research reports abbreviate the median by calling it "Md." or "Mdn." The second quartile is often denoted by Q_2.

The most widely used measure of central tendency is the arithmetic *mean*. You have been computing means for years, and you probably just called them averages. If you are working with a set of scores, their arithmetic mean is computed simply by adding the scores together and dividing by the number of scores. In most research and evaluation reports, you will find the mean denoted by the letter X with a line over it: $\overline{X}$. This is read as "X bar."

Which Measures When?

Three factors should be considered when you try to decide whether an author has used the right measure of central tendency: (1) the level of measurement of the data, (2) the shape of the score distribution, and (3) the stability of the measure of central tendency. We'll discuss these factors in order, since that's the way we'd consider them if we were evaluating the correct choice of a measure of central tendency.

Level of Measurement. To introduce the level of measurement issues, which relate to the *kind* of measurement involved, we'd like to give you some information and then ask you some questions. Consider the following data, concerning four fictitious persons:

Joe	Sally	Mary	Bob
60	70	110	120

The four numbers written below the names are IQ-test scores. To avoid pages of interesting, but diverting, discussion, let's agree that we'll *assume* IQ tests measure intelligence with perfect accuracy.

Given these assumptions, here are our questions. We ask that you respond affirmatively to only *one* of them:

(1) Notice that Bob's IQ-test score is twice as large as Joe's. Given this fact, are you willing to state that Bob is *twice as intelligent* as Joe?

(2) Notice that the difference in IQ score between Sally and Joe is 10 points. The difference in IQ score between Bob and Mary is also 10 points. Given this fact, are you willing to state that the *difference in intellgience* between Sally and Joe is the same as the *difference in intelligence* between Bob and Mary? (After all, 10 points is 10 points!)

(3) Notice that Bob has the highest IQ-test score, Mary is next, Sally's score is third from the top, and Joe's score is lowest. Given this fact, are you willing to state that Bob is *most intelligent*, Mary is second in intelligence, Sally is next, and Joe is *lowest in intelligence*? (That is, will you rank them by their scores?)

(4) Notice that Joe, Sally, Mary, and Bob all have different IQ-test scores. Given this fact, are you willing to state that these four people *differ in their intelligence*, but not state anything about the relative levels of their intelligence?

These four questions correspond to four different assumptions about the relationship between the results of measurement (the score on the IQ test) and the variable that is being measured (intelligence). Since various statistics incorporate assumptions like these, it is important to understand them.

Had you been willing to state that Bob was twice as intelligent as Joe because his IQ test was twice as large as Joe's, you would have been assuming that the IQ test measured intelligence at the

ratio level of measurement. This is the strongest measurement assumption you could make. With ratio-level measurement, a score that is twice as large as another corresponds to twice as much of the variable being measured as does the other score. In addition, a score of zero indicates that the amount of the variable is zero. In other words, if an IQ test measured intelligence at the ratio level, a person who scored zero on the test would have no intelligence at all. And a person who scored 180 would have three times the intelligence as a person who scored 60.

Many physical properties are measured at the ratio level. Height in inches, as measured by a yard stick, is an example of ratio-level measurement. So is weight in pounds, as measured with a bathroom scale.

The second question on our list asked whether you were willing to state that the difference in intelligence between Sally and Joe was the same as the difference in intelligence between Bob and Mary. Had you answered this question affirmatively, you would have been asserting that the IQ test measured intelligence at the **interval level** of measurement. Interval-level measurement assumes that a given interval on the score scale (10 points in this example) represents the same amount of the variable being measured, regardless of where the interval appears on the scale. Unlike ratio-level measurement, interval-level measurement does not imply that zero on the score scale represents an absence of the variable being measured. With interval-level measurement, zero is an arbitrary scale point that has no special meaning.

Temperature, measured in degrees Fahrenheit, is an example of interval-level measurement. The temperature difference between 65 degrees and 70 degrees *is* the same as the temperature difference between 80 degrees and 85 degrees, but zero on the Fahrenheit scale does *not* correspond to absence of temperature. Those of you above the Mason-Dixon line know only too well that zero degrees can seem quite warm after a spell of subzero weather. Zero degrees is just an arbitrary reference point.

Had you agreed with our third question, that Bob was most intelligent, Mary came next, Sally was third from the top in intelligence, and Joe was least intelligent, you would have been assuming that the IQ test measured intelligence at the **ordinal level**. Ordinal-level measurement assumes that you can rank-order the objects of measurement, from highest to lowest, on the basis of their scores. To say that Bob is most intelligent does not assume anything about the *size* of difference between his intelligence and Mary's. For instance, it does not assume that the difference between Bob's intelligence and Mary's is the same as the difference between Mary's intelligence and Sally's. Equal differences between ranks do *not* correspond to equal differences in scores. The ordinal-level measurement assumption is weaker than the interval-level assumption. It makes weaker demands on the results of measurement.

School grades provide a good example of ordinal-level measurement. An A is better than a B, and a B is better than a C. But the difference between an A and a B is not necessarily the same as the difference between a B and a C. (When we calculate "grade point averages" we *assume* grades are measured at the interval level, but that's often false; a teacher will often say that D work is only a little worse than C work, but F work is much worse than D work.)

If you disagreed with our first three questions and agreed with only the last, you were assuming that the IQ test measured intelligence only at the **nominal level**. You would be stating, in effect, that you would be willing to place the four persons into different intelligence categories, but would be unwilling to state who was more intelligent and who was less intelligent. You can think of nominal-level measurement as the weakest assumption you could make. You would be treating the IQ scores just like social security numbers; they serve as surrogate names for people, but nothing more. They don't represent differences in ability or any other variable that is pertinent to human existence.

Were we arbitrarily to assign numbers to categories of eye color: 1 = blue eyes, 2 = brown eyes, 3 = green eyes, and so on, we would have nominal-level measurement. The numbers wouldn't correspond to any property of eye color, except to say that people who had different numbers were in different eye color categories. For some people, this wouldn't even count as measurement; it would just be description. But, as we'll see in a moment, it's useful to consider it as a limiting case.

We have already suggested that various statistics incorporate particular assumptions about level of measurement. We'll now discuss those assumptions for measures of central tendency. Since the *mode* is merely the score value or category that has the highest frequency associated with it, this measure of central tendency makes use of only the nominal property of data. It can therefore be used with data that represent an underlying variable at any level of measurement—nominal, ordinal, interval, or ratio. Our eye color example is appropriate here. Suppose that you had recorded the eye colors of 20 people, using the scale we described earlier: 1 = blue eyes, 2 = brown eyes, and 3 = green eyes. When you computed the mode of the distribution, you found it to equal 2. You would than know that there were more brown-eyed people in the group than people with any other eye color. In contrast, a mean eye color of 2.57 would be meaningless, since it would not correspond to any eye color.

The *median* assumes that a set of data represents an underlying variable at least at the ordinal level of measurement. The median can therefore be used with data that measure at the ordinal level, the interval level, or the ratio level. If used with nominal-level data, the median will produce a meaningless value. Knowing that the median grade awarded in a class was a B is interpretable, since half the students in the class would then have earned a grade of B or below, and half would have earned a grade above a B. However, knowing that the median eye color was "brown" tells you nothing, since eye color is a nominal-level variable, and not an ordinal one.

The *mean* should be applied only to data that measure an underlying variable at the interval level or the ratio level. If the mean is applied to ordinal- or nominal-level data, the resulting value will be meaningless.

When you read research and evaluation reports that include measures of central tendency, we suggest that you ask yourself whether the author's choice of a statistic is consistent with your belief about the level of measurement of the data being described. If an author reports that a group's mean attitude toward their employer is 24.5, ask yourself whether you really believe that the attitude scale measures at the interval or ratio level. Do you believe that the interval between 15 and 20 represents the same difference in attitude as the interval between 25 and 30? If your answer is no, you should question the use of the mean.

Shape of the Score Distribution. If a score distribution is symmetric and has only one peak, as in Figures 1.12, 1.13, and 1.14, the mean, the median, and the mode will have exactly the same value.

Mo. M̄d. $\bar{X}$

Figure 2.1 Relationship of Central Tendency Measures in a Positively Skewed Distribution of Scores.

In this case, other factors should influence an author's choice of a measure of central tendency.

If a score distribution is bimodal and symmetric, as in Figure 1.15, the mean and the median will have the same value, and the distribution will have two modes. Each mode will correspond to a peak in the distribution. In this case, the modes will not be good indicators of the center of the distribution, but they will describe other important characteristics of its shape. Since the median and the mean will be equal, the choice of either one as a measure of central tendency should be made on the basis of factors other than the shape of the distribution.

If a distribution has only one peak and is not symmetric, the mean, median, and mode will all be different. If the score distribution is positively skewed, the mode will be smallest, the mean will be largest, and the median will be between the mode and the mean, usually closer to the mean. This is illustrated in Figure 2.1.

If a score distribution is negatively skewed, like the one shown in Figure 2.2, the mean will be smallest, the mode will be largest, and the median will be in between the two, again, usually closer to the mean.

When a distribution is highly skewed, the mean will not do a good job of representing the center of the distribution; either the median or the mode should be used instead. To see how the mean can give a false indication of the center of a skewed distribution, consider the following example. Suppose that you had a distribution of annual salaries for 11 people. Ten were first-year public school teachers, and one was the late J. Paul Getty, the oil magnate. Suppose that all 10 school teachers earned around $21,000 per year, and that Getty earned around $1,000,000 per year. This distribution of annual incomes would be very positively skewed. If we

$\overline{X}$ Md. Mo.

Figure 2.2 Relationship of Central Tendency Measures in a Negatively Skewed Distribution of Scores.

assume that the average income of the 10 teachers was $21,000, the mean income for the 11 people would be $21,000 times 10 plus $1,000,000, divided by the sample size of 11. The mean would then be $1,210,000/11 = $110,000. Now this figure vastly overestimates the average income of the teachers, and greatly underestimates Getty's income. It is nowhere near most of the incomes. In contrast, the median annual income of the 11 people would be close to the $21,000 average of the 10 teachers. Getty's income of $1,000,000 would just be treated by the median as a value that fell above the middle. It would not have the inordinate effect on the median that it did on the mean. Although the median would virtually ignore Getty's very high income, it would do a good job of indicating the center of the distribution of most of the scores.

A similar example of the effect of a skewed distribution on the mean was developed by Alexander Law (1982). Suppose that five people in an office made a contribution to the United Way Fund. Their contributions were $10, $1, $0.50, $0.25, and $0.25. Their mean contribution would be $12.00/5 = $2.40, whereas the median of their contributions would be $0.50. Except for that of the one generous contributor, most of the contributions are far better "represented" by the median than by the mean. In this case, the mode of the contributions would be $0.25, which is closer to the center of the distribution than the mean, but wouldn't be as good a measure of central tendency as the median.

Another of Law's examples provides further illustration of the effect of a few extreme scores on the mean, the median, and the mode. In Table 2.1, distributions of achievement test scores are shown for two groups, each consisting of 25 students. In the first group (Case 1), the students' scores ranged from a low of 60 to a high of 98. In the second group (Case 2), all students except the

TABLE 2.1: Achievement Test Scores For Two Cases (N = 25 for each case)

	Case 1			Case 2	
Student No.	Score		Student No.	Score	
1	98		1	98	
2	98		2	98	
3	97		3	97	
4	81		4	81	
5	80		5	80	
6	79		6	79	
7	78		7	78	
8	77		8	77	
9	75		9	75	
10	75		10	75	
11	73		11	73	
12	72	Range = 98 − 60	12	72	Range = 98 − 20
13	71	Median = 71	13	71	Median = 71
14	71	Mean = 73.6	14	71	Mean = 68.8
15	70		15	70	
16	68		16	68	
17	68	Mode = 68	17	68	Mode = 68
18	68		18	68	
19	67		19	67	
20	65		20	65	
21	65		21	65	
22	63		22	63	
23	61		23	21	
24	60		24	20	
25	60		25	20	

three who scored lowest earned the same scores as corresponding students in the first group. In Case 1, the student numbered 23 scored 61; in Case 2, this student scored 21. In Case 1, students numbered 24 and 25 scored 60; in Case 2, these students scored 20. Otherwise, all corresponding scores were identical in the two groups.

Notice that the median is exactly the same for both groups of students (the median score is 71). The mode is also the same for both groups (the mode is 68). However, changing only the lowest three scores in a group of 25 has caused the mean to drop from 73.6 for Case 1 to 68.8 for Case 2. This drop of almost five points shows clearly the effect that a few extreme scores can have on the mean. As Law noted, in Case 2, 60% of the students (15 out of 25) scored 70 or better. Yet the mean of this score distribution is only 68.8. With a distribution that is highly skewed, as in Case 2, the median does a far better job of representing the center of the distribution than does the mean.

Stability. Very often in research and evaluation work, an author will try to generalize his or her results beyond the sample of individuals who have been observed or measured. For example, when two mathematics curricula are being compared in an experiment, an author may conclude that Curriculum A is better than Curriculum B, not only for the samples of sixth-graders used in his or her experiment, but for sixth-graders in general. This is a form of inference that will be discussed in great detail in later chapters of this book, particularly in Chapter 6. However, it is relevant to the choice of a measure of central tendency, even when formal statistical inference is not used.

If a researcher really wanted to know whether Curriculum A was better than Curriculum B for all sixth-graders in a school system, he or she would, ideally, test the two curricula with every sixth-grader in the system. Usually, such large-scale experiments are impractical and are far too costly. What is done instead is to select representative samples from a list of all sixth-graders in the system, and then to use each curriculum with one of the samples. Measures of central tendency (usually means) on some outcome variable (typically a test score) are then compared, to decide which curriculum is better.

In this kind of experiment, average scores on the outcome variable for the *entire* population of sixth-graders in the school system are really the values of interest. Corresponding averages for the *samples* of sixth-graders are merely estimates of the population values. When two curricula are compared on the basis of sample averages, there is always the possibility that one average is higher than the other, not because one curriculum is better than the other, but because a particularly bright sample of students happened to be selected for that curriculum. Had other samples been chosen, perhaps Curriculum B would have been found to be better. To guard against drawing false conclusions, it is necessary to use representative samples, of course, but *also* measures of central tendency that do not fluctuate wildly from one sample to the next.

It is well known that some measures of central tendency are more *stable* than others, in the sense that they fluctuate less from one sample to another. The mean is the most stable of the measures of central tendency we have discussed. The median is less stable than the mean, but is far more stable than the mode.

You may be surprised by this, in light of our last example, where changing just three scores moved the mean substantially but did not affect the median. However, that was an artificial example, designed by us to make a key point. Taking real samples from the same population, we would find the median varying *more* than the mean.

Of the three measures of central tendency, the mode is, by far, the least stable. If independent samples of sixth-graders were selected from the population of all sixth-graders in a school system, the modes of their score distributions on an achievement test would fluctuate a great deal, from one sample to the next. The median would fluctuate somewhat, but not nearly as much as the mode. The mean would fluctuate least, only because of differences in the abilities of the sampled students. The mean is therefore the most stable of these measures of central tendency.

Summary

In this chapter we have tried to give you a sense of the meaning of three statistics that refer to "the center" of a score distribution. These measures of central tendency are defined differently, and will, therefore, often differ from each other in value.

Each of the statistics is a good measure of central tendency in some situations, and a bad measure in others. As a reader of research and evaluation reports, it is important that you know when a particular measure of central tendency has been used appropriately, and when that statistic can give a misleading indication of the center of a score distribution.

If a score distribution is reasonably symmetric, and measurement is at the interval level or the ratio level, the mean is the best measure of central tendency. It is the most stable of the measures, and will therefore do the best job of estimating a population average. If a distribution is highly skewed, and measurement is at the ordinal level, the interval level, or the ratio level, the median is the best measure of central tendency. It will do a better job of indicating the center of the distribution than will the mean. The median is better than the mode in this situation because it is a more stable statistic. If measurement is at the nominal level, and neither ordinal-level, interval-level, nor ratio-level measurement can be assumed, the mode is the only measure of central tendency that will make sense. Neither the mean nor the median will be useful in this situation.

In practice, it is often worthwhile to compute more than one measure of central tendency when several measures meet the assumptions of the data. If a distribution has more than one mode, the mean or the median will do a better job of describing the middle, but reporting the modes will let a reader know which scores have the highest frequencies. If a distribution is skewed, reporting both the mean and the median will often convey the degree of skewness.

Problems — Chapter 2

2.1 Suppose that you wanted to project your future annual administrative budget, adjusted for inflation, on the basis of your administrative expenditures during the past ten years. For nine of the past ten years, your budget fell between $90,000 and $110,000, but during one year you spent $210,000, including the cost of a major revision of your accounting systems by an outside consulting firm.

To project future administrative budget needs, would you likely be more accurate if you used:
   a. The average of the annual expenditures over the past ten years?
   b. The mode of the annual expenditures over the past ten years?
   c. The smallest of the annual expenditures over the past ten years?
   d. The median of the annual expenditures over the past ten years?
Explain the logic underlying your answer to this problem.

2.2 Recently, forty thousand high school juniors in a midwestern state were given a reading competency test as a high school graduation requirement. When the 120-item test was scored, it was found that the mean equaled 95.6, the median score was 98.2, and the mode of the distribution of scores was 101.4.

From these statistics, what would you conclude about the shape of the distribution of scores on the test?
   a. The distribution was negatively skewed.
   b. The distribution was symmetric.
   c. The distribution was positively skewed.
   d. The shape of the distribution cannot be inferred from the information given.

2.3 The distribution of payoffs at a race track is positively skewed, with a mode of $2.00, a median of $2.10, and a mean of $3.75. Given these statistics, which of the following are true statements? (Circle the letter of *each* statement that is true.)
   a. More than half the winners get less than a $3.75 payoff.
   b. Half the winners get less than a $2.10 payoff.
   c. Half the winners get less than a $2.00 payoff.
   d. The most frequent payoff is $3.75.

2.4 Suppose that a personnel consulting firm has administered a scale to measure the employee morale of all employees in each of the five departments in your administrative offices. They report that the average score of employees in Department A was 10, and the average score of the employees in Department B was 21. In their conclusion, they warn you that "The morale of employees in Department B was more than twice as high as that of employees in Department A." Answer yes or no to each of the following questions.
   a. Is the average an appropriate statistic to use in summarizing the central tendency of the employee morale data?
   b. Should you accept the conclusion that the morale of employees in Department B was more than twice as high as that of employees in Department A? Why might you challenge this conclusion?

c. Would you accept the conclusion that the average morale of employees in Department B was higher than that of employees in Department A? What measurement assumption would you have to make to accept this conclusion?

3.

Measures of Variability

How Spread Out Are the Scores?

Although statistics that indicate the center of a score distribution provide useful and important information about a group of scores, they certainly don't give a complete picture of the distribution. Two score distributions that have identical means, medians, and modes, such as those shown in Figure 3.1, can still differ from each other in important ways.

The distributions shown in Figure 3.1 are identical in their central tendencies. In addition, both are symmetric and both are unimodal. They differ only in the spread of their scores, the extent to which the scores differ or vary.

The statistics described in this chapter indicate the spread of scores in a distribution. They are called **measures of variability**. Each of the statistics we'll describe would have a larger value for Distribution B in Figure 3.1 than for Distribution A. As was true of

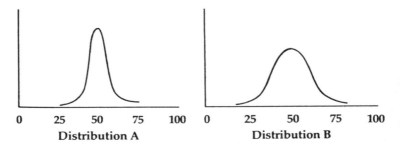

Figure 3.1 Two Score Distributions That Are Equal in Central Tendency, but Differ in Variability.

the measures of central tendency discussed in Chapter 2, the most frequently used measures of variability have different properties, and each provides the best indication of the spread of scores in a distribution in different situations. In this chapter we first define several measures of variability, then describe their properties, and finally discuss the appropriateness of the measures in various situations. We hope you'll be a better informed reader of research and evaluation reports when you finish this chapter. Remember that high variability reflects large individual differences, so you *must* know about variability before drawing any conclusions about individuals in a group from information about the group's average performance.

Measures of Variability

The simplest measure of the spread of a group of scores is called the **range**. The range is simply the difference between the largest score in a group and the smallest score in the group. For example, in Table 2.1, student number 1 of Case 1 scored 98 on an achievement test. Student 25, the lowest scoring student in this group, scored 60. For Case 1, then, the range is equal to 98 − 60 = 38. For Case 2 in Table 2.1, student number 1 scored 98 and student number 25 scored 20. The range of scores for Case 2 is thus 98 − 20 = 78.

In some statistics texts, and in some research and evaluation reports, you may find a range that is defined as (the highest score − the lowest score) + 1. This slight variation in the definition of range is of no practical consequence. It merely accommodates the real limits of the highest and lowest scores in a distribution. For example, in Case 1 of Table 2.1, the highest score, 98, has real limits of 97.5 and 98.5. The lowest score has real limits of 59.5 and 60.5. If the range were defined as the difference between the upper real limit of 98 and the lower real limit of 60, it would equal 98.5 − 59.5 = 39. This is the same as (98 − 60) + 1 = 39. This range is called the **inclusive range**, and the range that is defined as the difference between the highest and the lowest scores in a distribution is called the **exclusive range**. As we noted, these two definitions of the range are important only to statistical purists. For practical purposes either definition will suffice. We have mentioned both only because you might come across them in your study of the research in your field.

In Chapter 1 we introduced the concept of **percentiles**: statistics that divide a score distribution into two parts, so that a specified percentage of the distribution falls below the chosen statistic. Recall that we defined the 25th percentile, or first quartile, as the point on the score scale that divided a distribution so that 25% of the scores were less than or equal to that score value. We also defined the 75th percentile, or third percentile, as the point on the score scale that had 75% of the scores in a distribution less than or equal to it.

Two useful measures of variability can be defined in terms of the 25th percentile and the 75th percentile. One such measure is the **interquartile range**, which in some modern statistics texts is called the **hinge spread**. The interquartile range is equal to the difference between the 75th percentile and the 25th percentile. It indicates the spread of the *middle half* of a score distribution. Another, more widely used measure of variability is the **semi-interquartile range**. The semi-interquartile range is equal to half the difference between the 75th percentile and the 25th percentile. It is found merely by subtracting the 25th percentile from the 75th percentile, and dividing the difference by two. In most statistics texts and research reports, the letter Q is used to denote the semi-interquartile range. These measures are less sensitive than the range to the behavior of one or two exceptionally high or low scores, so, like the median, they give a better picture of the distribution for many purposes.

At this point in your statistical travels, if you read that a researcher had administered a 50-item test to a group of fourth-graders, and their median score was 35, you'd probably have some sense of where their distribution of scores was centered. However, if you read that the semi-interquartile range of their scores was 5, you might not know whether their score distribution was widely spread or very narrow. The following rule might help: If the score distribution was reasonably symmetric, half the scores in the distribution would fall between a score value equal to the median plus the semi-interquartile range (Mdn. + Q) and a score value equal to the median minus the semi-interquartile range (Mdn. – Q). In this example, the upper value (Mdn. + Q) = 35 + 5 = 40; and the lower value (Mdn. – Q) = 35 – 5 = 30. So if their score distribution was nearly symmetric, you would know that half the students scored between 30 and 40 on the test. That's a pretty narrow distribution.

What if the distribution wasn't symmetric? In that case, *more* than half the scores would fall between (Mdn. + Q) and (Mdn. − Q). In a highly skewed distribution, as much as 70% of the scores might fall between these two values. So (Mdn. + Q) and (Mdn. − Q) define values that will include *at least half* of a score distribution.

The most widely used measure of variability is the **standard deviation**. This statistic is intimately related to the mean and is almost always used as a measure of variability when the mean is used as a measure of central tendency. In fact, the standard deviation is a measure of the spread of the scores *around the mean*. The more the scores differ from the mean, the larger the standard deviation will be. If all of the scores in a distribution were equal (e.g., everyone scored 25 on a test), each score would equal the mean and the standard deviation would be 0. If everyone scored between 24 and 26, the standard deviation would be greater than 0, but it would be a small number, probably less than 1. If half the students scored 0 on a 50-item test, and the other half earned perfect scores of 50, the standard deviation would be a large number, because every score would be a long way from the mean (which is 25).

The standard deviation is related in a very simple way to another measure of variability that is used quite often in inferential statistics, but very little in descriptive statistics. This statistic is called the **variance**. The standard deviation is equal to the square root of the variance. For example, if a distribution of scores had a variance of 16, the standard deviation would equal 4. So the standard deviation can always be found from the variance, and the variance can always be found from the standard deviation. To find a variance from a standard deviation, merely square the standard deviation (multiply it by itself). For example, if a distribution of scores has a standard deviation of 6, its variance will equal 6 times 6 = 36.

In many research and evaluation reports, you will find the standard deviation denoted by the letter s, or the Greek version of the letter s, which is called sigma, and is written σ. The variance is often denoted by "s-squared"; that is, an s with a 2 printed half a line above it: s^2.

Interpretation of a standard deviation presents the same sort of dilemma as interpretation of a semi-interquartile range. What is a big one and what is a small one? If the standard deviation equals 10, is the distribution narrow or really spread out? Just as the semi-interquartile range was interpreted in conjunction with the median, the standard deviation is interpreted in conjunction with the mean. Here's an example. Suppose that, on a 100-item test, the mean score was 60 and the standard deviation was 10. We can interpret these results in several ways. First, for any score distribution, regardless of its shape, *at least* 75% of the scores will fall in an interval that ranges from two standard deviations below the mean to two standard deviations above the mean: $(\overline{X} - 2s)$ to $(\overline{X} + 2s)$. In this example, we therefore know that *at least* 75% of the students scored between $[60 - 2(10)] = 60 - 20 = 40$ and $[60 + 2(10)] = 60 + 20 = 80$. Another rule that applies to virtually all score distributions, regardless of their shape, is the following: *At least* 89% of the scores in the distribution will fall between score values that are three standard deviations below the mean and three standard deviations above the mean: $(\overline{X} - 3s)$ and $(\overline{X} + 3s)$. In this example, then, *at least* 89% of the students will score between $[60 - 3(10)] = 30$ and $[60 + 3(10)] = 90$. We have emphasized the words "at least" in stating and applying these rules because the percentages given are *very* conservative. In *most* score distributions, the percentage of scores that fall within two standard deviations of the mean (no more than two standard deviations below the mean and no more than two standard deviations above the mean) is far greater than 75%. Likewise, you will likely find that *far* more than 89% of the scores in a distribution will fall within three standard deviations of the mean.

This leads us to the second set of rules that apply only when a score distribution looks like the bell-shaped normal distribution we discussed in Chapter 1. If a score distribution is shaped like a normal distribution, the following rules apply: First, a little more than two thirds of the scores in the distribution (68%, to be more precise) will fall within an interval that is one standard deviation below the mean to one standard deviation above the mean. Second, slightly more than 95% of the scores will fall within an interval that is two standard deviations below the mean to two standard deviations above the mean. Finally, 99.7% of the scores in the distribution (almost all of them) will fall within an interval that ranges from three standard deviations below the mean to three standard deviations above the mean. These rules are summarized in the following table, and illustrated in Figure 3.2.

Some Characteristics of a Normal Distribution	
Interval	Percent of Scores Included
$(\overline{X} - s)$ to $(\overline{X} + s)$	68
$(\overline{X} - 2s)$ to $(\overline{X} + 2s)$	95
$(\overline{X} - 3s)$ to $(\overline{X} + 3s)$	99.7

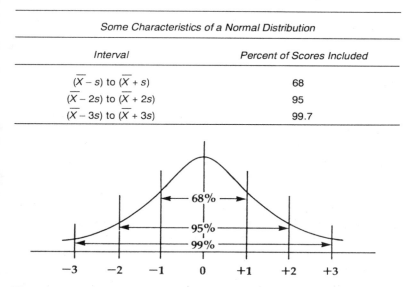

Figure 3.2 The Bell-Shaped or Normal Distribution Curve

Let's go back to our example of a 100-item test, administered to a group that had a mean score of 60 and a standard deviation of 10. If we assume that the distribution of scores is *normal* in shape, we can draw the following conclusions: First, 68% of the students have test scores that are between $(60 - 10) = 50$ and $(60 + 10) = 70$. Second, 95% of the students have test scores that are between $[60 - 2(10)] = (60 - 20) = 40$ and $[60 + 2(10)] = 80$. Finally, 99.7% of the students have test scores that are between $[60 - 3(10)] = (60 - 30) = 30$ and $[60 + 3(10)] = 90$. Let's summarize these data in a table like the one above:

Interval	Percent of Scores Included
50 to 70	68
40 to 80	95
30 to 90	99.7

From these data, you can see that knowing the mean and standard deviation of a distribution of scores tells you a good deal about the entire distribution. If you can assume that the distribution of scores is bell-shaped (and many distributions are), it is easy to define score intervals that will contain various percentages of the distribution.

Properties of the Measures

As was true for measures of central tendency, the measures of variability we have defined have different properties and are appropriate in different situations. The three considerations we applied to measures of central tendency in Chapter 2 also apply to measures of variability when deciding whether an author has used the right statistic. In that chapter we listed (1) level of measurement, (2) shape of the score distribution, and (3) stability as criteria to use in evaluating the appropriateness of a measure.

Level of Measurement. As was the case with the measures of central tendency discussed in Chapter 2, various measures of variability make use of different measurement properties of the data to which they are applied. Like the mean, the standard deviation should be applied only to data that measure an underlying variable at the interval level or the ratio level of measurement. The same is true of the range of the variance. Because it is based on percentiles, the semi-interquartile range will provide an interpretable measure of variability if it is used with data that measure at the ordinal level, the interval level, or the ratio level. There is no widely used measure of variability that is appropriate for nominal-level data.

Shape of the Score Distribution. If a score distribution is reasonably symmetric and unimodal, and measurement is at the interval level or the ratio level, the standard deviation is the most appropriate measure of variability. If a distribution is highly skewed, scores that are in the tail of the distribution (the part that has low frequencies associated with it) will be far from the mean, and will cause the standard deviation to become quite large. This large standard deviation will not give an accurate indication of the spread of scores in the distribution. In this case, the semi-interquartile range will be more appropriate than the standard deviation as a measure of variability, *provided* the scores in the distribution measure an underlying variable at least at the ordinal level of measurement.

Another situation in which the semi-interquartile range is more appropriate than the standard deviation is when a distribution is reasonably symmetric, with most of the scores concentrated around a central peak but with smaller concentrations of scores both well below and well above the central peak. For example, if most of the scores in a distribution fell between 40 and 60, but there were small concentrations of scores at 25 and 75, the standard deviation would be greatly affected by the few extreme scores. The standard deviation would become far larger than necessary to represent the variability of the scores that were concentrated between 40 and 60.

Stability. The standard deviation is the most stable of the measures of variability we have discussed. If independent samples were selected from a population and all of the measures of variability we have discussed were to be computed for each sample, the standard deviation would fluctuate least from sample to sample. This is very important when a sample standard deviation is used to estimate the standard deviation for a population. The semi-interquartile range is not as stable as the standard deviation. Its value would change more, from one sample to the next, than would the standard deviation. However, other advantages of the semi-interquartile range outweigh its relative instability in many situations.

The range is the least stable of the measures of variability we have defined. In fact, the range is so unstable that it should never be used as the sole measure of variability. Since the range is computed from only two scores, the highest and lowest, it is not surprising that it will fluctuate wildly from one sample to the next. In a sample of 1000 scores, the range ignores 998 and makes use of only the two extremes.

Summary

We have described five statistics that indicate the variability of a distribution of scores: the range, the interquartile range, the semi-interquartile range, the variance, and the standard deviation.

These five statistics have different properties and are appropriate for different situations.

Because it is the most stable of the measures of variability, the standard deviation is the preferred statistic in those situations where it will provide an accurate indication of the spread of a distribution. The standard deviation should be used only when measurement is at the interval level or the ratio level. It is most appropriate when a score distribution is reasonably symmetric and does not have concentrations of scores that are extremely large or extremely small.

The semi-interquartile range is the preferred measure of variability in a variety of circumstances. If the data measure an underlying variable at the ordinal level, but not at the interval or ratio levels, the semi-interquartile range is best. If a score distribution is highly skewed, or if it is symmetric but has small concentrations of extreme scores, the semi-interquartile range will give the most accurate indication of variability.

The range should be used as the sole indicator of the variability of a score distribution for only very informal purposes. Although it has the advantages of simplicity and computational ease, the range is a very unstable statistic. Because it ignores all but the two extreme scores, the range can be very misleading.

As was true in our discussion of measures of central tendency, we do not advocate concentrating on one measure of variability and ignoring others. Very often, an author can do a better job of describing his or her score distribution by reporting several measures of variability, such as the range and the standard deviation or the range and the semi-interquartile range.

As you read and review research and evaluation reports, be on guard for the use of misleading measures of variability. Don't draw conclusions about the variability of a score distribution just by considering the range. If you're convinced that the variable under discussion can be, or has been, measured only at the ordinal level, but not at the interval level or the ratio level, don't accept the standard deviation as a measure of variability. Look for a semi-interquartile range instead. Examine frequency polygons or frequency distribution tables to see whether reported measures of variability are reasonable, in light of the shapes of distributions. By thinking about the general appropriateness and plausibility of statistics as well as their numerical values, you will be better informed and less often misled.

Problems — Chapter 3

3.1 Look at the two frequency polygons shown below, for distributions of heights (in inches) of twelve-year-old girls and twelve-year-old boys. Assuming the distributions shown in these figures are correct, which of the following statements is true?

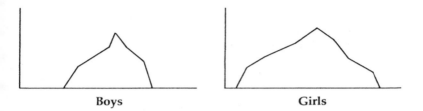

Boys   Girls

- a. The range of heights is larger for twelve-year-old boys than for twelve-year-old girls.
- b. The standard deviation of heights is larger for twelve-year-old girls than for twelve-year-old boys.
- c. The distributions of heights of twelve-year-old girls and boys are about equal in variability.

3.2 Suppose that a report on the effectiveness of an instructional program in mathematics provided the following statistics: When the program was used in 100 different schools, the median of the distribution of school average scores on a posttest of achievement was 28. The semi-interquartile range of the distribution of school average scores was 4. The distribution of school average scores was symmetric.

Between what two school average scores would the middle 50% of the distribution of school averages fall?

_____ and _____

3.3 Suppose that teachers in a large metropolitan school system are given contracts of different length, depending on such factors as years of experience, degrees held, rating at last evaluation, and field of specialty. Upon reading a report on personnel practices in that school system, you find that the distribution of lengths of teacher contracts is normal in shape, with a mean of 3 years and a standard deviation of 6 months.

Given these data, which of the following conclusions would likely be true? (Circle the letter of *each* true statement.)

    a. Hardly any teachers would have contracts longer then five years.

    b. Hardly any teachers would have contracts shorter than one year.

    c. The majority of teachers would have contracts with lengths between two years and four years.

    d. About half the teachers would have contracts of four years or shorter.

3.4 In a report on the entering freshman class at a local college, the Director of Admissions proudly wrote that the mean rank-in-high-school-class of students admitted in 1982 was 10.6, and the standard deviation of rank-in-high-school-class was 4.2.

    a. Do you see anything wrong with using these measures of central tendency and variability in describing the distribution of rank-in-high-school-class of entering freshman?

    b. What level of measurement is assumed when data are reported in terms of ranks?

    c. What statistics would be more appropriate for describing the central tendency and variability of a distribution of rank-in-high-school-class?

Central tendency:

Variability:

4.

Correlation

The General Idea

A great many questions in applied research and evaluation involve the degree to which two variables "go together." For example, a researcher might ask whether, and to what extent, students who earn high scores on an aptitude test also tend to earn good grades in school. An employer might ask whether, and to what degree, job applicants who earn high scores on a screening test tend to receive high ratings from their supervisors on the job. A psychologist might ask whether, and to what extent, examinees who earn the highest scores on an anxiety scale tend to earn the lowest scores on an examination. All of these questions are concerned with the degree of *covariation of two variables or measures.* That is, they are concerned with the tendency of the measures to vary together, in the sense that one increases as the other increases (in which case we say that the variables "covary positively"), or in the sense that one variable increases as the other decreases (in which case we say that the variables "covary negatively"). If they covary, one can predict one variable from the other, for example, college performance from test results.

This chapter is concerned with statistics that indicate the extent to which two variables covary. Such statistics are called **correlation coefficients**. In the remainder of this section we will elaborate on the nature of correlation. In the next section, we describe some properties of the most widely used correlation coefficient, called the **Pearson product-moment correlation coefficient**. In a final section, we introduce a number of other correlation coefficients that are used with variables that are measured at the ordinal and nominal levels of measurement, as well as some related statistics. As usual, our discussion will concentrate on the interpretation of results, and ignore the details of computation.

A graph called a **scatter diagram** or **scattergram** provides one of the most useful ways of seeing (or showing) whether, and to what degree, two variables covary. In a scatter diagram, one of the variables to be correlated is plotted on the horizontal axis, and the other is plotted on the vertical axis. Each individual's scores or measurements on the two variables are represented by a single point. The point is plotted directly above the individual's score on the horizontal-axis variable, and to the right of the individual's score on the vertical-axis variable.

A typical scatter diagram is shown in Figure 4.1. In this figure we have plotted the weights (in pounds) and heights (in inches) of 14 hypothetical persons. We have circled the point that represents a person who weighs 150 pounds and is 65 inches tall. Notice that the point for this person is plotted just above 150 pounds on the weight scale, and just to the right of 65 inches on the height scale. Try to find the weight and height of the person whose point is closest to the lower left-hand corner of the graph. If you said that this person weighs about 125 pounds and is about 62 inches tall, you'd be right!

If you focus your attention on the entire collection of points in the scatter diagram, you will notice that the points tend to "scatter" upward and to the right. This means that people who weigh more tend to be taller. It also means that taller people tend to weigh more. This relationship can be summarized by saying that, for this group of people, weight and height appear to *covary positively*. This summary statement does *not* mean that being tall causes increased weight, nor that being heavy causes increased height. It does mean that heavier people, on average, tend to be taller than lighter people. The "on average" in the last sentence is important. Even though weight and height *tend* to increase together for this group of people, there are several exceptions to the rule. One of our hypothetical people weighs about 140 and is 72 inches tall. Another weighs 165, but is only 70 inches tall. Scatter diagrams in which every person who has a higher score on one variable also has a higher score on the other variable are extremely rare. Exceptions to general trends are found in virtually all scatter diagrams that represent real data.

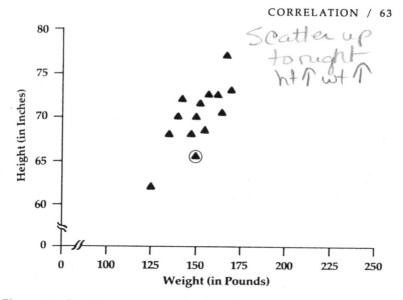

Figure 4.1 Scatter Diagram Showing Weights and Heights for 14 Persons.

We said that although height and weight tend to covary positively in the scatter diagram shown in Figure 4.1, you should not therefore conclude that increased height causes increased weight, nor that increased weight causes increased height. This point cannot be overemphasized. To say that one variable causes another is far stronger than saying that they covary, or equivalently, that they "are correlated." It's *usually* true that if two variables do not covary, one cannot cause the other, but the fact that two variables *do* covary does not often indicate a causal connection. Except for the clearly causal relationship between mosquitos and mosquito bites, it is safe to say that nothing is caused solely by a single factor in the real world of research and evaluation. Often, two variables are correlated because both are caused by other same variables. For example, were you to plot a scatter diagram with per-capita alcohol consumption in the United States on the *x*-axis, and average teacher salary in the United States on the *y*-axis, you would find a very strong positive relationship between these two variables over the years 1920 to 1980. In fact, an increase in alcohol consumption would almost always be accompanied by a corresponding increase in average teacher salary. But it would be wrong to conclude from this very strong relationship that teachers spent all of their salary increases on demon rum, and just as wrong to conclude that an alcoholically lubricated society was led by its inebriation to raise teacher salaries. More likely, the increase in these two variables over the years was caused by an increase in gross national product, coupled with inflation.

The Pearson Product-Moment Correlation Coefficient

The Pearson product-moment correlation coefficient, usually denoted r, provides a numerical summary of the kinds of relationships illustrated in scatter diagrams. When this statistic is appropriate, it indicates the degree to which two variables tend to covary. More specifically, the Pearson correlation coefficient r provides an indication of the tendency of points in a scatter diagram to fall right along a straight line.

.If the points in a scatter diagram fall *right on* a straight line that is angled upward, from lower left to upper right, the associated Pearson correlation coefficient is equal to +1.00. If the points in a scatter diagram fall *right on* a straight line that is angled downward, from upper left to lower right, the associated Pearson correlation coefficient is equal to –1.00. (It doesn't matter what the particular positive or negative *angle* of the line is, only that the points fall *on* it.) If the points in a scatter diagram were scattered uniformly throughout a circular pattern, there would be no tendency for one variable to increase or decrease as the other variable increased. The associated Pearson correlation coefficient would then equal zero.

The greater the tendency of points in a scatter diagram to fall along a straight line that is angled upward (a line that has *positive slope*), the closer the Pearson correlation coefficient will be to +1.00. The greater the tendency of points to fall along a straight line that is angled downward (a line that has *negative slope*), the closer the Pearson correlation coefficient will be to –1.00. These relationships are illustrated by the hypothetical scatter diagrams shown in Figure 4.2.

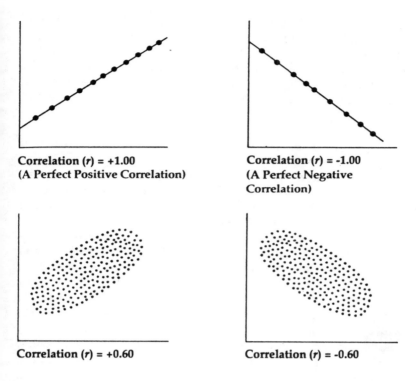

Correlation (*r*) = +1.00
(A Perfect Positive Correlation)

Correlation (*r*) = -1.00
(A Perfect Negative Correlation)

Correlation (*r*) = +0.60

Correlation (*r*) = -0.60

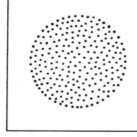

Correlation (*r*) = 0.00

Figure 4.2 Scatter Diagrams Associated with Pearson Product-Moment Correlation Coefficients of Various Magnitudes.

A Pearson correlation coefficient of +1.00 is called a *perfect positive correlation* and a coefficient of –1.00 is called a *perfect negative correlation*. These rare ascriptions of perfection stem from the ability of a researcher to predict the value of one variable perfectly, by knowing the value of the other variable (and the values of a couple of constant factors), when the correlation between the variables is either +1.00 or –1.00. But alas, perfection in research and evaluation is as elusive as perfection in other aspects of life. We've never seen a Pearson correlation coefficient of +1.00 or –1.00 outside a statistics book, and we'd be truly amazed if you were to find one.

Prediction of one variable from another is frequently of interest in research and evaluation. And the closer a correlation coefficient is to +1.00 or –1.00, the more accurately a researcher can predict the value of one variable by knowing the value of the other. The method most often used for prediction is called **regression analysis**, a topic that is discussed at length in Chapter 15. You will find that regression analysis and correlations are intimately related.

Whether a correlation coefficient is considered to be large or small depends on the usual behavior of the variables used to compute it, and on the group for which it is computed. Some statistics texts provide rules for evaluating the magnitude of a correlation coefficient, such as: "a correlation that is less than 0.30 is small, a correlation that is between 0.30 and 0.70 is moderate, a correlation that is between 0.70 and 0.90 is large, and a correlation that is greater than 0.90 is very large." Although such rules provide general guidelines to interpretation, they can be misleading in many specific situations. To tell whether a correlation coefficient is large or small, you have to know what is typical. For example, if a standardized reading achievement test were to be administered to a group of ninth-grade students, and another standardized reading achievement test were to be administered to the same students a week later, we would expect the correlation between their two sets of scores to be between 0.90 and 0.95. In this context, a correlation coefficient of 0.80 would be considered quite small, and a correlation of 0.90 would be considered moderate. In contrast, the correlation between high school graduates' scores on any of the widely used scholastic aptitude tests and their first-year college grade point averages is typically around 0.35. In this context, a correlation of 0.60 would be considered very high, and a correlation of 0.20 would be considered quite low. The best way to determine the "typical" size of a correlation coefficient for particular variables in a particular population is to read some research and evaluation reports in that area, especially those providing an overview of research.

One way researchers often express the strength of the relationship between two variables is by squaring their correlation coefficient. Suppose a group of students was administered a reading achievement test and a verbal IQ test. If the students' reading achievement scores and verbal IQ-test scores had a correlation of 0.80, a researcher might report the squared correlation as 0.80 times 0.80 = 0.64. This squared correlation coefficient is called a **coefficient of determination**. The coefficient of determination is useful because it gives the proportion of the variance of one variable that is predictable from the other variable. So we might say that 0.64 (or 64%) of the variance of the students' reading achievement scores is predictable from their verbal IQ-test scores. If two variables had a correlation of plus or minus 1.00, the corresponding coefficient of determination would equal +1.00. This would mean that 100% of the variance of one variable would be predictable using the other variable, and vice versa. This interpretation is consistent with our earlier comments on a perfect correlation of plus or minus 1.00. Conversely, suppose that two variables had a correlation of zero. Then the coefficient of determination would equal zero, suggesting that none of the variance of one variable was linearly predictable from the other variable. This too is consistent with our earlier comments. If two variables have a correlation of zero, there is no tendency for the points in their scatter diagram to fall along a straight line. Therefore, knowing a person's score on one variable would not help if we used linear regression to predict their score on the other variable. This interpretation of correlation coefficients is discussed in greater detail in the section of Chapter 15 that deals with regression analysis.

When you find correlations in research and evaluation reports, you might wonder *why* particular coefficients are large or small. Unfortunately, the answer is rarely simple. There are many reasons why a correlation coefficient might be large and many reasons why it might be small. Proper interpretation demands thoughtful consideration of many factors, and a good bit of caution. Finding a large correlation coefficient might mean that one of the variables being correlated has a major influence on the other; the relationship between the variables might be causal. Alternatively, a large correlation coefficient might result because the variables being correlated have a number of causes in common. In fact, the variables being correlated might be symptoms of other, underlying variables that have a more fundamental relationship. For example, the correlation between elementary school students' family income and their verbal intelligence would probably be quite large. But this does not mean that being verbally bright causes students to come from rich families, nor that being from a rich family causes verbal intelligence. Family income is most likely an indicator of an intellectually rich home environment, with many opportunities to practice verbal skills. And a score on a verbal intelligence test is, to some degree, an indicator of the quality of schooling a student has received. The strong relationship between these more fundamental variables might well explain the relatively high correlation between family income and verbal intelligence test scores. Correct interpretation of a large correlation coefficient thus requires knowledge of the real-world relationships that may influence the variables being correlated.

The correlation between two variables might also be large because the data used to calculate it came from several groups that differed on the variables being correlated. For example, the correlation between the weights and the reading achievement scores of a group consisting of 20 third-graders, 20 fourth-graders, and 20 fifth-graders would probably be quite high. This is because the fourth-graders would have a higher average reading achievement score and a higher average weight than the third-graders, and the fifth-graders would have a higher average reading achievement score and a higher average weight than the fourth-graders. For students in any one grade, however, the scatter diagram of weights and reading achievement scores would be nearly circular, and the corresponding correlation coefficient would be close to zero. But if the data for students in all three grades were taken together, the scatter diagram would be stretched out, and the corresponding correlation coefficient would be moderately large. This is illustrated in Figure 4.3.

When interpreting correlation coefficients in research and evaluation reports, it is therefore important to note the source of the data used to calculate the correlations. The correlation between

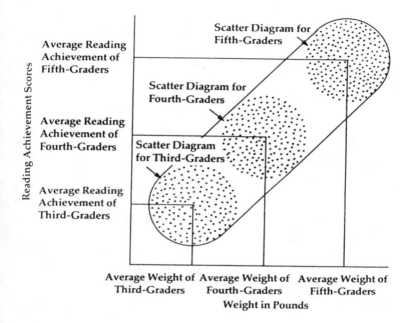

Figure 4.3 Scatter Diagrams of Weight and Reading Achievement for Students in Grades Three, Four, and Five.

two variables can be very different, depending on the group that supplied the data, as we have illustrated in Figure 4.3; it's near zero within one grade but high within the school.

Two variables can have a *small* correlation coefficient for many reasons. One possibility is that the data are related, but not *linearly* related; that is, although the points in the scatter diagram have no tendency to fall along a straight line, they do have a tendency to fall along a curve. This would indicate a *curvilinear relationship* between the variables, a topic that is discussed in the next section. For example, researchers have found that anxiety and achievement often have a curvilinear relationship. A small amount of anxiety appears to facilitate achievement so that, up to a point, an increase in anxiety is associated with an increase in achievement. But, beyond the point of facilitation, anxiety interferes with achievement, and becomes debilitating. So, as anxiety increases further, achievement decreases. A scatter diagram of scores on an anxiety scale versus scores on an achievement test would therefore follow a curve, and not a straight line. Because of this, the Pearson correlation coefficient between anxiety and achievement would probably be low.

Another reason a correlation coefficient might be low is because measurement is poor. If the tests, observation instruments, attitude scales, and other devices used to measure variables like achievement, attitudes, and behavior do not measure consistently, scores on these devices cannot be highly correlated. You can often detect this problem by examining the reliabilities of the devices being correlated. This reliability problem is discussed in Chapter 5.

Yet another measurement problem that might result in low correlation coefficients is called the "floor and ceiling effect." If a test that is very difficult is administered to a group, many of the resulting scores will be very low. Because many examinees will earn nearly identical low scores, the correlation between scores on that test and scores on any other variable will necessarily be low. To illustrate with an unlikely extreme: If everyone earned the same score on a test, there would be no high scores and no low scores, hence no difference in scores, hence no variance. That test would therefore be useless in predicting differences between scores (variance) on any other variable, and would therefore have a correlation of zero with any other variable. If scores on a test tend to pile up in the low end of the score scale, the test is said to have an "inadequate floor." The test does not measure differences in the ability of low scorers. A problem arises when a very easy test is administered to a group. Many examinees earn the highest possible score, because of the "inadequate ceiling" of the test. Again, the correlation between scores on the test and scores on any other variable will be low. If the difficulty of the test was more appropriate to the ability of the group being tested, the correlation between scores on the test and scores on other variables would undoubtedly be higher. By looking at a scatter diagram, you can often tell whether a variable is exhibiting a floor or ceiling effect.

Other Types of Correlation Coefficients

Although Pearson correlation coefficients are used more frequently than any other kind, they do not always give a complete picture of the relationship between two variables, and they are not applicable in all situations. The Pearson correlation coefficient indicates only the degree to which the points in a scatter diagram tend to fall along a *straight* line. This is called the *degree of linear relationship* between two variables. If the points in a scatter diagram tend to fall along a curve, such as an arc (a parabola), the Pearson correlation coefficient might miss their relationship entirely. An alternative correlation coefficient, called **eta**, indicates the degree of relationship between two variables regardless of whether the relationship is linear (i.e., the points in a scatter diagram fall along a straight line), or nonlinear (i.e., the points in the scatter diagram fall along a curve). Eta is denoted by the lowercase Greek letter η. A related statistic, **eta-squared**, indicates how well one variable can be predicted from another, either through a linear relationship or a nonlinear (curved) relationship. Eta-squared can be compared to the coefficient of determination, to estimate the extent to which two variables have a nonlinear relationship. In one of our earlier examples, involving prediction of students' reading achievement scores from their verbal IQ-test scores, the coefficient of determination was found to be 0.64. Suppose that eta-squared for these tests had been found to equal 0.90. In that case, 90% of the variance of reading achievement scores would be predictable from students' verbal IQ-test scores, either linearly or nonlinearly; and since 64% of the variance of students' reading achievement scores was linearly predictable from their verbal IQ-test scores, 90 – 64 = 26% of the variance of their reading achievement scores would be predictable nonlinearly.

We have already suggested that the Pearson correlation coefficient is applicable to data that measure underlying variables at the interval or ratio levels of measurement. Other correlation coefficients have been developed for use with data we can collect only at other levels of measurement. The **Spearman rank-order correlation coefficient** is widely used with data that measure underlying variables at the ordinal level. The Spearman correlation coefficient is interpreted just like the Pearson coefficient. Although the formulas for the two coefficients are different, the Spearman correlation coefficient should be thought of as the Pearson correlation coefficient applied to sets of ranks.

If applied to the *same* set of interval-level data, the Spearman correlation coefficient would be somewhat closer to zero than the Pearson correlation coefficient. When it is appropriate, the Pearson correlation coefficient should always be used because it makes use of the interval-level properties of the data. It therefore does a better job of indicating the degree of linear relationship between two interval-level variables. The Spearman coefficient throws away the *size* of the intervals, using only the ranks. But when you *have* only the ranks, you will be very happy to have the Spearman coefficient.

In research on testing, students' scores on individual test items are often correlated with their scores on the remainder of the test. Because test items are typically scored 0 (for a wrong answer) or 1 (for a right answer), special correlation coefficients are needed for this application. The **biserial correlation coefficient** and the **point biserial correlation coefficient** meet these needs. Each of these correlation coefficients can be used whenever one of the variables is scored 0 or 1, and the other variable is measured on an interval scale. The biserial correlation coefficient provides an estimate of what the Pearson correlation coefficient would be, if the researcher had true interval-level measurement for the 0-1 variable. This achievement of the biserial correlation coefficient is, to some degree, offset by the fact that it is based on a strong assumption that isn't always met in practice. The point-biserial correlation coefficient takes the 0-1 variable as it is, and doesn't incorporate any strong measurement assumptions. When its assumptions hold, the biserial correlation coefficient will usually be larger than the corresponding point-biserial correlation. Some researchers feel that it does a better job than the point-biserial coefficient in indicating the relationship between scores on test items and scores on the remainder of a test. The interpretation of such correlation coefficients is discussed in Chapter 5.

The evaluation of tests provides the context for some additional correlation coefficients. Correlations between examinees' scores on different test items are often useful guides when tests are to be improved. In this application, *both* of the variables to be correlated are scored 0 (for a wrong answer) or 1 (for a right answer). Two correlation coefficients have been developed for variables that are both scored 0 or 1: the **phi coefficient** and the **tetrachoric correlation coefficient**. The phi coefficient is equivalent to the Pearson correlation coefficient, applied to two variables that are scored 0 or 1. Because of this scoring, the formula for the Pearson correlation coefficient can be simplified to that of the phi coefficient. The tetrachoric correlation coefficient assumes that the two 0-1 items really measure underlying variables that have an interval scale. This coefficient attempts to predict what the correlation would be, if data on these underlying variables were available. Like the biserial correlation coefficient, the tetrachoric correlation coefficient is based on strong measurement assumptions that may not hold in practice. As was true for the Pearson correlation coefficient and all of the other correlation coefficients we have discussed so far, the phi coefficient and the tetrachoric correlation coefficient theoretically can assume values between −1.00 and +1.00. The extreme values indicate perfect correlation, and a correlation of zero indicates the absence of a linear relationship.

In many studies, researchers and evaluators attempt to predict one variable (called a *criterion variable*) from scores on *several* other variables (called *predictor variables*). For example, students' college grade point averages are often predicted from their high school grade point averages *and* their scores on several aptitude tests (such as the verbal subtest and the quantitative subtest of the Scholastic Aptitude Tests). In these studies, a statistic called the **multiple correlation coefficient** (usually denoted by R) is often used to describe the correlation between actual scores on the criterion variable and predicted scores on the criterion variable. The higher this correlation, the more accurate the prediction. Because of the way it is defined, the multiple correlation coefficient can assume values only between 0.00 and +1.00. If the multiple correlation coefficient were to equal +1.00, each person's predicted score on the criterion variable would equal their actual score on the criterion variable; in that case, prediction would be perfect.

Reports on studies involving multiple correlation sometimes contain a statistic called the **coefficient of multiple determination**. This coefficient is simply the square of the coefficient of multiple correlation, and indicates the proportion of the variance of a criterion variable that can be predicted using all of the predictor variables. For example, a coefficient of multiple correlation equal to 0.80 would have an associated coefficient of multiple determination equal to 0.64. This is sometimes described verbally by saying that the predictor variables "explain" or "predict" 64% of the variance of the criterion variable. The larger the coefficient of multiple determination, the better the prediction. The coefficient of multiple determination is usually denoted by R^2. Both the coefficient of multiple correlation and the coefficient of multiple determination are illustrated and discussed in greater depth in Chapter 15.

Summary

Correlation coefficients are statistics that indicate the degree of relationship between two variables. The Pearson correlation coefficient, like most correlation coefficients, indicates only the degree of linear relationship between two variables. In contrast, the eta coefficient indicates the degree of linear and nonlinear relationship between two variables.

Correlation coefficients must be interpreted thoughtfully and cautiously. There are many reasons why a correlation coefficient can be large or small. In general, a large correlation coefficient does not mean that two variables are causally related; there are many alternative explanations.

A variety of correlation coefficients has been developed for use with data that measure at the interval, ordinal, and two-category nominal levels of measurement. All of these coefficients can take on values between –1.00 and +1.00.

Multiple correlation coefficients indicate the degree of linear relationship between a single criterion variable and a number of predictor variables. These coefficients are discussed in Chapter 15.

Problems — Chapter 4

4.1 Suppose that you were to collect data on the ages and weights of 100 persons—both children and adults—who were attending a company picnic. If you were to calculate the correlation coefficient between the ages and the weights of these 100

persons, which of the following values is most likely to be the correlation you will find?
   a. A correlation of −0.90.
   b. A correlation of +1.00.
   c. A correlation of +0.02.
   d. A correlation of +0.50.

4.2   Suppose a research report gave the correlation coefficient between the IQ-test scores of students when they were in the second grade and their arithmetic achievement scores when they were in the third grade. The reported value was 0.60. The report also stated that the correlation between the number of days the third-graders were absent from school and their third-grade arithmetic achievement scores was −0.85. Given these data, which of the following are true statements? (Circle the letter of *each* true statement.)
   a. Number of absences during the third grade is a better predictor of third-graders' arithmetic achievement than are their second-grade IQ-test scores.
   b. Number of absences during the third grade is not as good a predictor of third-graders' arithmetic achievement as are their second-grade IQ-test scores.
   c. Second-grade IQ-test performance and number of absences during the third grade are equally good predictors of third-graders' arithmetic achievement.
   d. If a scatter diagram were drawn, using data on third-graders' absences and their arithmetic achievement scores, the scatter of points would go from the upper left corner of the graph to the lower right corner.

4.3   A report on the relationship between expenditures for public education and student achievement in school systems states that "the correlation between annual per-pupil expenditures and average student achievement test performance equals +2.7 for the 500 school systems in the sample." From this result, which of the following can you safely conclude is true?
   a. There was either an error in computing the correlation coefficient or a typographic error in reporting the result.

b. Higher student achievement attracts higher expenditures for public education.
c. There is a positive association between per-pupil expenditures for education and student achievement.
d. Spending more on education causes student achievement to increase.

4.4 The following is a scatter diagram that illustrates the relationship between level of debt and number of employees for a sample of Fortune 500 corporations. Assuming the data shown in the scatter diagram are representative of the entire Fortune 500 list, which of the following correlation coefficients is most likely to summarize the true relationship between debt level and number of employees for those corporations?

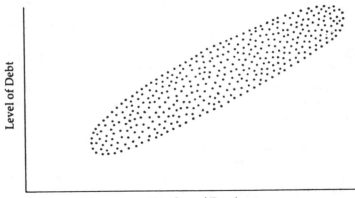

Number of Employees

a. +0.00
b. +0.60
c. −0.60
d. +1.00

5.

Some Fundamentals of Measurement

Measurement as the Basis for Statistics

Researchers in the physical and biological sciences have several distinct advantages, compared to their brethren in the social and behavioral sciences and those who conduct educational research. One major advantage is that physical and biological scientists can often observe the things they want to measure, while social and behavioral scientists often cannot. In educational research, most of the really important and interesting variables are *not* directly observable; many are psychological or social states—observable only through their manifestations. As you might imagine, not being able to see what you want to measure often creates thorny problems. In the terms of the title of this book, think of how difficult it would be to measure a professional baseball player's hitting ability if it was impossible to observe his performance at the plate. That's how it is most of the time in educational research, and much of the time in social and behavioral research.

Think of the variables most often used by educators to describe the behavior or performance of students. They talk about things like "intelligence," "motivation," "attitude," "aptitude," and "ability." None of these variables can be observed directly. We can stand a student next to a door frame and measure his or her height merely by comparing the distance from the floor to the top of the student's head with the distance shown by a tape measure. But we cannot measure a student's intelligence that way.

Intelligence, and all of the other variables in our list, are examples of what behavioral scientists call **constructs**. They are *constructed variables*. We label a person as intelligent because that person exhibits a certain consistent set of observable behaviors. Intelligence is the label applied to the concept *underlying* the behaviors. For example, intelligence is suggested by lucid speech and a large vocabulary, but vocabulary alone is not sufficient. Since the turn of the century, the most widely accepted measurement of intelligence is a person's performance on the set of problems that comprise an IQ test. The test gives us a chance to observe a person's responses to a set of problems that don't have obvious solutions. Collectively, those responses give an indication of the person's status with respect to the construct we call "intelligence."

Motivation is another key psychological construct. We cannot observe a student's motivation directly. However, we can observe that the student always comes to class on time and rarely misses a day of class, always completes assigned work on or ahead of time, always provides a careful and complete response to assigned work, often volunteers to do extra work, and usually volunteers answers to teachers' questions in class. To be sure, variables other than motivation, such as ability and health, affect these behaviors. But, taken together, we would normally describe a student who exhibited all of these behaviors as being "highly motivated." Thus we summarize these and other patterns of consistent behaviors under the label "motivation."

The use of constructs (rather than directly observable variables) in research and evaluation results in a host of measurement issues and, often, measurement problems. First, we have to concern ourselves with the extent of the relationship between certain of the variables we observe (e.g., performance on a vocabulary test) and the constructs we want to measure (e.g., intelligence). This is a **validity** issue. Second, we have to concern ourselves with the consistency of whatever measurement approach we use; for example, are we measuring motivation in such a way that a student who is determined to be "highly motivated" when one person does the measuring will be similarly assessed by someone else using the same approach? This is a **reliability** issue. Finally, we must concern ourselves with the development of appropriate **units** of measurement. It might be obvious that—in the U.S. today—we should measure students' heights in feet and inches.

But what units should we use for measuring motivation? Clearly, feet and inches won't do.

In the remainder of this chapter, we consider the issues of validity, reliability, and units of measurement in greater detail. If you are to be a knowledgeable judge of the results of research and evaluation studies in education and the social and behavioral sciences, it is essential that you learn how to judge the appropriateness and quality of the measurements that are the foundation of such studies. The raw data of educational and behavioral research are only as good as the processes used to produce them. Measurement plays a critical role in all such research. And we have by now developed some very useful statistical tools we can apply to evaluating various approaches to measurement.

Assessing Validity

When we collect data on a person for the purpose of research in education or the social sciences, we usually measure or observe a *sample* of that person's behavior. We might provide the person with a task to be completed or some set of stimulus materials that require a response. A traditional pencil-and-paper test is a good example. Alternatively, we might just observe the person in some naturally occurring situation, and count the incidences of some behavior or action. In recent years, much educational research has included observations of the incidence of specified students' or teachers' behaviors in classrooms. For example, a researcher might count the number of times, in a 15-minute period, that a teacher asks his or her students a direct question.

If research merely involved reporting the number of test items a person answered correctly, or the number of times a teacher asked his or her students a question, there would be few validity issues. Validity concerns arise because researchers interpret these observable behaviors as indicators of a person's status on more general constructs such as "ability" or "interest." By generalizing beyond observed behaviors that occur at a particular time and in a particular setting, researchers and evaluators create a multitude of validity issues. The most fundamental concern is the appropriateness of the interpretations of the results of measurement. Measurement procedures are not *inherently* valid, nor inherently invalid. It is the *interpretations* of measurement results that must be examined for validity.

The nature of measurement validity has been debated for decades, and many issues are still far from settled. Entire texts have been devoted to the theory of measurement, with discussion of the nature and assessment of measurement validity filling many of their pages. Our discussion here will be relatively brief, and concerned more with practical interpretation than with theoretical underpinnings.

Classical measurement books usually identify four types of evidence pertaining to measurement validity: **construct validity** evidence, **concurrent validity** evidence, **predictive validity** evidence, and **content validity** evidence. Recent contributors to the measurement literature, such as Messick (1989), have suggested that content validity evidence is really not concerned with measurement validation, and that the other three distinctions are about as confusing as they are helpful. Nevertheless, we think that the four types of evidence form a useful framework for critical reading of many research and evaluation reports. We will therefore discuss each one.

Construct validity evidence is at once the most fundamental and the most complex of the four types of evidence we have mentioned. (Messick, 1989, suggests that it encompasses all of validity, and subsumes the other three types.) Construct validity evidence is concerned with the total relationship between the results of a particular measurement or set of measurements and the underlying construct the researcher or evaluator is attempting to measure. In short, it addresses the question: "Does this measurement procedure really measure the construct it is claimed to measure?" For example, the question: "Does this IQ test really measure intelligence?" is asking about construct validity. As you might imagine, the question is very difficult to answer, and a conclusive answer is rarely found. All a researcher can do is try to amass a balance of evidence in support of the claim that the IQ test measures intelligence. Construct validity is never "proved"; it is merely accepted as long as supporting evidence strongly outweighs contrary evidence. A construct validation study is designed to determine whether a measurement procedure yields results that are consistent with theoretical expectations. For example, the theory of intelligence suggests that older children are, on average, more intelligent than younger children. If an IQ test is truly a measure of intelligence, older children should therefore earn a higher average score on that test than will younger children—and, indeed, on most IQ tests they do. Another theoretical expectation is that more intelligent children, on average, achieve better grades in school than do less intelligent children. The correlation between children's scores on the IQ test and their grade point averages in school should therefore be positive. If the correlation is positive, the construct validity claim—that the IQ test measures intelligence—is somewhat supported; if the correlation is close to zero or is negative, the claim to construct validity would have suffered a near-fatal blow.

No single piece of evidence is sufficient to establish the construct validity of a measurement procedure. A series of studies that examines every reasonable alternative interpretation of the results of measurement is necessary, before a construct validity claim is adequately supported.

When you read research and evaluation reports that contain discussions involving constructs, it is essential that you question the validity of the authors' claims. If authors state that one group had more positive attitudes than another, or that students in one academic program are less highly motivated than students in another, you must ask how these constructs were measured and critically question the authors' evidence that their procedures actually measured attitude and motivation.

At this point, you're probably wondering how you can possibly know whether the construct validity of a measurement procedure has been adequately demonstrated. Unfortunately, there is no simple answer. In any study, you can quickly note whether the author has even addressed construct validity issues—that is, whether there's any explicit discussion of the problem. When a researcher has used a commercially available measurement instrument, such as a test or an attitude scale, you can check such sources as the Buros Institute's *Mental Measurements Yearbooks*, the *Journal of Educational Measurement*, or *Educational and Psychological Measurement* for professional reviews that often include discussion of measurement validation. As in other aspects of research and evaluation, healthy skepticism on the part of the reader is fully warranted.

When a researcher has developed a new measurement procedure, he or she might provide evidence of its validity by amassing concurrent validity evidence. Let's consider an example. The Torrance Test of Creativity is one of the most widely accepted measures of what psychologists call "creativity" or "divergent thinking." Suppose that, in an evaluation of an educational program designed to foster creativity in children, you develop your own procedure for measuring "creativity." As evidence supporting this claim, you administer your measurement procedure *and* the Torrance Test of Creativity to a large sample of students who have participated in the new educational program. You then compute the correlation coefficient between students' scores on your test and their scores on the Torrance Test. You find that the correlation coefficient equals 0.90, suggesting that students who earn relatively high scores on your procedure also earn relatively high scores on the Torrance Test, and that students who earn relatively low scores on your measure also earn relatively low scores on the Torrance Test. Since the Torrance Test is an accepted measure of creativity, you can legitimately reason that your procedure also measures that construct.

The essential features of this example are common to all concurrent validation studies. Such studies involve an accepted measure of some construct, and a new, as yet unvalidated measure. The concurrent validity of the new measure is estimated by administering it, together with the accepted measure, to an appropriate group of subjects. The correlation coefficient between scores on the new measure and scores on the accepted measure is known as a validity coefficient. The closer the validity coefficient is to 1.00, the higher the concurrent validity of the new measure. Concurrent validation gets its name from the almost-simultaneous administration of the accepted measure and the new measure. In fact, the time interval between the two administrations need only be short enough that no systematic changes in the examinees' behavior are likely to take place. Concurrent validation is often part of a more general validation construct of a new measurement procedure. It should seem reasonable that a new measure of a given construct should give results that covary positively with older, accepted measures of that construct. High concurrent validity coefficients thus provide supporting evidence of construct validity.

The primary objective of many applied studies is the *prediction* of subjects' future performance or behavior. For example, a professional polling organization, such as the Gallup Poll, might survey registered voters several months prior to an election in an attempt to predict the election outcome. Such predictions are effective only to the degree that voters' responses to the survey questions indicate their future voting behavior. In an educational context, most selective colleges require that their applicants for admission complete an aptitude test, such as the *Scholastic Aptitude Tests* (*SAT*) or the *American College Testing Program Tests* (*ACT*). Colleges then use the applicants' test scores to predict their future college grade point averages (GPA), and admit only those applicants who are likely to exceed some minimum GPA.

In studies such as these, the correlation coefficient between the measure used for prediction (such as the score on the voters' survey questionnaire) and the measure used to indicate future performance (such as actual voting behavior at the time of the election) is called a **predictive validity coefficient**. The higher this correlation between the predictor variable (e.g., the voters' responses to the survey questionnaire) and the criterion variable (actual voting behavior), the more valid is the predictor.

Predictive validity evidence is of particular importance in situations involving selection of applicants, placement of applicants into appropriate positions (such as occupational specialties within the military or in industry), and in marketing studies that attempt to predict consumer behavior. As is true for all types of validation, a measurement procedure does not have any *inherent* predictive validity. Its predictive validity might be high when predicting some criterion variables, and low when predicting others. It might also be high for some groups of individuals and low for others. For example, it might be the case that people who say they intend to vote Democratic really do so a month later, whereas people who say they intend to vote Independent often change their minds. In that case, the predictive validity of a survey questionnaire would be high for Democrats, but low for Independents.

When interpreting a research study that involves predictive evidence of validity, make sure that the criterion variable and the group used to collect such evidence are relevant to your own interests and likely applications. Otherwise, you should regard evidence of predictive validity as being tentative for your own purposes.

The need for **content validity evidence** arises frequently in educational research and evaluation studies, but also in psychiatry and market or political research. In such studies, researchers or evaluators often want to generalize from an individual's (often a student's) performance on a particular test to that individual's ability to solve test problems in some larger **content domain**. For example, suppose that a test contains 20 items (a problem on a test is called an **item**) in which a student is shown four words. In each item, three of the words are spelled correctly and one is spelled incorrectly. The student must identify the word that is spelled incorrectly. In most uses of such a test, the researcher or evaluator would not be interested in the student's ability to discriminate between the *particular* 60 correctly spelled words and the *particular* 20 incorrectly spelled words that make up that test. What is really of interest is the student's ability to discriminate between *all* correctly or incorrectly spelled words that are, in some way, like the words used to make up the test. Researchers and evaluators routinely generalize from students' performances on a few specific test items to their hypothetical performances on all possible similar test items. The content validity issue focuses on exactly these generalizations. To be content valid, the items on the test must constitute a **representative sample** of the domain of items used to generalize the students' performances. For example, if all the words used in the 20 spelling items consist of two syllables and begin with a vowel, it would clearly be unreasonable to generalize the students' performances to all words in Webster's *New World Dictionary*. The test items would not constitute a representative sample of the words in the dictionary.

Unlike construct validation evidence, concurrent validation evidence, and predictive validation evidence, all of which are substantially statistical (e.g., correlation coefficients), content validation evidence is solely judgmental. The fundamental issue in content validation is whether the content of the test is consistent with the content of the domain of items or tasks for which the generalization is claimed to hold. In pursuing this fundamental question, one might ask whether *each type* of item for which representativeness is claimed is actually represented in the test. One might also ask whether each type of item is present in the test *in proportion to* its presence in the domain of content used for generalization. For example, if a mathematics test is claimed to measure students' abilities to solve computational problems involving the four basic arithmetic operations of addition, subtraction, multiplication, and division, then that test should not consist of 80% addition items, 10% subtraction items, 5% multiplication items, and 5% division items. The four types of items would normally make up approximately equal proportions of the test.

A good way to begin analyzing the content validity of a commercially available test is to obtain the test publisher's technical manual for the test. Most reputable test publishers provide a **test blueprint** or a **table of specifications** that shows how many items on the test were designed to measure each of the types of behavior the test is intended to assess. Comparison of the test blueprint with a desired domain of content is a useful beginning in assessing a test's content validity for a particular application.

Assessing Reliability

The **reliability** of a measurement procedure is the technical term for its consistency. It is well known that no measurement procedure—whether it is the use of a bathroom scale or the administration of an achievement test—is perfectly consistent. If you were to step on and off your bathroom scale five times in a row, chances are you would observe three or four different measurements of your weight. Depending on whether you placed your feet in exactly the same spot on the scale, and on the quality of the scale itself, the scale's indication of your weight might fluctuate by three our four pounds across the five measurements. The more consistent the indications of your weight, the more reliable is your bathroom scale. If the scale were to indicate exactly the same weight for you every time you stepped on and off (a highly unlikely occurrence), it would be totally consistent. We would then say that it was perfectly "reliable" *even though it might indicate the wrong weight every time* and thus give you an invalid weight. (In the *everyday* sense of "reliable" we would include validity, too; but in the technical sense, validity is a completely separate issue.)

When you observe the weight indicated by your bathroom scale, you are reading what measurement theorists call an **observed score**. This observed score can be thought of as consisting of two parts: one is your true weight (the **true score**), and the other is the result of a variety of factors that have nothing to do with your true weight (the **error component**). These other factors might include such things as the particular position of your feet on the scale (step too far forward, and the scale might read low; step too far backward and it might read high); the fact that you placed the scale on a thick rug instead of on the floor; and the tendency of the scale's springs to fatigue and recover depending on the rates at which you climb on and off the scale. In *every* measurement procedure, regardless of what is being measured or how it is being measured, the observed score that results from taking a measurement is equal to the sum of the true score and the error component. The reliability of the measurement procedure depends on the relative sizes of the true score and the error component. The larger the error component, the lower the reliability; the smaller the error component, the higher the reliability.

Measurement reliability is usually expressed as an index that can take on values between 0 and 1, much like a correlation coefficient. Unlike a correlation coefficient though, the reliability of a measurement procedure can never be a negative number. A reliability of 0 means that the observed scores consist entirely of error components. A reliability of 1 would mean that the observed scores consist entirely of true scores; in reality, however, observed scores are composed of both true scores and error components, and their reliabilities are less than 1.

Another statistic that is closely associated with reliability is called the **standard error of measurement**. The standard error of measurement is equal to *the standard deviation of the error components* in a set of observed scores. If the reliability is equal to one, there are no error components, and the standard error of measurement is equal to zero. If the reliability is equal to zero, the observed scores consist totally of error components, and the standard error of measurement is equal to the standard deviation of observed scores.

In many research and evaluation reports that include assessments of measurement quality, standard errors of measurement are provided, together with estimates of the reliabilities of measurement procedures. These standard errors of measurement can be interpreted by assuming that errors follow a normal distribution, as is commonly the case. For example, if a 50-item test were administered to a group of students and the standard error of measurement were reported to equal two points, you could draw the following conclusions from your knowledge of the normal distribution: Sixty-eight percent of the individuals tested would have true scores that were within one standard error of measurement (two points) of their observed scores. Ninety-five percent of the individuals tested would have true scores that were within two standard errors of measurement (four points) of their observed scores. Alternatively, suppose a given individual had an observed score of 30 on the test. You could then say that the chances were 68% that this person's true score was between 28 (one standard error of measurement below 30) and 32 (one standard error of measurement above 30). Also, the chances would be 95% that this person's true score was between 26 and 34.

Although reliable measurement procedures are always desirable in research and evaluation, your need for a particularly high level of reliability might depend on the nature of your research, since high reliability may be expensive and unnecessary. And, of course, reliability is not at stake when a true score is changing *on its own*. For example, if you were measuring weights using a bathroom scale, you would want the measurement procedure to provide consistent results at a particular time on a particular day. But you wouldn't be distressed if the scale showed different weights for people on Friday than it did on Monday. Since individuals' true weights change over a period of five days, the scale's indications of their weights should also change. In contrast, suppose that you administered an IQ test to a group of adults on Monday, and then administered the same test to them on Friday. Ignoring the possibility that they might recall the items and hence do better because they've had practice, you would expect the intelligence levels of these individuals to be exactly the same on Friday as they were on Monday. In this example, reliable measurement implies consistency over a five-day period. Consistency over time is known as **stability** of measurement, and should be high for stable variables.

A variety of methods have been developed for assessing the reliability of measurement procedures. Some of these procedures indicate consistency of measurement at a given time, and others indicate stability of measurement across a period of time. Whether a particular method for assessing reliability is appropriate depends on the purposes of the research or evaluation study in which it is used. We will now describe several of the most widely used methods of assessing reliability, and discuss the situations in which they are most appropriate.

Suppose you were interested in assessing the reliability of an IQ test, in the sense of providing stable measurement across a two-week period. One way you could handle this problem would be to administer the IQ test to a sample selected from the group of individuals you intend to use it with, and then administer the test to these same individuals two weeks later. You could then calculate the correlation coefficient between the scores resulting from the first administration and the scores resulting from the second. The correlation coefficient you obtained through this procedure would be called a **reliability coefficient**. The higher the correlation coefficient, the higher the reliability of the IQ test. The logic underlying this **test-retest method** of assessing reliability is as follows: If the measurement procedure is reliable, the person who scored highest on the first administration of the test should score at or very near the top on the second administration. The person who scored second highest on the first administration should score high on the second administration, and so on. In short, with reliable measurement, people ought to retain their relative scores from one administration of the test to the next. The greater the extent to which this occurs, the higher the reliability coefficient.

The test-retest method of assessing reliability has at least two potential flaws. If it is used with a measurement instrument like an IQ test, there is always the chance that examinees will either remember the items and do better on them the second time around *or* will remember the *answers* they gave to specific test items on the first administration, and give exactly the same answers on the second administration of the test. This kind of *memory effect* has nothing to do with the *true* reliability of the test, but will tend to increase the correlation between scores obtained on the two administrations. Therefore the *indicated* reliability of the test, when using the correlation between scores as its measure, will be spuriously increased. To handle this problem, publishers of commercially available tests often create several forms of their tests, so that one form can be administered initially and a second form, containing totally different items, can be used for the second administration. Test forms that are designed to be interchangeable are known as **parallel forms**, and the use of parallel test forms in a test-retest reliability study is known as the **parallel forms method** of assessing reliability.

The parallel forms method of assessing reliability has advantages beyond its elimination of potential memory effects. In most testing situations, a researcher or evaluator is interested in determining an examinee's performance on an entire *domain* of skill, rather than the few specific items on one test. A single test merely provides an estimate of how the examinee would perform by sampling from that domain. By using two parallel test forms in assessing reliability, the researcher can get a better estimate of the examinees' performances on the entire domain of items simply because more items are used. In other words, the parallel forms method of reliability estimation includes an important error component, namely the error due to selection of a specific, relatively small, sample of test items. The test-retest method, using a single test form, ignores this error component and might therefore provide an unrealistically high estimate of a test's reliability.

Both the test-retest and parallel forms methods of assessing reliability require that a group of individuals be measured twice. This is costly, time-consuming, and inconvenient. It is often difficult, if not impossible, to assemble the same group more than once. A number of reliability assessment methods that require data to be collected on only one occasion have been developed in response to these problems. We will describe the methods that are used most often.

Reliability assessment methods that require data to be collected on only one occasion are called **internal consistency methods**. Although these methods differ in methodological detail, each of them indicates the degree to which the components of a measurement procedure tend to assess the same underlying variable or construct. When applied to a test, these methods show the extent to which the items on the test tend to measure the same thing.

An easy way to increase reliability is by using a longer test; for example, giving both parallel forms at one sitting. If you wanted to measure a baseball player's hitting ability, you'd get a more reliable measure of this variable by calculating the average percent of times at bat that the player got a hit in both games of a doubleheader than by calculating the percentage for a single game. In this example, the two baseball games are analogous to two sets of test items, such as two parallel forms. You will obtain far more reliable information about an examinee's performance from twice as many test items administered at one time as you will from half as many, and in general, the greater the number of measurements involved in a measurement procedure, the more reliable the procedure. So the longer a test—up to the point where examinee fatigue sets in—the more reliable it will be, *provided* the added measurements assess the same variable as the initial ones. If you were trying to assess a ballplayer's hitting ability, you would not increase measurement reliability by counting the number of times he or she caught a fly ball. Fielding skill doesn't correlate highly with batting skill. The added measurements would have to assess hitting ability, just like the initial ones. Internal consistency reliability methods indicate whether, and to what degree, all of the measurements used in a procedure assess the same variable.

One of the simplest internal consistency methods for assessing reliability is called the **split-half method** or the **odd-even method**. In this procedure, we *make* two tests out of one. Thus, a group of examinees is given a test only once, but two scores are calculated for each examinee, one based on the odd-numbered items in the test, and the other based on the even-numbered items. These two sets of scores are then correlated, to determine whether examinees who score highest on the odd-numbered items also tend to score highest on the even-numbered items. This correlation coefficient is called the **split-half reliability coefficient**. The higher the split-half reliability coefficient, the more consistent are the items on the test (in the sense that the odd-numbered items measure the same variable as the even-numbered items).

Because the reliability of a measurement procedure increases as the number of measurements is increased, the split-half reliability coefficient will tend to underestimate reliability. For example, if it is applied to a 50-item test, the split-half method really indicates the reliability of two shorter tests—the 25-item halves, composed of the odd items and the even items, respectively. To estimate the reliability of the full 50-item test, it is necessary to adjust the split-half reliability coefficient using a formula known as the **Spearman-Brown prophecy formula**. When you see a reliability coefficient reported as a Spearman-Brown coefficient, you can be sure that the author has used the split-half method for assessing reliability, and then has applied the adjustment formula.

The split-half method of assessing reliability, like all internal consistency methods, will not show the stability of a measurement procedure over time. Nor will it reflect errors that arise from peculiarities in the administration of a measurement procedure on a particular occasion. A split-half reliability coefficient, when adjusted using the Spearman-Brown prophecy formula, might therefore overestimate the true reliability of a measurement procedure.

Two widely used alternatives to the split-half method of estimating reliability are named after the authors of the research paper in which they were first proposed. Both methods can be used only with procedures composed of a series of measurements that are scored 1 for a correct response and 0 for an incorrect response. These procedures are known as the **Kuder-Richardson Formula 20 method** and the **Kuder-Richardson Formula 21 method**. You will often find them abbreviated as KR-20 and KR-21. The KR-21 formula is sometimes used instead of KR-20, because it is simpler and easier to compute. However, it makes the assumption that each of the measurements that compose a procedure (or each of the items that compose a test) is equally difficult. This assumption is often violated in practice, resulting in an overestimate of true reliability.

The Kuder-Richardson methods of assessing reliability have all of the advantages and all of the pitfalls of the split-half method. They are sensitive to the same kinds of measurement errors, and ignore the same error components as well. They should never be used to assess stability of measurement, not in situations where the conditions of measurement are difficult to control, nor where speed of response is a major factor in performance. In any of these applications, they are likely to give a falsely inflated estimate of true measurement reliability.

It is not necessary to use the Spearman-Brown prophecy formula to adjust the reliability estimates obtained through use of the Kuder-Richardson procedures, as must be done with the split-half method. The correction for reduced test length is built into the KR formulas.

A final method for assessing internal consistency reliability was named after its developer, Lee J. Cronbach. It is known as **Cronbach's alpha**. Cronbach's procedure, like the other internal consistency methods, uses measurement data collected on a single occasion. Cronbach's alpha is a generalization of Kuder-Richardson Formula 20, in that the test items (or other components of the measurement procedure) do not have to be scored either 0 or 1. This improvement makes it possible to apply Cronbach's method to many measurement procedures other than tests, including attitude instruments in which each item requires a response on a five-point scale that might range from "Strongly Disagree" to "Strongly Agree."

In recent years, variants of Cronbach's alpha have been used in more sophisticated studies of reliability known as **generalizability studies**. In these studies, the components of measurement error—such as those due to instability and those due to peculiarities of measurement conditions—are analyzed separately. For example, in a study in which five judges were used to estimate the work attitudes of a group of employees on three different occasions in two different work settings, generalizability methods would make it possible to determine how much the reliability was affected by disagreements between judges, and how much it was affected by changes across time, or by inconsistency across work situations. This kind of information could then be used to design a more reliable measurement procedure.

Reporting the Scores

The score scales that are used in research in education and the behavioral sciences are often arbitrary or difficult to interpret. For example, suppose that a researcher used a 20-item attitude scale in which each item provided five responses ranging from "Strongly Disagree" to "Strongly Agree." It is traditional to give a score of 1 for a response of Strongly Disagree, and a score of 5 for a response of Strongly Agree. With 20 items, a respondent could earn a score that ranged from a low of 20 to a high of 100. This score scale is totally arbitrary. It would make just as much sense to give a score of 2 to a Strongly Disagree response, and a score of 10 to a Strongly Agree response. In that case, total scores would range from a low of 40 to a high of 200. If the original scoring system were used, but the attitude scale had 25 items instead of 20, the possible scores would range from a low of 25 to a high of 125. In all three cases, we could presume that a higher score on the scale indicated a stronger level of agreement. However, any numerical value on the score scale would be an artifact of the way the scale was constructed, and would have no absolute meaning.

This example illustrates the nature of observed scores that result in many research and evaluation studies in education and the behavioral sciences. To give meaning to the scores, it is necessary to transform them in some way. Various transformations have been developed for this purpose.

One way to give meaning to a person's raw score is through comparison with the scores earned by others. This is called a **normative interpretation** of scores. We discussed one such transformation, the percentile rank, in Chapter 1. If a person earned a score of 75 on our 20-item attitude scale, we could judge the relative value of this score by computing the person's percentile rank. For example, if a raw score of 75 corresponded to a percentile rank of 80, we could conclude that the degree of the person's agreement was at least as strong as that held by 80% of the other individuals who were assessed.

As we mentioned in Chapter 1, percentile ranks are group dependent. A given score might have a relatively high percentile rank in one group, and a relatively low percentile rank in another. Publishers of commercially available tests often report the "national" percentile rank associated with every possible raw score on their tests. These percentile ranks purport to indicate the percentage of examinees at a particular grade level or of a particular age throughout the nation who would earn scores that were less than or equal to each possible raw score. Percentile rank distributions of this kind are called **national norms**. In recent years, test publishers have encountered increasing difficulty in obtaining truly representative samples of examinees when developing their national norms. As a result, the samples used vary substantially from one test to the next, and so-called national norms are often not nationally representative, nor comparable between different tests.

Another type of normative transformation results in what are termed **standard scores**. A standard score is a score that is on a scale with a predefined mean and a predefined standard of deviation, selected for computational and interpretive convenience. Several types of standard scores are commonly used in educational and behavioral science research. They differ only in the definition of their means and standard deviations.

The most basic standard score is termed a z-score. The lower-case z is used here to denote a score scale with a mean value of zero and a standard deviation of 1.0. If a set of raw scores is transformed to z-scores, a raw score that is right at the mean will have a corresponding z-score of zero; a raw score that is one standard deviation above the mean will have a corresponding z-score of 1.0; and a raw score that is two standard deviations below the mean will have a corresponding z-score of –2.0.

One advantage of z-scores is that they allow comparison of an individual's relative performances on several different measures, even though the measures have totally different raw-score scales. For example, if a student scored 25 on a 40-item reading test, and 30 on a 50-item math test, we could not tell from these scores whether that student's performance was better in reading or math. However, if the student's z-score was 1.0 on the reading test and 1.5 on the math test, we could confidently conclude that, compared to the other students with whom he or she was tested, the student was doing substantially better in math than in reading.

Another popular standard-score scale has a mean of 50 and a standard deviation of 10. Scores on this scale are called Z-scores or T-scores. A person with a Z-score of 50 would be right at the mean of his or her group, and a person with a Z-score of 70 would be two standard deviations above the mean of his or her group. Similarly, a person with a Z-score of 20 would be three standard deviations below the mean of his or her group, since 20 is 3×10 or 30 points below the mean of 50.

Historically, T-scores were computed in such a way that their distributions were always normal in shape, whereas the shape of a distribution of Z-scores was identical to the shape of the distribution of raw scores from which they were computed. In recent years, this distinction between T-scores and Z-scores has been abandoned, and the two terms are used interchangeably.

Yet another standard-score scale was developed by the College Entrance Examination Board (CEEB) for reporting scores on its college entrance tests, including the *Scholastic Aptitude Tests* (*SAT*) and the *Graduate Record Examinations* (*GRE*). Originally, the CEEB scale had a mean of 500 and a standard deviation of 100. So a person who earned a score of 600 on one of the parts of the SAT or GRE would be one standard deviation above the mean of the distribution of those who completed that part of the test. Since examinees rarely score more than three standard deviations below the mean or more than three standard deviations above the mean of a distribution, virtually all examinees would earn CEEB scores between 200 and 800. For that reason, the College Entrance Examination Board reports scores that are outside the 200-to-800 range as being *at* the end points, and thus reports all scores as being in the 200-to-800 range.

When large samples of individuals are measured or tested, the resulting distribution of scores often follows the normal distribution. From our discussion of the normal distribution in Chapter 3, you might recall that specific percentages of the distribution fall within an interval that is one, two, or three standard deviations on each side of the mean. These facts can be put to good use in establishing relationships between percentile ranks and various standard-score scales, whenever scores are normally distributed. In 1980, the Psychological Corporation published a graph that summarizes many of these relationships. It is reproduced here as Figure 5.1.

Figure 5.1 shows the percentages of scores in a normal distribution that fall within score intervals that are one standard deviation wide, on each side of the mean of the distribution. For example, 13.59% of the scores will fall between score values that are one standard deviation above the mean and two standard deviations above the mean. Scores that are at the mean, or one, two, three, or four standard deviations above or below the mean, are shown for a number of standard score scales, including the z-score scale, the T-score scale, and the CEEB score scale that have already been discussed.

Other standard score scales shown in Figure 5.1 include the NCE scale (Normal Curve Equivalent scale), the stanine scale, the Wechsler scale for subtests, the Deviation IQ scale, and the Otis-Lennon School Ability Test scale. We will discuss each of these briefly. The NCE scale was developed for, and promoted by, the U.S. Department of Education, as a tool for evaluators of projects supported under Title I of the Elementary and Secondary Education Act of 1965. The NCE scale is a standard-score scale with a mean of 50 and a standard deviation equal to the seemingly strange value 21.06. This choice of standard deviation ensures that persons with a percentile rank of 1 will have an NCE score of 1;

Figure 5.1 The Normal Curve, Percentiles, and Selected Scores.

Source: The Psychological Corporation, Test Service No. 148, September, 1980. Printed by permission of the publisher, The Psychological Corporation.

persons with a percentile rank of 50 will have an NCE of 50; and persons with a percentile rank of 99 will have an NCE of 99, for any measure that has a normal distribution of scores. Although the advantages of the NCE scale are dubious, it continues to enjoy widespread popularity because the U.S. Department of Education requires its use in reporting the results of evaluations of projects supported under what is now Chapter I of the Education Consolidation and Improvement Act of 1981.

The word *stanine* is a contraction of the words standard and nine. This score scale was developed by the U.S. Air Force, but is now widely used by publishers of achievement tests intended for use in elementary and secondary schools. The scale has nine values—the whole numbers one through nine. Each stanine from two through eight represents an interval on the score scale that is one half a standard deviation wide. Stanine 5 is located around the mean, in the middle of the score distribution, and includes scores that are between one fourth of a standard deviation below the mean and one fourth of a standard deviation above the mean. Stanines 6 through 8 are located right above Stanine 5, and are also half a standard deviation wide. Stanine 9 is at the top of the distribution, and includes any score that is at least one and three fourths of a standard deviation above the mean. Therefore, any raw score that has a corresponding z-score of at least 1.75 is in Stanine 9. Stanines 1 three 4 are located below Stanine 5, and have definitions that are similar to those of Stanines 6 through 9.

The **Wechsler** scales for subtests apply to several of the most widely used, individually administered IQ tests. These include the Wechsler Adult Intelligence Scale (WAIS) and the Wechsler Intelligence Scale for Children (WISC). The scale is used with each of the subtests of the Wechsler tests, and has a mean of 10 and a standard deviation of 3.

The **deviation-IQ** scale is used with many group-administered IQ tests. It is defined so that the mean IQ of examinees in the publisher's national norm group is 100, and the standard deviation of IQ scores in this group is equal to 15. Therefore, a person with an IQ of 115 is one standard deviation above the mean of the national norm group. Provided the distribution of IQ scores is normal in shape, a person with an IQ of 115 would have a percentile rank of 84 in the national norm group. This is true because 50% of the group would score below the mean of 100, and another 34%

of the group would score between the mean of 100 and a score that was one standard deviation above the mean (115).

The Otis-Lennon School Ability Tests, like a number of standardized ability and IQ tests, use a standard-score scale with a mean of 100 and a standard deviation of 16. Thus an Otis-Lennon score of 100 would be right at the mean, a score of 116 would be one standard deviation above the mean, and a score of 84 would be one standard deviation below the mean. The tradition of using a standard-score scale with a mean of 100 and a standard deviation of 16 can be traced back to the Stanford-Binet IQ test, which, in turn, has its origins in the Binet IQ tests developed around the turn of the century.

The **grade equivalent scale (GE)** is, without doubt, the most widely used score transformation in educational research and evaluation studies. Its seeming, but deceptive, simplicity is responsible for its overwhelming popularity. The scale is based on a division of the school year into 10 equal units, each representing a "month." Since most school years are nine months long, the three summer months are regarded as equivalent to one month of schooling.

When an achievement test is administered and a student is reported to be scoring at grade equivalent 4.7, that student's performance, regardless of his or her actual grade level, is supposedly equivalent to the median performance of students who are beginning the seventh month of their fourth school year. Likewise, a grade equivalent score of 6.0 supposedly indicates performance that is equivalent to the median of the score distribution of students who are just beginning their sixth year of school. The score scale appears to be simple and straightforward.

The problems with grade equivalent scores arise from the way they are constructed. Typically, a test publisher will administer an achievement test intended for students at a particular grade level to a sample of students in that grade, and to samples of students one grade above and one grade below that grade level. Suppose that the test is administered to students in grades four, five, and six, during the eighth month of the school year. The median score earned by fourth-graders is then set equal to a grade equivalent score of 4.8; the median score of fifth-graders is GE 5.8; and the median score of sixth-graders is GE 6.8. These three score values are then used by the publisher to specify all other grade equivalent scores. A smooth curve that passes through the three points is used to define grade equivalent scores between 4.8 and 6.8, and to extend the scale below 4.8 and above 6.8. The process is subjective, assumes a good deal, and is liable to be very misleading.

Grade equivalent scores should be avoided whenever reasonable alternatives are available, and used with caution when they cannot be avoided. You should realize that a third-grader who earns a grade equivalent of 5.2 on a third-grade test in reading is not thereby proven ready for a fifth-grade reading group. He or she merely did *as well as some fifth-graders on a third-grade test*. Furthermore, grade equivalent scores are *not* on an interval scale. They are merely on an ordinal scale, so they should not be averaged, nor used to compute standard scores. Grade equivalent scores on one test are not equivalent to grade equivalent scores on another. Therefore, you cannot safely conclude that a student with a grade equivalent of 6.0 on a reading test and a grade equivalent of 5.5 on a math test is doing better in reading than in math.

Summary

Measurement is an essential component of research and evaluation in education and the behavioral sciences. In this chapter we have briefly described the fundamental measurement issues of validity, reliability, and scales for reporting scores. Since many of the variables that are measured in education and the behavioral sciences cannot be observed directly, the correspondence between the score that results from some measurement procedure and a person's status on an underlying variable (construct) must always be questioned. The validity of a researcher's interpretations of measurement is always a troublesome issue. The validity issues that arise in various research and evaluation contexts were discussed under the headings of construct validity evidence, concurrent validity evidence, predictive validity evidence, and content validity evidence.

Consistency of measurement, termed measurement reliability, is another essential feature of a good measurement procedure. In addition to defining reliability in terms of stability of measurement and internal consistency, we described the features of a number of procedures for estimating reliability. The test-retest method and the parallel forms method provide estimates of stability of measurement. The split-half method, the Kuder-Richardson formulas, and Cronbach's alpha provide estimates of internal consistency reliability.

Since most raw-score scales used in education and behavioral sciences research are arbitrary, score transformations are essential to interpretation of results in these fields. The score transformations described in this chapter include percentile ranks, grade equivalent scores, z-scores, T-scores, Deviation-IQ scores, and stanines. The relation of these (and other) score scales to each other and to the normal distribution was discussed and displayed graphically.

Measurement is an important and complex topic that has given rise to year-long graduate courses in universities throughout the nation and text material that encompasses many volumes. In this brief chapter we have merely "hit the highlights." But by paying careful attention to the fundamental issues of measurement validity, reliability, and scales of measurement discussed here, you can become a much more sophisticated and better-informed consumer of research and evaluation in your field. We urge you to question the results of measurement and accept authors' conclusions with appropriate caution and skepticism.

Problems — Chapter 5

5.1 You are considering the adoption of a new reading test for your school system. Publisher A lists the test-retest reliability of its reading test as 0.87. Publisher B lists the Kuder-Richardson Formula 20 (KR-20) reliability of its reading test as 0.91. If you are seeking the reading test that will provide the most stable measurement of reading skill over a specified time interval, whose test should you adopt?

    a. Publisher A's because its reliability was estimated using the test-retest method.

    b. Publisher B's because the reliability of its test is highest.

    c. Publisher B's because its reliability was estimated using the KR-20 method.

    d. It doesn't matter, because both tests have high reliability.

5.2 Publisher A reports performance on its mathematics achievement test in terms of the percentage of objectives each student has "mastered." Publisher B reports performance on its mathematics achievement test in terms of the percentile rank of each tested student. If you were to characterize the tests offered by these publishers as either norm-referenced or criterion-referenced tests, which of the following would most likely be an accurate characterization?

a. The tests of both Publisher A and Publisher B are most likely norm-referenced.
b. Publisher A's test is most likely criterion-referenced, and Publisher B's test is most likely norm-referenced.
c. Publisher A's test is most likely norm-referenced and Publisher B's test is most likely criterion-referenced.
d. The tests of both Publisher A and Publisher B are most likely criterion-referenced.

5.3 You are interested in adopting a test that will help in selecting students who are most likely to do well in an honors high school physics program. In reviewing the technical literature on available commercial tests, which of the following pieces of information should most influence your decision on the test to be adopted?

a. A widely used science aptitude test has a reported test-retest reliability of 0.85.
b. A newly developed achievement test in high school physics has a reported concurrent validity of 0.90 when used in conjunction with a widely accepted test of high school physics achievement.
c. A well-recognized science aptitude test has a reported predictive validity of 0.87 when a widely accepted test of high school physics achievement is used as a criterion measure.
d. A well-accepted test of high school physics achievement was found to have very high content validity when compared to the objectives of your honors physics curriculum by a group of science curriculum specialists.

5.4 Suppose that you wanted to explain the standardized test performances of students named Bob, Mary, and Joe when you held a conference with their parents. Bob's performance on a standardized English test gave him a T-score of 70; Mary's performance on a standardized Social Studies test give her a percentile rank of 87; and Joe's performance on a standardized Mathematics test give him a z-score of 0.25. All of these scores involve national norms. Which of the following interpretations would be most accurate?

   a. Bob and Mary performed well above average, compared to the national norm group, but Joe's performance was close to the national average.
   b. All three students performed well above average compared to the national norm group.
   c. Mary's performance was well above the average of the national norm group; Bob's performance would rate him about a C on the usual grading scale; and Joe's performance was just below average.
   d. In terms of their performance relative to each other, Joe did best, Mary did next best, and Bob did least well.

6.

Can You Trust the Conclusions?

A Brief Digression on the Design of Research Studies

In a society in which 50% of marriages end in divorce, and 75% of mothers must work outside their households to make ends meet, it is not surprising that many young children spend at least a portion of their weekdays without the care and supervision of an adult. Some researchers in child development have labeled such children pejoratively "latchkey children." Others, pointing to the absence of research-based evidence of the negative effects of children being alone or without adult supervision, term such youngsters "self-care children." Researchers in the field of child development and family relations continue to investigate the effects of having children spend part of their day without an adult.

Suppose that a study on this topic examined the anxiety levels, rates of delinquency, and school achievement of two groups of 50 young children, one group never having experienced time away from school without an adult present in their homes; the other having spent at least an hour a day without adult supervision. Assume the researchers reported a mean anxiety score of 25 for the adult-supervision children and a mean anxiety score of 27 for the self-care children, on a 50-point anxiety scale. Assume further that

TABLE 6.1: Results of a Comparison of Self-Care Children and Adult-Supervision Children

	Mean Anxiety Score	Percent Committing Delinquent Acts	Mean Reading Comprehension Score
Self-Care Children	27	9	20
Adult-Supervision Children	25	4	24

4% of the supervision children and 9% of the self-care children had committed at least one delinquent act resulting in intervention by school officials or public safety officials during the year of the study. Finally, assume that the mean reading comprehension scores of adult-supervision children and self-care children were 24 items correct and 20 items correct, respectively, on the 40-item Reading Comprehension subtest of the Metropolitan Achievement Tests. These results are summarized in Table 6.1.

From these results, the researchers concluded that (1) the effects of self-care on the anxiety levels of young children are negligible; (2) self-care results in increased rates of delinquency among young children; and (3) self-care results in a small average loss in the reading comprehension of young children.

Do you agree with these conclusions? Are the results trustworthy? Would you advise the parents of young children to avoid leaving their children in self-care arrangements on the basis of these results? These questions illustrate more general themes that prompt this digression from topics that deal principally, if not exclusively, with basic statistics.

Whenever we encounter conclusions that are drawn from empirical research studies, whether quantitative or not, we must consider their trustworthiness. Fortunately, issues surrounding the trustworthiness of research findings have been codified and enjoy a rich literature developed by thoughtful and insightful pioneers in the field of empirical research methods. We will examine some of the most important issues in sufficient depth to heighten your awareness. To gain deeper understanding we recommend that you invest time with Borg and Gall (1989, Chapter

15), Bracht and Glass (1968), Campbell and Stanley (1963), and Cook and Campbell (1979).

Internal Validity

Issues concerning the trustworthiness of conclusions based on empirical research can be classified in myriad ways, but a fundamental dichotomy is those that concern the validity of conclusions for the specific subjects (persons, schools, etc.) observed in the setting and circumstances where research data were collected (**internal validity**), and those that concern the generalization of those conclusions to other subjects, other settings, or other circumstances (**external validity**). In this section we will consider only issues of the first type, deferring external validity issues to the next section.

Think about the study involving 50 adult-care children and 50 self-care children. The researchers concluded that self-care caused negligible increases in children's anxiety, substantial increases in their delinquency, and small losses in reading comprehension for young children. Although it is indisputably true that these differences between 50 young children in adult-care and 50 young children in self-care were observed in this study, the researchers run into trouble when they unequivocally attribute these results to the care arrangements in which these children spent their after-school time. In effect, the researchers are asserting that differences in care arrangement *caused* the observed differences in anxiety, delinquency, and reading comprehension observed for these children. It is the assertion of cause that leads to questions of internal validity.

On what basis can the researchers conclude unequivocally that the differences observed were caused by, or even associated with, the care arrangements in which these children spent time outside of school? The answer is, they can't! Although it *might* be the case that differences in care arrangement produced the observed average differences in anxiety level, rates of delinquency, and reading comprehension score, many other factors could have contributed to these averages, and the causes of the observed differences could be totally unrelated to the children's care arrangements. In the words of Cook and Campbell (1979), to support a claim to causal effect it is necessary to consider a host of "plausible rival explanations" and demonstrate why these alternatives are unlikely to be operating.

Let's consider some alternative explanations. First, children whose parents place them in self-care arrangements might differ substantially from children whose parents consistently place them under the care of an adult, prior to the initiation of their after-school care. Parents who use self-care for their children might be fearful of having their children supervised by some other adult, might effectively transmit their anxiety to their children, and might thereby increase their children's anxiety. But what if this explanation could be shown to be implausible, if not impossible? It is still possible that, prior to the initiation of their care, the 50 children of parents who used self-care arrangements were more anxious than were their 50 adult-care counterparts. No causal explanation is necessary here. Two groups of 50 children selected from the same population of children will differ somewhat on many characteristics, it is possible that one group might contain children at one extreme while the other group contains children at the other extreme. Just as no two individuals are perfectly alike (although so-called "identical twins" come very close), no two groups of 50 children will be perfectly alike.

All well and good, you say, but what about the 2-to-1 difference in rates of delinquency? Again, the results cannot be disputed. But is care arrangement the culprit? What else can it be, you ask; that is, is there a plausible rival hypothesis? Try this one: It is well known that rates of delinquency among children are strongly related to the socioeconomic status of their parents. It is also likely that parents with greater economic need will be more likely than affluent parents to have their children look out for themselves after school. Female, single-parent heads of households who must work to support themselves and their children are least likely to afford the costs of after-school child care, and are therefore most likely to use self-care out of necessity. So it is not self-care versus adult-care that produced the marked differences in delinquency rates, we claim, just differences in economic status, and attendant differences in life opportunities that promote or inhibit delinquency among the young. This plausible rival explanation comes under the heading **selection**, in the list enumerated by Cook and Campbell (1979). That is, the members of the two groups being compared in the research were selected in such a way that they were different at the outset. It is these initial differences, not the experience or treatment that occurred between their selection and their assessment, that accounts for the differences found when the assessment was conducted. We cannot be certain that selection totally explains the differences observed in the care-arrangement study, but the claim is certainly plausible.

Selection of fundamentally different individuals for the groups that are to be compared in a research study often contributes to many plausible explanations of the results of that study. In this example, were it the case that the 50 children in self-care were of far lower socioeconomic status than the 50 children in adult-care, the history of the self-care children's experiences from the time of their selection to the time of their assessment would likely be far different from the history experienced during the same time period by the 50 children in adult-care. Low socioeconomic-status parents typically live in neighborhoods with far higher incidences of crime and delinquency, and in households that offer fewer of the amenities that facilitate children's academic performance, such as magazines, newspapers, and so on. Neighborhoods with higher incidences of crime are less safe, and might well foster higher levels of anxiety among the children who live in those neighborhoods. It is therefore quite plausible that the results observed in the research study—children in self-care having somewhat higher levels of anxiety, far higher rates of delinquency, and somewhat lower reading comprehension test scores—could be attributed solely to differences in these children's experiences (quite apart from their self-care) between the time they were first placed in self-care and the time their anxiety, delinquency, and reading achievement scores were assessed. Cook and Campbell (1979) term this kind of alternative explanation of research findings **selection-history**.

Let's consider yet another rival explanation. Suppose the researchers had not paid attention to the ages of the children in their study, other than to note that they were all of "elementary school age." If the children placed in self-care were, on average, a year older than the children placed in adult-care (not an implausible supposition, since most parents would be more likely to leave older children than younger children on their own), differences in age could, by themselves, explain the findings of the research study. Older children probably spend more time away from their homes without parental supervision, and are therefore more vulnerable to unsafe neighborhoods. Consequent increases in anxiety would be expected. Older children are also more likely than younger children to commit delinquent acts. And individual differences in reading comprehension typically increase as children get older, thus leading to greater deficits for children of low socioeconomic-status parents. Beyond these initial differences, however, children in different age groups mature at different rates, thus enhancing their initial differences when they are measured, say, a year later. This differential maturity between the 50 children in the self-care group and the 50 children in the adult-care group might well explain the findings of the study, even if the children were reasonably comparable in their anxiety, rates of delinquency, and reading achievement when the study began. Cook and Campbell (1979) would view this possibility as an example of **selection-maturation**.

So far we have introduced just a few of the many threats to internal validity of research conclusions enumerated by Borg and Gall (1989), Campbell and Stanley (1963), and Cook and Campbell (1979). We will illustrate others after we provide some answers to the questions that must be burning in your mind by this point: "So what do I do about all these plausible alternative explanations of research findings?" or, equivalently, "Can I ever trust the results of a research study?" The answer to the first question is "a lot can be done," and to the second, "most definitely."

Control underlies the answer to both questions. In research, control means designing a study so that many, if not all, potentially plausible alternative explanations of the findings are rendered implausible, or far less plausible. There are many approaches to control of alternative explanations. Let's consider a few of them, by reviewing each of the alternative explanations suggested for the care-arrangement study.

First, we proposed that the adult-care children were less anxious than the self-care children and were better readers than the self-care children because they came from higher socioeconomic-status families. In the research study in question, the researchers could have addressed this explanation by obtaining data on the socioeconomic status of the families of children in both groups. If they could show that the distributions of socioeconomic status of these families were very similar, this explanation would be far less plausible. Even better, if in designing their study, the researchers had intentionally selected pairs of children from families that had similar socioeconomic status—one child in each pair having spent time in self-care and the other having no time in self-care—this rival explanation would have been eliminated.

This second idea, selecting pairs of children from families with similar socioeconomic status, is an example of what researchers call a **matching design**. Although it is effective in creating groups of subjects who are similar in the characteristics on which they are matched (in this case, socioeconomic status), it is not necessarily effective in matching the groups on any other variables that might offer equally plausible alternative explanations for the research findings. For example, groups of children whose families are quite similar in socioeconomic status might still differ markedly in their average ages.

We suggested earlier that the children in self-care and the children in adult-care might have differed in their reading comprehension scores because of pre-existing differences; that is, because they had different levels of reading ability at the beginning of the study. The same claim could be made concerning anxiety and propensity to commit delinquent acts. Rival explanations involving pre-existing differences often can be refuted by using what are termed **pretest-posttest research designs**. In such designs, groups of subjects are measured or observed before the initiation of the treatment or condition on which they are to be compared, as well as at the end of the treatment period. If the groups can be shown to be comparable prior to the initiation of treatment, rival explanations involving selection *on the variables measured at time of pretest* are controlled. The emphasized phrase in the preceding sentence is very important. Just as in matching designs, groups that are comparable on one set of characteristics—in this case, average anxiety level, average propensity to commit delinquent acts, and average reading comprehension score—are not necessarily comparable in other ways. It might still be the case, for example, that the children placed in self-care were substantially older than those placed in adult-care arrangements. If that were the case, the selection-maturity explanation, discussed earlier, would still apply. Even though the two groups of children were comparable on the three variables used to assess the effects of care arrangement at the beginning of the study, the age difference between the groups would be a plausible rival explanation of the differences found at the end of the study.

As we have just shown, although a demonstration that the groups in a research study are comparable at the time they are pretested is a powerful method for controlling rival explanations, pretesting alone does not control *all* plausible rival explanations. In fact, pretesting can be the source of a rival explanation known as **testing effect**. Let's see how.

A fundamental tenet in the philosophy of science is known as **Heisenberg's Uncertainty Principle**. This principle states that the very act of measurement will affect the entity that is the object of measurement. This is particularly true when the entity is a person and when the attribute being measured is an affective characteristic, such as anxiety. So in the care-arrangement study, by giving an anxiety inventory as a pretest, the researchers might well be increasing the levels of anxiety of the children they are assessing. If pretested children in self-care arrangements exhibit a higher mean level of anxiety at the end of the study, the cause of their increased anxiety might be the *combination* of pretesting with an anxiety scale (which sensitized them to the increased risk of their self-care situation) and the self-care situation itself. This rival explanation suggests that the observed posttest difference in average anxiety would not have been found, had the children not been pretested.

The researchers who designed the care-arrangement study could refute testing effect as a rival explanation of their findings if they used a research design that involved four groups of children, rather than two groups. Had they used a **Solomon four-group design**, two groups of children would have been placed in self-care arrangements and the other two groups would have been placed in adult-care arrangements. One of the self-care groups would have been pretested and the other would not. Similarly, one of the adult-care groups would have been pretested and the other would not. The research groups would have been as shown in the following diagram:

Group 1	Pretest	Self-care arrangement	Posttest
Group 2		Self-care arrangement	Posttest
Group 3	Pretest	Adult-care arrangement	Posttest
Group 4		Adult-care arrangement	Posttest

To examine the effect of pretesting, that is, to estimate the testing effect, the posttest scores of the two groups that were pretested (Groups 1 and 3) would be compared to the posttest scores of the two groups that were *not* pretested (Groups 2 and 4). To examine the possibility that pretesting had a greater effect on students in self-care arrangements than on students in adult-care arrangements, the difference in average posttest score between Groups 1 and 3 (which were pretested) would be compared to the difference in average posttest score between Groups 2 and 4 (which were not pretested). If the difference in averages between groups that were pretested was the same as the difference in averages between groups that were not pretested, the researchers could refute the rival explanation that a testing effect caused their research findings.

In discussing the Solomon four-group design we have ignored the possibility that the children in self-care who were pretested were different from the children in self-care who were not pretested, and that similar differences might have existed for the two groups of children who received adult-care. In fact, all four groups could have differed at the time the study began, in ways that significantly affected their performances on the posttest measures.

Although there is no way of *ensuring* that the groups to be compared in a research study will be comparable to each other at the outset of the study, an excellent method for increasing the likelihood of comparability is through **random assignment** of subjects to groups. If subjects are randomly assigned to groups, we can be certain that these groups will differ from each other on any characteristic that could be measured only to the extent that the "luck of the draw" might result in some chance differences. Unlike matching designs, in which subjects that are alike with respect to one, two, or three characteristics are assigned to different groups, when random assignment is used, groups of subjects are *essentially comparable to each other on possible characteristics.* We have emphasized the term "essentially comparable" because random assignment typically does not result in perfect matching of the groups on any characteristic. However, the groups will differ only within the bounds of chance fluctuation.

The power of random assignment of subjects is so profound that researchers consider research designs that incorporate random assignment to be in a totally different class from those that do not. If random assignment is used in a research design, it is called an **experimental design**; if it is not, the design is generally termed a **quasi-experimental design**. The power of random assignment in empirical research is well described in a very readable chapter by Porter (1988).

One need not use a Solomon four-group design to benefit from the effects of assigning subjects to groups. Random assignment is an effective means of controlling threats to the internal validity of research findings whenever a study involves two or more groups of subjects. Although random assignment does not allow a researcher to refute all rival explanations, it renders many of them far less plausible. First, since randomly assigned subjects differ from each other only by chance, all rival explanations attributable to *selection effects* become implausible. For example, had the children in the care arrangement study been assigned at random either to self-care or adult-care, it would no longer be plausible that their posttest differences in anxiety, rates of delinquency, or reading comprehension were due to differences in the socioeconomic status of their families or to differences in their ages. Explanations that depend on *selection-maturity effects* can also be refuted when subjects are randomly assigned. Recall our earlier conjecture that the average anxiety score of self-care children was higher than that of adult-care children when the study ended, not because the self-care children had higher levels of anxiety to begin with, but because their age differences exposed them to a larger number of anxiety-inducing situations during the study. This claim would have no substance if the ages of the self-care children differed from those of the adult-care children only by chance. Similarly, rival explanations based on claims of *differing prior histories* for the various research groups are not viable when subjects are randomly assigned to groups. Our earlier supposition that children assigned to self-care were from families with lower socioeconomic status than were children assigned to adult-care, and that differences in family status resulted in differences in neighborhood safety and family academic support, which in turn resulted in differences in children's anxiety, delinquency, and reading achievement, would not be plausible had 100 children been randomly assigned—50 to self-care and 50 to adult-care.

You might rightly ask at this point whether it is reasonable to assume that the researchers could have assigned children at random, either to self-care or adult-care arrangements. The answer is, probably not. It is unlikely that parents would choose to have their children participate in a study that prescribed their after-school care arrangement for an entire year. For a variety of practical or ethical reasons, researchers are often faced with situations in which random assignment of subjects to groups is impossible. In such situations, quasi-experimental designs, rather than experimental designs, become the only possibility. It is in these very situations that knowledge of the kinds of rival explanations we have discussed so far becomes essential. A researcher armed with such knowledge can use other elements of research design, such as pretesting, to control plausible threats to internal validity. And a consumer of research with such knowledge can exercise healthy skepticism when the results of a research study are attributed unequivocally by the researcher to the conditions or treatments examined in the study.

How about a new example, and those other threats to internal validity we promised earlier? We thought you'd never ask! In the mid-1960s the federal government appropriated substantial new funding for school children they termed "educationally disadvantaged." What was then Title I of the Elementary and Secondary Education Act of 1965 has been perpetuated as Chapter I of the Education Consolidation and Improvement Act of 1981. Under the Act, federal funds must be used to supplement, rather than supplant, the instructional programs and other educational opportunities afforded educationally disadvantaged children. With new funding came new requirements for evaluation of the effects of the special programs supported by Title I, and ultimately, a veritable army of educational researchers turned evaluators.

Evaluation of programs supported under Title I presented a host of research design problems, not the least of which was the near impossibility of assigning students at random to Title I or conventional instructional treatments. The Title I legislation specified that the recipients of special educational programs had to be the neediest children in the school or school district operating the programs, thus ensuring that the children assigned to Title I were systematically different from the children assigned to conventional programs with whom they were compared.

It was not unusual in a Title I program to identify students with the very lowest achievement test scores as those most "educationally disadvantaged." Students in any comparison groups were therefore higher achievers at the outset than were the Title I students. This pretreatment difference made the explanation of posttest achievement differences between the groups very difficult. If it was found that Title I students had larger gains in achievement test scores than did the comparison students, could the Title I program take credit for the differences? Perhaps, but not necessarily. All of the threats to internal validity we have already discussed for groups that are not randomly assigned apply to this example as well. But another very real threat must be added to the pot.

As noted in Chapter 5, all achievement tests are less than perfectly reliable. Therefore, the achievement test score earned by any individual student will vary from one testing occasion to another, even if the achievement being measured has not changed at all. One effect of this unreliability is to produce systematic changes in the average achievement test score observed for a group of students, between the first time they are tested and the second time. Students whose initial test scores are low achieved those low scores in part because they had low achievement, but in part because of a host of factors that have little, if anything, to do with their true achievement levels: They might have been ill on the day they were tested. They might have been given test items that tapped specific bits of knowledge they could not bring readily to mind. They might have been unlucky in their guesses. If these same students had been retested within a few days, using another form of the achievement test that contained a different set of items, they would be far more likely to obtain higher scores than lower scores. This phenomenon is known as **statistical regression effect**. It is a plausible rival explanation of pretest-to-posttest gains on any variable that is assessed with less-than-perfect reliability, particularly when the group assessed was selected because of their initially low scores. Although there are formulas for estimating the magnitude of statistical regression effects, the best remedy is to avoid selection of one group of subjects because of their low pretest scores, and a comparison group of subjects because their pretest scores are higher.

A few enterprising evaluators of Title I programs found ways to use random assignment of subjects to special programs and comparison groups while adhering to the principle of serving the most educationally disadvantaged students. In situations where program funds did not permit treatment of all needy children in a given semester or school year, these researchers randomly divided the most needy children into a group that was served during an initial time period and a group that was served at a later date (say, during the next semester or the next school year). The group served later thus became a randomly equivalent comparison group during the initial time period.

Even with this innovative approach to Title I evaluation, random assignment of children to a treatment group and a comparison group did not eliminate all threats to the internal validity of the evaluation findings. As we noted earlier, it is not unusual for children who are the most educationally disadvantaged to come from families who are the most economically disadvantaged. Children of the poor are also among the most geographically mobile in our society, often attending a large number of schools before they graduate or drop out altogether. This mobility presented a special problem for Title I evaluators, and raised yet another threat to the internal validity of their conclusions. Even when they used random assignment of children to create their treatment and comparison groups, large numbers of children who were present at the time of pretesting had moved on by the end of the treatment period, and were no longer available for posttesting. So groups that were randomly equivalent at the outset of the study were no longer comparable at the end of the study. This threat to internal validity is known as **mortality**. It arises whenever subjects who leave one group during a study differ systematically from subjects who leave another group. Unfortunately, when substantial numbers of subjects defect during a study, mortality can pose the same threats to internal validity as do noncomparable comparison groups: selection, selection-mortality, selection-history, and so on.

Researchers have discovered procedures that sometimes remove, or greatly lessen, the threat posed by subject mortality. For example, if it could be shown that the pretest scores of children who left the Title I group were very similar to the pretest scores of children who left the comparison group, the threat posed by the mortality of these children would be greatly diminished. The same conclusion could be drawn if it were shown that the children left in the Title I group were very similar to the children left in the comparison group, on all variables that were measured when the study began.

Not unlike many researchers who work in field settings with human beings rather than in laboratories with rats and other lesser animals, evaluators of Title I programs encountered other perplexing threats to the internal validity of their conclusions. A particularly subtle one derived from the achievement tests that were often used as indicators of the effectiveness of a Title I project. These standardized achievement tests were often ineffective in distinguishing among the achievement levels of the severely economically disadvantaged children who were the target of the Title I program. This was most often the case when pretests were administered prior to the initiation of any special instructional program. Children often earned scores below the "chance score" on the tests, the score they would have earned had they guessed at random in response to the items. When an examinee scores below chance, the reliability of that person's assessment is effectively zero. After instruction, when posttests were administered, the children's scores often had increased to above-chance levels where assessment with the achievement tests was effective, since the tests provided reliable discriminations among the students' performances.

In situations like this, where the conditions of measurement effectively change the characteristics of the measurement instrument used, the validity of findings are threatened by what is termed **instrumentation effects**. The instruments are not measuring the same variable in the same way at pretest and posttest, so comparisons of posttest scores with pretest scores are not valid. Instrumentation effects are even more troublesome in comparative research, where one of the groups to be compared has extreme scores (either extremely low or extremely high) that are not well assessed by the measurement instruments used, and other groups' scores are less extreme.

It is often difficult to find a remedy for instrumentation effects. In the case of Title I evaluations, different levels of tests were sometimes used as pretests and posttests. For example, even though the achievement progress of third-graders was to be evaluated, a test designed for second-graders was sometimes used as a pretest and a test designed for third-graders was used as a posttest. The rationale for this approach was that the second-grade test was easy enough to permit the third-grade Title I children to score above the chance level, thus providing valid distinctions among their levels of achievement. Whether performances on the second-grade test could validly be compared to performances on the third-grade test posed another instrumentation-effect issue, which was frequently investigated and never well resolved. A study by Cleland and Idstein (1980), discussed at some length in Chapter 12, illustrates this body of research.

A unique category of threats to the internal validity of research that we have not discussed so far might be characterized as threats grounded in the vagaries of human nature. These threats are often subtle, and require particular sensitivity to the nature of human personality and response if they are to be detected. However, these threats can be anticipated. The clever researcher can sometimes structure research situations that minimize their influence, and the informed consumer of research can recognize situations in which they are likely to appear. This discussion is designed to help you join the ranks of informed consumers.

When research involving a treatment group and a comparison group is conducted in the same context, such as within a single school or a single industrial plant, normal communication processes can work to undermine the distinctions between the treatments received by the two groups. Teachers talk to each other—in the teachers' lounge, in the hallways, and when they have lunch. When a new instructional method embodied in an experimental treatment works particularly well, the teachers using that method are likely to describe it to their colleagues, who will then use it with the comparison-group students. Thus normal communication paths within the school often serve to diminish the distinction between the experimental treatment and the treatment received by a comparison group. The same problem arises when research is conducted in factories, offices, or any setting where those who administer or provide the treatments are likely to communicate, particularly when the treatment providers are a part of the regular work force in that setting. The result is an invalid comparison between the experimental and comparison treatments, *as planned or designed*. The researcher thought he or she was comparing apples and oranges, and wound up comparing two varieties of apples! This threat to validity is called **diffusion or imitation of treatments**.

The risk of diffusion or imitation of treatments can be reduced by constituting experimental groups and comparison groups in different contexts—different schools, different factories, and so on—but at the risk of thoroughly confounding the effects of treatments and the effects of contexts. For example, if an experimental Title I arithmetic program in one school were compared to the conventional arithmetic program in another school, any differences in student achievement found might be due to the two programs or due to differences between the schools in which they were applied. The cause of the achievement differences could not be attributed unequivocally, since the two potential causes would be thoroughly **confounded**.

Alternative approaches to reducing the threat of treatment diffusion or imitation would be (1) to secure the agreement of those administering the experimental treatment to keep its details under wraps, until the end of the research study, or (2) to alter the conditions of the research context so that on-the-job contact between those administering the experimental treatment and those administering the control treatment was minimized. The practicality of either of these approaches will vary substantially across research contexts. Minimizing contact between employees would be far easier to structure in a large factory than in a typical school. Conversely, agreements to keep the details of an instrumental treatment confidential would be far easier to secure from teachers, who would readily understand the importance of such confidentiality, than from factory workers who might not.

Even when diffusion of treatments cannot be reduced, researchers and consumers of research can increase the likelihood that it will be detected. A frequent error in research studies is the assumption that the treatments delivered to the research subjects were the treatments planned by the researcher. This is rarely the case, even when everyone participating in the study is well intentioned and conscientious. There is no substitute for rich description of the *actual* treatments delivered. These can be secured through direct observation, by having the treatment administrators keep logs or diaries, or by interviewing the treatment administrators during the study and at the end of the study. Informed consumers of research will seek evidence that the actual treatments delivered have been documented accurately.

The validity of research is sometimes undermined by the democratic value that promotes equality of opportunity. If an experimental treatment is perceived as providing enriched opportunities for those who receive it, administrators might strive to provide compensatory advantages for those who receive the comparison treatment. For example, in schools where Title I funds provide teachers' aides in experimental classrooms, principles might appeal to parent-teachers' organizations to provide volunteers to assist teachers in the comparison classrooms. The principals' motivation is not a desire to undermine the experiment, but their perception that the experimental students were being unfairly advantaged by having more adults in their classrooms.

This **compensatory equalization of treatments** cannot always be avoided, but it can always be documented through rich and thorough description of the treatments actually delivered to the experimental group and the comparison group. Documentation strategies were suggested earlier.

Remember the old song about the railroad construction worker John Henry, who "died with a stream drill in his hand?" According to the song, John Henry wasn't about to "let that steam drill beat him down," so he worked himself to death in a race to prove that he was better than the new technology of the time. Whether truth or fiction, the parable has led to the identification of a threat to internal validity known as the **John Henry effect** or, more properly, **compensatory rivalry of the comparison group**.

When a research study introduces an experimental treatment that is perceived to threaten the future livelihood or future well-being of workers or employees responsible for delivery of the comparison treatment, those employees might well exert extra effort, in an attempt to minimize the contribution of the experimental treatment. Although a researcher can do little to control such extra effort, he or she can do much to control the threat that the John Henry effect will unknowingly undermine the validity of the research. The key is good planning, and rich documentation of the treatments delivered to the experimental group and the comparison group. Prior to the introduction of the experimental treatment, the researcher can observe and document the typical operation of the comparison treatment, and its effects. For example, mathematics teachers' typical instructional delivery can be observed and documented, along with effects of such instruction, prior to the introduction of computers that might be perceived by teachers to undermine their authority and threaten their future livelihood. After the experimental computers have been introduced, the comparison teachers' instruction can still be observed and documented, so that it can be compared to their precomputer behavior as well as the instructional behavior of the teachers who used the experimental computers. Again, rich description of the experimental and comparison treatments, as actually delivered, is essential.

Yet another potential threat to internal validity derives from the curiosities of human nature: In some research settings, introduction of an experimental treatment that is perceived as providing great benefit or special privilege to the group that receives it might produce what could be termed a "reverse John Henry effect" on members of the comparison group. That is, providing special treatment to the experimental group and denying that treatment to the comparison group might have the effect of demoralizing members of the comparison group to the degree that their typical performance is diminished. This threat to validity has been labeled **resentful demoralization of the comparison group** (Cook & Campbell, 1979), and, when it operates, has the effect of making the experimental treatment look better than it should.

If an experimental group of students were to be given a computer laboratory to use in their mathematics classes, while comparison-group students were denied access to the laboratory, the latter group might label themselves "second-class citizens," decide that the school and their teachers did not value their mathematics performances, and, as a consequence of their perception, invest less time and effort in learning mathematics, thereby reducing their mathematics achievement test performances. Such actions would invalidate a comparison of the mathematics test performances of experimental-group students and comparison-group students, since any differences found could not be attributed solely to the experimental treatment. Unfortunately, as is true of the John Henry effect, even random assignments of students to experimental and control groups would not protect against this threat to validity.

Although it is difficult to preclude resentment and demoralization among members of a comparison group, the existence of such effects can be detected. At least three actions could be taken to detect the effects of demoralization. First, the pretreatment performance of the experimental group and the comparison group could be measured and documented. In the example just discussed, mathematics pretests could be administered to the group that was later given access to the computer laboratory and the group that was denied access. If the comparison group's performance decreased over the course of the research study while the experimental group's performance remained stable, demoralization of the comparison group would be evident. Second, an additional comparison group could be used, with pretest and posttest assessments taking place prior to the initiation of the experimental treatment. For example, the mathematics test performances of students taking the same mathematics courses could be assessed during the school year prior to the introduction of the computer laboratory. If the comparison students' pretest-to-posttest growth in achievement during the year of the computer laboratory was much smaller than that of the comparison students prior to the introduction of the computer laboratory, a demoralization effect would be suggested. Third, the behavior, as well as the outcome performance, of comparison-group members could be assessed. In the present example, if the amount of time comparison students devoted to mathematics homework diminished over the course of the research study, or the attendance rate of the comparison students diminished over the course of the study, resentment of the privileges afforded experimental-group students might well be indicated. Once again we see the value of noting what went on in a research study, in addition to determining what resulted.

As a consumer of research, you might be troubled by these "human foible" threats to internal validity, since you are powerless to redesign the research you consume. So be it. Better to be informed and troubled a bit than to be uninformed and totally gullible. By considering these threats to validity as possibilities, you can speculate on their likelihood in any specific research situation. Your task, after all, is to decide whether to believe researchers' claims that the outcomes of the research are unequivocally attributable to the conditions or treatments that were the focus of their study. And when you decide to move from research consumption to research production, you can guard against the more subtle threats to validity your less astute predecessors often ignored.

We have introduced a substantial range of threats to the internal validity of an empirical research study, and recommended some research designs and other procedures that can be used to control or detect such threats. It's been a long story, and a summary is in order. Table 6.2 is offered in the hope that it will help you "pull it all together."

External Validity

Even in the most immediately focused evaluation study, the interest of the researcher is rarely confined exclusively to the subjects on whom he or she has collected data, in the specific setting and period of time when the data were collected. More likely, the researcher will draw conclusions that carry an implicit, if not explicit, assumption that the results of the study can be **generalized**. The nature of the generalization made or implied will vary substantially in different studies, but often extends to "future times," or "subjects like these," or "settings or contexts like these." **External validity** is the label attached to the trustworthiness of such generalizations. Analyses of external validity consider factors that limit, and research design features and practices that enhance, the trustworthiness of such generalizations.

At this point you might be tempted to protest our contention that all research involves generalization. For example, you might think that evaluation studies are concerned solely with the subjects observed, the effects of treatments or programs at the time they were administered, and the context in which treatments or programs were applied. An evaluation of a fourth-grade reading text, used for the first time during the 1989-90 school year with all fourth-graders in the Atlanta public schools, appears to apply only to the students in Atlanta who used the text during that school year. However, the seeming interest only in the "here and now" is illusory. School administrators require evaluations of the effects of their policies out of more than idle curiosity. In this example, they would want to know, at a minimum, whether they should continue using the fourth-grade text next year. So the administrators are generalizing the results found with this year's

TABLE 6.2: Threats to the Internal Validity of Empirical Research Studies, Appropriate Control Methods, and Techniques for Detecting the Operation of Such Threats.

Type of Threat	Control Procedure	Detection Method
Selection	Random assignment	Examine pretest characteristics of experimental subjects and comparison subjects
Selection-History	Randon assignment	Examine pretest characteristics of experimental subjects and comparison subjects
Selection-Maturation	Random assignment	Examine pretest characteristics of experimental subjects and comparison subjects
Testing Effect	Use Solomon four-group design	Use Solomon four-group design
Statistical Regression	Avoid selection of extreme groups at pretest, or use statistical correction methods	Examine distribution of pretest scores of experimental subjects and, when used, comparison subjects
Mortality	Random assignment	Examine characteristics of those who leave the study
Instrumentation	Use measurement instruments that operate the same way over the entire scale needed	Look for below-chance scores and near-perfect scores on pretest and posttest measures
Diffusion of Treatment	Use preexperimental comparison or a comparison group in a different setting	Collect detailed data on experimental treatment and comparison treatment, as delivered
Compensatory Equalization	Use preexperimental comparison or a comparison group in a different setting	Collect detailed data on experimental treatment and comparison treatment, as delivered
John Henry Effect	Use preexperimental comparison group	Interview providers of comparison treatment, or compare with preexperimental performance of comparison providers
Resentful Demoralization of Comparison Group	Use preexperimental comparison group	Compare performance of comparison group with their preexperimental performance, or interview comparison group members

fourth-graders to next year's. Perhaps they are considering purchasing third-grade and fifth-grade texts from the publisher of the fourth-grade text. If they base their adoption decision on the outcomes of the fourth-grade evaluation, the administrators are generalizing not only to the following year, but to students in other grades as well.

Even when a researcher interprets his or her results only for the subjects, time period, and context used in a particular study, consumers of the results inevitably engage in generalization. If you were the Director of Public Housing in Detroit, why would you care about a study on reduction of vandalism that applied to only 20 housing units observed in Seattle during 1988? If the vandalism control methods that were studied worked well in Seattle, you'd be interested in their applicability to public housing projects in Detroit. You would generalize the results of the study *from* Seattle, *from* 1988, and *from* the 20 housing units studied, *to* Detroit, *to* the public housing projects where you had a vandalism problem, and *to* the year you intended to apply the Seattle treatment. Generalization of research results is of paramount importance to you as a consumer of research, even in situations where it is of lesser importance to the researcher who conducted the study.

When research is conducted for the purpose of contributing to a body of theoretical knowledge, in contrast to an applied purpose, generalization of conclusions will be central to the purpose of the researcher. For if no generalization were possible, there would be no theoretical contribution. Theoretical researchers attend to issues of external validity through their selection of subjects, their selection of treatments, and their selection of conditions of research. We will consider these strategies, along with some threats to external validity, in the balance of this chapter.

Perhaps the issue of external validity is nowhere clearer and more prominent than in research based on surveys. For in survey research, the goal of generalizing from a sample of respondents (the persons who have been interviewed or asked to complete a questionnaire) to a population of potential respondents (the larger collection of persons who are of central research interest) is explicit. An example is the Harris Poll, where the opinions on such things as "the quality of the job the President is doing," given by about 1500 carefully selected adults (the sample), are generalized to the adult population of the United States (the population of interest). Professional survey researchers always use procedures for selecting respondents that provide sound, scientific bases for generalization and methods for assessing the quality of such generalization.

Two principal threats to external validity in survey research are **bias error** and **random error**. Bias error occurs when the persons who have been interviewed or those who completed questionnaires are systematically different from persons in the population to which generalization is desired. Systematic differences can occur for a variety of reasons, such as the researcher having done a poor or careless job of selection, or because those who actually completed a questionnaire or those actually interviewed were a small, self-selected portion of the persons the researcher selected to complete a questionnaire or be interviewed.

Suppose, for example, that a researcher wanted to draw conclusions about the degree of financial stress experienced by families that are headed by single women, and wanted to generalize to the entire population of such families in the state of Georgia. In the researcher's design, data to inform these conclusions are to be collected by interviewing single women who are heads of households. Ideally, the researcher could obtain a list of all women in Georgia who were single and heads of households, and could then use a scientific procedure for selecting a sample from the list. In this ideal world, all selected women would agree to be interviewed, and would provide clear and complete responses to the researcher's questions. In reality, no list of single-female heads of households in Georgia exists, so selection of interviewees would have to be accomplished through referrals from such sources as social welfare agents, churches, women's groups, school systems, and so on. There would be no way of determining with certainty whether the collective characteristics of the referred women, including the degree of financial stress experienced by their families, was similar to, or systematically different from, that of the population of all such women in Georgia. Therefore, the potential for serious bias error would be great, and generalization from the sample of single-female heads of households to the population would be risky. Adding to the problem of external validity would be the likelihood that a number of the sampled females would refuse to be interviewed for any of a variety of reasons, including the possibility that their financial stress caused them to hold more than one job and therefore not be available for an interview. The latter possibility would surely bias the results of the survey by systematically excluding women whose families experienced the highest degree of financial stress.

Even if the survey could be conducted under the ideal conditions described earlier, results computed for the sample of women interviewed would differ from corresponding results for the entire population of interest. In particular, the average degree of financial stress experienced by the families of the sampled women would be somewhat different from the average degree of financial stress experienced by all women in the population. If two different samples of women were interviewed, the averages computed for each sample would differ from each other. The difference between the sample averages would result from a phenomenon known as **random sampling fluctuation**, a topic we will discuss in far greater detail in Chapters 7 and 8. At this point, we will merely note that it represents random error in estimating a quantity such as the average for a population, by using the average for a sample.

Unlike bias error, which is often difficult to control, random error can almost always be reduced by using a larger sample. Doesn't it seem likely that the average financial stress experienced by the families of 100 single Georgia women selected under ideal conditions would be closer to the average experienced by the families of *all* single women in Georgia than would the average for only 10 sampled women? Or that the difference between the averages of two samples of 100 would be smaller than the difference between the averages of two samples of 10? If your intuition says "yes," you are right on target. You can almost always reduce random error by selecting a larger sample, even though the bias error is usually unaffected by the size of your sample.

A few paragraphs ago we mentioned the possibility that some of the sampled women might refuse to be interviewed or refuse to complete a questionnaire. Refusal to participate is a problem that inhibits external validity in all kinds of research studies, not just in surveys. The crux of the problem is that those who agree to be studied are typically different from those who refuse. Since the population that is of real research interest includes both kinds of persons, generalizing from a sample of volunteers to a population containing participants and nonparticipants is certain to be erroneous.

Although there is no way to compel nonincarcerated individuals to participate in a research study, and thereby reduce the risk of bias error, there are ways to encourage that participation. Researchers can provide illustrations of the societal benefits that might result from the research, or can offer incentives to those who agree to participate in the research. Since some refusals are inevitable despite the best efforts of the researcher, it is important to keep accurate records on rates of refusals, and to compare the known characteristics of those who agree and those who refuse. As a knowledgeable consumer of research, you should seek information on the methods researchers used to identify and select their research subjects, and on rates of participation and refusal. Think hard about how the use of volunteers might bias the generalization of the study's results to the population that is of greatest interest to you.

Consumers of research often want to generalize findings from the types of organizations or settings used to conduct the research to an organization or setting that is of direct interest to them. You might ask, for example, whether the successful results of an innovative reading program, conducted in an inner-city elementary school with a low-income, predominantly Hispanic population, are likely to be experienced in your school, which is located in a middle-income suburb and enrolls mostly black students. The kind of external validity you demand extends *beyond* the bounds of the population that might be represented most immediately by the setting and sample studied. You want to generalize to a population that differs in ways often associated with reading performance from the sample used in the research.

Only logical analysis, based on careful attention to earlier research findings, will provide a basis for the kind of generalization you desire. You might reason that a reading program that works with children whose primary language is not English should work even better with children who have spoken English all of their lives. However, you would be ignoring the potential influence of nonstandard English. You might also recall that children from low-income families have traditionally experienced greater difficulty with reading than have children from more affluent families. You might therefore suspect that the innovative reading program would work better with children in your school than with children in the school originally studied.

Clearly, these deductions are fraught with dangers and over-simplifications. Although completely in English, the reading program might take advantage of Spanish-language idioms. The subject matter of reading passages used in the program might be central to the experiences of inner-city children and relatively foreign to children from the suburbs. More detailed study of the program would be essential prior to a decision to adopt it in your school. But the type of reasoning we have illustrated can help you address the issue of external validity, whenever you want to generalize from the context and sample of a research study to a different context and setting.

Researchers can do much to enhance the generalization of their findings from one context to another. An effective strategy involves systematic variation of the conditions under which the research is conducted. Had the study of the innovative reading program been conducted in several school systems that differed in prescribed ways, for example, one inner-city school system, one in a suburb, one in a rural area, one enrolling mostly black children, one enrolling mostly Hispanic children, one enrolling mostly white children, one that was racially balanced in its enrollment, and so on, the limits of generalization of the study's results would be far clearer. Consistent findings across all of these contexts would suggest safe generalizations to a wide variety of settings that were similar to any of these sites or to contexts that incorporated elements of several of them. For example, if the reading program was found to be successful in an inner-city school system with Hispanic students and in a suburban school system with black students, it would very likely be successful in an inner-city school system with black students.

If the reading program was substantially more successful in some of the contexts examined than in others, the *limits* of generalization would be revealed. Consistency of findings is not a prerequisite to increased knowledge of the external validity of a study. Even when differences in results are found, the researcher and consumers of the research are better informed.

As a consumer of research, you should consider the kinds of systematic variations that have been used in the studies you review. The greater the degree of variation, the more trustworthy the findings. Any evidence that the research produced consistent results in several settings increases the possibility that you would find the same result in the setting that is of interest to you. Evidence that the results varied across settings in describable ways should also help you to determine the results you would likely find, were you to conduct the study in a setting that is of interest to you. For example, if the reading program mentioned earlier produced consistently positive achievement effects for black students and Hispanic students in inner-city schools, but failed to produce positive effects for black students in a suburban school, you could reasonably assume that urbanism of school location was related to the program's effectiveness. Assuming that the positive effects found for the inner-city schools would generalize to Hispanic students enrolled in a suburban setting would not be warranted, because the research study provided no direct evidence for that combination of students and setting.

When the results of a study are inconsistent across settings or types of subjects, we say that an **interaction effect** exists—in this case, an interaction among the reading program, urbanism of school location, and ethnic background of students. The detection of interaction effects helps to define the boundaries within which research findings can be generalized, and consequently, the limits of external validity. We consider interaction effects in some detail in Chapter 14.

Beyond the effects of setting, organizational and physical context, and characteristics of research subjects, time period is another element that often limits the external validity of research findings. Consider drawing conclusions about the nature of discipline problems in today's public schools, on the basis of research studies conducted in the 1950s or the 1960s. School discipline problems of the 1950s included such weighty transgressions as chewing gum in class, talking out of turn, fistfights in the halls, writing graffiti on restroom walls, and so on. In today's schools, discipline problems center around abuse of illegal drugs and alcohol, assaults on other students and teachers, rape, teenage pregnancy, destruction of school property, robbery, and similar offenses. Problems of disruption have turned into problems of crime. Clearly, research on school discipline that was accurate in the 1950s and 1960s has little relevance to today's public schools; its generalizability over time is severely limited.

A less dramatic example of time-limited external validity arose in the use of a test of general aptitudes to predict workers' rated proficiency in a variety of jobs. As noted in Hartigan and Wigdor (1989), the effectiveness of the General Aptitude Test Battery in predicting supervisors' ratings of employees' job proficiencies was found to be substantially lower in studies conducted after 1983 than in studies conducted prior to that date. Although the reasons for the test's diminished predictive power are not well understood, suspicions include changes in the specific nature of jobs in the U.S. economy, or changes in characteristics of the examinee population that are not well characterized by their test performances. Whatever the reasons, it is clear that the external validity of the pre-1983 studies is limited, and that the predictive power of the General Aptitude Test Battery today is not well described by studies conducted more than six years ago.

The moral of these examples is twofold. First, researchers would be well advised to **replicate** earlier research studies to see whether results found today are consistent with results found in earlier periods. If so, generalization of earlier findings would be warranted. If not, useful limits of generalization would be established. Second, consumers of research would be well advised to be cautious in generalizing the findings of an earlier era to the social contexts and milieus found today. In prescribing caution we might be accused of "copping out," in much the same way as the air traffic controller who, when told by two pilots that he had just instructed them to land on the same runway from opposite directions, was heard to reply "y'all be careful, hear!" However, it is difficult to be more prescriptive about common sense. The first of our examples, generalizing from school discipline studies of the 1950s to the schools of today, is obviously fraught with dangers. The second, involving the predictive power of the General Aptitude Test Battery, is far less obviously time-bound. When considering the results of any research study that is more than a few years old, the informed reader should ask, How have conditions in the research setting (e.g., schools, factories, cities, colleges and universities, etc.) changed? Are the populations encountered today likely to be different from the sample used in the earlier study in ways that are substantially related to the phenomena studied? If the answers to these questions suggest that the phenomena studied are likely to operate differently in current institutions or with current populations, the findings of older studies should be generalized judiciously.

Summary

We have introduced two major questions in this chapter. First, can the results of a research study be attributed *solely* to the causes identified by the researcher? Second, can the results of a research study be generalized to subjects, contexts, and time periods other than the one studied? The first question is an internal validity question; the second, an external validity question.

Many issues of research design affect the internal validity of a research study. Control of plausible rival explanations for the research findings is essential to reaching trustworthy conclusions. Although it is virtually impossible to eliminate all rival explanations for the findings of a research study, many of the most plausible contenders can be controlled or eliminated by using such techniques as comparison groups, random assignment of subjects to experimental groups and comparison groups, and pretesting before experimental treatments have been applied.

External validity issues include generalization of the findings of a research study *from* the specific subjects, context, treatments, and time period studied, *to* larger groups of subjects of the same type, or to other types of subjects, contexts, treatments, or time periods. Techniques for controlling bias error and random error can be used to support generalizations to larger groups of the same type. Systematic variation of the conditions of study, across different contexts, treatments, and types of subjects, can be used to support claims that the findings of a study generalize in these ways. Conversely, when results are found to be inconsistent in the face of such systematic variation, the limits of external validity can be established and demonstrated.

For the consumer of research, skepticism and caution are the order of the day. The specific threats to validity and accompanying examples provided in this chapter should help you guide your skepticism and form appropriately tolerant limits of belief. A healthy dose of common sense, coupled with thoughtful consideration of the myriad ways in which internally valid studies might not generalize to other situations, should guide you in formulating appropriate conclusions concerning external validity. We wish you happy sleuthing as you begin the adventure of studying applied research.

Problems — Chapter 6

6.1 Researchers investigated the effectiveness of a public information program concerning a woman's right to select her own birth-control methods, including abortion, by (1) conducting a survey of public attitudes in a city with a population of 50,000; (2) operating the program (which included television commercials, newspaper advertisements, letters to the editor of the city newspaper, and distribution of brochures in public and commercial buildings) for five weeks; and (3) conducting a second survey of public attitudes to assess preprogram to postprogram changes.

Upon finding a 5% increase in attitudes favoring freedom of choice for women, the researchers concluded that the program had "caused a positive shift in attitudes." Assuming that a 5% increase represents an "important" change, which of the following statements is true? (Circle the letters of *all* true statements.)

a. The researchers are correct because an important change in public attitudes was observed in surveys conducted just before, and just after, the program had been conducted.

b. The researchers are incorrect because their research design did not include a comparison group that had no exposure to the program.

c. The researchers should not have concluded that their program caused the change in attitudes; other plausible explanations cannot be refuted on the basis of their research design.

d. Although it is possible that the program caused the change in public attitudes, "history" might have played a role as well. Therefore, researchers' conclusions are incorrect.

6.2 In a scientific study of the effects of anabolic steroids on the performance of college participants in track and field events, quarter-mile runners were divided into three groups—fast, average, and slow—based on their time in a quarter-mile run held just before the initiation of steroid therapy. After the athletes had used steroids under a physician's supervision for eight weeks, the runners were again timed in a quarter-mile run. From the results of their study, the researchers concluded that "Anabolic steroids increase the running speed of the slowest runners, decrease the running speed of the fastest runners, and have relatively little effect on the running speed of average runners."

Which of the following is the most plausible threat to the internal validity of these conclusions?

a. Statistical regression effect.
b. Selection-maturity effect.
c. Selection-history effect.
d. The John Henry effect.

6.3 Several Republican Administrations have proposed the use of education vouchers, through which parents could choose the schools their children attended and pay for their children's education in public or private schools, using government-supplied vouchers. One rationale advanced for the proposal is that the ability of schools to retain students through high school graduation would improve if parents could exercise choice in selecting schools. A group of researchers designed a study to examine the validity of the proposed rationale, by (1) allowing parents to obtain vouchers if they so desired; and (2) computing the proportion of ninth-grade students who graduated from high school within four years, (a) when their parents had used a voucher to pay for their high school education, and (b) when their parents had not made use of the voucher opportunity. The researchers found that 15% more ninth-grade students graduated from high school when their parents paid for their high school education with a voucher. Which of the following actions would be most effective in increasing the internal validity of this study?

a. Administering a standardized achievement test to all students in the study at the end of the ninth grade.
b. Randomly assigning parents to the voucher and no-voucher groups.
c. Collecting data on the socioeconomic status of parents who elected to use vouchers and parents who didn't use them.
d. Recording the ages at which school leavers in each group dropped out of school.

6.4 In a study of the effectiveness of preventive health care on overall health care costs, a medical care insurer in New York selected 200 of its clients at random, and then offered full reimbursement to half the selected clients for an annual physical examination for each member of the clients' families. Thus half the sampled clients were randomly assigned to a "free physical examination" group and the other half were randomly assigned to a comparison group in which the insurer's standard exemptions and restrictions were applied to all medical claims, including non-reimbursement of the costs of a physical examination in the absence of a specific medical condition. At the end of a two-year period, the average total claims of both groups were compared to determine the effectiveness of the preventive physical examination provision. It was found that total medical claims, including the costs of annual physical exams, were, on average, $150 lower for the experimental group. If you were the Director of Medical Services at a residential facility for senior citizens, and thus responsible for the costs and quality of medical services, could you safely generalize the results of the New York study to your client population? Circle the best of the following responses:

   a. Yes, because the clients in the New York study were not selected according to their ages; all ages were represented.

   b. No, because older adults have greater need for medical services than do younger adults; an annual physical would not prevent an older person from getting sick.

   c. Yes, because the New York study incorporated random selection of clients and random assignment of clients to experimental and comparison treatments. It is therefore a valid study.

   d. No, because the New York study did not report results for clients in specific age groups. The experiment might have had positive results overall at the same time it had negative results for clients in certain age groups.

7.

Elements of Statistical Inference

Inferential Statistics

A busy decision maker is often faced with information in the form of numbers that he or she must use in making important decisions, and sometimes the decision to be made requires *going beyond the numbers presented* to answer a series of "what if" or "is it also true" questions such as "what will happen to productivity if we wait one more year before adding extra staff?" In going beyond available data, one must use a form of **inference**, and because the numbers involved are statistics we call this statistical inference. Here are some more examples of what we mean, put in terms of a decision maker's problems.

1. A school system upstate used high-achieving sixth-graders to tutor struggling third-graders in reading. Suppose you are a school administrator and you've heard through the grapevine that it worked very well for them. How well did it really work? And is it likely to be effective in your school system? You'll have to look carefully at the data to answer even the first question, which calls for an evaluation. And then you'll have to *go beyond the data* to infer what would happen if you tried the approach in your school system.

2. At the most recent meeting of the American Management Association, you heard a talk on the relationship between employee assistance programs and worker absenteeism. The speaker claimed that factories with employee assistance programs helped supervisors to detect employees' problems, gave them a place to

refer employees who needed help, and helped employees to cope with their problems while the problems were still manageable. The result was rapid problem resolution with consequent reduction in lost work time. Just how strong were those relationships? What kinds of employee assistance services seemed to be effective? Should you invest in an employee assistance program at your workplace? Better look at the data very carefully! And then you'll have to **infer** from the data to your own setting and situation.

3. Although career education is no longer the darling of bold-thinking educational innovators, many still feel that high school students leave the twelfth grade with insufficient information on the world of work. They feel that these students have a vague understanding, at best, of the relationship between education and career opportunities. In the school system where you're superintendent, the career education program disappeared in 1986, along with performance contracting, new math, and strict accountability. In your view, some educational fads are best sent to an early grave, but others are abandoned too quickly, without ever getting a fair test. You'd like to see greater emphasis on the transition between school and work in your district's high school curriculum, and you've just been reading about an apparently successful career knowledge development program that was used in a school system in Pennsylvania. Once again, the old questions surface. How well did the program work in the Pennsylvania school system? You read that eleventh-graders who had been in the program a year knew more about career opportunities than did a similar group of students in schools who hadn't participated in the project. Did the project students' increased knowledge reflect a real project effect, or was it just due to the selection of especially bright students as project participants? Did the project students really know a lot more about careers at the end of the school year than at the beginning? Did they learn more than you'd expect them to just by growing a year older and going to school a year longer, even without the project? How sure can you be that the students' apparent gains in knowledge wouldn't just vanish were you to develop a similar project in your school system? Once again, these questions call for a hard look at relevant data. They also require inference beyond the data to a new situation or a new group of students.

All of us make inferences in our everyday lives. Sometimes we just play our hunches. (Ms. Jones has always supported me on personnel appraisal votes in the past; I assume she'll vote for my personnel recommendations again this year.) In other cases, we're more systematic in gathering information and in generalizing from that information. (I don't know how parents in my school system feel about our physical education program. I think we'll do a survey to get some information on parental opinions.) Regardless of the degree of formality or rigor you use in forming your inferences, as a manager paid to make decisions and implement policy, you can't get away from the necessity of going beyond the facts at hand. You must infer the likely actions of people, the likely consequences of your decisions, and the probable shape of the future in a world fraught with uncertainties.

This section of the book will teach you how statistics can be used in making formal inferences from numerical data. As in the first section, we will emphasize how to read and understand evaluation and research reports, and how to figure out what they do and don't say. We assume that you're too busy to compute your own statistics, and that you're not interested in learning a lot of fancy formulas. We assume that you are interested in knowing how to make sense out of all those numbers in evaluation and research reports. In fact, as a decision maker, you've got to be able to read and understand research and evaluation reports just to survive. The days of "flying by the seat of one's pants" are over. Research support for recommendations and decisions is often demanded by policy-making bodies, and, as we've noted, inferential statistical procedures are central to the vast majority of quantitative, empirical research studies.

Our Approach

Every field has its own vocabulary and its own set of basic concepts; inferential statistics is no exception. So we'll begin at the beginning, with some basic vocabulary and the fundamental ideas that are used in all formal statistical inference. That will be the dry part, where you'll wonder what inferential statistics has to do with becoming a more effective decision maker, and how it will help you understand evaluation and research reports; but it's only a couple of pages. Once we get through the basics, we'll move immediately to applications. You'll find that the same logic is used repeatedly in all applications of inferential statistics. So spending a good bit of time and effort on the next few chapters will pay off in the end. Once we get beyond fundamental concepts, every application of inferential statistics will be illustrated with data from a real research or evaluation report. You'll learn to read and understand the data tables, to form your own conclusions on what the data say, and to recognize when an author is handing you a line instead of the straight facts. Flushes of enthusiasm abound in evaluation and research reports, and you've got to be a knowl-edgeable reader to avoid getting bushwhacked. You don't want to propose a major programmatic change just because some over-zealous evaluator took poetic license with his or her data.

Some Basic Vocabulary

Two things go on in statistical inference: **estimation** and **hypothesis testing**. We either estimate or test hypotheses about various aspects—which we call **parameters**—of **populations**. In doing so, we use data collected from **samples** to compute various **statistics**. When we're doing estimation, the statistics we compute are called **estimates**. The formulas we use to compute them are called **estimators**. Now let's define all of these terms.

Population. Formally, a population is any collection of objects or entities that have at least one characteristic in common. Although we usually think of populations of people, in statistical work our populations can consist of schools, school systems, governmental units, pieces of furniture, library books, or any describable group of things or persons that share some common characteristic. In all of the inferential situations we describe later in the book, you will see that the population is that group of objects or persons about which we want to make some inference. That is, we really want to know some characteristic of a population, even though we haven't measured or observed every person or object that makes up the population.

Parameter. A parameter is some characteristic of a population. For example, if the population we're interested in consists of all fourth-graders enrolled in a school system, one parameter of that population is the fourth-graders' average IQ-test score. Another parameter is the percentage of fourth-graders who need remedial reading instruction. In statistical work, parameters are numbers that describe some important features of a population. Unless we've measured or observed every object or person in the population we're interested in, we won't know the true value of the population's parameters. So we use inferential statistics to infer the values of population parameters.

Sample. The simplest definition of a sample is that it is just a part of a population. A sample can consist of an entire population or any part of a population. In all statistical problems, a sample will consist of those objects or people we have observed or measured. For example, if the population we were interested in was all fourth-graders in a school system, and the parameter we were interested in was the average IQ-test score of all fourth-graders, our sample would consist of the fourth-graders who actually completed an IQ test. They would be the sample of persons who had supplied us with data.

Many samples are useless for statistical work. We want to do our best to avoid such samples. Think about the problem of determining the average IQ-test score of all fourth-graders in a school system. Suppose that you had given an IQ test to a sample of fourth-graders who were enrolled in a special program for gifted students. Their average IQ might be around 120. You wouldn't want to use their average IQ to infer the average IQ of all fourth-graders in the school system. Clearly, your estimate would be too high. The problem is that the fourth-graders in the program for the gifted don't fairly **represent** all fourth-graders in the school system. In statistical work, we want to use only samples that are representative of the populations we're interested in. Such samples are called **probability samples**, and have the following features in common. First, every person or object that is a member of the population has some chance (but not necessarily the same chance) of being a member of the sample. Second, before we select our sample, we can figure out the chances that any person or object, or group of persons or objects, might wind up in the sample. Third, we have defined our population so well that we can state without any question whether a particular person or object is or is not a member of the population. For the moment, don't worry too much about the second and third features of probability samples. The first feature is often the stumbling block when samples don't represent populations. In the example we've been considering, if all sampled students were in the program for the gifted, then fourth-graders who were not in that program wouldn't have any chance at all of being sampled. We therefore wouldn't have a probability sample, and we'd run into real trouble when we tried to infer the average IQ of all fourth-graders in the school system.

Statistic. A statistic is just a characteristic of a sample. It is a number that describes some feature of a sample (such as the average IQ-test score of a sample of fourth-grade students). A statistic can be used to infer the value of a population parameter. You've been introduced to lots of different statistics in the first part of this book. Means, standard deviations, ranges, semi-interquartile ranges, variances, medians, and correlation coefficients are all examples of statistics. Each is computed using the data collected on a sample. Each describes some feature or characteristic of a sample. The statistic can be calculated exactly; there's no risky inference involved.

So far, we've defined four terms: **population, parameter, sample**, and **statistic**. Just remember that the two terms that start with the letter "P" go together, and the two terms that start with the letter "S" go together. Parameters describe characteristics or features of populations. Statistics describe characteristics or features of samples. They often describe the same feature. For example, the average IQ-test score of a sample of fourth-graders is a statistic; it's *calculated exactly*. The average IQ-test score of the population from which the sample was selected is a parameter; it's what we usually have to *estimate*.

Estimate. An estimate is just a number. It is computed by using data collected from a sample, but it is *used* as a "best guess" about the value of a population parameter. Going back to the example we've used before, if you wanted to know the average IQ-test score of the fourth-graders in a school system, you might select a probability sample of, say, 100 of them, and administer an IQ test to all of the sampled students. If you computed their average IQ score, and it turned out to be 105.4, that number would be an estimate of the average IQ-test score of all fourth-graders in the school system (the population parameter of interest).

Estimator. An estimator is a formula used to compute an estimate. In the example just discussed, the estimator would be the formula for computing a sample average—add up the IQ-test scores for each sampled fourth-grader, and divide by the number of sampled fourth-graders.

Problems — Chapter 7

7.1 In a study of the relationship between investment and payoff, an economist wanted to estimate the correlation coefficient between current price and current dividend rate for all utilities stocks listed on the New York Stock Exchange. If the list of such stocks were considered to be a population, what would the correlation coefficient be called?
  a. A statistic.
  b. An estimate.
  c. A parameter.
  d. A sample.

7.2 When presidential election time rolls around, major polling companies, like the Harris Poll and the Gallup Poll, often provide predictions of election outcomes. They base their predictions on surveys of about 1500 prospective voters. The 1500 voters they survey constitute:
  a. A population.
  b. A parameter.
  c. An estimator.
  d. A sample.

7.3 When Harris Poll or Gallup Poll researchers gather data from potential voters on how they intend to vote in an upcoming presidential election, the researchers usually summarize their findings by computing the percentage of voters who said they would vote for Candidate A, the percentage who said they would vote for Candidate B, and so on. These percentages are examples of:

    a. Population parameters.
    b. Sample statistics.
    c. Population estimators.
    d. Sample parameters.

7.4   If a school superintendent wanted to know the mean IQ-test score of all sixth-grade students in a school system, it would not be necessary to test every sixth-grader. The population mean could be estimated by testing a sample of sixth-graders, and then using the mean IQ score of the sample to estimate the mean that would have been found, had all sixth-graders in the system been tested. The sample mean would be computed by summing the IQ-test scores of all tested sixth-graders, and then dividing the sum by the number of tested sixth-graders. This formula, used to compute the sample mean, is an example of:

    a. An estimator.
    b. A parameter.
    c. An estimate.
    d. A statistic.

8.

Nuts and Bolts
of Estimation

Estimation is the process of using data from a sample to infer the value of a population parameter. Like all forms of statistical inference, estimation involves the elements defined in the last chapter. The process of estimation is as follows:

1. The population that is of interest is carefully defined. It's important to realize that the way a population is defined will have a lot to do with the outcome of an evaluation or research study.

2. The relevant population parameter (or parameters) is defined. That is, we identify what we want to estimate. Examples include the one we've used earlier (the average IQ-test score of all fourth-graders in a school system), the proportion of windows in a district's schools that need to be replaced, the average and range of annual salaries of an agency's administrative staff members, and so forth.

3. A probability sampling procedure is used to select a representative sample of the population of interest. In most of the statistical work you'll encounter in evaluation and research reports, a particular probability sampling procedure, **simple random sampling**, will have been used. With simple random sampling, each member of a population has exactly the same chance of being sampled. In addition, the chance that a given member of the population is sampled doesn't depend at all on what other members of the population have been or will be sampled. In practice, simple random sampling is often assumed to have been used, regardless of the actual method used for selecting objects or persons for collection of data. Sometimes the assumption is appropri-

ate, and inferential statistical procedures work well. On other occasions, the assumption is totally unwarranted, and inferential statistics will produce badly distorted results. In a later section, we'll return to a discussion of this pitfall, and how to look out for it.

4. Data are collected (either through observation, measurement, or interview) from each member of the sample. The data collected are appropriate for estimating the population parameter (or parameters) that are of interest. If we were interested in the average IQ-test score of a population, we'd give each member of the sample an IQ test. If we were interested in the proportion of windows in a district's public schools that needed replacing, we'd record, for each sampled window, whether or not it needed replacing, and so on.

5. An appropriate estimator (formula) is applied to the data collected from the sample, to compute an estimate of the population parameter(s) in which we're interested.

The entire estimation process is illustrated by the drawing in Figure 8.1.

Two Types of Estimation

Two approaches to the estimation of population parameters are used in evaluation and research reports. The first, called **point estimation**, has been described in the preceding section. In point estimation, a population parameter is estimated using a single sample statistic. For example, a sample average (a statistic) is used to estimate a population average (a parameter). Or a sample standard deviation (another statistic) is used to estimate the value of a population standard deviation (another population parameter). In each case, a population parameter is estimated using a single estimate (called a point value) that is computed using the data from an observed or measured sample.

The other kind of estimation is called **interval estimation**. It involves the computation of **confidence intervals**. Regardless of the type of estimation used, the researcher or evaluator is trying to answer the question, "What is the value of a population parameter?" When point estimation is used, the form of the answer is, "I don't know for sure, but my best guess is (the value of the sample

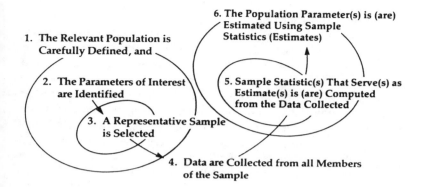

1. The Relevant Population is Carefully Defined, and

2. The Parameters of Interest are Identified

3. A Representative Sample is Selected

4. Data are Collected from all Members of the Sample

5. Sample Statistic(s) That Serve(s) as Estimate(s) is (are) Computed from the Data Collected

6. The Population Parameter(s) is (are) Estimated Using Sample Statistics (Estimates)

Figure 8.1   The Process of Estimation

statistic used as an estimate)." When interval estimation is used, the form of the answer is something like "I don't know the exact answer, but I'm 95% confident that the value falls between the following two numbers." The two numbers that are given in the interval estimation answer are called a **lower confidence limit** and an **upper confidence limit**, respectively. The interval between the lower confidence limit (LCL) and the upper confidence limit (UCL) is called a **confidence interval**.

Confidence intervals are widely misinterpreted in evaluation and research reports. It is important that you understand what they are and what they are not, so that you won't be misled. The explanation must, of necessity, be a little bit involved. At times it might read like a shaggy dog story and you may wonder whether it will ever end. But stick with it. Once you understand confidence intervals, you'll know a good bit about the logic of statistical inference. Many data tables in many research and evaluation reports will then seem a lot clearer.

To explain confidence intervals, we'll have to engage in a hypothetical discussion. It's important that you understand right off that the discussion is purely hypothetical. It's merely a teaching device, and won't have anything to do with actual practice. To keep fiction and reality clearly separated, let's briefly review the actual steps involved in estimating a population parameter. You begin by defining the population you are interested in and the parameter you want to estimate. Then you select a *single* probability sample from that population. After you collect data from all members of the sample, you compute an estimate of the population parameter. The estimate could be in the form of a single value (a point estimate) or in the form of a confidence interval (an interval estimate).

Suppose that you've identified the population you're interested in and the population parameter you want to estimate. For the sake of specificity, let's go back to the example we've used previously, and assume that you want to estimate the average IQ score of all fourth-grade students enrolled in the public schools in a school district. Let's assume that you're an administrator in that school district, and that you have 5000 fourth-graders in your population. Now you wouldn't have to test all 5000 students in order to estimate their average IQ score. In fact, it might be sufficient to administer an IQ test to a fairly small sample (say 100 students) and use their IQ-test performances to estimate the average IQ of the entire population. Here's the hypothetical part: Suppose that you selected a simple random sample of 100 fourth-graders, gave each one an IQ test, and when you computed their average IQ you found it equaled 105.2. You could use that number as a point estimate of the average IQ of all 5000 students, but in this case you want to form a confidence interval. Now let's suppose that you selected a second simple random sample of 100 students from the same population of 5000. Do you think that their average IQ would equal 105.2, just like the first sample of 100? You'd probably expect the average for the second sample to be similar to that of the first sample, but it would be surprising if the two averages were exactly the same. More likely, the average for the second sample would be a bit higher or a bit lower. For the sake of specificity, let's assume that the average for the second sample was 101.0.

Proceeding with this hypothetical example, let's assume that you were to select a large number of independent simple random samples from the population of 5000 fourth-graders. Each random sample would contain exactly 100 students, and after you had given all students in a sample an IQ test, you'd record their average IQ-test score, and you'd put them back in the population, so you wouldn't run out of students to sample. Remember, this is all

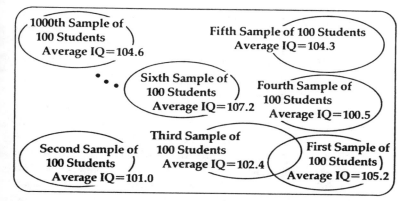

Figure 8.2 Hypothetical Example of Repeated Sampling and Estimation From a Population of 5000 Fourth-Grade Students

hypothetical, just to illustrate the logic and meaning of confidence intervals.

At this point, you'd have a long list of sample average IQs, one for each sample you selected. If you were to select 1000 samples, each with 100 students, before you got tired of the whole process you'd have a list of 1000 sample average IQs. Look at Figure 8.2 for an illustration of the results of this process.

From known statistical theory, we can tell what would happen if you were to treat the 1000 sample averages just like any set of data, and were to draw a frequency distribution of the 1000 scores. The shape of the frequency distribution would be a familiar bell-shaped curve, called a **normal distribution**. Furthermore, we know that the average of all 1000 sample averages would be exactly the same as the average IQ of the entire population of 5000 fourth-grade students. This is a very important point. It tells us that the average of all of our estimates would exactly equal the population parameter we're trying to estimate. (Statisticians pride themselves in being right, "on the average.") Finally, if we were to compute the standard deviation of the 1000 sample averages, we would find that it was related to the standard deviation of the individual IQ scores of the 5000 fourth-graders who make up the population. In this case, the standard deviation of the 1000 sample averages would be one tenth as large as the standard deviation of the individual IQ scores of those 5000 students. That's because each of our samples contains 100 students. In general, the standard deviation of the sample averages would equal the standard deviation of the original scores, divided by the square root of the sample size. If that last bit of information is a bit mind-boggling, don't worry about it right now. Just accept the information concerning this example, "on faith." Figure 8.3 shows what the frequency distribution of the 1000 sample averages would look like. To make the problem more concrete, we've assumed that the standard deviation of the individual IQ-test scores of the 5000 students in the population equals 15 points. That's close to the true value we'd find with most standardized IQ tests. Since the standard deviation of the frequency distribution of sample average is only one tenth as large as the standard deviation of the individual IQ scores, it would equal one and one half (or 1.5) points in this example.

We warned you that this was going to be a shaggy dog story. But don't give up yet. We're almost to the point, and once you see it, you'll understand a good bit of inferential statistics.

When a set of scores has a frequency distribution that follows a bell-shaped curve (the normal distribution), we know a lot about the scores. For example, a little more than two thirds of the scores (68% to be exact) will be less than one standard deviation from their average value. In this example, then, we know that 68% of the sample averages will fall in an interval that is 1.5 points below to 1.5 points above the average of their frequency distribution. However, we've already said that the average of the sample averages will equal the average IQ score of the 5000 fourth-graders. Remember that this is a population parameter we're trying to estimate. So 68% of the sample averages will be within 1.5 points of the population average. Another useful fact is that 95% of the sample averages will fall in an interval that is between two standard deviations below the average of their frequency distribution and two standard deviations above that average. In this case, two standard deviations equals three IQ points, since two times 1.5 equals 3.0. So 95% of the 1000 sample averages will fall no farther than three points from the average IQ score of the population of 5000 students. Again, this fact is illustrated in Figure 8.3.

The only tricky part of understanding confidence intervals is coming next, so read the next section carefully.

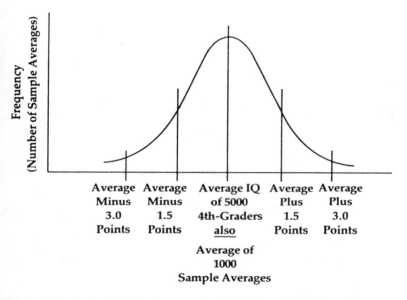

Figure 8.3 Hypothetical Frequency Distribution of 1000 Sample Averages (Each Sample Consists of 100 Fourth-Grade Students, Selected From a Population of 5000 Fourth-Grade Students)

Suppose that we consider any one of the sample averages that is no more than two standard deviations from the true average IQ of the 5000 students. One such sample average is shown in Figure 8.4. If we were to form an interval by adding two standard deviations to that sample average, and then subtracting two standard devistions from that sample average, the interval would contain the true average IQ of the 5000 students. Look at Figure 8.4 to verify this fact. If we had chosen to start with any of the 95% of sample averages that are within two standard deviations of the average of the frequency distribution, we could have said the same thing. The interval we would have formed would contain the true average IQ-test score of the 5000 students. Only if we chose one of the 5% of sample averages that was more than two standard deviations from the average of the frequency distribution, would our interval fail to contain the average IQ-test score of the population of 5000 fourth-graders. This is illustrated in Figure 8.5.

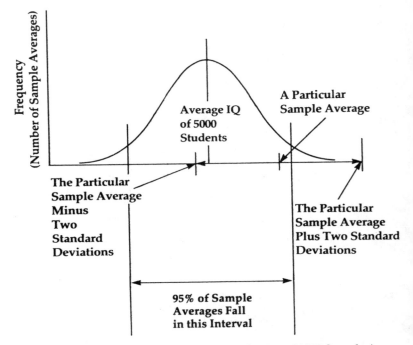

Figure 8.4   Hypothetical Frequency Distribution of 1000 Sample Average IQ Scores (A 95% Confidence Interval Around a Particular Sample Average Includes the True Average IQ of the Population of 5000 Fourth-Grade Students)

If you've followed the argument so far, you're about to understand confidence intervals. Let's go back to reality: In fact, we're going to select only one sample of 100 students, not 1000 samples. For that one sample, suppose we completed the following three steps: (1) We computed the sample average IQ score; (2) we added two standard deviations to that average (to compute an upper confidence limit); (3) we subtracted two standard deviations from that average (to compute a lower confidence limit). We could then say that we were 95% confident that the population parameter—the true average IQ of all 5000 fourth-graders in the school system—fell between the lower confidence limit and the upper confidence limit. Now we wouldn't know for sure that we were

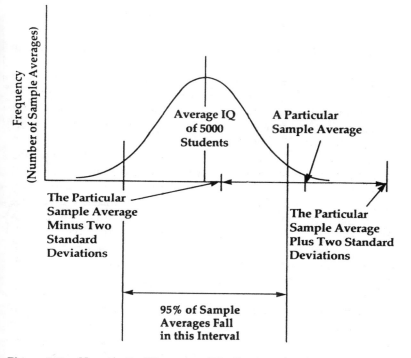

Figure 8.5   Hypothetical Frequency Distribution of 1000 Sample Average IQ Scores (A 95% Confidence Interval Around a Particular Sample Average Fails to Include the True Average IQ of the Population of 5000 Fourth-Grade Students)

making a true statement. We would know only that, had we selected 1000 independent samples of 100 students and followed the same procedure with each one, the true average IQ score for the 5000 fourth-graders would have been "captured" between the upper and lower confidence limits for 95% of those samples (that is, 950 out of 1000). The true average IQ score for the 5000 students would not have been captured between the upper and lower confidence limits for 5% of the samples (that is, 50 out of 1000). We have no way of knowing whether the one sample we selected was one of the "good" 950 for which the population parameter was captured by the confidence interval, or was one of the "bad" 50 samples for which the true average IQ score of the 5000 students was not captured by the confidence interval. Since our statement that the confidence interval captures the true average IQ would be correct for 95% of the intervals, we say that we have formed a "95% confidence interval."

The 95% figure is called a **level of confidence**. Although 95% is often used as a confidence level, it is not the only possibility. In some evidence and research reports, you will find 90% confidence intervals, 99% confidence intervals, and sometimes, 80% confidence intervals. The confidence level used should reflect the evaluator's or researcher's desire for assurance that he or she has captured the true value of the population parameter. The more assurance required, the higher the confidence level. However, given the same set of data, the higher the confidence level, the wider the confidence interval will be. For example, based on a single sample of 100 students, we might say that we are 95% confident that the average IQ of the entire population of 5000 students falls between 102.0 and 108.0. If we wanted a 99% confidence level and had the same sample of data, our confidence interval would range from 101.13 to 108.87. Notice that the 99% confidence interval is almost two points wider than the 95% confidence interval. In statistics as in life, you don't get something for nothing. If you want to be more confident without collecting more data, you have to widen the limits of your uncertainty (the confidence interval).

Interpreting Confidence Intervals in Research Reports

This logic we've just discussed is applicable to all interpretations of confidence intervals, regardless of the context in which they're encountered. We've discussed the interpretation of a confidence interval around a single sample average. That's just one of many possible applications. Confidence intervals can be constructed for the purpose of estimating any of a number of population parameters, such as correlation coefficients, standard deviations, variances, and medians, to name just a few. One frequent application is a confidence interval on the difference between two population averages. Let's explore that application.

Suppose that you were interested in the relative effectiveness of two reading curricula you were considering adopting for third-graders in a school system. Since the school system had been using the California Achievement Test (CAT) to assess third-grade reading achievement for the past several years, they wanted to select the curriculum that would maximize their third-graders' average score on the CAT. Suppose that you selected 100 students at random from the entire population of third-graders in the system, and then randomly assigned 50 third-graders to each of the two competing curricula for an entire school year. At the end of the year, the school system had the CAT administered to all 100 students, and found that the 50 students who completed Curriculum A had an average reading comprehension score that was five points higher than the average of those who completed Curriculum B. For the 100 third-graders in your experiment, you are sure that Curriculum A was more effective, on average, than was Curriculum B. But that's not what you're interested in. You'd like to have some reasonable assurance that Curriculum A would be better than Curriculum B (i.e., it would result in a higher average reading comprehension score) if you used it with the entire population of third-graders in the school system. You can get the assurance you want, based on the data collected in your experiment, by computing a confidence interval.

It is possible to compute a confidence interval on the average reading comprehension score of all third-graders using Curriculum A, minus the average reading comprehension score of all third-graders using Curriculum B. The details of the computational procedures are not important here; what matter is that the confidence interval can be computed. Suppose that, when a 95% confidence interval was computed, the lower confidence limit was 2 points and the upper confidence limit was 8 points. You could then be 95% confident that Curriculum A would yield an average reading comprehension score for the entire population of third-graders that was at least two points higher than the average that would have resulted had the school system used Curriculum B with all third-graders. In fact, the advantage in average score provided by Curriculum A might be as much as eight points, based on the data resulting from your experiment and a 95% confidence level.

Can you be sure that Curriculum A would be better, were the school system to use it with all of your third-graders? The answer is no. The level of confidence is 95%, not 100%. The only way to know for sure that one treatment is better than another would be to try both with the entire population of interest. Whenever you use statistical inference, some degree of uncertainty remains. That is the price you pay for collecting data from a relatively small sample, instead of the entire population. Can you say that the chances are 95% that Curriculum A would produce an average reading score for the population that was between two points and eight points higher than the average reading score that would result from using Curriculum B? Again, the answer must be no. Were Curriculum A to be used with all third-graders, and their memories to be wiped out prior to using Curriculum B, there probably would be some real difference between their average scores on the CAT Reading Comprehension Test. That difference might favor Curriculum A by two points to eight points, or it might not. You have no way of knowing for sure. If it does, your confidence interval is correct—that is, the difference between the averages for Curricula A and B would be between two points and eight points. Otherwise, your confidence interval is not correct. Recall that there is no way of knowing whether a particular 95% confidence interval provides a true statement or a false statement. All you know for sure is the following: Had you repeated the experiment over and over thousands of times, computing a confidence interval each time, the true difference between the average achievement resulting from Curriculum A and that resulting from Curriculum B would have been captured within 95% of the confidence intervals you computed.

When you see a confidence interval in an evaluation report or a research report, then, interpret it the same way. Realize that the true value of the population parameter under consideration might or might not be captured within the reported confidence interval. You can be sure, however, that a percentage of all possible confidence intervals, equal to the level of confidence, would capture the true value of the population parameter.

Confidence intervals have an added advantage. They provide information on the range of a researcher's or evaluator's uncertainty. In the example we just discussed, the confidence interval on the difference between reading comprehension averages had a lower limit of two points and an upper limit of eight points. Thus the experimental results leave you with a six-point range of uncertainty, at the 95% confidence level. Now it could be the case that a two-point difference in average scores is trivial, as far as you're concerned, whereas an eight-point difference is worth looking into. If that were the case, your experiment would have told you that Curriculum A was probably no worse than Curriculum B in terms of average reading comprehension score, but the difference in effectiveness might be trivial or it might be substantial. You can't know for sure on the basis of an experiment involving 100 students. But you can conclude that Curriculum A is a better bet than Curriculum B.

A Short Review Quiz

If you've survived this far, you've encountered a load of new vocabulary and some of the most challenging concepts in inferential statistics. It's probably a good time for a bit of review and the opportunity to test your grasp of the new material. In the following paragraphs, you'll find some hypothetical statistical information of the sort that you're likely to encounter in evaluation or research reports. Read each paragraph carefully, and write down your answers to the questions that follow. All of the answers are given at the end of the last set of questions. We know that, as a mature decision maker who sets an example for your peers and colleagues, you won't even be tempted to look at the answers in the book before you write down your own. Did we even suggest that wouldn't be fair?

Example A: The Effectiveness of an Inservice Science Education Program

In 1988 the Pomegranate, Ohio, Union School District conducted a series of inservice science education workshops for elementary school teachers to increase their awareness of curriculum materials on new developments in the physical sciences. The workshops had the parallel objective of increasing the teachers' knowledge of recent developments in the sciences that have immediate application to everyday life, such as medical applications of biotechnology (recombinant DNA applications, gene splitting, etc.) and computer applications of physics and chemistry (work with integrated circuits, transistor technology, etc.).

The success of the workshops in increasing teachers' knowledge of recent scientific developments was evaluated in part by administering a specially developed science awareness test to all participating teachers at the beginning of the first workshop, and then administering a parallel form of the test following completion of the last workshop. The evaluator reported the mean and standard deviation of teachers' scores on the pretest and the posttest, and then computed a 95% confidence interval on the teachers' mean "gain" from pretest to posttest. This approach to evaluation is not at all unusual, despite the fact that it is a very weak design, as you learned in Chapter 6.

The data reported by the Pomegranate Science Workshop evaluator are presented in Table 8.1. Review the data and then answer the questions.

TABLE 8.1: Results of Science Knowledge Evaluation for 30 Teachers Participating in Pomegranate Science Program Inservice Workshops

Pretest (25 items)	Posttest (25 items)	Gain
Average = 17.5	Average = 23.5	Average = 6.0
Standard Deviation = 4.3	Standard Deviation = 5.0	
95% Confidence Interval on Average Gain: (2.5, 9.5)		

Questions for Example A

1. What group constitutes the sample in this example?
2. Is it clear that the sample was chosen randomly from some population?
3. To what population might the 95% confidence interval refer?
4. What is the population parameter that is of central interest in this example?
5. How confident can you be that the average gain of the population falls between 2.5 points and 9.5 points?

6. If you conducted the Pomegranate inservice evaluation independently 1000 times, how many of the 1000 95% confidence intervals would not capture the average science achievement gain for the population?

Example B: Estimating the Budget for the Oak Park School District—The Need for Remedial Classes

At its last meeting, the Oak Park School Board recommended that any third- through sixth-grade student whose arithmetic achievement score fell below the 35th percentile on the national norms of the Metropolitan Achievement Test be considered for placement in a remedial mathematics class. To estimate the need for remedial mathematics classes, the Research Department reviewed the most recent test data of 100 randomly selected students in each of grades three through six. The proportions of students in these samples whose arithmetic achievement fell below the 35th percentile were calculated, and then multiplied by the total numbers of students in these grades, to estimate the numbers of students who, by the school board's criterion, needed remedial mathematics. These estimated numbers of students needing remediation were then divided by 25 (the average class size in the Oak Park District) to estimate the need for remedial math classes by grade. Ninety-percent confidence intervals on the number of classes needed in each grade were then computed. Results are shown in the following table:

Grade	Sample Size	Number <35%ile	Percent <35%ile	Estimated Number Needing Remediation	Estimated Classses Needed	LCL Classes	UCL Classes
3	100	20	20	1000	40	32	48
4	100	25	25	1200	48	42	54
5	100	28	28	1200	48	42	54
6	100	26	26	975	39	32	46

Questions for Example B

1. What are the populations in this example?
2. What are the population parameters in this example?
3. What is the point estimate of the number of fifth-graders who need remedial mathematics classes?
4. What is the point estimate of the number of remedial math classes needed for fourth-grade students?
5. What is the lower 90% confidence limit on the number of remedial math classes needed for third-graders?
6. What is the upper 90% confidence limit on the number of remedial math classes needed for fifth-graders?
7. If you were trying to get the school board to approve a budget you were reasonably certain would be adequate, how many sixth-grade remedial math classes would you have them include?

Answers — Example A

1. The 30 participating teachers constitute the sample in this example.
2. It is not clear that the sample was chosen randomly from some well-defined population. We can assume that it was not. You should realize that this situation is not at all unusual in research and evaluation, and that you'll encounter it in many research and evaluation reports. Here's how you handle interpretation. You are being asked by the author to assume that the sample he or she used is representative of some (unspecified) population. You must assume that the population is much like the sample in terms of its composition. For example, if you were to assume that number of years teaching was relevant to teachers' development of science awareness, then you would try to generalize the results shown for the sample to a population that was similar to the sample, in its distribution of years of teaching experience.
3. The population in this example is composed of all teachers who are potential participants in the science education inservice workshops.
4. The population parameter that is of central interest in this example is the average gain on the science awareness test that would be exhibited by the population of potential workshop par-

ticipants. Your particular interest might be in the average science awareness gain this population of teachers would experience, were the inservice workshops to be used in another school system.

5. You would have 95% confidence, since that is the level of confidence associated with the reported confidence interval.

6. We would expect 50 of the confidence intervals to fail to capture the average gain of the population, since 50 is 5% of 1000.

Answers — Example B

1. The relevant populations consist of all third-graders, fourth-graders, fifth-graders, and sixth-graders enrolled in the Oak Park School District.

2. The population parameters of interest are the numbers of remedial mathematics classes needed by Oak Park's third-graders, fourth-graders, fifth-graders, and sixth-graders.

3. The point estimate of the number of fifth-graders who need remedial mathematics instruction is 1200.

4. The point estimate of the number of remedial math classes needed for fourth-graders is 48.

5. The lower 90% confidence limit on the number of remedial math classes needed for third-graders is 32.

6. The upper 90% confidence limit on the number of remedial math classes needed for fifth-graders is 54.

7. You should have the school board budget for 46 remedial math classes for sixth-graders, since 46 is the upper 90% confidence limit on the number that will be needed. In that way, you can be reasonably sure that this aspect of the budget will be adequate, while at the same time not going too far overboard. In fact, you could readily justify your budget figure here, based on a sound statistical analysis: the school board would surely resonate to your scholarship and logic.

Compare your answers with those given here. If you answered at least 10 of the 13 questions correctly, you can probably assume that you have an adequate grasp of the fundamental vocabulary of statistical inference, and a fair understanding of the logic of point and interval estimation. Those accomplishments are reserved to relatively few individuals in the world, so you can be proud of yourself and move ahead to the task of understanding the logic of hypothesis testing. If you missed more than three questions, don't give up! The subject matter is not trivial. Go back to the beginning of the discussion on estimation and review. Or review the vocabulary, if you feel such a review would be helpful. Then re-read the examples and the questions that follow them, and reconsider your original answers in light of the ones we have provided. Then, after you work the following problems, go on to the next chapter and learn all about hypothesis testing.

Problems — Chapter 8

8.1 In a report on sources of revenue in medium-sized school systems throughout the nation, Spend and Squander (1987) estimated the proportion of funds available from such sources as local tax revenues, state foundation programs, and federal programs. They based their estimates on a survey of superintendents of 100 medium-sized school systems, randomly selected from the entire U.S. population of such systems. One kind of information provided in the report was a 95% confidence interval on the percentage of school system funds provided by state foundation programs. The interval was reported as ranging from 43.2% to 67.8%.

Which of the following is a correct interpretation of this information?

   a. If a medium-sized school system is randomly selected from the population of all such systems in the United States, the probability is 0.95 that the percentage of its funding provided by a state foundation program will be between 43.2% and 67.8%.

   b. The percentage of funding in all medium-sized school systems in the U.S. that is obtained from state foundation programs might or might not be between 43.2 and 67.8, but one can be 95% confident that this interval captures the true value.

   c. Five percent of the medium-sized school systems in the nation obtain more than 67.8% of their funding from state foundation programs.

   d. Ninety-five percent of the school systems in the nation obtain at least 43.2% of their funding, but no more than 67.8% of their funding, from state foundation programs.

8.2   Administrators in a school system wanted to know the average length of time microcomputers would last (until they needed major repairs) if the computers were purchased for use in classrooms. To obtain this information, the administrators leased 20 microcomputers from a major manufacturer, had them installed in a random sample of classrooms throughout the school system, and recorded the number of days of operation until each microcomputer suffered a major breakdown. The average turned out to be 19.4 days.

Which of the following provides the best description of this result?

  a. The value 19.4 is a point estimate of the average time until major repairs would be needed, were microcomputers to be installed in classrooms throughout the school system.
  b. The value 19.4 is a population parameter. It is the expected number of days until failure that would be experienced, if the school system were to install microcomputers in all of its schools.
  c. The value 19.4 is a lower confidence limit on the number of days until failure that would be experienced, were the school system to install microcomputers in all of its classrooms.
  d. The value 19.4 is nothing more than a sample statistic. It has nothing to do with the average number of days to failure that would be experienced, were the school system to install microcomputers in all of its classrooms.

8.3   Meteorologists always seek new variables that help predict weather phenomena. In one recent study, researchers quantified sunspot activity, on a scale of 1 to 10, and correlated this sunspot rating with total rainfall, during each week of a year. The correlation was +0.42, across all of the weeks in a year.

  a. Do you think that this study is an example of descriptive or inferential research? Justify your answer.
  b. If you were to consider this an inferential study, what would the population be?
  c. If you were to consider this an inferential study, what would the sample be?
  d. Would you describe the correlation of +0.42 to be a sample statistic or a population parameter?

8.4 Those who engage in games of chance involving sports usually inspect data on past performance very carefully. For example, in the not-so-distant past, the Dodgers and the Yankees have opposed each other in 28 baseball games. Of these contests, the Yankees won 21; 75% of the games. In predicting the outcome of future encounters, a sports enthusiast might use these data to compute a 95% confidence interval on the proportion of games the Yankees will win in an entire population of games that includes the future, as well as the past. Suppose that the 95% confidence interval ranges from 52% to 98%.

Which of the following conclusions is warranted on the basis of these data?

    a. The Dodgers will never win another game when they meet the Yankees in the future, since the lower confidence limit is greater than 50%.

    b. The probability that the Yankees win the game, the next time they meet the Dodgers, is at least 0.52.

    c. Since the upper confidence limit is 98%, a value that is less than 100%, the Dodgers have some small chance of winning future games.

    d. A person who engages in games of chance, on the basis of these data, would be better advised to bet on the Yankees than the Dodgers, since the lower confidence interval on the proportion of past and future games won by the Yankees is above 50%.

9.

The Logic of Hypothesis Testing

The Lay of the Land

If you understood the logic presented in the chapter on estimation, you've gone a long way toward an understanding of hypothesis testing as well. Not that the two forms of inference are identical. Indeed, they seek answers to fundamentally different questions. However, they both make use of concepts like statistics, parameters, samples, and populations. And distributions of sample statistics (such as the normal distribution of sample averages you encountered in the last chapter) play a crucial role in both procedures.

In estimation, the fundamental question we try to answer is, "What is the value of a population parameter?" In hypothesis testing, the fundamental question is, "Is it reasonable to believe that the value of a population parameter is x?" The x in that question is just a number, like 0, or 100, or some other value that makes sense in the context of a particular problem.

Hypothesis testing might be easier to understand if we consider a specific example. You're probably tired of it by now, but the example involving the average IQ-test score of all fourth-graders in a school system is as good as any, and at least it's familiar. To simplify the language of the presentation we'll assume that you're the superintendent of schools.

Let's suppose that you have an extensive achievement testing program in your school system, but your use of IQ tests is limited. Suppose that the average reading achievement of your fourth-graders has fallen far below that of previous years, and that you're searching for an explanation. You call a meeting of all fourth-grade teachers to explore the problem, only to have the teachers assert that your district is faced with an unusually dull crop of fourth-graders this year. The teachers suggest that the average verbal IQ of this year's fourth-graders is far different from the national average, and that's why reading achievement has suffered.

Your reaction to this distressing news is skepticism, since distributions of IQ-test scores don't change much from one year to the next unless a school system is affected by changes in its attendance area or substantial migration of families. Since your school system's boundaries and population have remained fairly stable, you decide to have your research department check out the fourth-grade teachers' claim.

Your testing budget is limited, as always, so you authorize testing a sample of 400 fourth-graders rather than all 5000 of them. To keep an open mind, you suggest that the research department begin with the assumption that your district's fourth-graders have an average verbal IQ that is exactly the same as the average for fourth-graders nationwide (100 points), and seek any evidence that refutes the assumption.

Regardless of whether you knew it at the time, you've called for a test of the **hypothesis** that the average verbal IQ of your district's fourth-graders is 100 points. The logic of your assignment to your research department is an exact parallel to that of **hypothesis testing**. You've begun with an initial statement of belief: an assertion that the average verbal IQ of your district's fourth-graders equals 100. Were the statement true, the fourth-graders' average IQ would be just the same as that of fourth-graders' throughout the nation. A statement of belief such as yours is known in statistical language as a **null hypothesis**. It is a statement about the value of a population parameter (in this case, the value of the average verbal IQ of the population of fourth-graders in your school district). In hypothesis testing, belief in the validity of the null hypothesis continues, unless evidence collected from a sample is sufficient to make continued belief appear unreasonable. You've instructed your research department to seek just such evidence.

You should realize that the population parameter involved in your hypothesis test has *some* true value, although you cannot know this value unless you test every fourth-grader in your school district. Now the average verbal IQ of all 5000 fourth-graders is either equal to 100, in which case your null hypothesis is true, or it equals some other value, in which case your null hypothesis is false. If your null hypothesis is false, an **alternative hypothesis**, in this case, that the average verbal IQ of your district's 5000 fourth-graders does not equal 100, must be true. There is a law in logic, called the "law of the excluded middle," that asserts that a thing must either be true or false. You can't have it both ways. Now that might appear obvious, but it's important to the logic of hypothesis testing. Remember, at the start of this example your fourth-grade teachers asserted that the average verbal IQ of your fourth-graders was not equal to 100. Your response was to instruct your research department to begin with the converse of the teachers' assertion—that is, a belief that fourth-graders' average verbal IQ equaled 100—and to seek evidence refuting that belief. In short, you asked your research department to attempt to "nullify" your initial statement of belief, in which case the teachers' assertion, that the fourth-graders' average verbal IQ does not equal 100, must be true. The law of the excluded middle guarantees it.

So far, we've illustrated two basic concepts in hypothesis testing—a null hypothesis and an alternative hypothesis—and the logic that connects them. The logic may seem indirect and cumbersome. If you want to examine a claim that fourth-graders' average verbal IQ is different from the national average, why not do it directly, instead of stating just the opposite (the null hypothesis), and then trying to show that the null hypothesis is unreasonable? There are several answers to this question. The best answer is that you can't "prove" anything using inferential statistics, least of all that a population average is different from 100. Furthermore, a wealth of statistical theory, coupled with some reasonable assumptions, allows you to examine the reasonableness of your null hypothesis, and thereby determine whether the alternative is a better bet. In short, we don't know how to go at the problem directly, and we do know how to tackle it indirectly. Although the logic may appear to be convoluted and cumbersome, it's sound.

The General Procedure

Like estimation, hypothesis testing is an inferential statistical procedure. To test a hypothesis, we use observations or measurements collected on a sample to decide whether or not our hypothesis about the value of a population parameter is reasonable. We decide either to continue believing that our null hypothesis is true, or we reject that belief and decide that the alternative hypothesis is true. The steps of the process are as follows:

1. Identify the population and the population parameter of interest.

2. Define a null hypothesis and an alternative hypothesis.

3. Collect data on a random sample of objects or individuals, selected from the population of interest.

4. Compute a sample statistic that is an estimate of the population parameter of interest.

5. Depending on the value of the sample statistic, decide that the null hypothesis is true, or reject the null hypothesis in favor of the alternative hypothesis.

Boiled down to its essentials, that's the process of hypothesis testing. As you might suspect, we've oversimplified it just a tad. There are a few important questions that we've conveniently ignored, such as: What happens if you make the wrong decision? How do you determine exactly when to reject the null hypothesis, and when to continue believing it's true? How large a sample should you take? We know you can hardly wait to have all of these questions answered, so read on! Your fondest desires will be realized!

Errors and Risks

The outcome of hypothesis testing is a decision; in the case of this example, a decision to continue believing that your district's fourth-graders have an average verbal IQ of 100 (the null hypothesis), or a decision to reject that belief, in favor of the alternative hypothesis that the fourth-graders' average IQ differs from 100. In general, the outcome of hypothesis testing is a decision to continue believing the null hypothesis, or a decision to reject the null hypothesis, in favor of a belief in the alternative hypothesis.

Reality exists, regardless of your decision. That is, the population average is either equal to 100 (in which case the null hypothesis is true) or it is equal to some value other than 100 (in which case the alternative hypothesis is true). Since the decision you will make in this example will be based on the test performances of only 400 fourth-graders, and not on the performances of the entire population of 5000, you might make the wrong decision. That is, you might decide that the average IQ of all 5000 fourth-graders is different from 100, when in fact, it equals 100. Such a mistake has a name in hypothesis testing. It is called a **Type I error**. A Type I error occurs when the null hypothesis is rejected even though it is true.

One of the joys of hypothesis testing is that the risk of making a Type I error can be set by the researcher or evaluator. You can design and adopt a decision rule that ensures that you will incur a very small risk of making a Type I error. The risk of making a Type I error is called the **level of significance** of the hypothesis test. The symbol that is used for the level of significance is a lower-case Greek letter alpha (α), so the level of significance is sometimes called the **alpha level** of the test. When you read an evaluation report or a research report and see that a particular statistic is "significant at the .05 level," the author is telling you that a null hypothesis was tested in such a way that the risk of making a Type I error was set at .05 (5%), and the null hypothesis was rejected in favor of the alternative hypothesis. If this last bit of information seems a bit opaque, don't be too concerned. There will be many more illustrations of hypothesis testing and interpretations of "significant" statistics in later sections of the book.

For the moment, let's get back to errors and risks. So far we've described one kind of error (Type I), the error that occurs when the decision maker decides that the null hypothesis is false (e.g., that the average verbal IQ of the district's fourth-graders is not equal to 100), when in fact it is true. This is the only type of error that can be made if the null hypothesis is rejected. Suppose, however, that the decision maker decided that the null hypothesis is true. In doing so, he or she will be rejecting the alternative hypothesis. In any given circumstance, that decision can be appropriate, or it can result in another type of error. If the alternative hypothesis is true, but the decision maker decides to stick with the null hypothesis, a **Type II error** results. In our present example, suppose that, on the basis of advice from the research department, the administrator decides that the average verbal IQ of his or her district's fourth-graders is equal to 100 when, in fact, the population average is different from 100. The administrator would have committed a Type II error. The risk of making a Type II error doesn't have a special name in statistics, but the Greek letter beta (β) is usually used to denote it.

Once again we've discussed a number of complex concepts that might not seem to hang together in a logical pattern. You may well be asking yourself: "Where are they going with all those hypotheses, errors, and risks?" Have faith! Remember that the logic of confidence intervals turned into a shaggy dog story, but we did get to the point eventually. The same thing will happen with hypothesis testing. If you stick with it, you'll finally be able to figure out all of those "*" and "**" marks next to the numbers in evaluation and research reports, and you'll understand the cryptic footnotes that say things like "$p < .05$" or "significant, alpha = .01." There now, doesn't that inspire you?

Let's review: In any hypothesis testing problem there are two hypotheses to deal with. The *null hypothesis* is an initial statement of belief about the value of a population parameter. The object of hypothesis testing is to decide whether it is reasonable to continue believing that the null hypothesis is true, or to reject that belief in favor of an *alternative hypothesis*. The decision is based on data collected from a sample that is randomly drawn from the population.

As in life, our decision can be either right or wrong. There are two ways in which we can be right, and two ways in which we can be wrong. If the null hypothesis is, in fact, true, we can be right by reaching that decision. We can be wrong by deciding that the null hypothesis is false, despite the fact that it is true. As we stated earlier, that kind of error is called a Type I error. The other possibilities occur if the null hypothesis is actually false and the alternative hypothesis is true. Here again, we can be right by reaching that decision. Or, we can be wrong by deciding that the alternative hypothesis is false, despite the fact that it is true. Again, that kind of error is called a Type II error. These four possibilities are summarized in the table shown below.

Earlier, we related one of the primary joys of hypothesis testing. The researcher or evaluator can control the risk of making errors.

THE POTENTIAL OUTCOMES OF A HYPOTHESIS TEST

The True State of Reality

		The Null Hypothesis is True	The Alternative Hypothesis is True
D E C I S I O N	**The Null Hypothesis is True**	Probability=$1-\alpha$ ☺	Type II Error (Risk β) ☹
	The Alternative Hypothesis is True	Type I Error (Risk α) ☹	Probability=$1-\beta$ ☺

One of the steps in hypothesis testing is to develop a decision rule—a rule that specifies what values of a sample statistic will lead you to continue believing that the null hypothesis is true, and what values of a sample statistic will lead you to reject the null hypothesis. It is possible to design the decision rule so that the risk of making a Type I error is as small as you want. Furthermore, if your sample size is large enough, you can make the risk of making a Type II error small at the same time you make the risk of making a Type I error small. In other words, it is possible to design a hypothesis test so that you make the right decision most of the time.

Decision Rules

Let's return to our example. Your research department followed your instructions, and dutifully administrated an IQ test to 400 fourth-graders who were randomly sampled from the 5000 in your school district. Suppose that the average IQ of the 400 sampled fourth-graders was 101.2. Now what should you do about your null hypothesis that the average IQ of the entire population of fourth-graders is 100? Well, 101.2 is pretty close to 100, isn't it? Don't you think it is quite possible to find a sample of 400 fourth-graders with an average IQ of 101.2 in a population of 5000 fourth-graders who have an average IQ of 100? Of course it is! So based on the data collected by your research department, you really don't want to reject the null hypothesis that fourth-graders in your school district have the same average IQ as fourth-graders throughout the nation.

Now suppose that the IQ-test results for the sample had been somewhat different. Let's say that the average IQ for the 400 sampled fourth-graders turned out to be 85.6. That's a long way from 100. Do you think that it is possible to find a sample of 400 fourth-graders with an average IQ of only 85.6 in a population of 5000 fourth-graders who have an average IQ of 100? Well, it's possible, but it's not at all likely. In fact it's so unlikely that the only sensible thing to do is reject your initial belief that the population of fourth-graders have an average IQ of 100. In other words, you ought to reject the null hypothesis, and conclude that your fourth-grade teachers are right. You do have a dull crop of fourth-graders this year!

So far we've discussed two possible outcomes of giving a sample of 400 of your fourth-graders an IQ test. In the first case, the average IQ of the sample was very close to the value you'd hypothesized for the population. The only rational behavior was to persist in your belief that the average IQ of the population was indeed equal to 100 (i.e., continue to believe that the null hypothesis was true). In the second case, the average IQ of the sample fourth-graders was substantially different from the value you'd hypothesized for the population. The only rational behavior was thus to reject your belief that the population had an average IQ of 100 (i.e., reject the null hypothesis). Both of these cases are so extreme that the appropriate decision was obvious. But what decision would you reach if the average IQ of the 400 sampled students was neither very close to, nor very far from, the hypothesized value of 100? For example, what if the sample average IQ turned out to be 103? Should you reject the null hypothesis or retain it? If you're like most people, your gut feelings aren't very strong either way. In fact, what appears to be a borderline decision might induce a bit of indigestion if you rely solely on your tummy to tell you what to do! What's needed is some reliable, scientific way of determining when you ought to retain the null hypothesis and when you ought to reject it. In short, you need a firm decision rule. What we're talking about is the kind of rule that says something like, "If the average IQ of the 400 sampled students is between 98.5 and 101.5, continue to believe that the null hypothesis is true; if the sample average IQ is either smaller than 98.5 or larger than 101.5, reject the null hypothesis." (At this point you're probably wondering where in the world those numbers came from. Hang in there, and we'll let you in on the secret.) Once you have a decision rule, you won't have to rely on your gut feelings, your antacid bills will go down, and you'll be able to justify your decision on scientific grounds.

Sampling Distributions

Now comes the story on how we came up with the decision rule we so glibly spouted in the last paragraph. As Johnny Carson often says, there's good news and bad news. The bad news is that it's a long story. The good news is that you've heard most of it before—back in the chapter on the logic of estimation.

Remember the hypothetical example in which we sampled over and over again from the same population of fourth-graders, each time computing the average IQ of the sampled students? Let's suppose that we were to do the same thing here. In the earlier example we selected samples of 100 students; in this example, to avoid boring you with total duplication, we'll select samples of 400 students. As before, we'll select a sample of students using simple random sampling; administer an IQ test to the sampled students; record their average test scores; and return the students' names to the population prior to selecting the next sample. Actually, we're going to draw a large number of independent samples (1000 samples is as good an illustration as any), and record the average IQ for each sample. When we finish, we'll have a list of 1000 sample averages.

Back in the chapter on estimation, you learned that the frequency distribution of the 1000 sample averages would look like a bell-shaped curve called the normal distribution. That's still true in this chapter. Also, it is still true that the average of the 1000 sample averages would be precisely equal to the average IQ of the 5000 fourth-graders in the population (the unknown population parameter). Let's assume, as before, that the standard deviation of the IQ scores of the 5000 fourth-graders is equal to 15 points. Then the standard deviation of the frequency distribution of sample averages (the standard error of the mean) would be equal to three fourths of a point (0.75). That number didn't pop out of the air by magic: it was found by dividing the standard deviation of the frequency distribution of IQ scores for individual fourth-graders (15 points) by the square root (20) of the sample size (400). The square root of 400 is 20, and 15/20 is three fourths or 0.75.

If, for the moment, we assume that the null hypothesis is true— namely that the population of 5000 fourth-graders has an average IQ of 100—we can draw a picture of what the frequency distribution of sample averages would look like. Take a look at Figure 9.1, and try to recall what you learned about normal distributions in the chapter on estimation. First, we said that 68% of the 1000 samples will have averages that fall within one standard deviation of the average of the population. If the null hypothesis is true, then we can conclude that 68% of the samples will have averages that are between 99.25 and 100.75. We found these values by adding 0.75 to 100, and by subtracting 0.75 from 100. It is also true that 95% of the samples will have averages that are between 98.5 and 101.5, because 95% of a normal distribution falls within two standard deviations of the population average. If the standard deviation of the distribution of sample averages is 0.75 points, the population average plus two standard deviations equals 100 + 1.5 = 101.5. Also, the population average minus two standard deviations equals 100 − 1.5 = 98.5.

The Risk of Making a Type I Error

We said earlier that you could set the risk of making a Type I error (the risk of rejecting the null hypothesis when it is true). In this example, you're really deciding the chance you want to take of concluding that the 5000 fourth-graders have an average IQ that is different from 100 when, in fact, their true average IQ equals 100. Or to put it another way, how big a risk do you want to take of concluding that the fourth-grade teachers were right, when in reality they were wrong? The answer to this question is called the *level of significance* of your hypothesis test.

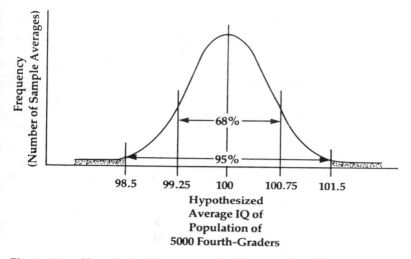

Figure 9.1   Hypothetical Frequency Distribution of 1000 Sample Averages, Assuming that the Null Hypothesis (Population Average = 100) is True (Each Sample Consists of 400 Fourth-Grade Students, Selected from a Population of 5000 Fourth-Grade Students)

A decision on an appropriate level of significance should take into account the seriousness of making a Type I error. The more serious the consequences of rejecting the null hypothesis when it is true, the smaller the risk you want to take of making a Type I error. In many research and evaluation studies, a level of significance equal to 5% (0.05) is used. This is based partly on tradition, and partly on thoughtful consideration. It says that the researcher or evaluator is willing to reject a true null hypothesis only 5% of the time. Or to put it another way, the researcher or evaluator is satisfied knowing that he or she will appropriately retain a true null hypothesis 95% of the time.

If we can adopt a 5% level of significance in this example, we can proceed to develop a decision rule.

Computing a Decision Rule

If we adopt a level of significance equal to 5% (0.05), our decision rule should be the one stated in the illustration above;

namely, reject the null hypothesis that the population average IQ equals 100, on the basis of data from a single sample of 400 students, only if the sample average IQ is either greater than 101.5 or less than 98.5.

Now where did those numbers come from? You can see the answer by looking at Figure 9.1 and considering the following logic. First, in setting our level of significance at 5%, we have stated that we are willing to run a 5% risk of rejecting the null hypothesis that the population average IQ equals 100, when the null hypothesis is true. From Figure 9.1, we see that, when the null hypothesis is true (i.e., when the population average IQ equals 100), 95% of the samples of 400 fourth-graders will have averages that fall between 98.5 and 101.5. This means that only 5% of the samples of 400 students will have averages that are either greater than 101.5 or less than 98.5 (in the shaded portions of the figure). If our decision rule is to reject the null hypothesis only if the average of the single sample that we draw is greater than 101.5 or less than 98.5, we can conclude that we will reject the null hypothesis, when it is true, only 5% of the time. This is exactly the outcome we sought. The decision rule we have stated conforms precisely to the level of significance we desired. You will find that decision rules in hypothesis testing are always a consequence of the desired level of significance (risk of making a Type I error), so the consistency we found in this example is no accident.

Another Example—And a Review

In the chapter on estimation we used an example that's characteristic of many decision situations in school systems and other organizations: you have to choose between two programs, projects, or products, either of which might be best. In our example in the last chapter, you were trying to decide which of two third-grade reading curricula should be adopted by a school system. We suggested that a confidence interval on the *difference* between the average California Achievement Test scores in reading be computed for the sample of third-graders taught using Curriculum A and those taught using Curriculum B. We examined the confidence interval to determine whether those taught using Curriculum A would do better or worse on the California Achievement

Test (CAT) than those taught using Curriculum B, and how large the average achievement difference was likely to be. We found that the confidence interval had a lower limit of two points, and an upper limit of eight points, in favor of Curriculum A. We concluded that Curriculum A was better than Curriculum B in terms of average score on the CAT, by an amount that might be trivial (two points) or substantial (eight points).

Hypothesis testing provides an alternative statistical approach to decision making when you have to choose between two programs, projects, products, or curricula, and it's impractical to try both possibilities with the entire population of students you're interested in.

To use hypothesis testing with the problem of choosing between Curricula A and B, you'd begin by defining a null hypothesis. Since you don't know which of the two curricula would provide a higher average score on the California Achievement Test for the school system's third-graders, your null hypothesis should be that the two curricula are equally effective. That is, you'd hypothesize that the population of third-graders' average CAT score would be exactly the same, regardless of whether they were taught using Curriculum A or Curriculum B. To express this hypothesis statistically, you would hypothesize that the difference between the third-graders' average CAT score using Curriculum A and their average CAT score using Curriculum B was equal to zero.

The alternative hypothesis in this example is the precise opposite of the null hypothesis. If two things aren't equal, they must be unequal. So your alternative hypothesis is that the average CAT reading core for third-graders will differ, depending on whether Curriculum A or Curriculum B was used. Now it's important to recognize exactly what we mean by this alternative hypothesis. What we're saying is the following: Suppose we were to have each third-grader in the school system study reading using Curriculum A, and then complete the CAT reading test. If we then calculated the average CAT reading score of all third-graders in your system, what we'd have would be a population parameter (the population average CAT reading score for all third-graders, taught using Curriculum A). Next, let's suppose we erased the memories of all of the school system's third-graders, so they had no recollection of being taught reading using Curriculum A, and instead we taught the entire population using Curriculum B. If at that point we were to administer the CAT reading test and then compute the students' average score, we'd have another population parameter (the population average CAT reading score for third-graders, taught using Curriculum B). The alternative hypothesis says only that these two population parameters would be different from each other, whereas the null hypothesis says that they would be equal. In practice, were we to decide to reject the null hypothesis in favor of the alternative hypothesis, we would be deciding that one of the two curricula was more effective than the other, at least as far as scores on the CAT reading test were concerned.

When we considered forming a confidence interval on the difference between third-graders' average CAT reading scores in the last chapter, we conducted an experiment to collect the data we needed. Recall that we first selected a random sample of 100 third-graders from the entire systemwide population, and then we randomly divided the sample between Curriculum A and Curriculum B. That is, we assigned 50 third-graders to A and 50 to B, for an entire school year. At the end of the year, we administered the CAT reading test to both groups, and computed the average score of those instructed using each curriculum. We used those sample averages (and some other numbers we didn't describe explicitly) to construct a confidence interval. Instead of computing a confidence interval on the difference between population averages, we could have used the same experimental data to test the null hypothesis that the two curricula were equally effective against the alternative hypothesis that they differed in effectiveness. In fact, it's generally true that the data collection procedure is exactly the same, whether we're constructing confidence intervals or testing hypotheses. It's what we do with the data once we've collected them that differs.

So far we've identified a population and the parameters that are of interest to us, and we've defined a null hypothesis and an alternative hypothesis. We've all taken the next step in hypothesis testing, which is to specify a plan for collection of data. If you look back to the section in this chapter headed "The General Procedure," you'll see that the last two steps in hypothesis testing are to compute a sample statistic that is an estimate of the population parameter of interest, and to reach a decision on whether or not the null hypothesis is true. Of course you know that we've left out a few important specifics in defining these "five easy steps to an ideal hypothesis test." We must specify the risk we're willing to take of making a Type I error (α), and then we've got to develop a decision rule. Deciding on an appropriate value for α is pretty easy, but coming up with a decision rule will take a good deal more thought and discussion.

In testing a hypothesis that concerns the difference between two population averages, the logical statistic to use would seem to be the difference between corresponding sample averages. So why don't we just compute the average CAT reading score of the 50 third-graders who were taught using Curriculum A, and the average CAT reading score of the 50 third-graders who were taught using Curriculum B, and then compute the difference between the sample averages? If the sample averages are very similar, the difference between them will be close to zero and it would seem reasonable to continue believing that the null hypothesis is true (that Curricula A and B are equally effective in terms of average CAT reading scores). On the other hand, if the 50 third-graders taught using Curriculum A had an average CAT reading score that was much higher or much lower than the average CAT reading score of the 50 students taught using Curriculum B, we would be justified in rejecting the null hypothesis in favor of an alternative hypothesis (that the two curricula are not equally effective). As in the example we discussed earlier, we have the sticky problem of finding an explicit decision rule. How different must the two sample averages be, to cause us to reject the null hypothesis in favor of the alternative hypothesis? We know the answer depends on where we set our Type I error level (α). But it also depends on how much the difference between sample means would fluctuate, were we to conduct our experiment over and over.

The logic used in developing a decision rule for this example is virtually identical to that used in the last example. To avoid complicating the description, we're going to make some assumptions that are a bit unrealistic, but not really troublesome. In particular, we will assume that we know the standard deviation of scores on the CAT reading test for the entire population of third-graders in your school system, and that this standard deviation would be exactly the same, whether the students were taught using Curriculum A or Curriculum B. If you want to dazzle your friends or your boss or your lover with a truly impressive word, tell them that you're going to assume you have *homoscedasticity*. Now wait, you don't have to run to the doctor for an immediate shot in the behind. Homoscedasticity just means equal spread or equal variability. So our assumption of equal standard deviations on the CAT, regardless of the curriculum we use, is a homoscedasticity assumption.

In this experiment, it will seem reasonable to take a very small risk of deciding that one of the curricula was better than the other if, in fact, they were equally effective. That's suggesting that we want a very small risk of making a Type I error. So let's set alpha equal to 0.01. In doing so, we're saying that we'll only have a 1% chance of rejecting the null hypothesis if the curricula are, in fact, equally effective.

As in the last example, we have to engage in a purely hypothetical discussion at this point in order to develop a decision rule. You're also going to have to accept a few things on faith. Here goes: Let's suppose we were to repeat our experiment of sampling 100 third-graders from the population of 5000 over and over, each time dividing the sample randomly into two groups of 50. With each repetition we'd teach one group using Curriculum A and the other using Curriculum B, and then administer the CAT reading test at the end of the school year. We'd compute the average CAT score for each group, and the difference between the averages. If we did this over and over, say 1000 times, we'd have a list of 1000 differences between an average score using Curriculum A and an average score using Curriculum B. This list of 1000 differences between sample averages would have a frequency distribution, just like any list of 1000 numbers. Fortunately, statistical theory tells us what the frequency distribution would look like, and we can use this information to develop a decision rule for accepting or rejecting the null hypothesis.

The frequency distribution of differences between sample averages would look like a normal distribution (our old friend, the bell-shaped curve). If the null hypothesis were true, the average of this frequency distribution would equal zero. This just says that if the population average of third-grader's CAT reading scores was the same, regardless of whether Curriculum A or Curriculum B was used (in which case the difference between these population averages would be zero), the difference between sample averages would fluctuate around an average value that also was equal to zero.

So far we know that the frequency distribution of the difference between sample averages would look like a normal distribution, and that its average would be zero, provided the null hypothesis was true. To construct a decision rule we need to know two additional facts: (1) the standard deviation of the frequency distribution, and (2) how many standard deviations from the average we'd have to go in order to include 99% of the distribution. (If we include 99% of the distribution, we'll only exclude 1%—an amount that is equal to our desired risk of making a Type I error.) To answer the first question, we're going to use some invention and some statistical theory. Our final result will be a standard deviation that is equal to 1.6 points. The invention part comes from assuming that, if we were to give all third-graders in the school system the CAT reading test, the standard deviation of their individual test scores would equal 8 points. The statistical theory part comes from a formula that tells us how to calculate the standard deviation of the difference between sample averages, if we know the standard deviation of test scores for individual students. The formula isn't really important here, so we're not going to impress you with it. If you really want to see it, you'll find it on page 232 of Glass and Hopkins (1984), and in lots of other introductory statistics books. The answer to the second question is 2.58: 99% of our 1000 repeated experiments would result in a difference between sample averages using Curricula A and B that would fall within 2.58 standard deviations of the average of the frequency distribution. This fact comes from what's known about all normal distributions.

Here we are again, in the thicket of another shaggy dog story. Let's review the facts we know so far: The standard deviation of the frequency distribution of sample mean differences equals 1.6 points. If we assume that the null hypothesis is true, the average of the frequency distribution will equal zero. And if we go 2.58 standard deviations on both sides of the average, we will include 99% of the frequency distribution. Now, 2.58 standard deviations is just 2.58 times 1.6 points, or 4.13 points. Hang on! A decision rule is about to leap right out at us! To see it, look at Figure 9.2, which illustrates the facts we've just summarized.

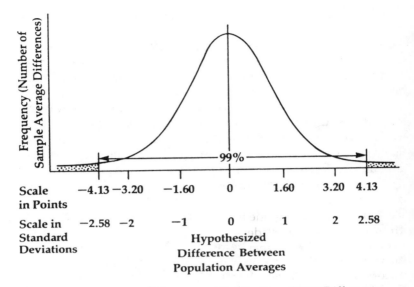

Figure 9.2 Hypothetical Frequency Distribution of 1000 Differences Between Sample Averages, Assuming that the Null Hypothesis (Difference Between Population Averages = 100) is True (Each Sample Consists of 100 Third-Grade Students, Randomly Split Between Two Curricula; Assumed Standard Deviation of Individual Scores is Eight Points)

Remember that we wanted only a 1% risk of rejecting the null hypothesis if Curricula A and B were, in fact, equally effective. So we wanted a decision rule that would cause us to retain the null hypothesis 99% of the time, if it was true. From Figure 9.2 we can see that our decision rule should be as follows: If the difference between sample averages is bigger than 4.13 points, either plus or minus, reject the null hypothesis. If the difference between sample averages is between −4.13 points and +4.13 points, continue believing that the null hypothesis is true. If we followed this decision rule, and if the null hypothesis were true, only 1% of the repeated experiments would result in a difference between sample averages that fell in the shaded portions of Figure 9.2, thus causing us to falsely reject the null hypothesis. Ninety-nine percent of the experiments would give us a difference between sample averages that was between −4.13 points and +4.13 points, causing us to

THE LOGIC OF HYPOTHESIS TESTING / 181

retain a true null hypothesis, just as we should. So once again, our decision rule is totally consistent with our desired risk of making a Type I error. The values –4.13 and +4.13 are known in statistical parlance as **critical values**, and the shaded regions of Figure 9.2 are called **critical regions**. In general, if the sample statistic falls in a critical region, we *reject* the null hypothesis.

It is important to clearly separate the hypothetical data-collection scenario we've described in this example from actual practice in a real hypothesis-testing situation. Once again we've used the illustration of selecting 1000 independent samples of 100 third-graders as a way of describing the frequency distribution of the difference between sample averages. In an actual hypothesis-testing situation, we'd select only one sample of 100 students, divide that sample in half, instruct one group of 50 students using Curriculum A, instruct the other group of 50 using Curriculum B, and collect achievement data from both groups. We would base our decision on whether to retain or reject the null hypothesis solely on the data collected from the *one* sample of 100 students, not on the data from 1000 samples. If the average CAT reading scores of the 50 students taught using Curriculum A differed by more than 4.13 points (in either direction) from the average CAT score of the 50 students taught using Curriculum B, we would reject the null hypothesis. If the two sample averages differed by less than 4.13 points, we would retain the null hypothesis. The discussion about 1000 samples of 100 students each was just a way of describing the basis of our decision rule.

Suppose that, when you conducted your experiment, you found that the 50 students who were taught using Curriculum A had an average CAT reading score that was 6.2 points higher than the average CAT reading score of the 50 students taught using Curriculum B. What would your decision be? Well, since 6.2 is larger than 4.13, you should reject the null hypothesis that the two curricula are equally effective. We would describe the 6.2-point difference between the sample averages by saying that it is "significant at the .01 level." This is just statistical shorthand for saying that we have tested a null hypothesis using a Type I error level of .01, and, on the basis of sample data, we have rejected the null hypothesis. Notice that the difference in sample averages (6.2 points) would fall in the shaded region of Figure 9.2 that is on the far right end of the curve. We've already said that we'll reject the null hypothesis if the difference between sample averages falls anywhere within either shaded area (critical region).

Suppose that we had been more tolerant of the possibility of making a Type I error and, instead of setting our alpha level at .01, we had set it at .05. This means that we would have been willing to run a 5% risk of making a Type I error. How would that have changed our decision rule? It's easy to determine our new decision rule because most of the computations wouldn't change at all. First, the frequency distribution of the difference between sample averages would be exactly the same. If the null hypothesis were true, the average of the frequency distribution would still equal zero. The standard deviation of the frequency distribution would still be 1.6 points. But instead of having the critical values 2.58 standard deviations from the average of the frequency distribution, they would only be two standard deviations from the average. Remember that 95% of the normal distribution falls between points that are two standard deviations below the average and two standard deviations above the average. By including 95% of the frequency distribution, we exclude only 5%, which is the new value we set for the risk of making a Type I error. In this example, since one standard deviation equals 1.6 points, two standard deviations would equal 3.2 points. So our new decision rule, with an alpha of .05, would be as follows: Reject the null hypothesis only if the difference between sample averages is larger than 3.2 points or smaller than –3.2 points. In other words, if the average CAT reading score of either sample of 50 third-graders differed from the average of the other sample by more than 3.2 points, we would reject the null hypothesis. We would then say that the difference between sample averages was "significant at the .05 level." The critical regions, the areas under the curve in Figure 9.2 that should be shaded, would fall to the right of 3.2 points and to the left of –3.2 points.

It is worthwhile to compare the decision rule and the critical values when we set alpha at .01 with the decision rule and the critical values when we set alpha at .05. With an alpha of .05, we would reject the null hypothesis if the average CAT reading scores for the two samples differed by more than 3.2 points. With an alpha of .01, the two sample averages would have to differ by at least 4.13 points before we would reject the null hypothesis. This shows that the difference between sample averages could be significant at the .05 level (that is, greater than 3.2), but might not be significant at the .01 level (greater than 4.13). For example, if the average CAT reading score of those taught using Curriculum B was 35.0, and the average for those taught using Curriculum A was 31.5, the difference would be 3.5 points. Since 3.5 is greater than 3.2, the difference would be significant at the .05 level, and we would reject the null hypothesis that the two curricula were equally effective at the 5% level of significance. However, 3.5 is less than 4.13, so the difference between sample averages would *not* be significant at the .01 level. In fact, if we were testing our null hypothesis at an alpha level of 1% (.01), we would retain the null hypothesis. In all hypothesis testing, it is always the case that significance at the .05 level does not necessarily mean the statistic is significant at the .01 level. However, a statistic that is significant at the .01 level will *always* be significant at the .05 level. If you take another look at Figure 9.2, you can see why this is true. In order to be significant at the .01 level, a statistic must be farther from the average of the frequency distribution than it need be if it is significant only at the .05 level. The further from the hypothesized value of a population parameter a statistic is, the smaller the alpha level at which it is significant.

Another Review Quiz

Well, it's that time again! Time to make sure that you have all those alphas, betas, hypotheses, risks, and errors straight in your mind, so you can really gobble research reports with confidence—authoritatively separating the wheat from the chaff (to put it most politely).

Once again, we'll provide a few hypothetical examples of research and evaluation reports that contain inferential statistical results of the form you'll encounter in the real world. There will be questions following each example. After reading each example carefully, write down your answers to the questions that follow. At the end of this thrilling exercise, you can compare your answers to those that follow the last example.

Example A: The Validity of a Teacher Selection Test

In the 1990s world of public education, where accountability and economy are the watchwords, assignment of blame is a favorite sport. For example, in your school system the board has suggested that low basic achievement scores can be attributed directly to inadequate screening of teachers at the time they are hired. Their proposed solution is to institute a teacher competency test, to be administered to prospective teachers as a part of the interview process.

In response to the board, you've begun a search for an existing teacher competency test that might meet your school system's needs. A computerized search of Educational Resources Information Center (ERIC) files yields an article on a test that was validated in a South Carolina school system. When you read the validation report, here's what you find:

The test was administered on an experimental basis to all applicants for teaching positions in a very large South Carolina school system, but applicants' scores were ignored when making hiring decisions because the validity of the test was unknown. At the end of one year on the job, the test scores of newly hired teachers were compared with teaching effectiveness ratings given by their principals. The instrument for rating teaching effectiveness had been in use in the school system for a number of years. The researchers selected a sample of 25 teachers who had scored between 0 and 50 on the competency test, and another independent sample of 25 teachers who had scored between 51 and 100 on the competency test. Statistics on principals' ratings of teaching effectiveness were computed and reported for both samples, and a hypothesis test was conducted to investigate the question of test validity. The data reported in the article were as shown in the table following the Questions for Example A.

Questions for Example A

1. What populations are of interest in this example? To what populations are inferences being made?
2. What is the null hypothesis?
3. What is the alternative hypothesis in this example?
4. What is the risk of making a Type I error in this example?

5. Explain the statement that follows the asterisk at the bottom of the table: "significant at the .01 level."

6. Do the data in the table support the researcher's contention that the competency test is a valid measure of teaching effectiveness? Why or why not?

7. What kinds of inferences would you be making if you recommended use of the competency test in your school system on the basis of the reported validity analysis?

Group:	Scored Between 0 and 50 on Competency Test	Scored Between 51 and 100 on Competency Test
Average Effectiveness Rating by Principal:	64.8	82.6
Standard Deviation of Effectiveness Ratings by Principal:	8.2	7.8
Difference in Average Effectiveness Ratings:	17.8*	

*Significant at the .01 level.

Example B: Teacher Salaries and Student Achievement—Are They Related?

In keeping with the old adage that you get what you pay for, an article in a recent issue of the *School Administrator's Quarterly* reported on a study of the relationship between elementary school teachers' salaries and the achievement of their students. A researcher in one of the largest school systems in California selected a random sample of 100 elementary school teachers from the list of 2571 teachers employed by the system, and looked up the sampled teachers' annual salaries. She then went to the system's achievement test files and recorded the average achievement of students in each teacher's class in four different subject areas: reading, spelling, arithmetic concepts, and arithmetic computation. The achievement scores reflected students' performances on system-developed criterion-referenced tests, and were scaled in terms of percentage of items correct, so that scores could be compared across grade levels.

Wondering whether there was any correlation at all between teacher salary and student achievement, the researcher computed a series of correlation coefficients between teachers' annual salaries and the average achievement of their students, with the following reported results:

Correlation between annual teacher salary and:	
Reading	.08
Spelling	.17*
Arithmetic Concepts	−.02
Arithmetic Computation	.20**

*significant, alpha = .10
**significant, alpha = .05

Questions for Example B

1. Four separate null hypotheses were tested in this example. Can you identify them?

2. What were the alternative hypotheses associated with these null hypotheses?

3. To what population was the researcher attempting to generalize?

4. What was the population parameter in the hypothesis test concerning the relationship between teacher's salary and students' reading achievement?

5. Discuss the meaning of the statement, "significant, alpha = .05."

6. Does it appear that teacher salary and student achievement are related?

7. Do these results suggest that raising teachers' salaries is a good way to increase students' achievement? Why or why not?

Answers — Example A

1. The populations that are of direct interest in this example consist of all first-year teachers in the South Carolina school system who scored between 0 and 50 on the competency test, and all first-year teachers in the system who scored between 51 and 100 on the competency test. These are the populations from which the researcher selected his samples. Formally, inferences always refer to the populations from which samples are drawn. If you considered these results in deciding whether or not to use the competency test for screening applicants in your school system, however, you would be assuming that it is reasonable to make inferences to the population of first-year teachers you might hire.

2. The null hypothesis in this example is that the average teaching effectiveness rating by principals is exactly the same, for the population of first-year teachers who score between 0 and 50 on the competency test and the population of first-year teachers who score between 51 and 100 on the competency test. Another way of stating the same thing is to say that the difference between average principals' teaching effectiveness ratings is zero, for the population of teachers who have competency test scores between 0 and 50 and the population of teachers who have competency test scores between 51 and 100.

3. The alternative hypothesis in this example is the converse of the null hypothesis: that the average principals' effectiveness rating for the population of teachers who score between 0 and 50 on the competency test differs from their average effectiveness rating for the population of teachers who score between 51 and 100.

4. The risk of making a Type I error in this experiment is 1% or .01. We know this because the footnote to the data table reads "Significant at the .01 level." Although statistics books also advise that the researcher establish a Type I error level (α) prior to conducting an experiment, that isn't always done in practice. As often as not, the researcher will conduct an experiment, compute a sample statistic, and compare it with critical values that correspond to various alpha levels. The smallest alpha level at which significance was reached will then be reported.

5. The statement that follows the asterisk at the bottom of the table implies that the null hypothesis of no difference between population averages was tested using a Type I error level of .01 (or

1%), and that the null hypothesis was rejected in favor of the alternative hypothesis.

6. The data presented in the table support the researcher's contention that the competency test measures teaching effectiveness, but they certainly don't provide absolute proof. It is clear that sampled teachers who earned competency test scores in the upper half of the range (between 51 and 100) received teaching effectiveness ratings that averaged 17.8 points higher than those received by sampled teachers who scored in the lower half of the competency test range (between 0 and 50). The finding of significance at the .01 level assures us that a difference in sample average ratings as large as 17.8 points would have occurred less than one time out of 100 (.01 = 1/100), if the averages for the populations had been equal. Thus we can be reasonably certain that principals give higher ratings to teachers who score in the upper half than they do to teachers who score in the lower half of the range on the competency test. However, we have to ask whether the principals' ratings are valid. That is, are teachers who receive higher ratings from principals really more effective teachers? In what ways are these teachers more effective? If you give it a little thought, you will see that the question of test validity is very complicated, and that it's not answered by the results of a single experiment.

7. If you recommended the use of the competency test in your school system on the basis of the validity analysis reported in the example, you would be making several inferences. First, you would be assuming that the relationship found for first-year teachers in the South Carolina school system would also be found in your school system. Second, you would be assuming that the principals in the South Carolina school system were able to identify which teachers were truly more effective. You would be accepting the validity of the principals' ratings, and the validity of the competency test.

Answers — Example B

1. Each of the four null hypotheses tested in this example concerns the correlation between teachers' annual salaries and the average achievement of their students. The first null hypothesis tested is that, for the population of elementary school teachers in

the California school system, the correlation between teachers' annual salary and students' average reading achievement equals zero. That is the same as hypothesizing that teachers' salaries and students' reading achievement are not linearly related. The other null hypotheses also state that correlation coefficients equal zero. Respectively, they assert that teachers' salaries are not correlated with students' spelling achievement, arithmetic concepts achievement, and arithmetic computation achievement. Again, correlations of zero are hypothesized not for the sample of 100 teachers, but for the entire population of elementary school teachers in the large California school system where the research was conducted.

2. The alternative hypotheses are all of the same form. They state that, for the population of elementary school teachers in the large California school system where the research was conducted, the correlations between teachers' salaries and students' achievement (in reading, spelling, arithmetic concepts, and arithmetic computation respectively) are not equal to zero.

3. The researcher is attempting to generalize to the population of elementary school teachers in the school system from which the sample was selected. In discussing her results, however, it would not be unusual (although not absolutely correct) for the researcher to sound as though she is attempting to generalize to all elementary school teachers in the nation. The reader has to be cautious in accepting a researcher's or evaluator's conclusions. Overgeneralization in research and evaluation reports is, unfortunately, common. As an informed reader, you must pay attention to the population that was actually sampled, and be cautious in generalizing beyond that population to the particular population that might be of interest to you. This is an external validity issue, as discussed in Chapter 6.

4. The population parameter in the hypothesis test concerning the relationship between teachers' salaries and students' reading achievement was the population correlation coefficient between these two variables; it was the correlation for the population of all elementary school teachers in the California school system and the students they taught.

5. The statement "significant, alpha = .05," the footnote with two asterisks at the bottom of the data table, refers to the correlation between teachers' salaries and students' arithmetic computation scores. It means that the null hypothesis that teachers' salaries

and students' arithmetic computation scores have a correlation coefficient of zero would be rejected, if tested at a Type I error level of 5%. The hypothesis test refers to the correlation between these variables for the population of all elementary school teachers and their students in the large California school system.

6. It appears that teachers' salaries are related to students' achievement test scores in some subjects, but not in others. Because there are no asterisks beside the correlations for reading scores and arithmetic concept scores, we can infer that those correlations were not significant at the .10 level. In other words, when the researcher tested the null hypothesis that, for the entire population of elementary school teachers and their students in the school system, these types of achievement were not correlated with teachers' salaries, the null hypotheses were retained. In contrast, the null hypotheses that teachers' salaries were uncorrelated with spelling achievement and arithmetic computation achievement were rejected. This suggests that it is unlikely that the population values of the correlations between teachers' salaries and students' achievement in spelling and arithmetic computation are equal to zero. It does not tell us how large the correlations are likely to be for the entire population, however. The correlations could be so small that they are trivial, even though they are different from zero.

7. These results certainly don't suggest that raising teachers' salaries is a good way to increase students' achievement. In the first place, just because two variables are correlated, we cannot state that one variable causes the other. That is, we don't know whether high-achieving students are assigned to older (therefore better paid) teachers, or whether highly paid teachers are more effective, and therefore produce students with higher achievement. It could also be the case that teachers' salaries and students' achievement are correlated with each other only because they are both correlated with some third variable. For example, it could be that students from wealthier homes have higher achievement scores, and are assigned to schools with higher-paid teachers. If this were the case, economic status would be responsible for the correlation, so that paying teachers more probably wouldn't affect student achievement at all.

Okay, those are our answers. Compare yours with ours and see how you made out. We gave you 14 questions in all. If you answered at least 10 of the 14 correctly on your first try, we would think you were doing very well, and that you had a pretty firm grasp of the logic of hypothesis testing. In case you haven't noticed, the material in this chapter isn't your ordinary bedtime reading. It's heavy and complicated, so you can be very pleased with yourself. If you didn't quite make our somewhat arbitrary cut score, don't despair. Give it another shot. First, check your understanding of the vocabulary at the beginning of the chapter. Finally, take the quiz again. When you finish, be sure to compare each question with your answer and our answer. Note the similarities and differences. If you haven't realized already, there's a good bit of new information in our answers (sneaky devils, aren't we?).

This chapter ends our introduction to the theory of statistical inference. You should have enough vocabulary and sufficient understanding of basic concepts by this point to get into interpretation of real research and evaluation reports. In the chapters that follow, we will try to help you interpret and fully understand the results sections of a number of real evaluation and research reports. These examples differ in the types of statistical inferences they report and the types of parameters involved in the inferences. They constitute a carefully selected sampling from the files of the Educational Resources Information Centers (ERIC). Once you learn to interpret the results presented in the remaining chapters of the book, you'll be able to read and understand a very large percentage of the quantitative research and evaluation literature. You'll be among a small minority of decision makers who can truthfully make that claim.

Problems — Chapter 9

9.1 In a report on performance on the Verbal Subtest of the Scholastic Aptitude Test (SAT), Psycho and Metric (1986) stated: "Those of high socioeconomic level had a mean score of 590, while those of low socioeconomic level had a mean score of only 480. The difference of 110 points was significant at the .05 level."

Based on this report, which of the following statements are true? (Circle the letter of *each* true statement.)

a. One can be 95% certain that socioeconomic level is one of a number of causes of SAT performance.
b. In comparing populations of students of low and high socio-economic level, one can be 95% confident that the difference between their average SAT scores would be at least 110 points.
c. Assuming the students tested were randomly sampled from their respective populations, it is very unlikely that the average SAT score of the population of low socioeconomic-level students is the same as the average SAT score of the population of high socioeconomic-level students.
d. In this study, the authors apparently tested the null hypothesis that populations of low socioeconomic-level and high socioeconomic-level examinees had equal average SAT scores, using a Type I error probability of 0.05.

9.2 Aged and Wise (1990) reported on a study of the relationship between age of school building and the dropout rate in a sample of 76 elementary schools. They found a correlation of 0.21, which was "significant at the 0.10 level."
a. To what population might the authors be generalizing?
b. What null hypothesis are the authors testing?
c. What alternative hypothesis is implied by the authors' statement?
d. Can you be certain that a correlation of 0.21 would be significant at the 0.05 level?

9.3 The Gallup Poll recently reported that 37% of the moviegoing public was between the ages of 14 and 18, whereas only 24% was between the ages of 19 and 25. As is typical of Gallup's work, this report was based on a survey of people in both age groups. In a test of the null hypothesis that equal proportions of the populations of both age groups attended movies, it was found that the test statistic fell into the critical region (alpha equaled 0.01).
a. What was the alternative hypothesis in this study?
b. Should the null hypothesis be rejected or retained?
c. Was the test statistic significant at the 0.05 level?

9.4   Think of an evaluation study involving two competing curricula, where the objective is to maximize student motivation. Suppose that you can conduct the study using random samples of students selected from a particular school system, and that a good method of measuring student motivation is available to you.

   a. State an appropriate null hypothesis.
   b. State an appropriate alternative hypothesis.
   c. Describe a Type I error in the context of this study.
   d. Describe a Type II error in the context of this study.

10.

Inferences Involving Averages

The Path Ahead

This chapter is a prototype for all that follow. In this chapter we'll examine research and evaluation studies in which the focus of inference is two population averages. In subsequent chapters, we'll examine studies in which inferences focus on standard deviations, correlation coefficients, or more than two averages. When more than two averages are involved, the appropriate statistical procedure is called the *analysis of variance*. Analysis of variance (ANOVA) is of sufficient importance to rate a chapter all its own. In fact, we think it's so important that we're going to give it two. We'll then complete this marvelous tome with an investigation of studies involving a few of the fancier statistical procedures you're likely to run into in your wanderings through evaluation and research reports: regression analysis, analysis of covariance, and factor analysis.

Our goal in these chapters is not to expose you to more statistical theory (the chapters you've already plowed through on your way to this one gave you enough of that). Rather, we hope you'll gain facility in reading and interpreting the statistical portions of evaluation and research reports by studying a series of structured examples.

The bulk of each chapter contains excerpts from real evaluation and research reports. We begin each chapter by discussing the types of inferences it treats, and then we move immediately to presentation of a number of studies that involve those types of inferences. Each study begins with a synopsis of its purposes and an overview of its design. We then present data tables and other statistical results from the authors' original work, together with the authors' interpretation of those data. At this point, we'll help you to see the precise inferential process the authors used—what the population is, what the parameters are, the hypotheses or confidence intervals involved, and the level of significance or level of confidence the authors used. Finally, we'll interpret the data, help you to see the ways in which the study is weak or strong, and discuss the assumptions you'd be making were you to apply the study's results to your own local setting. We know that sounds like a heavy load. But it's like olives and oysters: Try one and you'll see they're not so bad. Try two and you might even like them.

This chapter contains examples of inferences involving two population averages. In the discussions that follow, you will see that two basic research questions are usually addressed in these studies. The researcher is either concerned with the difference between the averages of two populations, or with the difference between the averages of a single population on two different occasions (such as before treatment and after treatment). The inferential questions that apply will be made clear in the discussion of each study.

A Final Evaluation of a Career Education Program

Purpose of the Study. Kershner and Blair (1975) conducted an evaluation of the third-year operation of a career education program developed by Research for Better Schools, Inc. The program was intended to provide secondary school students with cognitive skills, career experiences, and personal perspectives "which aid in the selection and pursuit of adult life goals." Various community resource sites and a large urban high school were used to provide students with instruction in career exploration and specialization, career guidance, and basic skills. The bulk of the third-year program participants were eleventh-graders, but the program also served some students in the ninth, tenth, and twelfth grades.

Evaluation Design. The evaluation was extensive, if not complex. It involved five groups of students, three of which were labeled experimental groups (groups that received some program treatments), and two of which were labeled control groups (groups that did not receive program treatments). One of the experimental groups consisted of students who were chosen during the third year of program operation to replace other students who had dropped out. All students who were available for assessment at the beginning of the school year as well as at the end of the school year completed a large number of assessment instruments. These instruments included standardized measures of career maturity, self-acceptance, and achievement, in addition to specially developed measures of career attitudes and school attitudes. Demographic information was collected only once during the year, through an additional instrument called the Student Demographic Data Questionnaire.

We will consider only a small portion of the evaluation in the present example. We will focus our attention on an assessment of the attitudes of students who had either been in the program for two years, or who had been members of a control group for a period of two years. Thirty-six experimental students who were participating in the program for their second year were assessed at the beginning and end of the 1974-75 school year. Twenty-five control group students completed the same instruments during the same time periods. The groups were composed of "returning students," and were not constructed through random assignment. Thus it is possible that the groups differed in their attitudes and on other important variables, prior to the initiation of program treatments.

Students' attitudes were measured through an Assessment of Student Attitudes Scale (ASA) that provides scores for five educational foci: education in general, the school curriculum, school resources, school counseling, and learning environments in general. The attitudes of second-year experimental and control group students toward all five foci were assessed at the beginning and end of the 1974-75 school year. Results are shown in the following data table.

Authors' Data Table. Table 40 in the Kershner and Blair (1975) report (p. 64) provides data on student attitudes. It is reproduced here as Table 10.1.

TABLE 10.1: Assessment of Student Attitudes, Second Year Students

Adminis-tration	Subtest	Group Experimental (E2) n = 36	Control (C2) n = 25	"t"
Pretest	ASA Education in General	33.53	34.88	.70
	ASA School Curriculum	33.47	35.88	1.76
	ASA School Resources	33.67	33.16	.92
	ASA School Counseling	34.28	31.44	1.19
	ASA Overall Attitude Toward Learning Environments	33.67	33.64	.02
Posttest	ASA Education in General	36.81	32.44	3.76
	ASA School Curriculum	36.78	33.08	2.16
	ASA School Resources	35.81	31.88	2.30
	ASA School Counseling	37.81	29.04	4.51
	ASA Overall Attitude Toward Learning Environments	36.47	31.48	4.99

Critical value for two-tailed t-test, df $\geq$ 30, = 1.697
Critical value for one-tailed t-test, df $\geq$ 30, = 1.310

Authors' Interpretation. Kershner and Blair conclude from this table that there were

> no pretest differences between the E2 (experimental) and C2 (comparison) groups. The posttest analyses indicated that the E2 group had a significantly more positive attitude than the C2 group on all subtests of the ASA.
>
> There is overwhelming support for the hypotheses that experimental students gain significantly more positive attitudes toward learning than do the control students. (p. 64)

The Nature of the Inferences. From the authors' interpretation, it is clear that some hypotheses were tested to develop the results presented in Table 10.1. Just what were those hypotheses? What parameters were involved? How can the results be generalized? What is the level of significance? All is about to be revealed to you!

The data in Table 10.1 illustrate the results of testing 10 different null hypotheses against 10 different alternatives. Five of the hypothesis tests involve pretest data, and five are based on posttests.

In each case, the authors are acting as though their experimental and control groups had been randomly sampled from a population of students who might have participated in the career education program. Although they acknowledge the nonrandom selection of students, their statistical procedures largely ignore that fact. So the population to which the authors implicitly generalize their results is the population of students who might have participated in the program. In effect, the authors are asking, "What if the population of potential participants had been divided in half through some random procedure, one half being assigned to the program and one half being excluded? Would the halves differ in their preprogram attitudes, as measured by the ASA? Would the halves differ in their postprogram attitudes?"

The first five null hypotheses that the authors test state that the average pretest attitudes of the population of students who might have been assigned to the program are equal to the average pretest attitudes of the population of students who might have been excluded from the program. In short, the null hypotheses assert that there are no differences between the average pretest attitudes of the halves of the student population that might have been treated and untreated. For example, the first null hypothesis (the one represented by the first line of data in Table 10.1) stated that, at time of pretest, the average ASA attitude toward "Education in General" is equal, for the population of potential program participants and the population of potential nonparticipants. The last five lines of the table represent the results of testing five similar null hypotheses, at the time of posttesting.

In the footnote to their table, the authors provide critical values for two types of alternative hypotheses. The value labeled "Critical value for two-tailed t-test" applies to alternative hypotheses of the following form: "The average attitude of the population of potential program participants differs from the average attitude of the potential population of untreated students." The value labeled "Critical value for one-tailed t-test" applies to alternative hypotheses of the form: "The average attitude of potential program participants is higher (more positive) than the average attitude of the potential population of untreated students." The first kind of alternative hypothesis, where it is asserted that the averages differ without saying which average is larger, is called a **nondirectional alternative hypothesis**. The second kind of alternative, where one of the two averages is asserted to be larger then the other, is called a **directional alternative hypothesis**.

In this example, the authors don't state the level of significance they are using in their hypothesis tests. However, by knowing the type of hypothesis testing procedure they used, and by referring to an appropriate set of statistical tables, we were able to determine that the critical values they gave corresponded to an alpha level of 0.10. Thus they were willing to take a 10% risk of making a Type I error in testing each of their null hypotheses. We determined that alpha level by looking in a table of Student's t-distribution. We knew which kind of table to look in because of the t-statistics given in the last column of Table 10.1, and because of the nature of the null hypotheses tested.

In this analysis, the authors have used a statistical procedure known as Student's t-test for independent samples. It is an appropriate statistical procedure for testing null hypotheses that involve the equality of two population averages. Its logic and underlying principles are identical to those we discussed in the last chapter, although it differs in its computational details from those we've examined earlier. Basically, the procedure compares the averages of two samples that were selected independently of each other, and asks whether those sample averages differ enough to believe that the populations from which they were selected also have different averages. The more the sample averages differ, the larger the t-statistic will be. If the t-statistic is larger than the critical value that corresponds to the desired alpha level, the null hypothesis of equal population averages is rejected. Look at the data in Table 10.1 to see what we mean. In testing the null hypothesis that average ASA attitudes toward "Education in General" were equal at time of pretest, for the populations of potential program participants and potential control students (i.e., nonparticipants), the authors compared the average score of 33.53 for the experimental group with the average score of 34.88 for the control group. The t-statistic of .70 for this comparison was smaller than the directional critical value of 1.310 and was also smaller than the nondirectional critical value of 1.697. Thus the null hypothesis of equal population averages would not be rejected in favor of either alternative hypothesis (directional or nondirectional). In contrast, look at the comparison of average ASA attitudes toward "Education in General" at time of posttest. The average attitude of the experimental group has increased to 36.81, while the average attitude of the control group has decreased to 32.44. The difference in average attitudes of the two samples is 4.37 points, which yields a t-statistic of 3.76. This t-statistic is larger than both the directional critical value and the nondirectional critical value corresponding to an alpha level of 0.10. Thus we would reject the null hypothesis that the populations of potential program participants and nonparticipants have equal average attitudes toward Education in General, at the time of posttest. Since we have compared the t-value of 3.76 to critical values for both nondirectional and directional tests, we could either conclude that the average attitudes of these populations differ, or that the average attitude of the population of potential participants exceeds that of the population of potential nonparticipants.

We have not discussed the computation of the mysterious t-statistic in this example, nor do we intend to do so. For our purposes, and we hope for yours, detailed computations are irrelevant. However, if you need those details, they can be found in a host of the applied statistics texts, such as Glass and Hopkins (1984), Hays (1981), Hinkle, Wiersma, and Jurs (1988), or Shavelson (1988).

You will encounter many t-tests in your travels through evaluation and research reports. The comparison of two population averages is undoubtedly the most ubiquitous of inferential statistical procedures. In each case, you can probably recognize the test by the inclusion of a t-statistic somewhere in the author's data table. If the reported t-value exceeds the critical value that you will probably find at the foot of the data table, or if the t-value has at least one "*" associated with it, together with an appropriate, explanatory footnote, you can conclude that the null hypothesis of equal population averages should be rejected in favor of a directional or nondirectional alternative hypothesis.

Our Interpretation of Results. The real focus of the analyses reported in Table 10.1 is whether or not the experimental group had more positive average attitudes than did the control group, at the time of posttesting. For each of the five attitudes tested, the difference between sample averages was statistically significant at the 0.10 level, and the difference in sample averages favored the experimental group. Whether or not the differences in sample averages were large enough to be substantively important is a question that the authors did not treat. The differences in sample averages range from 3.70 points (for the ASA attitude toward "School Curriculum") to 8.77 points (for the ASA attitude toward "School Counseling"). These differences are large enough that we can reject a hypothesis that corresponding differences in population averages are equal to zero. But they give us no assurance that the differences in population averages would be large enough to be substantively significant. That is a judgmental question that cannot be answered through inferential statistics.

The five null hypotheses that involve pretest attitude measures were conducted solely to determine whether or not the experimental group and the control group were reasonably similar at the beginning of the school year. Since the experimental group and the control group were not selected randomly, it would be unreasonable to assume that they were chosen from populations that had identical average attitudes prior to the experimental treatment. The hypothesis tests at the beginning of the school year allowed the authors to conclude that null hypotheses of equal ASA attitudes would not be rejected at time of pretest, except for attitudes toward "School Curriculum." (For that one attitude, the control group had a significantly higher average score then did the experimental group, at the beginning of the school year). These hypothesis tests strengthen the authors' assertion that posttest differences in average attitudes can be attributed to the career education program.

Assumptions Needed to Generalize. Were you to use these experimental results as a basis for adopting the career education program in your school system, you would be making a number of assumptions. Clearly, you would feel that the attitude scales used by the authors measured important outcomes of career education. You would also have to assume that the average differences in attitudes exhibited by the experimental and control groups at the time of posttesting were of substantive importance. Finally, you would have to assume that similar average differences in attitudes would be realized by high school students in your school system. That last assumption is, undoubtedly, the most tenuous, since it presumes that the program could be installed just as effectively in your school system as it was in Philadelphia, and that your school staff would be just as effective in running the program. However,

the same kinds of questions arise whenever a previously successful curriculum is adopted in a new setting.

Relationships Between Teacher Attitudes and Teacher Behavior

Purpose of the Study. This study considers the questions of how
teachers' attitudes toward mathematics, toward teaching as a profession, and toward students relate to their behaviors in the classroom, as judged by students and outside observers. The author
(McConnell, 1978) viewed this question as one of several links in a
chain that relates teachers' attitudes to students' attitudes toward
mathematics and education in general. He reasoned that the only
way teachers' attitudes might be communicated to students, and
thereby influence the attitudes of the students, would be through
teachers' overt behaviors as they conducted their classes. By investigating the ways in which teachers' attitudes relate to their
classroom behaviors, McConnell hoped to establish the first link
in the overall chain of relationships.

Research Design. McConnell made use of a variety of measures
of teachers' attitudes and behaviors in collecting data on a sample
of 47 ninth-grade algebra teachers. One set of measures, the
Teacher Opinion Inventory Scales (TOI) was used in the National
Longitudinal Study of Mathematical Abilities (a nationwide study
of mathematics instruction in elementary and secondary schools)
in the late 1960s. That earlier study was designed to secure data on
the attitudes of a nationally representative sample of teachers, a
fact that is particularly relevant to the portion of McConnell's
study we will discuss here.

In collecting his data, McConnell was not able to randomly
sample his 47 ninth-grade mathematics teachers from some well-
defined population. That's not an unusual situation, and his study
should not be faulted because he was forced to conduct his research within realistic, if unfortunate, bounds. In fact, McConnell
is to be lauded because he specifically examined the representativeness of his sample, a consideration that is all too frequently
missing in published educational research. It is this aspect of his
research that we will discuss here.

McConnell examined the representativeness of his sample of 47 mathematics teachers by comparing the averages and standard deviations of their scores on the Teacher Opinion Inventory with those of the 637 ninth-grade teachers assessed in the National Longitudinal Study of Mathematical Abilities (NLSMA). He reasoned that the NLSMA sample was designed to represent the population of ninth-grade teachers throughout the United States and, if the data for his sample were comparable to the data from the NLSMA sample, it would be safe to generalize his results to a nationwide population of teachers.

Author's Data Table. Table 5 in the McConnell (1978) paper (p. 12) contains means, standard deviations, and reliability coefficients for the seven scales that compose the Teacher Opinion Inventory. Data are presented for the 47 ninth-grade mathematics teachers in McConnell's study (in the columns headed "This Study"), and for the 647 ninth-grade teachers in the National Longitudinal Study of Mathematical Abilities (in the columns headed "NLSMA"). The entire table is presented here as Table 10.2, just as it appeared in the original paper, even though we will examine only a small portion of the data it contains.

Author's Interpretation. Among McConnell's discussion of the results shown in his table is the following:

> The second test in checking the representativeness of this sample of teachers was comparison of the means to the NLSMA means. The NLSMA results were assumed to define the population mean and standard deviation. A z-test . . . was used to test whether the sample of teachers in this study could be assumed [to have been selected] from the NLSMA grade nine population.

> Two scales had means significantly different from the NLSMA ninth grade means: TOI4, "Non-Authoritarian Orientation" and TOI7, "Need for Approval." The teachers in this study scored higher on "Non-Authoritarian Orientation" and lower on "Need for Approval." . . . The majority of tests showed that this sample could have come from the population defined by the NLSMA grade nine data.

The Nature of the Inferences. In his discussion of results, McConnell does a good job of defining the purpose of the statistical tests represented by the data shown in Table 10.2, but he presumes

TABLE 10.2: Means, Standard Deviations, and Reliabilities From the Teacher Opinion Inventory on the Sample of 47 Teachers in This Study and 637 Ninth-Grade Teachers From the NLSMA y - Population Sample

Code	Scale	This Study			NLSMA[a]			z-test
		Mean	SD	r[b]	Mean	SD	r[b]	
TOI1	Theoretical Orientation	39.25	5.93	.66	39.58	7.16	.69	−.30
TOI2	Concern for Students	34.16	5.35	.67	33.25	6.25	.69	.95
TOI3	Involvement in Teaching	31.67	5.29	.55	31.24	6.36	.67	.44
TOI4	Non-Authoritarian	23.37	4.47	.66	20.37	5.15	.63	3.82*
TOI5	Like vs. Dislike	14.23	1.02	.08	13.77	1.80	.57	1.68
TOI6	Creative vs. Rote	42.21	4.96	.47	43.64	6.62	.67	−1.42
TOI7	Need for Approval	37.27	5.02	.63	39.27	5.76	.72	−2.28*

a Wilson, Cahen, Begle (1968)
b Reliabilities (Cronbach Alpha)
* Significant at .05 level: z (.05) = 1.96

that the reader can deduce just what hypotheses were tested, and how the analyses were conducted. A little clarification might be in order.

Each line of the table reports the results of an hypothesis test involving population averages. Thus, seven hypothesis tests are considered in Table 10.2. For each of the seven TOI scales, Mc-Connell tested the null hypothesis that the average scale score of the hypothetical population from which he might have sampled the 47 teachers in his study was equal to the average scale score of the population of NLSMA teachers. If these null hypotheses were retained, he would conclude that his sample of 47 teachers could be treated as though it were drawn from the NLSMA population. Thus the parameter in each hypothesis test was the average scale score of the hypothetical population from which the 47 sampled teachers could have been selected. The sample statistic that serves as an estimate of this parameter was the average scale score of the 47 teachers. From the footnote at the bottom of the table, we can see that the level of significance (alpha) McConnell used in each of his tests was 0.05.

In the first hypothesis test, the null hypothesis was that the average score of the hypothetical population on the TOI1 scale ("Theoretical Orientation") was equal to 39.58, which is the mean on that scale for the 637 teachers in the NLSMA population. The alternative hypothesis was that the average score of the hypothetical population was different from the mean NLSMA score of 39.58.

In testing this null hypothesis, McConnell conducted a z-test, a statistical procedure that is virtually identical to the one described in the first example in Chapter 9. The value –.30 in the column headed "z-test" is an example of a **test statistic**. The null hypothesis would be rejected only if this test statistic fell in the critical region of an appropriate sampling distribution. Just as in the example in Chapter 9, the appropriate sampling distribution is the normal distribution, and the critical regions fall beyond z-values of plus or minus 1.96. Since –.30 is larger than –1.96 and smaller than +1.96 (that is, it lies between the two critical values), it does not fall in either critical region. Thus, the null hypothesis is retained. The appropriate conclusion is that we cannot reject the hypothesis that the 47 teachers in McConnell's study were sampled from a population that has an average TOI1 score that is equal to that of the NLSMA teachers.

Notice that the z-test value for the "non-Authoritarian" scale (TOI4) equals 3.82, and that it has an "*" beside it. Since 3.82 is larger than 1.96, the difference between the average TOI4 score of the teachers in McConnell's sample and the average TOI4 score of the teachers in the NLSMA sample is significant at the 0.05 level. Thus the null hypothesis must be rejected, and McConnell appropriately concluded that his sample of teachers differed from the NLSMA teachers on this attitude scale.

Our Interpretation of Results. We feel little need to elaborate on our interpretation of the results presented in Table 10.2, since we agree fully with the interpretation given by McConnell. On five of the seven TOI scales, the statistical evidence supports retention of the null hypotheses that the sample of 47 teachers was drawn from a population that has average scores that were equal to those of the NLSMA population. On two of the scales, TOI4 and TOI7, the averages of the 47 teachers differ significantly (at the 0.05

level) from those of the NLSMA teachers. In one case (TOI4) the 47 teachers have a significantly higher average (you can tell this by comparing the means given in the table, and because the number in the "z-test" column exceeds 1.96), and, in the other (TOI7), the 47 teachers have a significantly lower average.

By way of apology, we should note that we have not concentrated on the most interesting aspects of McConnell's study in this example. In fact, the example has little to do with the central purpose of his study. However, we'll remedy that oversight in the chapter on inferences involving correlation coefficients, when we consider the relationships among teachers' attitudes on the various TOI scales.

We have also ignored a good bit of the data shown in Table 10.2. The numbers in the columns headed "SD" (for standard deviation) and "r" (for reliability) are useful for several purposes. We have ignored them solely because they aren't essential to this example.

Since the question of generalizing these results to another school system is not appropriate here, we will omit such discussion.

Evaluation of a Beginning Teacher Development Program

Purpose of the Study. This study, reported by Gunter (1985), was designed to evaluate the effectiveness of the Florida Beginning Teacher Evaluation Program by comparing the posttreatment characteristics of samples of teachers who participated in the year-long teacher development program, with the characteristics of teachers who did not participate. Although the program served beginning teachers throughout the State of Florida, data were collected in only three Florida school systems (Lee County, Hillsborough County, and Marion County) that volunteered to participate in the study. The author notes that voluntary participation by only three Florida school systems might limit the generalizability of her findings: "Three limitations on [sic] the study are noted. First, the study was limited by the sample which might have precluded the representativeness that a larger sample would have provided" (p. 40).

The study explored six research questions, stated in the form of null hypotheses (p. 41):

1. There is no difference between participants in the Beginning Teacher Evaluation Program and nonparticipants in their absentee rate.

2. There is no difference between participants in the Beginning Teacher Evaluation Program and nonparticipants in their scores on a job satisfaction inventory.

3. There is no difference between participants in the Beginning Teacher Evaluation Program and nonparticipants in performing the Generic Competencies.

4. There is no difference between participants in the Beginning Teacher Evaluation Program and nonparticipants in their intent to continue in the profession.

5. There is no difference between participants in the Beginning Teacher Evaluation Program and nonparticipants in their ratings for continued employment.

6. There is no difference between participants in the Beginning Teacher Evaluation Program and nonparticipants in the numbers of effective teaching behaviors demonstrated.

Since the same methodology was used in testing each of these null hypotheses, we will restrict our discussion to the last one.

Evaluation Design. The Florida Beginning Teacher Program was evaluated by administering a large number of assessment instruments to matched samples of teachers, with less than one year of teaching experience, who were employed by the three named school systems. Samples of teachers who had participated in the Florida Beginning Teacher Program and teachers who had not participated in the program during their initial year of teaching were matched by the evaluator on age, race, sex, whether they had graduated from a university in Florida or outside of Florida, highest level degree held, level of teaching (elementary, middle, or high school), and subject area taught (academic, fine arts, exceptional child, or vocational education). Most analyses were based on matched samples composed of 77 pairs of teachers. The analysis we will discuss was based on a matched sample of 36 pairs of teachers.

All assessment instruments were administered at the end of the teachers' initial year of teaching. The evaluation thus used a post-test-only design without random assignment of subjects to exper-

TABLE 10.3: Teaching Behaviors Observed on the *Summative Observation Instrument* (n = 36 pairs)

Behavior	x	SD	SE Mean
Effective*			
Participants	38.62	23.98	4.00
Nonparticipants	37.73	19.40	3.23
Ineffective**			
Participants	2.95	5.63	.94
Nonparticipants	8.00	11.67	1.94

*$p = .852$
**$p = .033$

imental and comparison groups. The author described the design as a "causal-comparative" study. This designation indicates that the author wanted to say that the program caused any posttreatment differences between the experimental teachers and the comparison teachers, but clearly recognized that the groups of teachers had not been assigned randomly. The author recognized the strong possibility that selection played a major role in producing any posttreatment differences found. The author matched subjects on selected variables in an attempt to compensate for her inability to assign them randomly to the experimental and comparison groups.

Author's Data Table. Table 6 in the Gunter study, containing data on the frequencies with which participating and nonparticipating teachers exhibited effective and ineffective teaching behaviors, as measured by Florida's *Summative Observation Instrument*, is reproduced here in its original form as Table 10.3. The table appeared on page 52 of Gunter's report.

Author's Interpretation. Gunter comments as follows on her research question concerning the frequency with which participating and nonparticipating teachers exhibited effective and ineffective teaching behaviors, and on the results shown in her table:

Are there differences between the two groups in the amount of effective teaching behaviors exhibited on the *Summative Observation Instrument* of the Florida Performance Measurement System? Data on classroom performances were collected from 37 pairs of teachers in the study using the *Summative Observation Instrument* of the FPMS. All teachers who were participants in the Beginning Teacher Program from the counties represented in this study were required to be observed using this instrument; however, one county declined to participate in this aspect of the study, and one county reported incomplete data, yielding data from 37 matched pairs. These data were reported in number of effective and ineffective teaching behaviors recorded in classroom observations of teachers in the study.

The null hypothesis was tested using the *t*-test for near nonindependent pairs to determine if teachers in either group demonstrated more effective teaching behaviors at the .05 level of significance. An obtained *t*-value of .18 with 36 degrees of freedom led to a conclusion of no significant difference between the groups. Teachers in the Beginning Teacher Program had a mean number of effective teaching behaviors observed of 38.62. Teachers who were nonparticipants in the Beginning Teacher Program had a mean number of 37.73 effective teaching behaviors observed. The observations were made by persons who have been trained in the Florida Performance Measurement System. The null hypothesis was also tested using the *t*-test for nonindependent pairs to determine if the teachers in either group demonstrated more ineffective teaching behaviors at the .05 level of significance. Teachers who were in the Beginning Teacher Program demonstrated significantly fewer ineffective teaching behaviors at the .033 level of significance as evidenced by an obtained *t*-value of 2.19 with 36 degrees of freedom. Teachers in the Beginning Teacher Program had a mean number of 2.95 ineffective behaviors reported in their observations. Nonparticipants had a mean number of 8 ineffective behaviors reported in their observations. Table 6 (Table 10.3 here) presents the observation data.

In this study the *Summative Instrument* was used by trained observers during classroom observations lasting approximately 20 minutes. The null hypothesis was tested to detect possible differences between the two groups in the number of effective behaviors recorded during the observations. This test yielded no significant differences in the number of effective behaviors of the two groups. However, when the null hypothesis was tested to detect possible differences between the two groups in the number of ineffective behaviors recorded during the observations, teachers who participated in the Beginning Teacher Program demonstrated significantly fewer ineffective behaviors at the .05 alpha level.

These data indicate that both groups appear to perform in the classroom using a repertoire of teaching behaviors which have been identified by research as being effective. Beginning Teacher Program participants, however, demonstrate significantly fewer ineffective behaviors than nonparticipants. A possible explanation of this might be attributable to the training given to participants in the Beginning Teacher Program. In has been shown in the literature that teacher behaviors such as those on the *Summative Instrument* can be demonstrated and taught in training programs.

The Nature of the Inferences. The author used a statistical procedure known as a **paired-difference** *t*-test or a *t*-test for dependent groups to test two null hypotheses. Both null hypotheses were of the same form. Together they stated that there was no difference between the potential population of teachers who would participate in the Florida Beginning Teacher Program and the potential population of teachers who would not participate in the program, or the average number of effective or ineffective teacher behaviors they would exhibit in a 20-minute classroom observation. The alternative hypotheses were the direct converse of the respective null hypotheses: that there would be some differences between corresponding population averages for program participants and nonparticipants. As we noted earlier, the evaluator's desire was to attribute to the Florida Beginning Teacher Program any differences between averages that were found to be statistically significant.

The paired-difference *t*-test gets its name from the fact that it is used to compare average scores of samples of individuals who are paired in some way (such as siblings, mothers, daughters, persons who are matched in terms of particular characteristics, etc.) or to compare the average scores of a single sample of individuals who are assessed at two different times (such as pretreatment and posttreatment). This is in marked contrast to the *t*-test for independent groups we encountered in the first example in this chapter. In that example, as in every application of the *t*-test for independent groups, the two samples whose averages were compared were assumed to have been selected independently.

Apart from the difference in sampling procedures, the paired-difference *t*-test operates just like the other hypothesis testing procedure we have discussed. The sample data are used to compute the value of a test statistic, labeled t, and this computed value is compared to some critical values to determine whether to retain or reject the null hypothesis. The null hypothesis is also of the form: There is no difference between population averages. The corresponding alternative hypothesis is either nondirectional (in which case the alternative is merely that there is some difference between population averages), or directional (in which case the alternative hypothesis is that one of the population averages is larger than the other). An appropriate directional alternative hypothesis in this example would be that the average number of ineffective behaviors of potential program participants is smaller than the average number of ineffective behaviors of the population of potential nonparticipants.

Instead of reporting the significance of her findings for a particular Type I error level (alpha), Gunter summarized the results of her hypothesis tests—as shown in Table 10.3—by reporting the proportion (area) of the appropriate t-distribution that would fall to the right (i.e., be larger than) the values of the t-statistics she computed. Thus, for the hypothesis test involving the frequency of effective teaching behaviors, Gunter reported "$p = .852$." This footnote should be interpreted as follows: If Gunter's null hypothesis were true—both populations (potential program participants and potential nonparticipants) would exhibit the same average number of effective teaching behaviors in a 20-minute observation period—852 times out of 1000 (because $852/1000 = .852$), we would expect to find t-statistics that were larger than the value she found. Thus the value of the t-statistic she found was not at all unusual, and does not suggest that the null hypothesis is false.

Conversely, for the hypothesis test involving the frequency of ineffective teaching behaviors, Gunter reported "$p = .033$." This footnote should be interpreted as follows: If Gunter's null hypothesis were true—both populations (potential program participants and potential nonparticipants) would exhibit the same average number of ineffective teaching behaviors in a 20-minute observation period—only 33 times out of 1000 (because $33/1000 = .033$), would we expect to find t-statistics that were larger than the value she found. Thus the value of the t-statistic she found was very unusual, and strongly suggests that the null hypothesis is false. Adopting an alpha level of .05, as Gunter did, for rejecting null hypotheses, we would certainly reject on the basis of a p-value equal to .033.

Our Interpretation of Results. Gunter is refreshingly cautious in her interpretation of the findings of her study. In other parts of her report that we have not cited, she carefully enumerates the weaknesses of the design she was forced to use because of the kinds of data available to her. She also enumerates the most likely threats to the validity of a conclusion that the Florida Beginning Teacher Program caused the significant difference between the numbers of ineffective teaching behaviors observed for program participants and nonparticipants: Gunter warns that the relationship she found might not be causal. She notes that matching subjects on age, sex, race, and so forth will permit her to refute claims that these "third variables" were the real causes of the differences she found, but will not protect her against claims for other potential third variables, such as differences in the abilities of the participating and nonparticipating teachers or differences in the preservice education of participating and nonparticipating teachers.

Despite the problems of internal validity we have just reviewed, the results for "frequency of ineffective behaviors" certainly warrant further scrutiny. Not only was the difference between the averages for program participants and nonparticipants statistically significant, it appeared to be substantively important. The nonparticipants exhibited two-and-a-half times the number of ineffective behaviors as did the program participants, which appears to be a nontrivial difference in performance. However, our seeming enthusiasm must be tempered by the realization that Gunter has told us little about the *Summative Observation Instrument*, except that the behaviors it measures are "research-based." Careful review of the content of the instrument would certainly be warranted, before we let our passion and fervor run away with us.

Assumptions Needed to Generalize. Can you safely conclude that you would find results similar to Gunter's, were you to export the Florida Beginning Teacher Program to a school system of your choice? Probably not. First, realize that results were reported only for 37 pairs of beginning teachers in two self-selected Florida school systems. As Gunter observed, her sample was small and not obviously generalizable. Second, the threats to internal validity we noted earlier cast a good bit of doubt on the causal influence of the program, even in the school systems where it was evaluated. And we know nothing of the gravity of the "ineffective teaching behaviors" exhibited by the nonparticipants in the program. In short, you'd have to assume a great deal, were you to assert that the Florida Program would be beneficial in a school system of your choice. Although we're sometimes of a betting persuasion, we wouldn't put our money on this horse until we had a far closer look at its pedigree.

Summary

In this chapter we've presented portions of three actual research and evaluation studies. Each example involved the use of statistical hypothesis testing to compare two population averages. In discussing these examples, we hope we've helped you to identify the statistical hypothesis involved, the logic of the statistical procedures in the context of the particular studies, and appropriate interpretations of the data presented. When you read other studies that incorporate t-tests and z-tests, you will find that their structure is virtually identical to that of the examples considered here. To be sure, the details will differ. But the fundamental logic, and much of the statistical language, will be exactly the same. We suggest that you try your hand at reading a few evaluation studies involving comparisons of averages now, while the material in this chapter is fresh in your mind. Look at the authors' data tables, and form your own conclusions concerning the significance of the results. Only then would we suggest that you read the authors' interpretations. You may be pleasantly surprised by your new-found caution and expertise.

Problems — Chapter 10

10.1 In summarizing a study of the relative effectiveness of two types of product sales campaigns, an author used the following data table:

Campaign	Mean Sales	t
Radio	$120,000	
Newspaper	$ 92,000	
		4.62**

**Significant at .01 level

  a. What null hypothesis was tested in this study?
  b. What alternative hypothesis was tested in this study?
  c. Discuss the meaning of the two "**" attached to the t-statistic of 4.62.

10.2 What is the difference, if any, between a t-test for independent samples and a paired-difference t-test?

10.3 What is the difference, if any, between a nondirectional alternative hypothesis and a directional alternative hypothesis?

11.

Inferences Involving Correlation Coefficients

The Nature of the Inferences

Chapter 4 describes *correlation coefficients* as statistics that indicate the degree of relationship between measures of two characteristics of some group of persons or objects. For example, by calculating a correlation coefficient, you could learn whether students who earned the highest scores on a reading test were also likely to earn the highest scores on a mathematics test. Or whether, among American women, shoe size was consistently related to height (do women with the smallest feet tend to be the shortest, and vice versa?). If you want to be persnickety, you'll recall that correlation coefficients don't do a good job of indicating all types of relationships among variables, they merely tell whether plotted points that represent measurements of both variables tend to fall along a straight line. Statisticians and researchers would say that correlation coefficients reflect only the degree of *linear relationship* between two variables.

Educational researchers and evaluators have an abiding fascination with how things go together. They're forever posing titillating questions like "How does learning relate to instruction?" or "How is intelligence related to social class?" or "How does use of repeated drill and practice relate to arithmetic achievement?" Answers to all of these questions can be found in correlation coefficients. As you might imagine, correlations abound in the educational research and evaluation literature.

In this chapter we'll concern ourselves with correlation coefficients as population parameters. In particular, we'll examine studies in which something about the value of a population correlation coefficient is inferred from the value of a corresponding sample correlation coefficient. The logic of inferences involving correlation coefficients is basically the same as the logic you've encountered earlier, in the chapter on averages. Both point estimation and confidence intervals can be used to estimate the value of a population correlation coefficient. And hypothesis testing can be used to examine the belief that a population correlation coefficient is equal to a particular value. Formal inferential procedures also exist for examining the hypothesis that the correlations between two variables are the same, in two different populations. For example, it is possible to test the hypothesis that the correlations between scores on a reading readiness test administered in kindergarten and scores on a reading achievement test administered in the first grade are the same, for boys and for girls.

The kind of correlation inference that you'll encounter most frequently in research and evaluation reports is a test of the null hypothesis that a correlation coefficient equals zero. If the null hypothesis were true, it would mean that the variables being correlated would have absolutely no linear relationship when data were gathered from all members of the population. In virtually all research and evaluation studies where this null hypothesis is tested, the researcher fervently hopes and expects that the null hypothesis will be rejected, in which case he or she will conclude that the sample correlation used in the hypothesis test is "significant," and that there is some reasonable assurance of a relationship between the measured variables in the population to which generalizations are being made.

The following examples consider the significance of correlation coefficients in a number of research contexts. Although the statistical procedures used in each example are the same, the contexts vary enough to make interpretation of results a bit different in each case.

Are High School Sophomores' Ego Identities Related to School Factors and Cognitive Factors?

Purpose of the Study. Many educators view the fundamental purpose of high school as preparing students to function successfully in adult roles following their high school graduation. Educators now realize that successful adult functioning requires more than the acquisition of knowledge and appropriate cognitive development. Successful emotional development is also required. With this realization has come renewed emphasis on the role of the high school counselor and attention to components of a student's high school experience that will foster his or her positive emotional growth and development. Unfortunately, these components are understood far less than are activities that foster cognitive growth. Even the characterization of students' emotional status and development, and our knowledge of personal and school-related factors that are associated with students' emotional status, are at a stage of relative infancy.

Ego identity is one construct that can be used to characterize a high school student's description of his or her conception of self. In the work of Frederick Erikson, an adolescent who is experiencing an *ego identity crisis* is likely to have conflicts involving such component constructs as trust versus mistrust, autonomy versus shame and doubt, initiative versus guilt, industry versus inferiority, intimacy versus isolation, generativity versus stagnation, and integrity versus despair. A student who consistently describes himself or herself in terms of the more positive elements of these construct pairs is more likely to function successfully as an independent adult than is one whose self-description includes the more negative components of these pairs.

Among other objectives, the study by Wrabel (1985) sought to determine the degree to which high school sophomores' ego identities were related to a number of cognitive and school-related factors, including their cognitive quantitative ability (CQA), their cognitive verbal ability (CVA), their high school grade point average (GPA), and their normed test achievement (NTA). Through this study, Wrabel attempted to discover better known and more frequently measured constructs that might predict students' ego identities. The author suggested that such knowledge would be of value to high school counselors, as well as other school personnel.

Research Design. Wrabel (1985) collected data from a sample of 202 sophomores in the only suburban high school in a community of 31,000 people outside Cleveland, Ohio. His sample of students volunteered to participate in his study and were given permission to do so by their parents. The sampled students constituted over 84% of a sophomore class of 240. Most of the sampled students were 15 years old, white, and middle class. The sample was balanced in terms of gender. Absence on the day of data collection and lack of parental permission were the principal reasons the other 16% of the class did not participate in the study.

Counselors at the selected high school administered the "3-R's Verbal Abilities, Quantitative Abilities, and Achievement Tests: Ohio Version, Form A, Level 15/16" to all high school sophomores in the study on a single day during the fall semester. Health teachers at the school administered the "Rasmussen Ego Identity Scale: Revised Short Form" to participating students during the same week that the students completed the ability and achievement tests. Students' grade records were used, together with a formula that considered the number of Carnegie units associated with each course they had completed, and the standard or honors status of each course, to compute their grade point averages.

Once data on all variables had been obtained for each participating student, Pearson product-moment correlation coefficients between each pair of variables were computed and were tested for statistical significance. Because he was interested in examining the consistency of relationships between the variables for male and female students, Wrabel computed and tested correlation coefficients separately, and collectively, for students classified by gender.

Author's Data Table. Table 2 (p. 73) of Wrabel's report provides correlation coefficients among students' ego identity scores, cognitive verbal ability scores, cognitive quantitative ability scores, normed test achievement scores, and grade point averages. Portions of the table report correlations between these variables for male students, female students, and all students regardless of gender. Results of numerous hypothesis tests are also reported in the table.

Wrabel's Table 2 is reproduced here, just as it appeared in his report, as Table 11.1. Notice that each section of the table contains correlation coefficients arrayed in a triangular pattern. This arrangement appears frequently in research and evaluation reports because correlation coefficients are commutative. That is, the correlation between two variables is the same, regardless of the order in which the variables are listed. Thus the correlation between ego identity and cognitive verbal ability is exactly the same as the correlation between cognitive verbal ability and ego identity. For this reason, the upper half of each section of the table would contain totally redundant information, and is typically left blank.

Notice also that the correlations that appear along an imaginary diagonal line from the upper left corner to the lower right corner of each section of the table are equal to 1.00. This is because these values all represent correlations of a variable with itself. In theory, a variable is perfectly correlated with itself, although we know that less-than-perfect reliability results in somewhat lower correlations in practice.

Author's Interpretation. Wrabel's interpretation of his correlational results was succinct. He occasionally compared his findings with those of previous studies in which relationships among variables similar to those he explored had been examined. Wrabel's summary is cited below in its entirety:

An examination was made to determine if any significant correlations existed among ego identity (EI), cognitive verbal ability (CVA), cognitive quantitative ability (CQA), normed test achievement (NTA), and grade point average (GPA). The Pearson product-moment correlations for both males and females were significant between NTA and CQA, NTA and CVA, CQA and CVA, GPA and CQA, GPA and NTA, and GPA and CVA. The findings were in agreement with those of Cross and Allen (1970). It may be concluded that a meaningful relationship exists among cognitive ability and academic achievement factors when males and females are considered separately. EI and CQA were significantly correlated (0.20, $p < 0.05$) for males but the strength of relationship was weak. A significant positive correlation (0.22, $p < 0.05$) was identified between EI and GPA for females. This finding is congruous [sic] with the earlier finding of Hummel and Roselli (1983). Since the strength of the relationship between EI and GPA for females is slight, it may only be concluded with caution that these two variables are related among females.

Nine Pearson product-moment correlations were significant when all subjects were studied together. The data in Table 2 [Table 11.1 here] demonstrated significant correlations between NTA and CVA, NTA and CQA, CQA and CVA, GPA and NTA, GPA and CQA, and GPA and CVA. These findings are partially in harmony with those of Chang (1982). It may be concluded from the findings that a healthy relationship exists among cognitive ability and academic achievement factors for all subjects. When further analyzing these data, significant positive relationships of modest strength were found between EI and GPA (0.21, $p < 0.01$), EI and CVA (0.18, $p < 0.01$), and EI and NTA (0.15, $p < 0.05$); these findings are consistent with those of Crook (1982). It may be concluded with caution that EI and GPA, CVA, and NTA show a tendency to be mildly related.

The Nature of the Inferences. Whenever you find a table of correlation coefficients like Table 11.1, where some correlations have one or more asterisks beside them, it means that the author tested each correlation for statistical significance. That is, for each correlation coefficient in the table, the author tested the null hypothesis that the corresponding correlation, in the population to which he or she wished to generalize, is equal to zero. Unless otherwise stated, the alternative hypothesis is that the corresponding population correlation coefficient is not equal to zero.

In Table 11.1 you might note that some correlations don't have any asterisks beside them, some have one, several have two, and a number have three. Just because a correlation coefficient doesn't rate any asterisks doesn't mean that testing its significance was ignored. It just means that the null hypothesis that the corresponding population correlation was equal to zero was not rejected, at the level of significance indicated for a single asterisk (in this case, 0.05). Thus, in Table 11.1, the correlation 0.19 between Cognitive Verbal Ability and Ego Identity for Males was not found to be significant at the 0.05 level; we would not reject the null hypothesis that for male sophomore high school students similar to the ones sampled, the population value of the correlation between Cognitive Verbal Ability and Ego Identity was equal to zero. The correlation between Cognitive Quantitative Ability and Cognitive Verbal Ability was reported as 0.72 for males. This

TABLE 11.1: Intercorrelations Among the Variables of Ego Identity, Cognitive Verbal Ability, Cognitive Quantitative Ability, Normed Test Achievement, and Grade Point Average for Male, Female, and All Subjects

Variables	Ego Identity	Cognitive Verbal Ability	Cognitive Quantitative Ability	Normed Test Achievement	Grade Point Average
			Males		
Ego Identity	1.00				
Cognitive Verbal Ability	0.19	1.00			
Cognitive Quantitative Ability	0.20*	0.72***	1.00		
Normed Test Achievement	0.14	0.82***	0.80***	1.00	
Grade Point Average	0.19	0.38***	0.46***	0.46***	1.00
			Females		
Ego Identity	1.00				
Cognitive Verbal Ability	0.16	1.00			
Cognitive Quantitative Ability	0.03	0.66***	1.00		
Normed Test Achievement	0.13	0.84***	0.78***	1.00	
Grade Point Average	0.22	0.51***	0.49***	0.57***	1.00
			All Subjects		
Ego Identity	1.00				
Cognitive Verbal Ability	0.18**	1.00			
Cognitive Quantitative Ability	0.12	0.69***	1.00		
Normed Test Achievement	0.15*	0.83***	0.82***	1.00	
Grade Point Average	0.21**	0.44***	0.46***	0.51***	1.00

***$p < 0.001$
**$p < 0.01$
*$p < 0.05$

correlation has three asterisks beside it. The footnote to the table indicates that it is therefore statistically significant, with "$p < 0.001$." Thus, for a population of male high school sophomores similar to the ones sampled by Wrabel, were you to test the null hypothesis that the correlation between Cognitive Quantitative Ability and Cognitive Verbal Ability was equal to zero, you would reject that null hypothesis at an alpha level of 0.001 (0.001 corresponds to 1/10 of 1%, a very small risk of committing a Type I error).

The results of significance tests for other correlation coefficients in Table 11.1 should be interpreted similarly. No asterisks means that the correlation coefficient is not significant at the 0.05 level; one asterisk means that the null hypothesis (that the corresponding population correlation equals zero) would be rejected at an alpha of 0.05; two asterisks means that the null hypothesis would be rejected at an alpha of 0.01; and three asterisks means that the null hypothesis would be rejected at an alpha of 0.001. You will find similar shorthand in many tables of correlations in a great many research and evaluation reports. The definitions of one asterisk, two asterisks, and so forth, might be different, however. For example, one asterisk might mean the correlation is significant at the 0.10 alpha level; two might mean it is significant at the 0.05 alpha level; and so on. You have to read the footnotes carefully to determine the definitions that are applicable to the correlations in a particular table.

Our Interpretation of Results. Wrabel has done a reasonably accurate, if concise, job of interpreting the results of this portion of his study. His principal finding, that paper-and-pencil measures of students' cognitive abilities and achievement are highly related, is consistent with a wealth of previous research and not at all unexpected. The moderate correlations (in the 0.40s and 0.50s) that he observed between students' cognitive ability test performances and their high school grade point averages are also consistent with previous research.

Wrabel urges caution in interpreting the correlations he observed between a measure of ego identity and various measures of students' cognitive abilities, achievement test scores, and grade point averages. It would be more accurate to say that these correlations were all quite small, and consistently bordered on the trivial. Although some of the correlations were statistically significant, the only supportable conclusion from these results is that, in a population of high school sophomores like those in the observed sample, a number of the corresponding correlations would be different from zero. These correlations might, however, differ from zero by trivial amounts. None of Wrabel's findings would support the contention that students' measured ego identities are strongly—or even moderately—related to measures of their cognitive abilities, achievement test performances, or grade point averages. Indeed, Wrabel makes no such claims.

As in many studies in the educational research and evaluation literature, the issue of external validity is equivocal in this study. Wrabel did an adequate job of describing the sample of 202 high school sophomores to whom he administered his measurement instruments. In fact, he provided a far richer description than is found in many studies. However, Wrabel's sample consisted of volunteers from a single suburban high school. The students he measured were not sampled in any scientific way from a larger population, and the results he reported do not obviously generalize to a readily identifiable population of high school sophomores. When interpreting studies such as this one, the burden falls to the reader to consider the nature of the sample used by the researcher, the methods used by the researcher to secure his or her sample, and characteristics of the sample (such as voluntary participation, collection of data at a single site) that might limit the external validity of the researcher's findings. Review of the external validity considerations discussed in Chapter 6 should be helpful in grappling with these issues.

Relationships Between Teacher Attitudes and Teacher Behavior

Purpose of the Study. In the chapter on Inferences Involving Averages, we discussed a study by McConnell (1978) that investigated relationships between teachers' attitudes and their classroom behaviors. Students and outside observers rated certain classroom behaviors of ninth-grade algebra teachers. McConnell examined the relationships between these ratings and teachers' self-reported attitudes toward teaching as a profession, toward mathematics as a subject, and toward students. His objective was to explore one portion of a theory that related teachers' attitudes to students' attitudes.

Research Design. As we stated in Chapter 10, McConnell collected data on a purposefully selected sample of 47 ninth-grade algebra teachers. He asked teachers to complete several previously used teacher opinion scales and other attitude measures. He had two adult raters observe teachers' classroom behaviors during four 30-minute visits conducted at intervals throughout the school year. In addition, he had students rate teachers' behaviors in order to determine how they viewed their teachers' actions in the classroom.

McConnell's paper contains a large number of data tables that bear on several interrelated research questions. We will restrict our attention to two specific questions in our review of inferences involving correlation coefficients. First, McConnell was concerned with the consistency of raters' evaluations of teachers on their third and fourth visits to their classrooms. Correlations between ratings of teachers' behaviors during successive classroom observations are measures of reliability. If teachers' behaviors were inconsistent across time, or if raters were unable to evaluate teachers' behaviors consistently, it would be unlikely that their rated behaviors would correlate with their attitudes or with anything else. A measure that is unreliable is essentially useless, since it is not a consistent indicator of behavior, nor will it relate consistently to any other measure. In short, a measure that does not correlate with itself cannot correlate with anything else. McConnell was therefore wise in investigating the reliability of his teacher observation scales.

The second issue we will examine lies at the heart of McConnell's research. He summarized his findings on the relationships between teachers' behaviors and attitudes in a two-page table containing only those correlation coefficients that were significantly different from zero when tested at an alpha level of 0.05. You will see that he found a large number of statistically significant correlations.

Author's Data Tables. Table 2 (p. 4) in the McConnell paper contains correlations between the averages of two rater's scores for each teacher on their third and fourth visits to the teachers' classrooms. Although 47 teachers participated in some phases of his study, McConnell obtained behavior ratings for only 43 ninth-grade teachers.

Correlations between selected teacher behavior measures and selected teacher attitude measures appear in Table 8 of the McConnell paper. The table is quite long, and covers pages 18 and 19 of his report. In an earlier study (McConnell, 1977), the author investigated relationships between teacher behaviors and measures of student learning and attitude change. A column headed "Import" in Table 8 summarizes some of the findings of that study, by reporting the number of times each teacher behavior measure was found to be significantly correlated with some measure of student learning or attitude change. Other columns in Table 8 provide the name of each teacher behavior measure (including the code for the variable in McConnell's coding scheme), the name of the category that contains the behavior measure, the "Source" of the measurement (either adult observers or pupils' ratings), the number and title of the associated teacher attitude measure, and the size and level of significance of the correlation coefficient between a teacher behavior measure and a teacher attitude measure.

Tables 2 and 8 of the McConnell paper are reproduced below, just as they appeared in the original document, as Tables 11.2 and 11.3.

Author's Interpretation. McConnell's interpretation of the results presented in Table 11.2 is quite limited. He notes that "Difficulty of Lesson was notably unstable across the two visits. The other nine [behavioral ratings] were adequately correlated" (p. 4).

McConnell's interpretation of the results shown in Table 11.3 is extensive, and we will cite only a portion of it here. On page 24 he concluded:

This study has shown that teacher attitudes are related to behavior patterns which are discernible by observers. The teachers who were more satisfied with teaching as a profession and who liked their subject more (in this case, mathematics) were rated as being clearer, more varied in presentations, more enthusiastic, more task-oriented, more indirect in the sense of using student ideas, more apt to ask higher cognitive questions, and less critical of students. The teachers who were more opposed to strict discipline and class control were viewed as being less clear, not providing as many chances for students to learn algebra, and providing less emphasis on logic and analysis.

TABLE 11.2: Correlations Between Item Scores on the Process Rating Sheet on Class Visits 3 and 4 for 43 Classes

Item		r
PR1	Clarity	.382*
PR2	Variability	.375*
PR3	Enthusiasm	.636**
PR4	Business-like	.533**
PR5	Uses Student Ideas	.398**
PR6	Criticism	.565**
PR7	Structures Lesson	.347*
PR8	Higher Cognitive Questions	.595**
PR9	Probing Questions	.332*
PR10	Difficulty of Lesson	−.147

*$p < .05$
**$p < .01$

McConnell suggests that his findings have implications beyond the field of mathematics, even though his study was limited to a small sample of ninth-grade algebra teachers in 13 high schools. He notes that the attitudes found to be important to successful teaching of algebra have analogues in other subject areas, and that the behaviors he found to be related to teacher attitudes are not unique to algebra teaching. Finally, McConnell notes the importance of including measures of teacher behavior in further research on the relationships between teacher attitudes and student attitudes.

The Nature of the Inferences. The inferences involving correlation coefficients that appear in the McConnell study are statistically identical to those examined by Koffler (1977), although they differ in their substantive implications. For each of the ten behavior rating scales listed in Table 11.2, McConnell has tested the null hypothesis that, in a hypothetical population of ninth-grade algebra teachers, the observers' ratings of a teacher on the third visit to his or her classroom would be uncorrelated with corresponding ratings resulting from observations on the fourth classroom visit. If the null hypothesis were true for a particular rating scale (e.g., for the "Clarity" scale), it would mean that an observer's evaluation of a teacher's clarity would be totally unstable from one classroom visit to the next. The rating scale would therefore be valueless as an indicator of a teacher's instructional clarity. Presumably, although teachers are more or less clear from one day to the next, their relative positions on a clarity scale would not fluctuate so wildly that the clarity ranking of a teacher on one visit to his or her classroom would have no relationship to the clarity ranking of that teacher on the next visit. Were the null hypothesis to be retained, we would be forced to conclude that observers' ratings of teachers' clarity were totally unstable across time.

For each hypothesis test summarized in Table 11.2, the alternative hypothesis is that the population value of the correlation coefficient is not equal to zero. Unless otherwise indicated, in tests involving correlation coefficients you should always assume that the alternative hypothesis is nondirectional.

Note that McConnell did not select a particular Type I error level (value of alpha) in conducting the hypothesis tests reported in Table 11.2. Rather, he reports the significance of each correlation coefficient when compared to critical values that are appropriate to two values of alpha (0.05 and 0.01). If a correlation coefficient has one asterisk beside it, you may conclude that it is significant at an alpha level of 0.05; if it has two asterisks beside it, you would reject the null hypothesis that the corresponding population correlation equals zero at an alpha level of 0.01. The one correlation coefficient that has no asterisks (the –.147 for Difficulty of Lesson) was not found to differ significantly from zero when the null hypothesis was tested using an alpha level of 0.05. We know this because 0.05 is the largest value of alpha used in any significance test reported in Table 11.2.

In constructing Table 11.3, McConnell has selected only those correlations between rated teacher behaviors and self-reported teacher attitudes that were significant at the .05 level. In the column headed "r" he has reported the value of each sample correlation for the 43 teachers observed in his study. In the column headed "Sig." he has reported the probability that a correlation at least as large as that reported in the "r" column would be found, for a sample of size 43, if the corresponding population correlation were equal to zero. Another way to interpret the numbers in the "Sig." column is as follows: They are the largest values of alpha at which we would reject the null hypothesis that the corresponding population correlations were equal to zero. For example, were we

TABLE 11.3: Correlations Between Teacher Behavior Measures and Teacher Attitude Measures (Significant at the .05 Level) Grouped by Categories of Teacher Behavior for 43 Teachers

	Teacher Behavior Measure			
Category	*Name*	*Description*	*Source*	*Import*
Clarity	PR1	Clarity	Obs.	6[a]
	RCLART	Clarity	Pupils	6
Variety/ Variability	PR2	Variability	Pupils	0
	RVART	Variability	Pupils	0
Enthusiasm	PR3	Enthusiasm	Obs.	0
	TCSZ	Exciting-Stimulating	Obs.	6
	RENTMST	Enthusiasm	Pupils	5
Business-Like Task-Oriented	PR4	Businesslike	Obs.	4
	TGSY	Responsible-Steady	Obs.	1
	RTASKT	Task-Orientation	Pupils	6
Use of Student Ideas	PR5	Uses Student Ideas	Obs.	0
	RUSET	Use of Ideas	Pupils	0
Criticism	PR6	Criticism	Obs.	1
	RCRITT	Criticism	Pupils	0

	Teacher Attitude Measure		
TOI #	Title	r	Sig.
1	Theoretical Orientation	.26	.047
3	Involvement in Teaching	.44	.001
5	Like vs. Dislike	.31	.023
4	Nonauthoritarian Orientation	−.26	.047
3	Involvement in Teaching	.33	.017
5	Like vs. Dislike	.30	.035
6	Creative vs. Rote	.28	.034
—	None	—	—
2	Concern for Students	.34	.014
3	Involvement in Teaching	.48	.001
5	Like vs. Dislike	.26	.044
2	Concern for Students	.38	.024
3	Involvement in Teaching	.36	.011
5	Like vs. Dislike	.34	.013
3	Involvement in Teaching	.36	.010
3	Involvement in Teaching	.40	.001
5	Like vs. Dislike	.33	.015
6	Creative vs. Rote	.27	.030
3	Involvement in Teaching	.30	.005
6	Creative vs. Rote	.32	.018
—	None	—	—
3	Involvement in Teaching	.31	.020
5	Like vs. Dislike	.31	.022
6	Creative vs. Rote	.20	.028
—	None	—	—
1	Theoretical Orientation	−.20	.031
3	Involvement in Teaching	−.20	.025
5	Like vs. Dislike	−.41	.033
6	Creative vs. Rote	−.37	.007
2	Concern for Students	−.28	.037

Table 11.3 continued

| Category | Teacher Behavior Measure | | | | |
	Name	Description	Source	Import
Structures Lesson	PR7	Structures Lesson	Obs.	1
	RSTRUCT	Structuring	Pupils	0
Questions	PR8	Higher Cognitive Questions	Obs.	3
	PR9	Probing	Obs.	1
	RQUEST	Questioning	Pupils	1
Difficulty	PR10	Difficulty of Lesson	Obs.	0
	RDIFFT	Difficulty	Pupils	0
Other	TCSC	Concrete, Practical	Obs.	0
	TCSK	Democratic, Kindly	Obs.	0
	ROPPT	Opportunity to Learn	Pupils	2

[a]"Import" indicates the number of significant correlations which were achieved between the teacher behavior measure and the criteria of pupil learning and attitude change in McConnell (1977).

to test the null hypothesis that the population correlation between observer ratings of teachers' "Clarity" and teachers' self-reported "Theoretical Orientation" was equal to zero, we would reject that null hypothesis at an alpha level of .047. Therefore, the sample correlation between these variables is significant, just beyond the .05 level. (The correlation barely made Table 11.3, using McConnell's criterion.) In contrast, the .44 correlation between observer ratings of teachers' "Clarity" and teachers' self-reports of their "Involvement in Teaching" is significant at the .001 level. This means that the null hypothesis that the corresponding population correlation was equal to zero would be rejected, even if the researcher were willing to run only a .001 risk of making a Type I error. (Note that .001 corresponds to 1/10 of 1%.)

As was true for the hypothesis tests reported in Table 11.2, the alternative hypotheses implied by the significance tests reported

Table 11.3 continued

	Teacher Attitude Measure		
TOI #	Title	r	Sig.
3	Involvement in Teaching	.33	.033
—	None	—	—
3	Involvement in Teaching	.49	.034
5	Like vs. Dislike	.35	.001
6	Creative vs. Rote	.35	.010
—	None	—	—
—	None	—	—
—	None	—	—
3	Involvement in Teaching	.20	.033
—	None	—	—
—	None	—	—
4	Nonauthoritarian Orientation	−.20	.035

in Table 11.3 are nondirectional. Thus the alternative to each null hypothesis is that the population correlation is not equal to zero.

Our Interpretation of Results. The significance tests reported in Table 11.2 are very unusual. Correlations that represent measurement reliability (called reliability coefficients) are typically treated as sample statistics, and are rarely subjected to a test of the hypothesis that their corresponding population values equal zero. Rejection of the null hypothesis that a population reliability coefficient equals zero provides little comfort that the corresponding sample coefficient is sufficiently large. Ideally, one would like all reliability coefficients to equal 1, a situation that is never realized in practice but is sought nonetheless. If a reliability coefficient equals 1, the corresponding measurement procedure is perfectly stable. Exactly the same result would be obtained if a person were measured repeatedly, under identical conditions, as long as that person's true status had not changed. If a reliability coefficient equals zero, measurement is totally unreliable, in the sense that the results of measurement are totally unrelated to a person's true status. If you think about these definitions, you will soon realize why you wouldn't jump for joy even if you were certain that a population reliability coefficient wasn't equal to zero.

The sample reliability coefficients reported by McConnell range from barely tolerable to moderately respectable. The one negative value (−.147 for "Difficulty of Lesson") is totally unacceptable, of course. In this case, it is comforting that the null hypothesis of total unreliability was not rejected. The coefficients that range in the .50s and .60s are not at all unusual for short rating scales, and are quite respectable. The coefficients in the .30s are troublesome, despite their statistical significance. Reliability coefficients limit the degree to which a scale will correlate with another variable. If measurement reliability is too low, a researcher might not be able to determine whether or not the measured variable is actually related to any other variable.

The correlation coefficients reported in Table 11.3 although statistically significant at the .05 level, are modest in size. They are undoubtedly limited by the reliabilities of the variables being correlated, and might represent far stronger relationships between the underlying variables. As McConnell suggests, they do support the contention that observers' ratings of teachers' classroom behaviors are related to teachers' reported attitudes. At least for the ninth-grade algebra teachers in McConnell's study, and quite likely for a larger population of algebra teachers as well, linkages between teachers' attitudes and observed behaviors are clearly established.

McConnell's suggestion that teachers' behaviors be considered in any study that attempts to explain relationships between the attitudes of teachers and students is quite reasonable, and, within the limits of generalizability of his study, well supported by his findings.

Generalizing the Results of This Study. Two factors limit the generalizability of McConnell's findings. First, his sample is composed of ninth-grade algebra teachers at 13 suburban high schools. Although McConnell compared his sample to teachers in the National Longitudinal Study of Mathematical Ability (NLSMA), he found differences on some characteristics and did not have the opportunity to examine a number of other important characteristics. So the populations to which one may safely generalize his findings remains unclear.

The second question that arises in generalizing from McConnell's results concerns the statistical treatment of his data. As is often true in correlation studies, a great many correlation coefficients were subjected to statistical hypothesis tests. If enough hypothesis tests are conducted, some significant correlation coefficients will be found, even though all corresponding population coefficients are equal to zero. For example, if 20 correlations are tested for significance at an alpha level of .05, we would expect to find that one of those correlations (5% of the 20) was significant, even if all population correlations were equal to zero. It is not clear from McConnell's paper how many correlation coefficients he tested for significance. In Table 11.3 alone, he reports 33 that are significant at the .05 level. Undoubtedly, this exceeds the number that we would expect to find just by chance, but we have no way of knowing with certainty.

So, in generalizing McConnell's results, you can probably conclude with a fair degree of assurance that some self-reported attitudes of ninth-grade algebra teachers are related, at least to a modest degree, to observers' ratings of their classroom behaviors. Whether these relationships generalize to teachers in other grades or to teachers of other subjects is an open question. Logic and substantive theory, rather than inferential statistics, will have to guide you in generalizing further.

Summary

In this chapter we have presented examples of one type of inference involving correlation coefficients. Although correlation coefficients are sometimes subjected to other inferential procedures, it is most common to test the null hypothesis that their corresponding population values equal zero.

We hope you will use the examples presented in this chapter as a guide to help you interpret the many similar studies you will find as you read research and evaluation literature. Although the substance of specific inferences will differ greatly, you will find a large number of research and evaluation reports that incorporate null hypotheses, alternative hypotheses, and statistical language that are just like the ones we've discussed here. Hopefully, your journeys through the literature of your field will now be less mysterious.

Problems — Chapter 11

11.1 A study of the relationship between years of formal schooling and reading habits was conducted in the late 1980s. One of its results was a 90% confidence interval on the correlation between years of schooling and number of books read per year, based on a survey of 436 adults in New York state. The lower confidence limit was +0.35 and the upper confidence limit was +0.47.

  a. To what population does this confidence interval apply?
  b. Can you conclude, on the basis of these data, that additional formal education results in adults reading more books?
  c. Had the author of the study computed a 95% confidence interval using the same data, would it have been wider than +0.35 to +0.47, or would it have been narrower?
  d. Could the author have used the same data to test the null hypothesis that years of formal schooling and number of books read per year were not correlated? Can you tell, by looking at the confidence interval, whether the null hypothesis would have been retained or rejected?

11.2 Jones and Stockton (1988) examined the relationship between teacher salaries and student reading achievement in 120 elementary school classes in North Carolina. They concluded as follows: "The correlation between teacher's annual salary and average student reading achievement in grades one through five was +0.02; this correlation was not significant at the 0.10 level."

  a. What null hypothesis were the authors testing in this study?
  b. Did they reject or retain their null hypothesis?
  c. To what population might these results generalize?
  d. What critical assumptions would be necessary, to generalize these results to a larger population?

11.3 In an experiment involving quantitative aptitude, mathematics achievement, and gender, Wright and Stanley (1984) computed correlation coefficients between the mathematics aptitude scores and mathematics achievement scores of independent samples of 85 fourth-grade boys and 88 fourth-grade girls. They reported their results in the following table:

Boys	Girls
Mathematics Aptitude with Mathematics Achievement $r = 0.79*$	Mathematics Aptitude with Mathematics Achievement $r = 0.62*$

*signif. at 0.05
**difference not signif. at 0.10

   a. To what null hypotheses does the footnote with one "*" refer?

   b. To what null hypothesis does the footnote with two "**" refer?

   c. To what populations might these results generalize?

11.4 Describe an inferential statistical study in your own context that involves at least one correlation coefficient.

   a. Define the research question you might want to investigate.

   b. Identify the population and the population parameter that are central to your research study.

   c. State a null hypothesis and an alternative hypothesis that are relevant to your study.

   d. What conclusions would you reach, were you to reject the null hypothesis?

12.

Inferences Involving Statistical Independence

The Nature of the Inferences

Suppose that a test of anxiety was administered to every member of a population of adults, and that the population was then divided into those who had low scores and those who had high scores. That is, each member of the population was placed either in a low-anxiety category or in a high-anxiety category, depending on his or her score. Next, suppose that all of the low-anxiety persons and all of the high-anxiety persons were given a test of problem-solving skill. Assume that this test was used to classify each person as a poor, average, or good problem-solver. Would the percentages of low-anxiety persons in each problem-solving category be the same as corresponding percentages of high-anxiety persons in each category? If so, we would say that, for the population of adults, anxiety and problem-solving ability were **statistically independent** variables. If not, we would say that the two variables were **statistically dependent**.

Research questions that are similar to the one posed in this example arise frequently in education and social science research. The answers to such questions tell us whether knowing how a person is categorized on one variable is at all useful in predicting how they should be categorized on the other. If two variables are statistically independent, they are not related in any way at all—either linearly (as might be indicated by a correlation coefficient) or nonlinearly. So that knowing how a person is categorized on one variable provides absolutely no hint as to how they might be

236

categorized on the other. In contrast, if two variables are statistically dependent, knowing a person's status on one variable is useful in predicting their status on the other.

The example we used to begin this chapter was decidedly unrealistic, since we assumed that we could secure measurements of the anxiety and problem-solving ability of everyone in the population. In real life, the opportunity to measure everyone in the population of interest is extremely rare. Far more often, we can obtain measurements only for some sample of persons that we hope is representative of the population of interest. Using the data gathered from our sample, we must make an inference to the population in order to decide whether two variables are statistically independent or statistically dependent. These are the kinds of inferences we consider in this chapter.

When dealing with the hypothesis tests involving the statistical independence of two variables, the null hypothesis is always that the two variables are independent. The alternative hypothesis is just the converse: that the two variables are statistically dependent. When the variables under consideration are categorical in nature, as is often the case, the appropriate statistical procedure is called the **chi-square test**.

When a chi-square test of independence is conducted, the statistical procedure is applied to data in the form of a **contingency table**. "Contingency table" is a fancy name for the simplest of two-dimensional tables. The categories of one variable form the rows of the table, and the categories of the other variable form the columns. The cells of the table merely show the numbers of sampled individuals who fall into each category of one variable and each category of the other. Not convinced that it's simple? Look at the following example. Suppose that you sampled 100 children, and it turned out that 55 were boys and 45 were girls. Let's assume that you had each child run a 100-yard dash, and that you categorized each child as fast, medium, or slow, depending on how many seconds the child took to run 100 yards. If 30 children were slow, 40 medium, and 30 fast, the resulting contingency table might be as follows:

	Slow	Medium	Fast	Total
Boys	20	30	5	55
Girls	10	10	25	45
Total	30	40	30	100

From the contingency table you can see that there were 20 slow boys and only 10 slow girls. There were 5 fast boys, and 25 fast girls. In short, the numbers in the body of the table tell you how many of the children in your sample fell into each combination of sex and speed categories.

By looking at the data in the table, it is clear that there were proportionately more fast girls than there were fast boys. For the sample, then, sex and speed for the 100-yard dash are dependent variables. Knowing a child's sex gives you information that is useful in predicting the child's running speed. The corresponding inferential question is whether the same relationship holds for the population from which the sample of 100 children was chosen. Were you to conduct a chi-square test using the data in your contingency table, you would be testing the null hypothesis that, in the population of children, sex and speed in running the 100-yard dash were statistically independent. The alternative hypothesis would be that the two variables were statistically dependent. The more dependent the two variables were in the sample, the larger the chi-square statistic would be. If the statistic was large enough, it would exceed the critical value associated with a selected alpha level, and you would reject the null hypothesis of independence.

In the examples that follow, you will see that tests of statistical independence arise in many different research and evaluation contexts. However, the data are always summarized in the form used in this example and the resulting chi-square tests differ only in numerical detail.

Do Boys and Girls Differ in Average Intellectual Growth During Adolescence?

Purpose of the Study. From the time of Lewis Terman's famous longitudinal studies of genius in the 1930s to Hernstein's studies of the correlates of intelligence in the 1970s, it has been apparent that the IQ-test performances of adolescent boys tend to be relatively stable while the IQ-test performances of adolescent girls tend to decline. In this study, Campbell (1974) investigated the phenomenon further and explored the possibility of personality differences between girls whose early adolescent IQ scores declined and girls whose early IQ scores were sustained. She was particularly interested in evidence that social expectations accounted for the IQ score decline among some girls.

Research Design. Campbell secured two sets of IQ-test scores for 471 high school seniors who attended one of two public high schools or two parochial schools in New York. She selected the schools purposefully, and was careful to obtain data from all sections of the state and from schools that varied in the urbanism of their attendance areas. The students for whom she obtained data volunteered to participate in her study, but she reports that only two refused to participate when asked. Although the population to which one might generalize Campbell's results is not clear from her study, the possibility of biased sampling due to the use of volunteer students would seem to be remote.

Campbell examined the school records of the high school seniors in her sample to determine their IQ-test scores during the seventh grade (her definition of the beginning of adolescence). She then had each student complete the same type of IQ test he or she had completed as a seventh-grader. Most of the students completed the Otis Quick Scoring Mental Abilities Test, and the others completed the Lorge-Thorndike Intelligence Test. In addition, Campbell had the girls in her sample complete several personality and attitude instruments.

Author's Data Table. Campbell determined the standard error of measurement of the tests used in her study by consulting appropriate test publishers' technical reports. She then classified each high school senior as an IQ gainer, an IQ loser, or as a person whose IQ remained constant, depending on whether the difference between their seventh-grade and twelfth-grade IQ-test scores was, respectively, a positive change that exceeded one standard error of measurement, a negative change that exceeded one standard error of measure, or a change in either direction that was less than one standard error of measurement.

TABLE 12.1: The Number of Young Men and Women Experiencing Changes in IQ Scores Greater Than the Standard Error of Measurement Over Adolescence

	Gained (No./%)	Lost (No./%)	Remained Constant (No./%)
Young Men	60/33.2	40/22.2	81/44.6
Young Women	56/19.3	84/29.0	150/51.7

*The differences between groups are significant: $\chi^2 = 11.77$, df = 2 $\boxed{p < .005}$ — *rejecting null* $@$ .005

$(r-1)(c-1)$ 2×3 *table*.

Table 2 (p. 5) of Campbell's paper reports the number and percentage of young men and young women in her study who were classified as having lost, gained, or remained constant in IQ, from the seventh grade to the twelfth grade. Campbell's Table 2 is reproduced here, just as it appeared in her paper, as Table 12.1.

Author's Interpretation. In another analysis of her data, which we shall not discuss in detail, Campbell tested the null hypothesis that the average change in IQ-test score was the same, for the populations of girls and boys. She used a two-sample *t*-test, similar to those discussed in Chapter 10. Her interpretation of the results shown in Table 12.1 is combined with an interpretation of the results of the *t*-test.

Campbell points out that 19.3% of the young women gained in IQ during adolescence, while 33.2% of the young men gained over the same period. She also notes that 29.0% of the young women declined in IQ score, while only 22.2% of the young men experienced an IQ decline. She concludes that the patterns of IQ loss and gain for boys and girls were significantly different at an alpha level of .005. She states:

> It would thus appear that the first hypothesis was substantiated and that during adolescence young women declined in intellectual abilities, as measured by IQ scores, in greater numbers and to a greater degree than did young men. (p. 5)

The Nature of the Inference. In Table 12.1, Campbell presents not only sample statistics on the numbers and proportions of adolescent boys and girls who gained, lost, or remained constant in

IQ-test score, she reports the results of a chi-square test of the null hypothesis that sex and change in IQ score are independent variables. The inferential results are summarized in the footnote to the table.

The chi-square statistic (represented by the Greek letter X with a "2" one-half line above it) was reported as 11.77. Without going into the derivation of this statistic, it might be useful to outline its origins. Suppose that we had data on the sex and change in IQ of every adolescent in the population of interest. Assume further that we used these data to construct a two-way table like Table 12.1. If sex and change in IQ were statistically independent variables, the proportions of adolescents represented in each cell of our constructed table would have a specific relationship to the proportions represented in each row and each column of the table. In fact, the proportion in each cell could be found by multiplying the proportion in that cell's row by the proportion in that cell's column. For example, suppose that 50% of the adolescents in the population were boys, and 50% were girls. In that case, the proportion in the boys' row would be .5 as would the proportion in the girls' row. If 30% of all adolescents had gained in IQ, the proportion in the gainers' column of the table would be .3. If sex and change in IQ were statistically independent, the proportion of boys who gained in IQ would equal .15. We found that number by multiplying .5 (the proportion of boys in the population) by .3 (the proportion of IQ gainers in the population). If the variables that define the rows and columns are statistically independent, the proportion in every cell of a two-way table constructed from data for an entire population will equal the product of the proportion of cases in the cell's row and the proportion of cases in the cell's column.

Notice that the discussion in the last paragraph assumed that we had data for every adolescent in our population of interest. In reality, we're far more likely to have data for only a sample of adolescents. We would then construct a table like Table 12.1 using our sample data. Now even if the proportion of cases in each cell of a table constructed from data for an entire population was equal to the product of appropriate row and column proportions, we might not find the same relationships in a table constructed from data for a sample. You know that data fluctuate from sample to sample, and that sample results don't represent population results perfectly. The chi-square statistic compares actual sample results with what would be expected, if the variables used to construct the table were statistically independent in the population, and the sample results represented the population data perfectly. The greater the differences between the actual sample proportions and the proportions that would be expected if the variables were statistically independent, the larger the chi-square statistic gets. The larger the chi-square statistic, the less likely it is that the variables are statistically independent in the population. If the statistic becomes so large that the probability of having statistically independent variables is extremely small, we reject the null hypothesis of independence. Just like the statistics you've encountered in earlier chapters (e.g., the z-statistic and the t-statistic), the chi-square statistic has a known frequency distribution. It is possible to refer to this frequency distribution and define the critical value associated with any desired alpha level. If the chi-square statistic computed from the sample data is larger than the critical value associated with our selected alpha level, we reject the null hypothesis of statistical independence in favor of the alternative hypothesis that the variables are statistically dependent.

In describing the chi-square statistic and its distribution, we've oversimplified a bit. There is actually a whole family of chi-square distributions. The one we use in deciding whether to reject a null hypothesis of independence depends on the number of rows and columns in our contingency table. Each chi-square distribution is known by its **degrees of freedom**. The origin of this curious term is not important to our discussion. When a chi-square statistic is used to determine whether two variables are statistically independent, degrees of freedom will always depend on the number of rows and columns in the contingency table. In particular, its degrees of freedom will equal (number of rows − 1) × (number of columns − 1). Notice that Table 12.1 has two rows and three columns. Campbell's chi-square statistic should therefore have (2 − 1) × (3 − 1) = 1 × 2 degrees of freedom. The part of the footnote to her table that says "df = 2" indicates the two degrees of freedom.

When Campbell tested the null hypothesis that sex and change in IQ score were independent in the population from which her sample had been selected, she rejected the null hypothesis at the .005 level of significance. You can tell that by noting the "$p < .005$" in her footnote. To reach her conclusion, Campbell compared her computed chi-square value (11.77) with a table of critical values of the chi-square distribution for two degrees of freedom. Her value was larger than the critical value for an alpha level of .005.

As we have already noted, it is difficult to identify the population to which Campbell intends to generalize her findings. She candidly reports that schools were selected for her study, in part, because they had the sort of data she needed and were willing to participate. In addition, student participants were volunteers. Campbell selected her schools from widely varying geographic areas, different types of control (public and parochial), and different levels of urbanism. This approach ensures that generalizability will not be severely restricted, but it does not ensure representativeness. In her interpretation of results, one might infer that Campbell would like to generalize her findings either to all adolescents in New York state or to all adolescents in the United States. There is little information in her paper that clearly supports or refutes such generalization.

Our Interpretation of Results. We have already sprinkled editorial comments liberally in our discussions of the design of Campbell's study and the nature of the inferences she treats. There is very little to add.

Campbell's operational definitions of IQ gainers, IQ losers, and those with constant IQ scores seem quite sensible to us. It would be foolhardy to define as a "gainer" everyone whose IQ score increased at all, regardless of the size of the gain. It is well known that IQ tests are less than perfectly reliable, and that some gain or loss will occur on retesting, due to error of measurement. By using a criterion of a gain larger than the standard error of measurement to define a "gainer," and a loss larger than the standard error of measurement to define a "loser," Campbell has appropriately handled the problem of the unreliability of IQ tests.

The use of seventh grade as an operational definition of the beginning of adolescence and the twelfth grade as an operational definition of the end of adolescence is certainly subject to challenge. The age ranges of students in these grades are fairly large; and ages of maturity vary substantially across adolescents. We cannot suggest an alternative design that would have handled these problems more effectively without being very complicated. But it would have been helpful to report the age distributions of the students when they were tested as seventh-graders and as twelfth-graders.

In a data table that we have not discussed, Campbell reports that young men gained an average of 1.62 IQ score points and that young women lost an average of 1.33 points. This difference is fairly small, despite its statistical significance. The data in Table 12.1 appear more convincing to us. The relationship between sex and change in IQ score is clearly statistically significant. The sample data suggest substantively important sex differences as well. Fourteen percent more boys than girls were IQ gainers, and 7% more girls than boys were IQ losers. These are large differences whose significance goes beyond the rejection of a null hypothesis. Causes should be sought, and if at all possible, ameliorating treatment should be applied.

We will not discuss the generalization of this study's findings to other contexts, since specific programs or treatments are not involved.

In-Level Versus Out-of-Level Testing of Special Education Students

Purpose of the Study. Publishers of standardized achievement tests provide different levels of their tests for use in various grades. For example, Level 16 of Form E of the California Achievement Tests is intended for use with sixth-graders, Level 15 for use with fifth-graders, and so on. Different levels within the same test series typically incorporate subtests with the same title (e.g., Reading Comprehension, Arithmetic Computation, etc.), but the levels differ in their specific content, the difficulty of their items, and the reading ability they require.

U.S. schools commonly promote students from grade to grade on the basis of their ages as much as their abilities. As a result, many sixth-graders read no better than the average third- or fourth-grader. Such students have great difficulty with levels of standardized tests intended for their grade (called in-level tests) and, in fact, do no better than would be expected had they merely chosen a response to each of the test's multiple-choice items by guessing at random. In-level tests are particularly troublesome for many special education students.

Cleland and Idstein (1980) examined the use of out-of-level tests with special education students. (A test that is intended for students in a grade below the examinee's current grade is called an out-of-level test.) In particular, the authors investigated the largely untested claim that measurement validity could be increased by administering tests that were one to two grades below special education students' current grade levels. They reasoned that measurement validity would be increased if the use of out-of-level tests resulted in a larger proportion of students whose scores were above the "chance level." The chance level is the score students would be expected to earn had they guessed randomly in choosing their response to each test item.

Research Design. Cleland and Idstein administered the Reading Vocabulary, Reading Comprehension, and Math Computation subtests of the 1977 edition of the California Achievement Tests (CAT) to 74 sixth-grade special education students in two elementary schools. They randomly assigned students to each of six groups that differed in the levels and order of the tests administered. The first group of students received Level 16 (the sixth-grade level) of the tests, followed by Level 15 (the fifth-grade level). The second group received the same tests, but in reverse order. The third group received Level 16 of the tests, followed by Level 14 (the fourth-grade level). The fourth group received the same tests as the third group, but in reverse order. The fifth and sixth groups of students received Levels 14 and 15 of the tests. Group Five received Level 15 first, and Group Six received Level 14 first. Sixth-grade teachers administered the tests as a part of their school district's regular testing program, after receiving instructions on the nature of the experiment and proper procedures for test administration. All students who did not complete two tests in sequence were eliminated from the study.

Authors' Data Table. The authors determined that order of test administration had an effect on students' performance only for the Reading Comprehension subtest. They therefore restricted their analyses of Reading Comprehension results to students' scores on the first test of each two-test sequence. For the other two subtests (Reading Vocabulary and Math Computation) they combined data for a given test level, regardless of whether students had received that level first or second in the testing sequence.

TABLE 12.2: Contingency Tables for Reading Comprehension, Reading Vocabulary and Math Computation at the Chance Level

	Test Level			
	I	O_1	O_2	Totals
I Reading Comprehension				
Chance	6	5	5	16
Above Chance	17	19	21	57
Total	23	24	26	73
II Reading Vocabulary				
Chance	17	12	12	41
Above Chance	31	38	38	107
Total	48	50	50	148
III Math Computation				
Chance	2	2	4	8
Above Chance	26	26	28	80
Total	28	28	32	88

Table 5 in the Cleland and Idstein paper (p. 8) contains a contingency table for each of the three subtests used in their study. Students are classified as scoring at or below the chance level (labeled "Chance") or "Above Chance" on each of three test levels. Level "I" denotes the in-level test battery (Level 16); Level "O_1" denotes the out-of-level test intended for fifth-graders (Level 15); and Level "O_2" denotes the out-of-level test intended for fourth-graders (Level 14). Table 5 is reproduced here, exactly as it appears in the Cleland and Idstein paper, as Table 12.2.

Author's Interpretation. Table 12.2 presents only one of several analyses Cleland and Idstein conducted in their investigation of the effects of out-of-level testing on the test performance of special education students. However, we will restrict our attention to Table 12.2, and their interpretation of the results contained in that table. The authors state that the chi-square analyses of data in the contingency tables shown in Table 12.2 "were not significant for Reading Comprehension ($\chi^2 = .360$, df 2, $p > .05$), Reading Vocabulary ($\chi^2 = 1.55$, df 2, $p > .05$) or Math Computation ($\chi^2 = .707$, df 2, $p > .05$). . . . Therefore, more students did not score above chance level as a result of taking an out-of-level test." In short, the authors conclude that out-of-level testing does not significantly increase the percentage of special education students who score above the chance level on standardized tests. In their summary, they advise caution in using out-of-level tests with special education students.

The Nature of the Inference. Cleland and Idstein have tested three null hypotheses in their analysis of the data shown in Table 12.2. First, for the Reading Comprehension subtest of the CAT they tested the null hypothesis that the percentage of special education students scoring at or above the chance level was statistically independent of the level of the test used. The alternative hypothesis was that scoring level (at or below chance versus above chance) and test level were statistically dependent. Second, they tested the same null and alternative hypotheses for the Reading Vocabulary subtest of the CAT. Finally, they examined the same hypotheses for the Math Computation subtest of the CAT. A chi-square test of independence was employed in testing each hypothesis. Since each contingency table in Table 12.2 has two rows and three columns, the appropriate degrees of freedom for each hypothesis test are $(2 - 1)(3 - 1) = 2$, as the authors note in their "df 2" statements. The "$p > .05$" comments in the authors' parenthetical summaries of the chi-square tests indicates that a Type I error level (alpha) of .05 was used for each hypothesis test.

It is clear just by looking at the contingency tables that, for the sample of students used in the experiment, test level has little relationship with the proportion of students who score at or above chance. For each subtest, the numbers of students listed in the "Chance" row is fairly constant, regardless of the level of test used. The same is true for the numbers of students listed in the "Above Chance" row of each table.

In testing their null hypotheses, Cleland and Idstein are attempting to generalize to some population of special education students. Each null hypothesis states that scoring level and test level are statistically independent variables in some population of special education students. Since Cleland and Idstein give very little information on the students used in their study, it is difficult to generalize from their findings. They tell us that students in their study were classified as "special education students," and were enrolled in the sixth grade in one of two elementary schools in the New Castle, Delaware County School District. However, they give no information on how the two elementary schools were selected, how students were selected within the two schools, or the basis for designating students as "special education students." Presumably, there is some population of special education students to which the authors' findings generalize. That population cannot be defined clearly from the information given in the paper.

Our Interpretation of Results. Cleland and Idstein have investigated an important and interesting problem. The selection of appropriate levels of standardized tests for special education students is a difficult problem facing administrators and testing coordinators in many school systems. From the data shown in the Table 12.2, it appears that use of out-of-level tests might not be helpful.

We have already noted the difficulty in generalizing from the results of this study, and will not belabor the point further. We have one additional quarrel with the authors' methodological procedures. One of the requirements of the chi-square test is that the numbers in the contingency table represent different individuals or units. For example, the six students listed as scoring at or below the chance level when given Reading Comprehension Test Level I should not be the same students as the five listed as scoring at or below the chance level when given Reading Comprehension Test Level O_1. For the Reading Comprehension data shown in Cleland and Idstein's table, this requirement is satisfied since they only used data for the test administered first in each testing sequence. However, the chi-square analyses of data for the Reading Vocabulary and Math Computation tests are suspect because the numbers shown in different cells of the contingency tables represent the same students. For example, a given student might have scored "Above Chance" when he or she completed Level I of the Reading Vocabulary subtest, and at "Chance" when completing Level O_1 of that subtest. Since each student's performance is reflected twice in the contingency tables for Reading Vocabulary and Math Computation, the numbers in those tables cannot come from independent samples. One of the basic requirements of the chi-square test has thus been violated, and any interpretation of the Reading Vocabulary or Math Computation data Table 12.2 is suspect.

Generalizing to Another Setting. Even if the problems we have noted did not exist, several strong assumptions would be required in order to generalize the results of the Cleland and Idstein study to another setting. You would have to assume that the sample of students used in the study fairly represented the special education students in the other school system. You would be generalizing across settings, definitions of special education, and, most likely, grade levels and test batteries. The study provides no assurance that similar results would have been found for students in some grade other than the sixth, or for test batteries other than the California Achievement Tests. "Special education student" is a broad label. It means very different things in different school systems. In some states it includes gifted students, and in others only students who are mentally retarded, physically handicapped, or emotionally disturbed. Despite these limitations, the authors' recommendation of caution in using out-of-level tests with special education students is consistent with their findings. However, this study is less than definitive, and you would be well advised to seek additional evidence before concluding that out-of-level testing of special education students is unwarranted, and will typically lead to the same results as in-level tests.

Evaluation of a Chapter I Supplementary Reading Program

Purpose of the Study. Lewis (1985) reported the results of an evaluation of the supplementary reading program for elementary school students that was operated by the Cincinnati, Ohio, Public Schools under Chapter I of the Education Consolidation and Improvement Act (ECIA). As noted earlier, the ECIA is the successor to the Elementary and Secondary Education Act of 1965, a federal law through which school systems receive funds to provide supplementary instruction to educationally disadvantaged children in schools serving large proportions of pupils from economically disadvantaged families.

The purpose of this study was to determine whether the Growth in Academic Performance Component of the ECIA Chapter I program had achieved a variety of objectives specified in federal guidelines and by school system personnel. In particular, the federal guidelines provide the following goal for ECIA Chapter I reading programs (Lewis, 1985):

Project children who are in Growth in Academic Performance classes for a full year will gain, on average, seven (7) normal curve equivalents in reading achievement in the six (6) months between administrations of a nationally recognized reading test. (p. 3)

The Cincinnati Public Schools' objectives for the project were as follows:

1. Project pupils will have as positive attitudes toward themselves as nonproject pupils.

2. Project pupils will have as positive attitudes toward school as nonproject pupils.

3. Opportunities for parent involvement will be provided through these means: (1) District Advisory Council and local school councils, (2) home and school visits, (3) inservice training, (4) volunteer service for school activities, and (5) workshops.

4. Inservice training will be provided for all project personnel continuously throughout the school year. Parents are invited and encouraged to participate in these inservice meetings. (p. 3)

In this example, we will restrict our attention to the methods used to examine the second of the objectives specified by the Cincinnati Public Schools.

Evaluation Design. Under the Growth in Academic Performance component of the ECIA Chapter I program, supplementary reading teachers and instructional assistants were provided in 51 public schools and 26 nonpublic schools in Cincinnati. The schools selected for service were those with student bodies that exceeded the systemwide average proportion of children who received free or reduced-price lunches, or with at least 25% of their pupils eligible to participate in the Chapter I program because their scores on a standardized reading achievement test were below the 34th percentile of an appropriate national norm distribution.

Children served by the project were in Grades 1 through 6, but were heavily concentrated in Grades 1 and 2. On average, 4,245 children in public schools and 646 children in nonpublic schools were served each month. Eligible children in nonpublic schools were selected for the project provided their school was within the attendance area of an eligible public school.

The project provided participating children with 45 to 50 minutes per day of supplementary reading instruction. Each Chapter I teacher worked with five or six groups of 5 to 8 children per day, and coordinated his or her instruction with each child's regular classroom teacher. The instructional rooms used for the Chapter I project contained a variety of "appropriate and stimulating reading materials to capture the interest of the children. Through the year, children were given several reading books through the 'Reading is Fun-damental' program to develop interest in reading as a personally satisfying experience" (Lewis, 1985, p. 6).

To evaluate the second of the local project objectives concerned with children's attitudes toward school, each project school "identified the regular classroom at each grade level which contained the highest proportion of project children" (Lewis, p. 10). An attitude survey called the "Smiles Survey" was administered to all children in the selected classrooms. The survey contained three sets of items that purportedly addressed children's attitudes toward self, attitudes toward school, and attitudes toward learning. We will consider only the second set of items, since analyses of results for the other two sets paralleled those used with the second set.

Author's Data Table. Table 5 in the Lewis study, containing percentages of Chapter I students and nonproject students who responded positively ("Smile") and negatively ("Frown") to each of six items on the Smiles Survey concerned with students' attitudes toward school, is reproduced here in its original form as Table 12.3. The table appeared on page 12 of Lewis's report.

Author's Interpretation. In interpreting the results shown in his table, Lewis commented as follows:

> The responses of the project and nonproject children to items concerning school are given in Table 5 [Table 12.3 here]. Project children were significantly more positive on one of the six items in this section. They felt better about the rules at their school. The nonproject children were significantly more positive on three of the six items. The nonproject children felt better about the way they were treated by their teacher, felt better about their school and were less likely to want to change their schools. The results show that overall, the nonproject children were more positive about school than the project children. The objective on attitudes toward school was not met in the primary grades, and an additional analysis indicated that both project and nonproject students gave lower responses than last year on five of the six items in this section. (p. 10)

TABLE 12.3: Results of the Attitudes Toward School Items, Smiles Survey, Primary Grades, 1984–85

	Chapter 1 Students		Nonproject Students		Chi-Square	Signif. Level
	Smile (N = 1525)	Frown	Smile (N = 1929)	Frown		
1. How do you feel when it's time to go to school?	61%	39%	58%	42%	3.3	ns*
2. How do you feel about your school?	79%	21%	83%	17%	7.9	p < .01
3. How do you feel about the way your teacher treats you?	72%	28%	77%	23%	11.8	p < .001
4. How do you feel about the rules at your school?	67%	33%	64%	36%	4.5	p < .05
5. How do you feel about going to some other school?	47%	53%	39%	61%	22.5	p < .001
6. How do you feel about asking your teacher for help?	85%	15%	85%	15%	0	ns*

*ns = not significant

And in his summary to the evaluation report, Lewis stated:

Attitudes of Chapter I students toward self, school, and learning were not as high as nonproject children at similar grade levels. Discrepancies between responses by these two groups were not great in magnitude, but the objective calling for equivalent attitudes was not achieved.

Based upon these findings, the following recommendations are presented for consideration by project administrators:

a. Additional attention should be given to improving the attitudes and self-concept of students in this project. (p. 19)

The Nature of the Inferences. Lewis tested six separate null hypotheses to produce the results shown in his table. For each of the six questions listed in Table 12.3, he tested the null hypothesis that the two variables, project participation status (participant vs. nonparticipant) and attitude (positive or negative) were statistically independent. His alternative hypothesis in each test was that the two variables were statistically dependent. Although Lewis displayed the data for each hypothesis test in a single row of Table 12.3, when he tested each hypothesis he treated his data as though they were contained in a contingency table with two rows and two columns. From the sample sizes and percentages shown for the first question in Table 12.3, Lewis's first contingency table can be reproduced as follows:

	Number of Smiles	Number of Frowns
Chapter 1 Students	930	473
Nonproject Students	1119	810

A similar contingency table could be constructed from the data displayed in each row of Table 12.3, and the chi-square test of independence would be applied to each of these contingency tables, just as in the earlier examples in this chapter.

Although Lewis did not specify the level of significance (alpha) he used in testing the six hypotheses he examined, we can infer from Table 12.3 the largest alpha level that he used as a criterion of statistical significance from the values shown in his "Signif. Level" column. Since the largest value in that column is "$p < .05$," we can assume that the two statistical tests marked "n.s.*" produced results that were not statistically significant for an alpha of .05. Notice that Lewis chose not to report the results of his statistical tests as merely "significant at an alpha of .05" or "not significant at an alpha of .05." Instead, he reported for each test the smallest alpha level at which the results were statistically significant. For example, for Question 3, "How do you feel about the way your teacher treats you?", Lewis reported "$p < .001$," indicating that he would have rejected the null hypothesis that students' project participation status and attitude were statistically independent even with a Type I error level of .001.

In most research and evaluation reports that include the results of hypothesis tests, the ubiquitous asterisk (*) is used to indicate a finding of statistical significance, with multiple asterisks used to indicate smaller Type I error levels. In contrast to this common practice, Lewis has chosen to footnote his nonsignificant results and to indicate the smallest alpha level corresponding to each of his statistically significant results. Although this notation is a bit unusual, it should not be confusing in the context of Table 12.3.

Our Interpretation of Results. This aspect of Lewis's study leaves much to be desired, both methodological and substantively. First, despite findings of statistical significance for four of the six questions in the Smiles Survey concerning students' attitudes toward school, the differences in percentages of Chapter I students and nonproject students who marked "smile" were typically trivial. These results thus illustrate a situation in which differences between students in an experimental group and a comparison group were statistically significant, but not substantively significant. Lewis's findings of statistical significance are, for the most part, an artifact of the very large samples of students who responded to his survey. With 1525 Chapter I students and 1929 nonproject students, very small differences between these samples would support the contention that the populations from which the samples were selected must differ as well. That is, a small amount of statistical dependence for the sample data will lead to rejection of the null hypothesis of independence for the population from which the sample was selected. However, the amount of dependence in the population might well be trivially small and substantively insignificant.

Second, although Lewis found that a significantly smaller percentage of students who participated in the Chapter I project than nonproject students marked "Smiles" for three of the six questions (Questions 2, 3, and 5), his evaluation design does not permit the attribution of these differences to the Chapter I project. Other than their assignment to classes that enrolled large proportions of project participants, Lewis tells us little about the characteristics of children who participated and did not participate in the Chapter I project. We know that the Chapter I students had lower reading scores than did the nonproject participants, but we know nothing about the other aspects of their lives that might substantially influence their attitudes toward school and their teachers. It might well be the case that the Chapter I students were from families that were more economically deprived, more frequently from single-parent households, more frequently residing in neighborhoods that affected their general attitudes toward life, and so forth, than were the nonproject students. In short, since the Chapter I students were not randomly selected from the population of students at the schools examined in Lewis's study, one cannot rule out the strong possibility that some factor other than participation in the Chapter I project results in their more frequent tendency to mark "Frown" in response to Questions 2 and 3, and a presumably negative "Smile" in response to Question 5. There remains the additional issue of how negative these students' attitudes would have been, had they not participated in the Chapter I project. It is possible that the Chapter I project had a substantial effect on the attitudes toward school of the participating students, even though a somewhat smaller percentage of them marked "Smile" in response to some of the questions.

Our third concern involves an important measurement issue. Presumably the Smiles Survey would have us interpret a large proportion of smiles in response to Question 5, "How do you feel about going to some other school?" as an indicator that the responding children have a negative attitude toward school. However, the validity of this inference is questionable. If a child responds "Smile" when answering this question, that response could be interpreted in a variety of ways in addition to the obvious interpretation that the child is unhappy with his or her present school. Perhaps the child looks forward to the adventure associated with new surroundings, or the possibility of meeting new students and making new friends. Or, the child knows that a brand new school has been built in another part of the city and wants the opportunity to attend that school. In short, the inference derived from the interpretation that the test constructors intended is not the only plausible one, and the validity of their inference is questionable. We raise this issue to remind you of the importance of measurement validity when the results of a research or evaluation study are interpreted. You should routinely think about the measurement instruments used in the study, the evaluation provided by the author concerning the validity of those instruments for the purposes and desired interpretations of the study, and the plausible rival interpretations of the results in response to those instruments.

Thinking further about the questions in the Smiles Survey, consider Questions 3 and 6. These questions ask students about their feelings toward their teacher. These questions are potentially confusing for the Chapter I students in Lewis's study, since these students had two teachers—a regular classroom teacher and a Chapter I reading teacher. It is not possible to tell which of these two teachers the Chapter I students were thinking of when they answered Questions 3 and 6, or whether the questions were so perplexing that their confusion influenced their responses. In this case, lack of clarity in the statement of the questions (as the survey was used in this evaluation) raises an important validity concern.

Finally, we hesitate to raise a statistical issue that you'll probably wish we hadn't (since it's a bit complicated) and, perhaps, we'll wish we'd left alone as well. But plunging courageously ahead, we'll bring it up anyway. The issue can be illustrated as follows. Suppose you were to test 100 independent null hypotheses, each with a Type I error level (alpha) of .05. How many of these null hypotheses would you expect to reject falsely, even if they were all true? To find the answer, remind yourself that an alpha of .05 means that you are incurring a 5% risk of deciding that a finding is statistically significant, even when the null hypothesis (of no difference, or no effect, or statistical independence) is true. Since 5% of 100 is 5, the answer is that you would expect to reject falsely 5 of the 100 null hypotheses.

Now Lewis has tested only six null hypotheses in Table 5, not 100 of them. He used an alpha level of .05 for each of his null hypotheses, which means that the probability he would not commit a Type I error for any single test was (1 − .05) or .95. Had his tests been independent of each other (i.e., had each of them been based on a different sample of students), the probability that Lewis would have committed no Type I errors for any of his six tests can be found by multiplying the probability of no Type I error for each test—.95 times .95 times .95, and so forth—until all six .95 values had been multiplied together. The resulting value would be 0.735. This is the probability that none of Lewis's six hypothesis tests would have resulted in a Type I error being committed. That is, for none of the six tests would Lewis have concluded that project participation status and students' attitudes toward school or their teacher were dependent variables, when they were actually independent variables. Now, the probability that Lewis would have committed a Type I error in one or more of his six tests can be found by subtracting 0.735 from 1 (1 − .735) =

.265. So, by conducting six hypothesis tests, each with a Type I error probability (alpha) of .05, Lewis has incurred a large risk (.265, which is larger than .25, or one in four chances) that he will commit a Type I error for at least one of his tests. We chose to discuss this problem, despite its obvious complications, not because Lewis's study is fatally flawed or particularly unusual in this regard. Rather, the problem of increased risk of finding statistically significant results when the null hypothesis is true (a Type I error), as a consequence of conducting a large number of hypothesis tests, arises in many research and evaluation studies. You should be aware of this problem and the associated danger of being misled (along with an unsuspecting author who is not as statistically erudite as you).

Assumptions Needed to Generalize. To safely generalize these results of Lewis' study to some other population you would have to assume that the other population, and the conditions of instruction of that population, were similar to those found in Lewis's sample. As noted in the preceding section, students' attitudes toward school are produced by a multiplicity of factors that operate inside and outside their schools. Since Lewis provides little background information on the students in his sample, it would be difficult to determine whether some other population was comparable to his sample in ways that are likely to influence students' attitudes toward school.

Clearly, the Chapter I experiences of the students in Lewis's sample constitute a relatively small portion of their typical school day. So understanding the limits of generalization of his findings would require knowledge of the regular education program these students experienced, as well as the nature of their Chapter I experiences. Lewis does a good job of describing the structure of the Chapter I reading program in the Cincinnati Public Schools, but does not provide any information on the regular instructional program in these schools. Therefore, generalization of his findings to some other population of students and schools would require explicit assumptions concerning comparability even though he provides little supporting information. Generalization in these circumstances is obviously perilous. In defense of the Lewis study, it should be noted that the author probably intended that his results be generalized only to the population of Cincinnati Public

School students in the year he conducted his study or, at most, to populations of such students in succeeding years.

Summary

We have examined three research and evaluation studies in this chapter that were concerned, at least in part, with the statistical independence of two or more variables. In each of these studies, the authors displayed their sample data in the form of one or more contingency tables (two-way tables in which one variable formed the rows of the table and the other formed the columns). A chi-square test was used to arrive at a decision on whether the variables were statistically independent or dependent in the population from which the sampled persons had been selected.

As you read the research and evaluation literature in your area of specialty, you will find many studies that are similar to those we have discussed here. Whenever you see a contingency table together with associated chi-square values, you can assume that the author has conducted a test concerned with statistical independence. Hopefully, by reading the paper or report, you will be able to determine not only what was done, but whether or not it was appropriate. We also hope you will be able to discern whether the author's interpretation of results is sensible and consistent with the supporting data. Once again, we wish you happy hunting.

Problems — Chapter 12

Jefferson and Jackson (1842) conducted a study of the relationship between voters' political party affiliation and their position on extension of the Voting Rights Act of 1834. They surveyed a random sample of 100 Republicans, 100 Democrats, and 100 Independents, and reported the following results:

	Republicans	Democrats	Independents
In Favor of the Voting Rights Act	30	90	80
Opposed to the Voting Rights Act	70	10	20

*Chi-square (2 df) = 93.0; signif. @ .05 level.

12.1 What null hypothesis were Jefferson and Jackson testing?

12.2 To what population were Jefferson and Jackson attempting to generalize their results?

12.3 Assuming that they acted in accordance with their findings, did Jefferson and Jackson retain or reject their null hypothesis? Support your conclusion by citing relevant data.

12.4 In a study on the relationship between academic major and attitudes toward education, Vetters and Clark (1980) administered a standardized attitude scale to independent samples of 50 students with each of four academic majors: sociology, psychology, education, and political science. They classified each student as having a "positive attitude," "neutral attitude," or "negative attitude." In reporting their results, the authors stated: "The chi-square on 6 df equaled 7.04, which was not significant at the 0.10 level."

a. What null hypothesis were the authors testing in this study?
b. What decision did the authors reach on retaining or rejecting their null hypothesis?
c. Making assumptions that you consider to be appropriate, interpret the results of this study in your own words.

13.

One-Way Analysis of Variance

The Nature of the Inferences

In Chapter 10, on Inferences Involving Averages, we discussed a number of research studies and evaluations in which the investigators tested the null hypothesis that two populations had the same average. In this chapter we'll also consider studies in which the investigator wants to compare population averages. However, the statistical procedures used in these studies permit more than two population averages to be compared at the same time.

As an example, suppose that you were considering the installation of a program in a school system. Three commercial text publishers had tried to convince you that theirs was not only the most effective program, but the flashiest and most interesting as well. When you compared costs, you found that all three programs were competitive, so that effectiveness would have to be the deciding factor in selecting one of the three. Since computer literacy was to be introduced in grade four, you wanted to select the best program for all fourth-graders. You defined "best" as the program that would produce the highest average score on a test of knowledge of basic computer operations. The average was to be based on the performance of all fourth-graders in the school system.

In this hypothetical example you are really interested in the relative sizes of the three population averages. Let's label the three curricula A, B, and C (isn't that novel and creative of us?). Now you really want to know what the average score on the test of computer operations would have been if the entire population of fourth-graders in the school system had been taught using Curriculum A; what the population average would have been had they been taught using Curriculum B; and what the population average would have been as a result of using Curriculum C. Presumably, you would select the curriculum that resulted in the highest average fourth-grade score on the test of basic computer operations.

One statistical approach to this problem is to hypothesize that the population averages would have been identical, regardless of the curriculum used. The logical alternative to this hypothesis is that the three population averages differ. The statistical procedure used to test the null hypothesis of identical population averages against the alternative hypothesis that the population averages differ is called the **Analysis of Variance**, often abbreviated ANOVA. Although ANOVA is intended for use in testing hypotheses involving three or more population averages, it is also an alternative to the *t*-test for independent samples, when testing the null hypothesis that two population averages are equal. You will encounter several examples of the application of analysis of variance to two populations later in this chapter.

Many evaluation reports and research papers discuss problems that are similar in form to our hypothetical example on computer literacy. The number of curricula to be compared (or, more generally, the number of population averages to be compared) might differ, but the general structure of the problems will be virtually identical. The null hypotheses will state or imply that some number of populations have identical averages. The alternative hypotheses will state or imply the inequality of at least two population averages. In testing the null hypothesis against the alternative, the researchers will proceed as though they had collected data on random samples of individuals, selected from each of the populations of interest. Using ANOVA, the variation in the averages of these samples, from one sample to the next, will be compared to the variation among individual observations within each of the samples. A statistic termed an *F*-ratio will be computed. It will summarize the variation among sample averages, compared to the variation among individual observations within samples. This *F*-statistic will be compared to tabulated critical values that correspond to selected alpha levels. If the computed value of the *F*-statistic is larger than the critical value, the null hypothesis of equal population averages will be rejected in favor of the alternative that the population averages differ.

In the examples that follow, we will describe the null hypotheses and alternative hypotheses in detail, and give considerable attention to the methods the authors used in deciding whether or not to reject their null hypotheses of equal population averages.

In-Level Versus Out-of-Level Testing of Special Education Students

Purpose of the Study. In the preceding chapter (on Inferences Involving Statistical Independence) we discussed a study by Cleland and Idstein (1980) on the use of out-of-level testing with special education students. The authors used several types of statistical analysis, including one-way analysis of variance, in investigating their research questions. We will therefore return to their study here, to consider their exploration of the hypothesis that special education students will demonstrate the same average score, regardless of the level of test used to measure their achievement.

To summarize briefly, the purpose of the Cleland and Idstein study was to determine whether the achievement of special education students could be measured more validly by administering achievement tests that were designed for students who were in lower grade levels (out-of-level tests). The authors reasoned that measurement validity would be greater if fewer students scored below the so-called "chance level" on out-of-level tests than on in-level tests. Additional details on the purposes of the study were provided in the preceding chapter.

Research Design. We will review Cleland and Idstein's research design briefly here, and suggest that you refer to the chapter on Inferences Involving Statistical Independence for additional details. The authors tested 74 special education students from two elementary schools in a Delaware school system. They administered three subtests of the California Achievement Tests (CAT) to each of six randomly assigned groups of students. All tested students were sixth-graders who had completed the Reading Comprehension, Reading Vocabulary, and Mathematics Computation subtests of the CAT. Two of the groups completed sixth-grade tests and tests designed for fifth-graders; two of the groups completed sixth-grade tests and tests designed for fourth-graders; the last two groups completed tests designed for fifth-graders and tests designed for fourth-graders. The order of administration of the tests was reversed within each pair of groups. Sixth-grade teachers administered all tests as a part of the school system's regular testing program.

Authors' Data Tables. Cleland and Idstein reported the results of their hypothesis tests in Table 3 of their paper. However, we will also examine data for their samples, shown in their Table 2. Table 2 reports sample averages (means) and standard deviations (SD's) of scores on all three subtests for students who completed sixth-grade levels of each subtest (labeled "I" for in-level testing), for students who completed fifth-grade levels of the subtests (labeled O_1 for the first set of out-of-level tests), and for students who completed fourth-grade levels of the subtests (labeled O_2 for the second set of out-of-level tests). These sample data will be useful in interpreting the results of analyses of variance, shown in Table 3.

Tables 2 and 3 are reproduced below, exactly as they appeared in the Cleland and Idstein paper on pages 5 and 6, respectively as Tables 13.1 and 13.2.

Authors' Interpretation. In their interpretation of the results shown in Table 13.2, Cleland and Idstein noted that the

> results of the analyses of variance show significant differences for reading comprehension ($F = 3.03$, df 2/143, $p < .05$) and math computation ($F = 4.86$, df 2/85, $p < .01$). Reading vocabulary showed numerical differences but these were not statistically significant ($F = 2.44$, df 2/145, $.05 < p < .10$). . . . In all three subtests, students tested at their assigned grade level scored numerically higher than those tested below grade level. The general trend was that the further one tested out-of-level from grade six, the lower the NCE scores became. (pp. 5-6)

The Nature of the Inference. Table 13.2 summarizes the results of three separate and identical analyses of variance—one for each subtest. In each case, Cleland and Idstein tested the null hypothesis that average achievement test scores would be the same, for the populations of special education students who could have been

TABLE 13.1: Means and Standard Deviations for Reading Comprehension, Reading Vocabulary, and Math Computation Scores

	Test Level					
	I		O_1		O_2	
Test	Mean	SD	Mean	SD	Mean	SD
Reading Comprehension	23.38	(12.97)	23.18	(11.30)	18.26	(10.84)
Reading Vocabulary	25.27	(13.52)	19.66	(12.40)	21.62	(12.21)
Math Computation	27.04	(11.19)	21.36	(11.25)	17.34	(13.38)

TABLE 13.2: Analysis of Variance for Reading Comprehension, Reading Vocabulary, and Math Computation Scores

Test	Source	SS	df	MS	F
Reading Comprehension	Total	20,420	145	—	—
	Between Groups	830	2	415	3.03*
	Within Groups	19,590	143	137	—
Reading Vocabulary	Total	24,220	147	—	—
	Between Groups	792	2	396	2.44
	Within Groups	23,428	145	162	—
Math Computation	Total	13,756	87	—	—
	Between Groups	1,408	2	704	4.86**
	Within Groups	12,348	85	145	—

*$p < .05$
**$p < .01$

tested using the in-level form of the test (I), the fifth-grade level of the test (O_1), and the fourth-grade level of the test (O_2). The alternative hypothesis was that the population averages would differ, for at least one pair of populations (either those tested with I and those tested with O_1, or those tested with I and those tested with O_2, or those tested with O_1 and those tested with O_2).

In our earlier discussion of this study, we noted that Cleland and Idstein were attempting to generalize their results to some population of special education students. We also noted how difficult it would be to identify or describe an appropriate population of generalization because the authors describe neither their sampling procedures nor their samples of tested students. We must be content with the conclusion that out-of-level testing appears to result in significantly lower average performance for some population of sixth-grade special education students on some subtests of the CAT. However, the nature of that population is not clear.

The largest level of significance (alpha level) Cleland and Idstein chose to regard as appropriate for rejection of a null hypothesis was .05. We can discern this from their interpretation of the Reading Comprehension results and the Reading Vocabulary results. In the former case, the F-statistic in the body of the table (3.03) has an asterisk beside it, and the corresponding footnote indicates that the probability of observing an F-statistic at least this large, given that the null hypothesis was true, is less than .05. In the interpretive statement quoted above, the authors did not regard the F-statistic resulting from the Reading Vocabulary analysis to be statistically significant, even though the probability of observing an F-statistic that large or larger was between .05 and .10. Finally, the F-statistic resulting from the analysis of the Math Computation data (4.86) was so large that it exceeded the critical value corresponding to an alpha level of .01. Once again, the footnote "$**p < .01$" provides the necessary evidence.

Without going into a great deal of detail, we think it would be worthwhile to discuss the logic of analysis of variance and the meaning of the overabundant shorthand that appears in Table 13.2. The reasoning behind the analysis of variance is as follows: If two or more populations have identical averages, the averages of random samples selected from those populations ought to be fairly similar as well. The sample averages probably wouldn't be identical simply because of sampling fluctuations. You know that sample statistics vary from one sample to the next, and are rarely equal in value to their corresponding population parameters. However, large differences among the sample averages would cause us to question the hypothesis that the samples were selected from populations with identical averages.

So, in testing the null hypothesis that our samples had been selected from populations that had the same averages, we wouldn't want to reject that hypothesis simply because the sample averages differed by a small amount. The question immediately arises, how much should the sample averages differ before we conclude that the null hypothesis of equal population averages is untenable? In analysis of variance, the answer to this question is obtained by comparing the variation among the sample averages to the variation among observations within each of the samples. Only if the variation among the sample averages is substantially larger than the variation within the samples, do we conclude that the populations must have had different averages.

The various statistics reported in Table 13.2 result from the application of the logic we have just described. We will discuss them one at a time. Note that three sections of Table 13.2 are identical in format. They differ only in the values of their numerical entries, and that is because each section refers to the different subtest. Let's consider the column headings first. The column headed **source** contains three entries "Total," "Between Groups," and "Within Groups." These are three "sources" of variation in the subtest scores of all students who completed each level of the subtests. The next two columns are headed "SS" and "df." The "SS" is shorthand for **sum of squares** and the "df" is shorthand for **degrees of freedom**. The sum of squares is a statistic that reflects variation; the more variable a set of scores, the larger the sum of squares will be. Unfortunately, the sum of squares also depends on sample size, so that it isn't a "pure" indicator of variation. This is where degrees of freedom come in. The numbers in the df column depend on sample size or on how many population averages are being compared, depending on whether we are talking about degrees of freedom *within* groups or *between* groups. For within groups, it's primarily the sample size that determines degrees of freedom; for between groups, it's the number of averages being compared. The degrees of freedom are used to adjust the sums of squares for sample size and number of groups, thereby forming **mean squares** (those are the numbers in the "MS" column). The mean squares can be compared with each other to determine whether most of the variation in the original data is between individuals in the same group, or between the sample averages. The sums of squares can't be compared directly because they depend on sample size as well as on variation.

All this might be sounding a bit thick and pointless by now, but have faith, since we're almost out of column headings. The last one in the table is "*F*." The number in the "*F*" column is called an "*F*-statistic." It's the test statistic used to determine whether the population averages are significantly different. In other words, the

F-statistic is compared to a critical value in an appropriate table to determine whether or not the null hypothesis that all populations have the same average should be rejected. If the computed F-statistic is larger than the critical value that corresponds to a selected alpha level, the null hypothesis is rejected. If the computed F-statistic is smaller than the critical value, the decision must be to stick with the null hypothesis.

Let's discuss the numbers in the top section of Table 13.2. Those in the row labeled "Total" were computed using the Reading Comprehension scores of all 146 students for whom data were available, regardless of the test level the students completed. The 20,420 in the SS column represents all of the variation in the data, regardless of test level. The number in the degrees of freedom associated with the total SS (df) column (145 here) will always equal one less than the total sample size. The numbers in the row headed "Between Groups" result from differences between the averages of the samples being compared. The more the sample averages differ from each other, the larger will be the number in the sum of squares (SS) column. The number of degrees of freedom (df) in the Between Groups row will always equal one less than the number of populations being compared in the study. Since three populations are being compared in this study, df between equals 2. The number in the mean square (MS) column, 415, is just the number in the SS column, 830, divided by the number of degrees of freedom, 2. Stick with it: there's only one more row to talk about, and then you'll know what all of the numbers mean!! All of the numbers in the "Within Groups" row of the table result from variation among the scores of students who are in the same sample. In this example, the more the Reading Comprehension scores of students who completed tests of the same level differ from each other, the bigger the sum of squares (SS) within groups. For example, had there been more variation among the scores of those who completed Level I of the tests, the 19,590 in the SS column would have been a larger number. The number in the degrees of freedom (df) column, 143 in this case, depends on the total sample size and the number of populations being compared. It always equals the total number of persons for whom data have been collected, minus the number of populations being compared. Just as was the case in the Between Groups row, the mean Square (MS) is just the sum of squares divided by the degrees of freedom

(19,590/143). The more the scores within a sample differ from each other, the larger the MS Within Groups row will be.

We've given you a lot of facts so far, but we haven't really appealed to your logic. Here it comes. We've said that the more the sample averages differ from each other, the larger the MS Between Groups will be. Also, the more the scores in a given sample differ from each other, the larger the MS Within Groups will be. Now, you might think that a large enough MS Between Groups would suggest that the samples couldn't have been selected from populations that had the same average. After all, samples drawn from populations with the same average shouldn't have sample averages that are all that different. So far, your logic is right on target. However, there's one little hitch. Suppose that the scores within each of the groups were highly variable, just because people tended to differ a lot on the phenomenon being measured (e.g., Reading Comprehension). If that were the case, the sample averages might also differ quite a bit, even though the samples had been selected from populations with the same average. To guard against this possibility, we compare the Mean Square Between Groups to the Mean Square Within Groups. Only if the MS Between Groups is much larger than the MS Within Groups do we decide that the samples couldn't have come from populations with the same average. The F-statistic, as we've noted above, is just the MS Between Groups, divided by the MS Within Groups. If it's larger than a critical value that corresponds to our chosen alpha level, we reject the null hypothesis of equal population averages. You don't have to worry about computing the critical value. It can be found in a table headed "F-Distribution" in the back of almost any statistics book.

We've asked you to wade through a lot of terminology and numbers in this discussion, not because we felt that it was mandatory that you understood every number in the first section of Table 13.2. We invested this much in our writing and your reading because you'll find thousands of studies that present data in tables structured exactly like Table 13.2. This table is an example of what is termed an **analysis of variance table**. Analysis of variance tables may differ in fine detail, but they are always identical in basic structure. If you understand one, you can understand all of them. So the investment in this example is well worth our effort, and yours, too. If you aren't too sure of where the MS Within Groups came from, go back and read this section again. As you try to read one of the many research and evaluation reports that use analysis of variance, at some time in the future, you'll be glad you spent time now.

Our Interpretation of Results. Apart from questions of generalizability, we agree with Cleland and Idstein's interpretation of the results shown in Table 13.2. For some population of sixth-grade special education students, average performances on the Reading Comprehension and Math Computation subtests of the California Achievement Tests do depend on the level of the subtests used. We have already discussed the difficulty of attempting to define that population of students, given the sparse information the authors provided on their sampling procedures and their samples.

If you will take a moment to study the data shown in Table 13.1, we think you will see why significant differences between population averages were found for the Reading Comprehension and Math Computation subtests, but not for the Reading Vocabulary subtest. First of all, notice that the difference between the largest sample average (23.38) and the smallest sample average (18.26) is more than five points for the Reading Comprehension subtest. Notice also that the standard deviations of scores within the three samples are comparatively small. The largest standard deviation is 12.97 points, but those for the other two samples are close to 11 points. Thus the sample averages differ quite a bit, and the scores within samples are relatively homogeneous. This combination of conditions produces the fairly large *F*-statistic shown for Reading Comprehension in Table 13.2 (3.03). Second, study the data for the Reading Vocabulary subtest shown in Table 13.2. Notice that the largest and smallest sample averages differ from each other by more than five points. You might therefore wonder why the *F*-statistic for Reading Vocabulary, shown in Table 13.2, was not larger. The answer lies in the size of the standard deviations within the three samples. All are larger than 12, and one is 13.52. These larger standard deviations result in a large Mean Square Within Groups, thus negating the large Mean Square Between Groups produced by sample averages that differ from each other. The result is an *F*-statistic (2.44) that is smaller than the critical value for an alpha of .05. The very large *F*-statistic (4.86) for the Math Computation subtest results from the combined effect of having sample averages that differ from each other by as much as 10 points (See Table 13.1) and relatively small standard deviations within two of the three samples. The Mean Square Within Groups is therefore moderately small, and the Mean Square Between Groups is quite large.

Generalizing to Your Setting. We have discussed generalization of Cleland and Idstein's findings at some length in the chapter on Inferences Involving Statistical Independence. We suggest that you refer to that chapter for a review of the issues.

An Evaluation of an Urban Day Care Program

Purpose of the Study. This report presented the results of an evaluation of the Get Set Day Care Program that was operated by the School District of Philadelphia in the early 1970s. Since the author of the report was not identified, we will refer to the report as "Get Set (1972)."

The purpose of the evaluation was to compare the achievement of children who had participated in the Get Set program for at least two years with the achievement of children who had no previous nursery school experience. The evaluation examined just one of several potential program outcomes. The Get Set Program was comprehensive, in that it included health services, nutrition enrichment, social services, extensive parental involvement, and psychological services. A series of inservice training workshops were provided for about 300 teachers and 300 teacher aides who had no previous training in early childhood education. However, no evaluation of the effectiveness of these program components was provided in Get Set (1972).

Evaluation Design. The evaluator hypothesized that "the Get Set Day Care children with two years of previous Get Set Day Care experience will perform better on the Stanford Early School Achievement Test than the children with no previous Get Set Day Care experience in the kindergarten program" (p. 2).

To examine this research hypothesis, the author administered the Stanford Early Achievement Test to 1391 kindergarten pupils who had been in the Get Set Day Care program for at least two years and 702 kindergarten children who had neither Get Set nor any other nursery school experience.

The Stanford Early Achievement Test has four parts, labeled Environment, Mathematics, Letters and Sounds, and Aural Comprehension. Performance on these four parts is aggregated to form a composite score. We will consider the author's analysis of children's composite test performances.

Author's Data Table. Table 3 (p. 8) in the Get Set (1972) report provides statistics on the composite test performances of children in the author's treatment group (those with at least two years of Get Set experience) and children in the author's control group (those with no previous nursery school experience). In addition, Table 3 shows the results of an analysis of variance of the composite test performance data, and a separate analysis of the significance of differences in treatment-group and control-group performances on Reading and Mathematics subtests. We will not discuss the Reading and Mathematics test results here. We have included them in Table 3, reproduced here as Table 13.3, only to provide an exact duplicate of the author's table.

Author's Interpretation. The author's interpretation of the results shown in Table 13.3 is limited in detail but grandiose in its inferences. The author states (p. 4) that "The study indicated that Get Set Day Care experiences promote the child's ability to learn in the school environment, particularly in the areas of reading and mathematics." The conclusion of the report is as follows: "Get Set Day Care experiences help children develop concepts in learning that are basic for a child when the child enters school. The children learn reading readiness skills and mathematics skills while attending Get Set Day Care. The children have the ability to learn and are learning" (p. 5).

The Nature of the Inference. The type of inference underlying the data shown in Table 13.3 is identical to those discussed in our previous chapter on Inferences Involving Averages. The null hypothesis is that the average composite score on the Stanford Early Achievement Test is the same for the population of children who could have had at least two years of Get Set Day Care experience and the population of children who could have had no prior nursery school experience. The alternative hypothesis is that these two population averages are different.

This null hypothesis could have been examined by using a *t*-test for independent groups (as illustrated in the studies discussed in Chapter 10), but the author chose to use analysis of

TABLE 13.3: Stanford Early Achievement Test Composite Score Language Arts and Mathematics

	Treatment Group Children with Get Set Day Care Experience A	Control Group Children with No Previous Get Set Day Care Experience B	
Sample Size	1391	702	
Mean Score	84.090	78.179	
Standard Deviation	19.289	20.936	

	Analysis of Variance		
	Sum of Squares	df	Mean Square	F Ratio
Within Groups	824481.312	2091	394.300	
Between Groups	16297.824	1	16297.824	41.334
Total	840779.136	2092		$p = .001$

	Get Set Children Percentile Rank	Children with No Get Set Experience	Significance
Reading	62	33	.001
Mathematics	53	12	.001

variance instead. When only two population averages are being compared, choice of the *t*-test or analysis of variance is arbitrary, since the results will be exactly the same. If one procedure results in a finding of statistical significance, the other will as well. If one procedure leads to support of the null hypothesis, the other procedure will merely confirm that decision.

We have described the populations underlying the inferences as consisting of "children who could have participated in the Get Set program" and "children who could have had no prior nursery school experience." These descriptions are admittedly loose. But the design of the study does not permit greater specificity. The author has presumably administered the Stanford Early Achievement Test to all kindergarten children in the Philadelphia School System who fell into either participation category during the 1971-72 school year. So you might think that data have been collected from all members of the populations of interest in that school year, and that there is no inference to be made. However, decisions on the efficacy of education programs should depend on their performances over a period of years, not just their apparent effects in a single year. So we might reason that the 1971-72 populations constitute random samples from populations of children who might be eligible for participation in the Get Set program in future years. The inference then applies to these larger populations.

The "$p = .001$" in the "Analysis of Variance" section of Table 13.3 indicates that the author used a very small alpha level (.001 equals $1/10$ of 1%) in testing the null hypothesis that the average composite scores on the Stanford Early Achievement Test were equal for the two populations. The very large F-statistic (41.334) exceeded the critical value corresponding to this small alpha level. As we noted in the previous example in this chapter, the degrees of freedom figures in this analysis of variance table can be verified by considering the number of population averages being compared and the sizes of the samples being compared. The degrees of freedom (df) between groups is, correctly, equal to 1, since there are only two populations under consideration. The total df is, appropriately, one less than the total sample size (1391 plus 702). And finally, the df Within Groups is just equal to the difference between the df Total and the df Between Groups. Note that the form of the analysis of variance table is virtually identical to that shown in the previous example.

Our Interpretation of Results. We have no quarrel with the statistical procedures used in the Get Set (1972) evaluation report. The analysis of variance appears to have been carried out correctly. However, we strongly question the author's interpretation of the study's results.

In his or her interpretation, the author suggests not only that children who participated in the Get Set program achieved a significantly higher average score on the Stanford Early Achievement Test, but that the Get Set program caused that higher achievement. That could be the case. But the evidence provided in the Get Set (1972) evaluation report is less than compelling. You should immediately realize that the author's treatment group and experimental group were not randomly assigned. This suggests the possibility that Get Set participants were more able than their nonparticipant counterparts at the time they enrolled in the program. Since Get Set is a preschool program, it is clearly voluntary rather than compulsory. Only children with parents who care enough about their children's development to enroll them in the program, and then give of their own time, constitute the treatment group. These children might well be regarded as advantaged at the outset. They might have shown superior performance on the Stanford Early Achievement Test in kindergarten just because of the support of their parents. We thus have at least one viable rival interpretation of the Get Set results. There are many others, including differences in the aptitudes of children who enroll in the program and those who do not; differences in the transiency rates of parents who enroll their children in preschool programs (i.e., it's really family stability that produces increased preschool achievement); the development of test-taking skills, rather than superior achievement, by program participants; and so forth.

The design of the Get Set evaluation unfortunately permits each of these rival interpretations to be entertained as viable alternatives to the conclusion that Get Set caused the apparent increases in preschool achievement. Without random assignment of children to the treatment group and a true control group, or the use of a much stronger nonexperimental evaluation design, there is no sound basis for claiming that the program resulted in greater achievement than would have been realized in the absence of the program.

Generalizing to Your Setting. Suppose that the Get Set evaluation had been designed differently, and that you could clearly attribute the superior performance of the treatment group to the effects of the Get Set program. What assumptions would be required to generalize these findings to your own setting? First, you would have to assume that the sample of children used in the Get Set evaluation was representative of the population of preschool children in your school system. Second, you would have to assume that the Get Set program could be replicated in your school system. This would require investment of the same time and dollar resources (at least proportionately) as in Philadelphia, and the same level of commitment and capability on the part of teachers, counselors, psychologists, nutritionists, and administrators as was realized in Philadelphia. Finally, you would have to be convinced that the Stanford Early Achievement Test was a valid measure of the kinds of outcomes that you would expect from a successful day care program.

Given the limitations in the **internal validity** of this study (i.e., one cannot causally attribute the results of the study to the treatment), the question of generalizability of results is moot for practical purposes. It will always be the case that internal validity is a necessary ingredient in the generalizability of research findings. If a research or evaluation study is not internally valid, generalizability of its findings is out of the question. However, there is no assurance that the findings of an internally valid research study will be generalizable to your setting. You have to address both questions separately, and achieve satisfactory answers to both before you apply research findings on your own home ground.

An Evaluation of an Experimental Assessment Center for Army Cadets

Purpose of the Study. Assessment centers are frequently used in management training programs for the purpose of helping managers and potential managers assess their strengths and weaknesses. Typically, the principal purpose of an assessment center is assessment, as the name implies. Less frequently, an assessment center is used as an integral part of an education program for the principal purpose of helping participants to develop management skills. In these relatively rare circumstances, the primary function of the assessment center is educational, and assessment is viewed as an important side benefit to the extent that it contributes to the development of more effective managers.

In this study, Butler, Wilson, and Priest (1984) evaluated the effectiveness of an experimental assessment center that was made a part of the leadership development curriculum for cadets in the United States Military Academy at West Point. The objective of the assessment center was to expose cadets, through carefully designed simulations, to the job requirements of the second lieutenant position in the U.S. Army, the initial military rank the cadets would hold upon graduation from West Point. In addition to collecting substantial amounts of "soft" data on the effectiveness of the assessment center from cadets and assessors who participated in the experiment, Butler et al. examined the relationship between the preparticipation leadership performance ratings and skill and behavior ratings collected during the assess-center exercise, for 66 participating cadets. We will restrict our comments to their analysis and interpretation of these data.

Research Design. The subjects of the Butler et al. (1984) research were 66 cadets enrolled in the U.S. Military Academy who were between one and two years from graduation. The cadets were divided into three groups, depending on their scores in the U.S. Military Academy's leadership performance rating system. The leadership performance of Academy cadets is rated by tactical officers, academic instructors, immediate cadet supervisors, cadet supervisors next removed, and cadets of the next senior class. Individual ratings of a cadet are combined through weighted averaging across six dimensions, and the combination yields an overall rating. In the current experiment, leadership performance ratings were completed prior to the cadets' participation in the assessment center.

During their assessment center participation, each of the 66 cadets was rated on 12 junior-officer skills by three Army officers who had received special training in assessment. A five-point scale that ranged from 1 (much less than acceptable) to 5 (much more than acceptable) was used to evaluate the performance of the cadets on each of the 12 skills. Butler et al. indicate that the cadets were rated in terms of their capabilities as future second lieutenants, with careful consideration of the job requirements of that position, and were not evaluated by comparing them to each other.

To investigate the concurrent validity of the assessment center, Butler et al. divided the 66 cadets into three groups: those whose leadership performance scores were less than 2.00; those whose leadership performance scores were between 2.00 and 2.99; and those whose leadership performance scores were at least 3.00. The authors reasoned that cadets who scored higher in leadership performance prior to their participation in the assessment center should receive higher scores on measures of the 12 training dimensions used in the assessment center. A finding to the contrary would call into question the effectiveness of the assessment center or the validity of the measures used to examine the junior-officer potential of the cadet participants.

Authors' Data Table. Butler et al. (1984) report the results of their analyses of the concurrent validity of the assessment center measures in the form of a summary data table. Their Table 1 (which

TABLE 13.4: Means and Standard Deviations on Twelve Skills

Junior-Officer Skills	Cadets Lowest in Military Leadership		Cadets in Middle in Military Leadership		Cadets Highest in Military Leadership		F
	X	SD	X	SD	X	SD	
Oral Communication	3.06	.66	3.44	.87	3.88	.80	5.37**
Oral Presentation	3.00	1.06	3.40	.87	4.12	.80	8.48**
Written Communication	2.88	.60	3.04	.84	3.71	1.16	4.95**
Initiative	3.18	.88	2.92	.91	3.62	.92	3.75*
Sensitivity	2.82	.73	3.16	.80	3.25	.74	1.67
Influence	2.82	.95	3.12	.97	3.42	1.10	1.72
Planning & Organizing	3.18	.64	2.96	1.06	3.42	.97	1.46
Delegation	2.88	.93	2.80	1.12	3.25	1.15	1.15
Administrative Control	2.18	.81	2.48	.96	2.67	1.20	1.14
Problem Analysis	2.65	.61	2.72	.79	3.21	.83	3.54*
Judgment	2.82	.81	2.84	.62	2.96	.91	0.20
Decisiveness	3.35	.86	3.24	.83	3.46	.88	0.40
Overall Average	2.90	.40	3.01	.49	3.41	.58	6.15**
N	17		25		24		

df = 2,63
**p < .01
*p < .05

appeared on page 6 of their paper) is reproduced here as Table 13.4.

Authors' Interpretation. According to Butler et al. (pp. 5-6), the authors

> expected the group high in cadet leadership to perform best on junior officer skills measured by the AC [assessment center], and the group lowest in cadet leadership to perform worst. Table 1 [Table 13.4 here] presents AC performance information of the three subgroups of cadets. Using one-way analysis of variance to test for differences in the overall averages of the 12 skills for the three groups indicated a significant difference ($F = 6.15$, df = 2/63, $p < .01$).

In their summary of findings, Butler et al. interpreted the results shown in Table 13.4 by stating:

Furthermore, the concurrent validity study shows that individuals who perform well as cadets, in terms of the cadet performance rating, also tend to have already developed many of the skills needed by second lieutenants and, were still between one and two years away from commissioning as second lieutenants. (p. 7)

The Nature of the Inference. Table 13.4 is in a form that is untypical for research studies that make use of analysis of variance. Instead of using the traditional ANOVA table that was found in the two studies described earlier in this chapter, Butler et al. summarized the results of their 13 one-way analyses of variance by reporting means and standard deviations of scores for three samples of cadets and the value of an *F*-statistic resulting from these data for each of their 13 dependent variables. For each of the dependent variables (e.g., oral communication), the authors tested the null hypothesis that mean scores would be identical for three populations of cadets: those who received scores less than 2.00 (lowest scorers); those who scored between 2.00 and 2.99 (middle scorers); or those who scored greater than 2.99 (highest scorers) in the U.S. Military Academy's leadership performance rating system. It is important to realize that the groups of 17 lowest scorers, 25 middle scorers, and 24 highest scorers who provided the data shown in Table 13.4 were regarded as randomly sampled cadets from potential populations of lowest, middle, and highest scorers. The 13 analyses of variance that are summarized in Table 13.4 were interpreted by the authors as though their results generalized to these populations.

The alternative hypotheses associated with the *F*-statistics that Butler et al. displayed in Table 13.4 were identical in form for each of their 13 analyses of variance. In each case, the alternative hypothesis was that at least two of the populations of cadets would differ in population average score on the dependent variable in question. For example, the first row of Table 13.4, with oral communication as the dependent variable, summarizes the results of an analysis of variance in which the alternative hypothesis was that at least two of the populations of cadets who were lowest in military leadership score, of midrange military leadership score, or highest in military leadership score would differ in average oral communication score.

From the footnote to Table 13.4, we can see that Butler et al. used a Type I error level of 0.05 as the largest value they associated with statistical significance. That is, they chose to reject a null hypothesis that the average scores of the three populations of cadets were equal, only if corresponding sample means and standard deviations produced an F-statistic that was statistically significant at the 0.05 level. Otherwise, they retained the null hypothesis of equal population averages.

Rather than testing all 13 of their null hypotheses by using a Type I error level of 0.05, the authors chose to report F-statistics that were statistically significant at the 0.05 level or the more stringent 0.01 level. Although strict statistical dictum would have researchers select the one level of significance they will use in reporting the results of their hypothesis tests prior to collection of data, in modern practice researchers frequently use several levels of statistical significance in reporting their findings. This practice is encouraged by modern computer programs that provide precise levels of significance associated with the test statistics they produce. For example, several computer programs provide all of the statistics contained in a standard analysis of variance table in addition to the precise proportion of the appropriate F-distribution that corresponds to values larger than the F-statistic computed from the sample data. Some researchers therefore include statements like "$p = 0.0328$" in footnotes to their analysis of variance tables. This statement indicates that the null hypothesis would have been rejected, had a Type I error level of 0.0328 been used. Since the value cited is smaller than 0.05 but larger than 0.01, the reader can conclude that the reported test statistic is significant at the 0.05 level, but not at the 0.01 level.

Our Interpretation. The authors of this study have been unusually economical in reporting the results of their research. Rather than providing the results of their 13 analyses of variance in 13 separate ANOVA tables, they have chosen to restrict their report to means and standard deviations by group, and the F-statistics that resulted from these data, for each of their 13 dependent variables. The authors' economy is justified by the compactness of Table 13.4 and the argument that all statistics contained in a standard ANOVA table could be computed from the data given in each row of Table 13.4.

More troubling than the compactness of their report of results is the authors' economy in interpreting their findings. Other than noting that the averages of their "Overall Average" dependent variables were significantly different at the 0.01 level, the authors provide little interpretive comment on their findings. Even the computation of this dependent variable is not described explicitly. The authors merely state that it is an "overall average" of 12 skills. They do not indicate whether they simply added the 12 skills scores for a cadet and divided by 12, or weighted the 12 skills scores in some way, when they computed an Overall Average score.

Butler et al. provided no information on how the 66 cadets in their study were selected from the classes of third- and fourth-year students at the U.S. Military Academy. Classic jokes about never volunteering in the military notwithstanding, it is possible that the 66 cadets volunteered to participate in the assessment center. It is also possible that the 66 constituted a group that was special in some way, such as all cadets who were enrolled in a particular class at a convenient hour of the day. Such "convenience samples" are typically not representative of the populations from which they were selected. If the cadets who participated in the study either volunteered or were selected because they constituted a convenience sample, the results of this study could not be generalized safely to the entire population of third- and fourth-year cadets in the U.S. Military Academy.

As you review the results in Table 13.4, notice that four of the F-statistics have two asterisks (**) beside them, two of the F-statistics have one asterisk (*) beside them, and seven of the F-statistics have no asterisks. This means that the authors found statistically significant differences among assessment center skills scores for less than half of the dependent variables (assuming we include the "Overall Average") in this count. This finding calls into question the authors' conclusion that "individuals who perform well as cadets, in terms of cadet performance rating, also tend to have already developed many of the skills needed by second lieutenants" (p. 7). There was a clear association of this type for some assessment center skills (such as oral communication and oral presentation) but none for others (such as planning and organization, and delegation). It is interesting that the strongest associations were found for communication skills that are less clearly indicative of the construct of "leadership" and the weakest associations were found for such skills as planning and organizing, administrative control, judgment, and decisiveness, skills that are more obviously associated with common conceptions of leadership ability. Weighting these skills equally in determining an overall average is, perhaps, a less useful strategy than combining them in a way that emphasizes skills that are more often regarded as indicative of sound leadership ability.

In discussing their procedures, Butler et al. do not indicate whether the assessors who rated their sampled cadets during the assessment center exercise had access to the results of the cadets' prior leadership score ratings. One would strongly hope that they did not, since prior knowledge of the cadets' leadership scores would surely influence the ratings the assessors provided during the experiment. When you read reports of experiments such as this, it is important to think about procedural details that might have undermined the validity of the research, and to search for statements that describe such procedures. In the absence of such statements, healthy suspicion is in order.

Finally, you should be aware that in conducting 13 analyses of variance, the authors incurred a large risk that at least one of them would be statistically significant, just by chance. Put another way, the risk of committing a Type I error is very large for the entire set of 13 analyses of variance, even though the authors chose to use a Type I error level of 0.05 for each analysis. A simple example should convey the logic underlying this statement: Suppose the authors had conducted only two hypothesis tests, each with a Type I error level of 0.05. For each one, the probability that a Type I error had *not* occurred would be 0.95. Therefore the probability that no Type I errors had occurred for either hypothesis test would have been (0.95)(0.95), that is, the product of the 0.95 values, which equals 0.9025. If the probability of no Type I errors is 0.9025, the probability of at least one Type I error is $(1 - 0.9025)$, which equals 0.0975. Therefore, for the two hypothesis tests, the risk of committing a Type I error is almost 10%, not the 5% implied by the authors' use of 0.05 for their alpha level with each test. When 13 hypothesis tests are conducted, each with a Type I error level of 0.05, the risk of committing at least one Type I error is $1 - (0.95)^{13}$, which equals 0.49. This means that Butler et al. had almost a 50% chance that one or more of their analyses of variance would produce statistically significant results, just because of chance. Their effective Type I error level for the entire set of 13 hypothesis tests was 0.49.

The discussion in the last paragraph assumed that the results of the 13 analyses of variance were independent of each other. That was not the case here, since the same 66 cadets were used in each analysis and the dependent variables used were undoubtedly correlated with each other. Nonetheless, the point illustrated is still valid, and is still of concern. The only practical way to guard against very large Type I error levels for an entire set of statistical tests is to use a very small Type I error level for the individual tests. Had Butler et al. used an alpha of 0.01 for each of their analyses of variance, their risk of committing one or more Type I errors for all 13 tests would have been 0.12, just 12%. This value is far smaller than the 0.49 that resulted from their using a Type I error level of 0.05 for each of their tests.

Generalizing to Your Setting. Before considering this topic we must note, in fairness to the authors, that they do not propose the generalization of their findings beyond the U.S. Military Academy at West Point. However, were you to consider generalizing their findings to a civilian setting, you would have to consider several factors. First, is "leadership" a generalizable construct? Are the characteristics of leadership the same in your setting as they are in the U.S. Army? Second, would the instructional techniques used in a military assessment center be transportable to your setting? The military has a clear chain of command and strict requirements for obedience. Most civilian organizations differ substantially in these characteristics. Thus a leadership development activity that was effective in the U.S. Military Academy might not be effective in any civilian setting. Third, cadets at West Point are college students. They are younger and less experienced than persons likely to be employed in most civilian sector organizations, such as school systems or corporate management divisions, where leadership skills are at a premium. Thus, for a variety of reasons, even if the internal validity of the Butler et al. research was beyond question, the generalizability of their findings beyond the context of their research (apart from the academies operated by the other military service branches) would be suspect.

Summary

We have discussed three research and evaluation studies that incorporated analysis of variance to test a null hypothesis of equal population averages. In each case, the alternative hypothesis was that the population averages were different.

Note that the inferential results in two of the studies were summarized in the form of an analysis of variance table. Both of the analysis of variance tables contained the same basic information, although the arrangement of the tables varied a bit. You will find the same basic structure and information in all analysis of variance tables, as you encounter other studies that use this form of analysis.

When you read reports of research that incorporate the analysis of variance, keep these points in mind. Remember also that the analysis of variance presumes that data have been collected from independent random samples selected from each population of interest.

Once again, we hope you can now read and understand research and evaluation studies with greater clarity, confidence, and appropriate wariness—believing what is true, and rejecting the inevitable falsehoods that plague research and evaluation in every field.

Problems — Chapter 13

In 1989, Neymann and Pratt reported the results of a study on the effectiveness of alternative methods of teaching beginning statistics at the college level. They randomly selected 75 students from among those registering for beginning statistics courses in the psychology department of a major university, and assigned independently selected groups of 25 students to each of three teaching methods: Traditional Lecture, Self-Paced Programmed Text, and a Discovery-Laboratory Method.

The authors administered a common final examination to the three groups, and reported their results in the following analysis of variance table:

	Sum of Squares	df	Mean Squares	F
Between Groups	162	2	81.00	5.67*
Within Groups	1028	72	14.28	
Total	1190	74		

*signif. @ 0.05; $_{.95}F_{(2,72)} = 3.13$

13.1 What null hypothesis and what alternative hypothesis were the authors testing in this study?

13.2 Assuming that the authors acted in accordance with the results reported above, what decision did they reach on retention or rejection of the null hypothesis? Support your answer by citing relevant data.

13.3 Interpret the results of this study in your own words. What assumptions are necessary to the interpretation you have made?

13.4 Describe a research or evaluation study in your own context in which one-way analysis of variance (ANOVA) would be an appropriate method of data analysis.
  a. Define the research question you might want to investigate.
  b. Identify the population(s) and population parameters that are central to your research study.
  c. State a null hypothesis and an alternative hypothesis that are relevant to your study.
  d. What conclusions would you reach, were you to reject the null hypothesis?

14.

Two-Way Analysis of Variance

The Nature of the Inferences

All of the problems we discussed in Chapters 10 and 13 (Inferences Involving Averages and One-Way Analysis of Variance) were similar in one respect: each analysis involved *one* **independent variable** (such as type of curriculum or treatment) and *one* **dependent variable** (such as student achievement or teacher attitude). In this chapter we'll consider problems that are somewhat more complex because they involve *more than one independent variable*. The problems are therefore more realistic and more interesting. But we will stick to a single dependent variable, so that the waters don't get too murky.

We introduced a one-way analysis of variance in the last chapter by discussing the hypothetical problem of selecting the best of three computer literacy programs. We suggested that a school administrator should purchase the curriculum that would result in fourth-graders achieving the highest average score on a test of basic computer operations. We began with the null hypothesis that the three candidate curricula were equally effective; that is, that the population of fourth-grade students in the school system would earn the same average score regardless of the curriculum selected. The alternative hypothesis was that at least one of the three curricula was more effective than the others.

Let's consider the problem of selecting a computer literacy curriculum a bit further. We'll first examine the instructional approaches used in the three curricula, and then consider the aptitudes and preferences of students who might be instructed using the curricula. Suppose that the three candidate curricula differ markedly in the way they present information about computer operations. Curriculum G presents information in a predominantly *graphic* form, with lots of pictures, charts, and graphs. Curriculum V is highly *verbal* in its presentation. It uses lengthy verbal descriptions, but very few pictures. Curriculum S presents material in highly *symbolic* form, with equations that emphasize the relationships between computer inputs and outputs.

Now it is well known that students differ in their preferences for the form in which new information is presented, and in the efficiency with which they learn information that is communicated in various forms. Some students are highly visual learners. Their most efficient learning mode is through study of graphs and pictures. Other students learn very little from visual materials, and do best with simple prose explanations. They are verbal learners. Still others learn most efficiently by studying relationships among symbols. Equations convey a great deal of meaning to such students, and provide useful summaries of important relationships. These facts suggest the possibility that no one computer literacy curriculum may be best for all students. Curricula G, V, and S might provide the most efficient learning mechanism, and the highest possible achievement, for different groups of students.

Using one-way analysis of variance, we were able to examine the possibility that one of the three curricula were more effective than the others for the entire population of fourth-grade students. Recall that our null hypothesis was just the converse: that all three curricula were equally effective. One-way ANOVA did not permit us to explore the possibility that one curriculum might be best for one type of student, while another curriculum might be best for others. Using **two-way analysis of variance**, we can still entertain the possibility that one of the three curricula is an overall winner, but in addition we can examine the more intriguing possibility that different curricula are best for different types of students. We can even consider the possibility that students' preferences for a particular type of instructional material (graphic, verbal, or symbolic) influence average achievement on the test of computer operations, regardless of the curriculum material used. In short, two-way ANOVA facilitates the examination of a far richer set of evaluation and research questions than does one-way ANOVA.

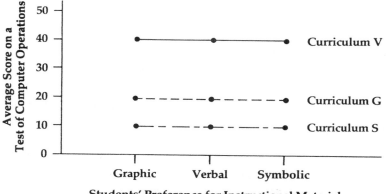

Figure 14.1 Illustration of Main Effect Due to Type of Curriculum, No Main Effect Due to Students' Preferences, and No Interactions

That's not to say it is always better, or more appropriate. Both one-way and two-way ANOVA are useful in particular evaluation and research settings.

The research questions that we can investigate using two-way analysis of variance might be easier to understand by considering the following set of figures. Each figure illustrates one of a number of possible relationships among the type of curriculum used, students' preferences for different types of instructional materials, and students' average performance on a test of computer operations. In each of the figures, average achievement on the computer operations test is shown on the vertical axis, students' preferences for instructional materials are indicated on the horizontal axis, and type of curriculum used is indicated in the body of the figure.

Figure 14.1 illustrates the possibility that the three curricula differ consistently in their overall effectiveness, regardless of students' preferences for various types of instructional materials. Since each type of student has the same overall average achievement, this figure also suggests that the preference variable has no effect on students' performance on the test of computer operations. Using statistical language, we would describe the results shown in Figure 14.1 by saying three things: First, there *is* a **main effect** due to type of curriculum used. Second, there is *no* main

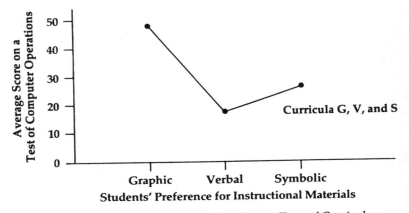

Figure 14.2 Illustration of No Main Effect Due to Type of Curriculum, a Main Effect Due to Students' Preferences, and No Interactions

effect due to preference for type of instructional material. Third, there is *no* **interaction** between type of instructional material and students' preferences. We'll discuss these terms in some detail when we've finished describing the figures. In the meantime, you should realize that we'd describe Figure 14.1 in exactly the same way, regardless of which curriculum won the achievement race. For example, if Curriculum S had resulted in the highest average achievement, and Curriculum V the lowest, we would still say that there was a main effect due to curriculum, and no other effects. The flat, parallel lines that connect the average achievements of each group of students are the key to this description.

Another possible experimental outcome is that the three curricula are equal in their *overall* effectiveness, that none of the curricula is more effective than any other if you ignore students' preferences for types of instructional materials, but that students differ in their average performance on the test of computer operations, depending on their preferences for types of instructional materials. Statistically speaking, with this outcome we would say that there is *no* main effect due to curriculum, that there *is* a main effect due to students' preferences for types of instructional materials, and that there is *no* interaction between curricula and students' preferences. This outcome is illustrated in Figure 14.2. Note that in Figure 14.2, the average score for students *with a given instructional*

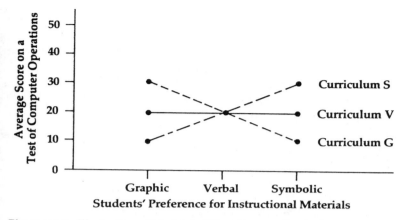

Figure 14.3 Illustration of No Main Effects Due to Curriculum or Students' Preferences, but an Interaction Between Curriculum and Students' Preferences

preference is the same, *regardless of the curriculum* used. However, students with a *preference for graphic instructional materials* have a higher average score than do students who prefer either verbal or symbolic materials. Again, we'd give the same statistical description of these results—a main effect due to students' preferences, no main effect due to curriculum, and no interactions—whichever group of students had the highest average achievement. The key here is that all three curricula resulted in identical average achievement for students with a given preference.

A third possible experimental outcome is illustrated in Figure 14.3. This figure illustrates the interesting possibility that no one curriculum is any more effective than any other when scores on the computer operations test are averaged across all fourth-graders in the population; that students with a preference for a particular type of instructional material have the same average score as students with a preference for any other type of material; but that *some combinations* of curricula and student preferences result in far higher achievement or far lower achievement than do other combinations. We would describe this outcome statistically by saying that there are *no* main effects due to curriculum or to student preferences, but that there *is* an interaction between type of curriculum and student preferences. Note that Curriculum G appears to

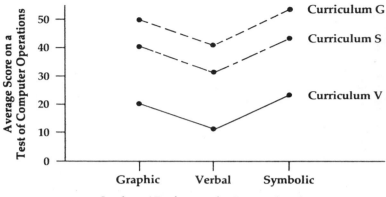

Figure 14.4 Illustration of Main Effects Due to Type of Curriculum and Students' Preferences for Instructional Materials, but No Interaction Effect

be particularly effective when used with students who prefer that type of instructional material, that Curriculum S is particularly effective when used with students who prefer symbolic materials, and that type of curriculum appears to have no effect for students who prefer verbal instructional materials. This figure illustrates just one of many possible outcomes that would be described as illustrating "no main effects, but an interaction" between the independent variables. The labeling of the curriculum lines could be interchanged, for example, without altering the basic description.

Each of the figures we've discussed so far illustrates one of the three effects that are possible in two-way ANOVA: a main effect due to one of the two independent variables, or an interaction effect between the independent variables. These effects can also be present in combination, and additional figures are needed to illustrate these possibilities. For example, a main effect due to each of the independent variables (type of curriculum and students' preference for instructional material) could be present, although there was no interaction between the independent variables. In this case, the three curricula would result in different average achievements for the entire population of fourth-grade students; the average achievement of students who preferred verbal materials would differ from the average achievement of students who preferred graphic or symbolic materials; but differences in the effectiveness of two curricula would be the same, for all three groups of students. Figure 14.4 illustrates this experimental outcome. Here again, we would describe the results shown in Figure 14.4 the same way—there are main effects due to type of curriculum and students' preferences, but no interaction—regardless of which curriculum was most effective, or which group of students had the highest or lowest average achievement. The key to the description is that the lines that join the average achievements for a given curriculum are parallel to each other. Because of this parallelism, the difference in average achievement between students taught using Curricula V and S, or any other pair of curricula, is the same for all groups of students. If the lines had not been parallel, specific combinations of curricula and student preferences would result in particularly high or particularly low average achievement, which we would describe as an interaction effect.

Three additional figures would exhaust the range of possible outcomes we have not yet illustrated. Two figures would show a main effect for one of the independent variables, in combination with an interaction effect. The third figure would show a "grand slam": a main effect due to each of the independent variables, in combination with an interaction effect. On the assumption that you've probably grown tired of looking at illustrative figures by now (regardless of your personal affinity for graphic instructional materials), and that you've grasped the general idea of how main effects and interactions make themselves evident in figures of this sort, we will skip the two intermediate possibilities, and end this section with an illustration of all three effects that can be present in two-way ANOVA. In Figure 14.5, the sets of average achievements are arranged to show a main effect due to type of curriculum; a main effect due to students' preference for instructional material; and an interaction between type of curriculum and students' preferences. Note that the lines that connect the average achievements associated with a given curriculum are not parallel in this case. In fact, when Curriculum G is used with students who prefer graphic materials, the resulting average achievement is very high—far higher than would result from mere addition of the effect due to use of Curriculum G with all students and the effect due to students who prefer graphic materials. In contrast, the use of Curric-

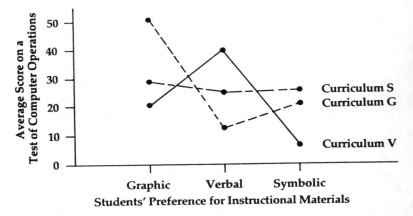

Figure 14.5 Illustration of Main Effects Due to Type of Curriculum and Students' Preferences and an Interaction Between Type of Curriculum and Students' Preferences for Type of Instructional Material

ulum V with students who prefer symbolic materials results in exceptionally low average achievement. Here again, the combination of curriculum and students' preferences is the cause of the extraordinary achievement outcome. Neither independent variable would produce such results on its own, and the sum of the two effects (use of Curriculum V and preference for symbolic materials) is far exceeded by the effect of the combination.

In describing the results shown in Figure 14.5, we have implicitly defined an interaction effect. It is an effect due to a combination of independent variables that exceeds the sum of the main effects of the independent variables taken individually. An interaction effect is sometimes called a **synergistic effect**. In a homely but dramatic way, the combined effect of a lighted match and spilled gasoline illustrates synergism or interaction. Neither the presence of a match nor the presence of gasoline produces an explosion or fire. But in combination, the effect of the two variables is dramatic.

Two-way analysis of variance is an inferential procedure, as is one-way ANOVA. It makes use of data collected from several samples to test hypotheses about the parameters of the populations from which the samples were drawn. Three null hypotheses can be tested using two-way ANOVA: first, that one of the independent variables has no main effect; second, that the other independent variable has no main effect; and third, that there is no interaction effect between the independent variables.

Going back to our computer literacy example, let's discuss the applicable null hypotheses, and their implications. The first null hypothesis would be that there is no main effect due to type of curriculum. What we mean by this is as follows: had all fourth-grade students in the school system been taught using Curriculum G, Curriculum V, or Curriculum S, their average score on the test of computer operations would have been exactly the same. In other words, type of curriculum has no influence on student achievement on the test of computer operations. The population parameter being considered here is the average test score of all fourth-grade students in the school system. Our null hypothesis is that this parameter is unaffected by the type of curriculum used; the average that would result from use of Curriculum G is equal to the average that would result from use of Curriculum V, which is equal to the average that would result from use of Curriculum S. The alternative hypothesis is that the average test score would be different, depending on the type of curriculum used. More specifically, if there is a main effect due to type of curriculum, at least one choice would result in a larger or smaller average score, for all fourth-graders in the school system.

The second null hypothesis that could be tested in this example is that there is no main effect due to students' preference for type of instructional material. Unfortunately, this statement is a little bit complicated, and our explanation will have to be correspondingly long-winded. Suppose that it were possible to conduct a survey of all fourth-graders in the school system, and that each student were to specify his or her preference for graphic, verbal, or symbolic instructional materials. You could then divide the population of fourth-graders into three subpopulations, each identified with a preference. Suppose that you could instruct all fourth-graders with a preference for graphic materials, using each of the three curricula, administer the test of computer operations after you'd used each curriculum, and then wipe out the students' memories of having been instructed and tested. If you averaged the three test scores for each student who preferred graphic materials, and then averaged the averages for all students in the subpopulation, you'd have a grand average achievement for the subpopulation of students who preferred graphic materials. In exactly the same way, it would be possible to calculate a grand average achievement for the subpopulation of students who preferred verbal materials, and to calculate a grand average for the subpopulation of students who preferred symbolic materials. At this point you'd have three subpopulation averages. The null hypothesis that there is no main effect due to students' preference for type of instructional materials states that these subpopulation averages are all equal. The alternative hypothesis is that one of the subpopulations has a higher average score on the test of computer operations than do the other subpopulations.

We have already discussed the third null hypothesis that can be tested using two-way ANOVA—the null hypothesis that there is no interaction effect between type of curriculum and student's preference for type of instructional materials. However, the concept of an interaction effect is novel, and it bears additional consideration. Perhaps the simplest way to describe the null hypothesis of no interaction effect is as follows: It states that if any subpopulation were to be instructed using any one of the three curricula, the resulting average achievement could be calculated from the main effect due to that subpopulation, and the main effect due to that curriculum. In other words, if there is no interaction effect, the main effects can merely be added together to determine the combined effect of the two independent variables. The alternative hypothesis, that there is an interaction effect, means that some combination of the two independent variables produces a result that is not equal to the sum of the main effects. In the case of the computer literacy program, for example, an interaction would be present if the subpopulation of students who preferred graphic instructional materials, when instructed using Curriculum G, earned an average score on the test of computer operations that exceeded the grand average of all students in the population, when taught using all three curricula, by more or less than the sum of the following two differences: (1) the difference between the average score of students who preferred Curriculum G and the average score of all students in the population when taught using all three curricula; and (2) the difference between the average score of all students in the population when taught using Curriculum G and the average score of all students in the population when taught using all three curricula. This is a long-winded way of saying that the effect of using Curriculum G with students who prefer Curriculum G is greater, or smaller, than the sum of the main effect due to Curriculum G and the main effect of preference for Curriculum G. If this is true, there is an interaction due to the combination of Curriculum G and preference for Curriculum G.

You will find that our computer literacy example is a model for the inferences considered in the real studies that follow. In each study, the authors test null hypotheses on main effects of independent variables and on interactions between independent variables. In the second study, the authors consider three independent variables rather than two. They conduct what is called a **three-way analysis of variance**. We have included their study in this chapter to illustrate the generality of the principles introduced in discussing two-way ANOVA. Using those principles, it is possible to test null hypotheses on the main effects of, and interactions among, any number of independent variables. More null hypotheses are involved, and the interpretations become more complex, but the basic statistical approach is identical.

A Final Evaluation of a Career Education Program

Purpose of the Study. In Chapter 10 we discussed an evaluation of the third-year operation of a career education program by Kershner and Blair (1975). We'll return to that example here, to describe a component of the evaluation that made use of two-way analysis of variance.

Kershner and Blair conducted a summative evaluation of a career education program that was developed and operated by Research for Better Schools, Inc. The program was designed to provide secondary school students with "cognitive skills, career experiences, and personal perspectives which aid in the selection and pursuit of adult life goals" (p. 6). The program focused on three areas of instruction: career exploration and specialization, career guidance, and basic skills. Many of the instructional activities took place in a large urban high school, and others took place at various community resource sites. Most of the program participants were eleventh-graders, but students from grades nine, ten, and twelve were also served.

The evaluation had several purposes. Among them was the goal of comparing the attitudes of program participants with those of students in control groups toward various aspects of career planning and knowledge. In this example we will limit our attention to this goal.

Evaluation Design. The evaluation involved assessments of the pretreatment and posttreatment status of students in three experimental groups, and parallel assessments of the status of students in two comparison groups. Instruments used by the evaluators included measures of career maturity, students' self-acceptance, school attitudes, achievement, and career attitudes.

One of the experimental groups (labeled E1) and one of the control groups (labeled C1) were randomly selected for evaluation of the program during its third year of operation. Another experimental group (labeled E2) and another control group (labeled C2) were not selected randomly, but participated in the program during two years of its operation. The third experimental group (labeled E3) consisted of students who had been selected during the third year of program operation to replace those who had dropped out of the evaluation. The results we will consider in this example involve only the randomly selected experimental and control groups (E1 and C1).

Kershner and Blair administered a 15-item Attitude Toward Career Knowledge Scale (ATCK) to all students in groups E1 and C1 at the beginning and the end of the third year of the program. Their purposes were to compare the attitudes of experimental and control group students both prior to treatment and at the end of one year of program participation. Their results are shown below.

Authors' Data Table. Table 30 in the Kershner and Blair report (1975; p. 67) contains the results of two-way analyses of variance using the pretest and posttest performances of experimental and control group students on the Attitude Toward Career Knowledge Scale. It is reproduced here as Table 14.1.

Authors' Interpretation. Kershner and Blair interpreted the results shown in Table 14.1 as follows:

> The analysis of variance of the ATCK pretest scores indicated no between group difference. There was a significant grade difference which reflected a possible grade linked development of career maturity. The posttest analysis of variance indicated significant grade

TABLE 14.1: Attitude Toward Career Knowledge, E1 and C1 Groups — Analyses of Variance

Source	df	MS	F
		Pretest	
Grade	3	108.2237	3.9814
Group	1	10.0928	0.3713
Grade x Group	3	14.7952	0.5443
Error	184	27.1823	
		Posttest	
Grade	3	222.4236	7.9037
Group	1	164.7753	5.8552
Grade x Group	3	46.6252	1.6568
Error	184	28.1417	

Critical value $F_{(1,180}$; alpha = .10) ≥ 2.74
Critical value $F_{(3,180}$; alpha = .10) ≥ 2.12

and group differences; E1 posttest performance on the ATCK was significantly higher than C1 performance. The grade differences were again identified and reinforced the stratification used in the analyses. (p. 67)

The Nature of the Inferences. The data in Table 14.1 illustrate the results of testing six different null hypotheses. Three of the hypothesis tests involve pretest data, and the other three involve posttest data. In each case, the authors are treating their experimental and control groups as though they had been randomly sampled from populations of students who might have participated in the career education program.

In another portion of Table 30, which we have not reproduced here, Kershner and Blair show separate average pretest and posttest scores on the ATCK for experimental and control group students sampled from grades 9, 10, 11, and 12. They also show average pretest and posttest scores for all students in the experimental and control groups, regardless of grade level, and average scores for students at each grade level, regardless of group membership.

From the data in Table 14.1, we can tell that the authors were interested in analyzing the effect of two independent variables—grade level and treatment—on average ATCK scores. They examined not only the main effects of these two independent variables, but a possible interaction effect as well. The two portions of Table 14.1 reproduced here show the results of separate but parallel analyses using pretest scores and posttest scores as dependent variables.

The first null hypothesis tested was that grade level had no main effect on ATCK pretest scores. This hypothesis reflects the following *hypothetical* scenario: Suppose that the authors could take an entire population of ninth-graders who were eligible to participate in the career education program, and divide it in half. One half of the population would be randomly selected for participation in the career education program, and the other half would be selected for the control group. Before any students had participated in the program, the authors would administer the ATCK to every ninth-grader in the population and record their average score. The authors would then complete the same procedure using tenth-graders, eleventh-graders, and twelfth-graders. The null hypothesis states that the average pretest ATCK scores of the ninth-graders, tenth-graders, eleventh-graders, and twelfth-graders would be exactly the same. That is the precise meaning of the statement that "grade level has no main effect on ATCK pretest score." The alternative hypothesis would be that grade level *does* have a main effect on pretest score. This is equivalent to stating that the average pretest score of the population of students in one grade will be different from the average pretest score of the population of students in at least one other grade.

Kershner and Blair rejected the null hypothesis that grade level had no main effect on pretest score. They took this action because the F-statistic associated with the source labeled "Grade" in the pretest analysis of variance table (the number 3.9814) was larger than the critical value for an alpha level of 0.10. The appropriate critical value (2.12) is shown in the footnote at the bottom of Table 14.1. The degrees of freedom shown for this critical value of the F distribution (3, 180) were found from the value 3 in the df column for Grade, and the value 184 in the df column for Error. (Tables of the F distribution don't list critical values for every choice of degrees of freedom. Often a researcher must use the critical value associated with degrees of freedom that are close to the desired value. Using the next smaller value for degrees of freedom in the denominator is a conservative decision, so Kershner and Blair appropriately used 180 instead of 184). In case you've forgotten what degrees of freedom and F-statistics are, you can refresh your memory by looking back to Chapter 13, on one-way analysis of variance.

The second null hypothesis that Kershner and Blair tested was that their treatment had no main effect on pretest score. This null hypothesis might seem strange to you, since at the time the pretest was administered, none of the students had received a "treatment"; neither the students in the experimental group nor the students in the control group had participated in the career education program at that point. The function of this hypothesis test was to provide statistical assurance that the random assignment of students to the experimental and control groups had been effective. Had the null hypothesis been rejected, the authors would have concluded that the experimental and control samples had been chosen from populations of students that differed in their average scores on the Attitude Toward Career Knowledge Scale at the beginning of the school year. Fortunately, the null hypothesis that the populations of potential experimental and control students had identical average scores on the ATCK at time of pretest was retained. We can substantiate the appropriateness of the authors' conclusion by noting that the F-statistic for Group (0.3713) is much smaller than the critical value (2.74) for an alpha of .10 shown in the footnote to Table 14.1. This critical value is for an F distribution with 1 degree of freedom in the numerator (the value shown in the df column for Group) and 180 degrees of freedom in the denominator (a value that is just smaller than the 184 shown in the df column for Error).

The final null hypothesis tested for the pretest dependent variable was that grade level and treatment had no interaction effect. The F-statistic associated with this test is shown in the Grade × Group row of the Pretest section of Table 14.1. Once again, the F-statistic (.5443) is much smaller than the associated critical value (2.12) corresponding to an alpha level of 0.10, so the null hypothesis of no interaction effect was retained by the authors. Notice that the Grade × Group source has three degrees of freedom associated with it. It is no accident that the degrees of freedom associated with this interaction is the product of the df values associated with the independent variables (Grade and Group) that form the interaction (in this case $3 = 3 \times 1$). Degrees of freedom associated with an interaction term will always equal the product of the degrees of freedom associated with the sources that form the interaction. The critical value 2.12 was appropriate here because the interaction term Grade × Group had 3 degrees of freedom and the Error source had 184 degrees of freedom associated with it.

Had the Grade × Group interaction been statistically significant, it would have meant that the random assignment of students to experimental and control groups was flawed in at least one grade. This is true because the alternative hypothesis in this case is that the difference between average pretest ATCK scores for potential experimental group and control group students in one grade was not equal to the corresponding difference for students in at least one other grade. Since there was no main effect due to Group, a significant interaction effect could only be interpreted as a significant control group versus experimental group difference in at least one grade.

The section of Table 14.1 headed "Posttest" contains the results of three hypothesis tests that parallel those described above for the pretest dependent variable. The row labeled "Grade" contains the results of a test of the null hypothesis that grade level had no main effect on average posttest score. As the authors stated, this null hypothesis was rejected. The F-statistic shown for Grade (7.9037) is substantially larger than the critical value (2.12) associated with an alpha level of 0.10 for an F distribution with 3 degrees of freedom in the numerator and 180 degrees of freedom in the denominator.

In rejecting the null hypothesis that grade level has no main effect on posttest score, the authors are stating that the average ATCK scores of the populations of potential program participants from which the samples of ninth-graders, tenth-graders, eleventh-graders, and twelfth-graders were drawn are not equal. At least two of these populations have different average scores.

The second null hypothesis tested in this section was that participation in the career education program had no effect on average posttest ATCK scores. As the authors report, this null hypothesis was also rejected. Since the null hypothesis concerning a main effect due to treatment was retained for the pretest dependent variable, and students were randomly assigned to treatment and control groups, the authors are on reasonably firm ground in concluding that the career education program was effective in influencing students' attitudes toward career knowledge.

The relevant statistics for the main effect of treatment (i.e., Group) on average posttest scores are the F value of 5.8552 and the critical value for an alpha level of 0.10 in an F distribution with one degree of freedom in the numerator and 180 degrees of freedom in the denominator (2.74). Since the F-statistic exceeded the critical value, the null hypothesis of no treatment effect was rejected.

The final null hypothesis tested by Kershner and Blair was that grade level and treatment had no interaction effect on average posttest score. This null hypothesis was retained, since the associated F-statistic (1.6568 shown for the Grade × Group source) was smaller than the critical value of 2.12 shown in the footnote to Table 14.1.

Had the null hypothesis of no interaction effect been rejected, the authors would have concluded that their treatment was more effective for students in one grade than for students in at least one other grade. In fact, they might have found that the career education program influenced the average ATCK scores of experimental group students in one or more grades, but had no such influence for students in the remaining grades. In statistical terms, a significant interaction effect would have meant that the difference between the average posttest ATCK scores of the populations of potential experimental and control group students varied across grade levels. For example, the difference between experimental and control population averages might have been larger for tenth-graders than for twelfth-graders.

Our Interpretation of Results. We agree fully with the authors' conclusion that the career education program had a statistically significant influence on the participating students' attitudes toward career knowledge, as measured by the ATCK. Whether or not this influence is educationally or substantively significant is another question. This latter question could be examined more adequately by computing a confidence interval on the difference between the average posttest ATCK scores of the experimental and control populations. Upon examining this confidence interval, you would have to decide whether the difference in average scores was large enough to be important. As is always the case, statistics can facilitate a judgment on the question of substantive significance, but do not provide an answer to that question. In the final analysis, statistics are only part of a complete evaluation; you would have to interpret the statistical results in light of your knowledge of the dependent variable.

Assumptions Needed to Generalize. Were you to use these experimental results as a basis for adopting the career education program in your school system, you would be making a number of important assumptions. These assumptions were described at length in Chapter 10, when we last considered the Kershner and Blair (1975) study. You might want to review that discussion at this point.

An Evaluation of a Multicultural Education Program

Purpose of the Study. Alexander and Brown (1978) conducted a unique evaluation of a multicultural education program operated by the Houston, Texas, school system. The purpose of the program was to provide elementary school students with diverse cultural experiences in order to increase their respect for persons of other cultures and to promote their understanding and acceptance of persons of other races. We'll discuss the statistical and testing aspects of the evaluation, even though it involves a three-way analysis of variance. This kind of analysis differs in detail, but not in spirit, from the two-way ANOVA that is the subject of this chapter.

The program exposed students to the cultures of six different nations or continents—Africa, China, Germany, India, Mexico, and the United States. Each culture was presented in a separate classroom, and involved students in the geography, attire, art, music, dance, lifestyle, language, food, games, and crafts of the region represented.

Students who participated in the program were selected from grades two through six. Equal numbers of black, Anglo, and Mexican-American students participated in the program.

The purpose of the evaluation was to determine whether program participation led to changes in students' attitudes toward children of other racial-ethnic groups. In particular, the evaluators tried to determine whether program participants became more accepting of students of other racial and ethnic backgrounds.

Evaluation Design. Alexander and Brown used a simulation game to assess the pretreatment and posttreatment attitudes of students in an experimental group (program participants) and a control group. The game consisted of having students place three six-inch dolls in a scale model classroom. One of the dolls represented a white child, one represented a black child, and one represented a Mexican-American child. The dolls were distinguished by color and other physical features, and the evaluators confirmed that the students made the correct racial-ethnic classifications. Each student in the experimental group was told to identify one of the dolls as himself or herself. The student was then told that his or her doll had to wait in the model classroom for the instructor to come, and that the two children represented by the other dolls also had to wait. The student was instructed to place the doll representing himself or herself anywhere in the model classroom, and then to place the dolls representing the other two children anywhere in the classroom. Each student in the control group was given the same instructions, except that these students were told that they had to wait for a bus driver to take them back to school. Each student participated in the exercise independently.

When a student had finished placing the dolls, their positions were noted on a piece of paper that formed the floor of the model classroom. The total distance between the dolls was used as a measure of proximity.

The doll placement exercises were conducted twice: once prior to the experimental students' participation in the multicultural education program, or the control group students' participation in a school function of similar duration that did not feature culturally related experiences or instruction, and once immediately following such participation.

There were 270 program participants, randomly selected from students in grades two through six. Ninety of the participants were Anglo, 90 were black, and 90 were Mexican-American. The control sample consisted of 90 students sampled in the same proportions from each racial-ethnic group, and each of grades two through six. The authors did not indicate the population from which participants were sampled, nor did they state that control-group students were randomly sampled.

Alexander and Brown assumed that students who placed dolls of racial or ethnic groups other than their own closer to their own doll would be more accepting of students of other races and cultures than would students who placed the other dolls farther from their own. They thus used proximity of doll placement as a measure of racial and cultural acceptance.

The dependent variable used in the Alexander and Brown evaluation was the total distance between the dolls in the pretreatment measure, minus the total distance between the dolls in the post-treatment measure. The authors reasoned that a change in students' acceptance of children of other races and cultures would be indicated by closer placement of the dolls in the postmeasure than in the premeasure. A positive pre-minus-post difference in total distance would therefore correspond to a positive change in student attitude.

Authors' Data Table. Alexander and Brown conducted a three-way analysis of variance, using the pre-minus-post difference in total distance scores as their dependent variable. Their independent variables were grade level (grades two, three, four, five, and six), racial-ethnic group membership of students (white, black, and Mexican-American), and instructional experience (multi-cultural education or control group participation). Table 1 in the Alexander and Brown paper (1978; p. 8) contains the results of their analysis. It is reproduced here, just as it appears in the paper, as Table 14.2.

Authors' Interpretation. Alexander and Brown concluded, on the basis of the results shown in Table 14.2, that type of instructional experience had a significant main effect, that racial-ethnic group had a significant main effect, and that grade level of student had a significant main effect. They reported that, on average, students who participated in the multicultural educational experience placed the dolls eight centimeters closer together in the posttest than they had in the pretest. In contrast, students who were members of the control group placed the dolls only an average of 0.59 centimeter closer together in the posttest than in the pretest. The authors stated that the scores of "students who participated in the [multicultural education experience] were significantly different from the scores of students participating in the neutral school function [control-group students]" (p. 7).

The Nature of the Inferences. Table 14.2 summarizes the results of testing seven different null hypotheses. We will discuss them in order.

Alexander and Brown first tested the null hypothesis that students' racial-ethnic group had no effect on the average value of

TABLE 14.2: Analysis of Variance Summary Table

Source	SS	df	MS	F
Ethnicity	732.38	2	366.91	3.66*
Grade	1056.49	4	264.13	2.64
Instructional Experience	4784.87	1	4784.87	47.83*
Ethnicity by Grade	680.78	8	85.04	.85
Ethnicity by Instruction	38.91	2	19.46	.19
Grade by Instruction	1478.66	4	369.66	3.69*
Ethnicity by Grade by Instruction	1020.96	8	127.60	1.27
Within	33011.39	330	100.04	

*$p < .05$

the dependent variable (change in the proximity of the dolls). To understand the meaning of this hypothesis, it is again necessary to construct a hypothetical scenario. Suppose that the students assigned to the experimental group and the control group had been sampled from three populations that differed only in their racial-ethnic background: a population of Anglo second- through sixth-graders, a population of black second- through sixth-graders, and a population of Mexican-American second- through sixth-graders. Suppose further that each population had been divided in random halves. One half of each population had completed the doll placement exercise, then had participated in the multicultural education program, and then had completed the doll placement exercise again. The other half of each population had completed the doll placement exercise, then had participated in the control group experience, and then had completed the doll placement exercise again. Finally, suppose that the evaluators had computed the average value of the dependent variable for each population. There would be one average change in doll placement distances for students in the Anglo population, one average change for students in the black population, and one average change for students in the Mexican-American population. The null hypothesis states that these average changes would all be equal. The alternative hypothesis is that at least one of these average changes would differ from another.

The authors rejected the null hypothesis that students' racial-ethnic group had no main effect on the dependent variable. In doing so, they compared the F-statistic for Ethnicity (3.66) with the critical value of an F distribution with two degrees of freedom in the numerator and 330 degrees of freedom in the denominator, corresponding to an alpha level of 0.05. Since 3.66 was larger than the critical value, the authors rejected the null hypothesis at the 0.05 level of significance. We can tell that Alexander and Brown reached this decision because the 3.66 value in Table 14.2 has a "*" beside it, and the footnote to Table 14.2 explains that the "*" indicates a probability value (alpha level) that is less than .05.

In a similar fashion, Alexander and Brown tested, and rejected, null hypotheses that grade level of students and instructional experience had no main effects on the dependent variable. Their null hypothesis concerning grade level applies to populations of students from grades two, three, four, five, and six who might have participated in either the multicultural education program or the control group experience. Interpretation of this null hypothesis requires a hypothetical scenario that is similar to the one we've just presented, in which half of each population was randomly assigned to the multicultural education programming and the other half was assigned to the control group experience. The null hypothesis states that the average score on the dependent variable would be exactly the same for students at each grade level. The alternative hypothesis states that the average scores would be different, for at least two of the populations of students from different grades.

The null hypothesis that instructional experience has no main effect on the dependent variable is the one most important to the evaluation. This null hypothesis presumes that, if populations of students from each grade level and each ethnic group had been divided in half randomly, and if one half of each population had been assigned to the multicultural education program and the other half to the control treatment, the two halves of the populations would have exactly the same average score on the dependent variable. The alternative hypothesis is that the average score of students who had been assigned to the multicultural program would differ from the average score of students who had been assigned to the control treatment.

Since the F-statistic associated with instructional experience (47.83) is larger than the alpha = .05 critical value of the F distribution for one and 330 degrees of freedom, the difference between the sample average values on the dependent variable was declared to be significant at the .05 level; that is, the null hypothesis was rejected.

Alexander and Brown tested three null hypotheses concerning interactions between pairs of independent variables. The first was that students' racial-ethnic group and grade level would not interact in their effect on the dependent variable. The meaning of this null hypothesis is as follows: Suppose that populations of black, Anglo, and Mexican-American students had different average scores on the dependent variable. According to the null hypothesis, the differences between their average scores would be the same, regardless of the students' grade levels. This null hypothesis was retained, because the associated F-statistic (.85) did not exceed the critical value of an appropriate F distribution for an alpha level of .05.

The second null hypothesis concerning an interaction stated that students' racial-ethnic group and instructional experience would not interact in their effect on the dependent variable. To understand the meaning of this null hypothesis, assume once again that the authors had three populations of students (one of each racial-ethnic group represented in the study) and that half of each population had been randomly assigned to each instructional experience. Suppose that the halves of each population that were assigned to the two instructional experiences had different average scores on the dependent variable. The null hypothesis states that these differences would be exactly the same for the black, Anglo, and Mexican-American populations. Since the F-statistic associated with this null hypothesis (.19) did not exceed its corresponding critical value, the null hypothesis was retained.

The third null hypothesis involving an interaction between two independent variables was rejected. The results in Table 14.2 show that there was a significant grade level by instructional experience interaction, since the associated F-statistic (3.69) has an "*" beside it.

The null hypothesis that there was no grade level by instructional experience interaction means the following: Suppose populations of students in each of grades two through six had been divided randomly in half, with one half assigned to the multicultural education program and the other half assigned to the control treatment. The null hypothesis states that, for students in each grade, the two halves of the population would have average scores on the dependent variable that differed by exactly the same amount. In other words, if the null hypothesis were true, it would mean that the difference between the effectiveness of the experimental and control treatments would be exactly the same for second-graders as it was for third-graders, and as it was for fourth- through sixth-graders.

Since this null hypothesis was rejected, we can surmise that the experimental treatment resulted in a greater change in doll placement distance for students in some grades than for students in others.

The final null hypothesis tested in this study involved what is called a **three-way interaction**. The null hypothesis states that there is no interaction effect of students' racial-ethnic group membership, grade level, and the instructional experience to which they were assigned. Three-way interactions are very complicated, and they can be described in a variety of ways. Perhaps the simplest explanation in this study is as follows: The data in Table 14.2 show that there was an interaction between students' grade level and their instructional experience. The null hypothesis that there is no three-way interaction states that the interaction between students' grade level and instructional experience is exactly the same for populations of students in each racial-ethnic group. This is an admittedly terse explanation. Because a full explanation would require many additional pages, we will take the easy path of referring you to a traditional statistics text (Glass and Hopkins, 1984) for more information. The null hypothesis that there was a three-way interaction between the independent variables was retained, since the associated F-statistic (1.27) was smaller than the alpha = .05 critical value in an appropriate F distribution.

Well, we've finally considered all seven null hypotheses represented by the results shown in Table 14.2. The authors chose not to interpret any of the hypotheses involving interactions, since they were concerned primarily with main effects and only one null hypothesis involving an interaction was rejected. This decision is, perhaps, warranted in this study. However, *interaction effects can often render main effects uninterpretable*, so it is generally foolhardy to ignore interactions. Although it is highly unlikely in this study, it is possible that students in one grade who were assigned to the control group experience exhibited greater average change on the dependent variable than did students who were assigned to the multicultural education program. For students in other grades, just the reverse might be true. This could happen even though there was a main effect due to instructional experience. To understand fully the meaning of main effects and interactions, it is often necessary to construct graphs similar to those shown in Figures 14.1 through 14.5.

You may have wondered about the row in Table 14.2 that is labeled "Within." The data in this row of the table represent the variation in the dependent variable within each of the groups in the experiment. In some studies, this row of the ANOVA table is labeled **error** or **residual**, instead of "Within." The terms are synonymous in this application.

Our Interpretation of Results. In many ways, Alexander and Brown did an excellent job of discussing the implications of their findings. They are particularly sensitive to questions concerning the validity of their doll placement exercise as a measure of racial attitudes.

As in all evaluative research, it is necessary to go beyond statistical information when judging the educational implications of the results. In the case of this study, we must be concerned, as were Alexander and Brown, with the meaning of a main effect due to instructional experience. Also, because it is not certain that the experimental and control groups were randomly sampled from the same populations, we must be cautious in stating that the multicultural education program alone was responsible for the main effect. Finally, the populations from which the samples were selected are not well described, so we are uncertain about the generalizability of the results of this study. Perhaps most important, we have no idea how much of a change in student attitudes is represented by the change in doll placement distances the authors found.

The measurement approach used in this study is unusual and imaginative. Measuring attitudes is very difficult, and is doubly difficult when young children are involved. Nevertheless, it is the responsibility of the evaluators to demonstrate that the changes they found represent real and important differences in students' attitudes toward children of other races and cultures.

Assumptions Needed to Generalize. Were you to use the results of this study as a basis for adopting the multicultural education program in your setting, you would have to make several strong assumptions. First, you would have to assume that it was important to change students' attitudes toward children of other races and cultures. Second, you would have to assume that the doll placement exercise was a valid measure of students' attitudes. Third, you would have to assume that the changes observed in this study represented important modifications of students' attitudes. Finally, you would have to assume that the program was transportable; that is, that the results found in this study would be likely to occur in your own setting. These are all strong assumptions. We would therefore encourage you to be appropriately cautious about any generalizations to your own situation—even without looking at costs, alternatives to, and side effects of the program.

A Study of Perceptions of the Roles of Women

Purpose of the Study. In 1984, White and Lewis presented the results of a study in which they investigated changes in perceptions of appropriate roles for women over the course of a decade. They collected responses to the *Attitudes Toward Women Scale* (Spence & Helmreich, 1972) from samples of male and female junior high school students, and from both parents of the sampled students, in the spring of 1974 and the fall of 1983. The authors were interested in determining how, if at all, attitudes toward women's roles had changed over the decade between their initial data collection and their second data collection and, more particularly, if changes had been similar or dissimilar in the four groups of respondents they surveyed.

Research Design. The design used in this study was ecologically longitudinal, but individually cross-sectional. By this we mean that the authors collected their data at two widely spaced times in the same institutional setting (in the case of this study, in the same junior high school), but used different samples of individuals the first time and the second time they collected data. As a result of this design, the authors can describe differences between the perceptions of respondents associated with the junior high school from $Time_1$ and $Time_2$, but they cannot interpret their data as though the data indicated changes in the perceptions of individuals over this time period.

White and Lewis reported that they selected a random sample of boys and girls from classes in grades seven, eight, and nine in a single junior high school in a small city, in the spring of 1974. After they obtained permission from the students' parents, they asked the students to complete a modified version of the Attitudes Toward Women Scale (ATWS) that had been rewritten to eliminate language that would be unfamiliar to junior high school students. The students completed the 20-item instrument during the school day, under the supervision of one of the authors. Students were then asked to take copies of the instrument home to their parents, and to deliver a written request that their mother and father also complete the instrument and have their child bring it back to school. In 1974, the authors collected responses from 30 girls, 30 boys, 29 mothers, and 24 fathers.

In the fall of 1983 the authors administered the same instrument to samples of girls and boys in the same junior high school and mailed copies of the scale to the mothers and fathers of the students they sampled. They had parents mail the completed instruments to one of the authors, rather than relying on the students to return them. Although White and Lewis do not report their 1983 sample sizes by group, it is possible to determine from their analysis of variance table (which is reproduced below) that their total 1983 sample size was 129, compared to 113 in 1974. This was accomplished as follows: The degrees of freedom in the row marked "Total" in White and Lewis' (1984) analysis of variance was 241. Since the total degrees of freedom is always one less than the total sample size used in the study, it was determined that the authors' total sample size was 242. The sample size in 1983 was then calculated by subtracting, from 242, the total of the reported group sizes for which data were obtained in 1974.

The modification of the Attitudes Toward Women Scale used by the authors consisted of 20 five-option items in a Likert scale format (e.g., with options ranging from 1—"strongly disagree"— to 5—"strongly agree"). Half the items were phrased positively, and the other half were phrased negatively, to avoid a phenomenon known as a "response set" in which respondents tend to agree with positive statements regardless of their content. The range of possible scores on the instrument was thus from 20 to 100, with a

TABLE 14.3: Comparisons of Groups of Girls, Boys, Mothers, and Fathers from 1974 and 1983 in Their Responses to an Opinionnaire About Girls and Women, Using a Two-Way Analysis of Variance Procedure

Source	SS	df	MS	F	p
Groups	5919.644	3	1973.215	28.82	< .01
Years	1781.074	1	1781.074	26.01	< .01
Interaction	725.528	3	241.843	3.53	< .05
Error	16021.342	234	68.467		
Total	24447.587	241			

higher score indicating a less traditional attitude toward women's roles.

Authors' Data Table. White and Lewis reported the results of a two-way analysis of variance of respondents' total scores on the modified Attitudes Toward Women Scale in their Table 2 (p. 11). Their table is reproduced here as Table 14.3.

Authors' Interpretation. The authors reported that they found a "significant main effect for groups," meaning that the average scores on the scale found for the four groups (girls, boys, mothers, and fathers) differed significantly, and a "significant main effect for time," meaning that the average of scale scores found in 1983 differed significantly from the average of scale scores found in 1974. They also reported that the magnitude of the difference for girls differed from that of the other three groups, and resulted in a statistically significant interaction effect. The patterns of average scores on the modified ATWS found in 1974 and 1983 were displayed in a graph that White and Lewis labeled Figure 1 (p. 12). We have reproduced that graph as Figure 14.6, because it so clearly illustrates the nature of the significant interaction effect that was present in the data.

White and Lewis concluded that since three of their groups (all except girls) had higher average scores in 1983 than in 1974, and since higher scores indicate less traditional attitudes than do lower scores, "some real changes are occurring in views of female roles" (p. 5). They suggested that the "home environments" for boys and girls might be changing (p. 5), since mothers scored higher than girls in 1983, and fathers scored higher in 1983 than in 1974. The authors then speculated on the processes underlying

Figure 14.6 Display of Means of Responses to the Opinionnaire About Girls and Women by Girls, Boys, Mothers, and Fathers in 1974 and 1983

their findings, and compared their results to those of other researchers who investigated attitudes toward women's' roles.

The Nature of the Inferences. Table 14.3 contains a summary of the results of three hypothesis tests. Table 14.3 is in the form of a standard analysis of variance (ANOVA) table, in that it is composed of columns headed Source (of variance), SS (sums of squares), df (degrees of freedom), MS (mean squares), F (a column of test statistics), and p (the proportion of the appropriate F-distribution that falls above the reported test statistic). Each row of the table contains results for a different source of variance—that is, a different contributor to variation in individuals' scores on the modified Attitudes Toward Women Scale.

In the first row of the table, we see the results of testing the null hypothesis that there were no differences among the average scores of the four populations sampled, when those averages are computed for both years in which data were collected. To be certain (or at least increase the likelihood) that this statement is clear, let's consider just two of the populations—junior high school girls and junior high school boys. Suppose it had been possible to collect scale scores for all girls who attended junior high school in Wyoming (the likely state in which the authors conducted their study, since that is where they both live) in 1974 and 1983. The population mean for girls would have been the average of the ATWS scores of all of these girls. Likewise, had it been possible to collect scale scores for all boys who attended junior high school in Wyoming in 1974 and 1983, the population mean for boys would have been the average of the ATWS scores of all of these boys. Think about collecting data from the entire population of mothers of these girls and boys, and from the entire population of fathers of these girls and boys. These two populations would have yielded two more population averages on the ATWS. The null hypothesis tested in the first row of the ANOVA table is that all four population average scores on the ATWS—for girls, boys, mothers, and fathers—were equal. The alternative hypothesis was that *at least one* of the population averages differed from the others.

In the second row of the ANOVA table, we find the results of testing the null hypothesis that the average score on the ATWS for all four populations in 1974 is equal to the average score on the ATWS for all four populations in 1983. The alternative hypothesis is that these two population averages, the overall average for 1974 and the overall average for 1983, are different. It is essential to understand that the averages hypothesized to be equal in this hypothesis test apply to all four of the groups under consideration in this research—girls, boys, mothers, and fathers. Were it possible to compute the population average for 1974, we would secure a score on the ATWS from every Wyoming junior high school girl and boy, and from each of their mothers and fathers, and average all of these scores together. The resulting value would be one of the population means specified in the null hypothesis. The other population mean would be the same average score, based on data collected from the same four populations in 1983.

The row of the table labeled "Interaction" contains the results of a somewhat more complex hypothesis test that can be described in several ways. Perhaps the easiest way to think about it is to consider, for each of the populations defined by gender and age— girls, boys, mothers, and fathers—the difference between the population average score on the ATWS in 1983 and the population average score on the ATWS in 1974. Conceptualized this way, there would be a difference in population averages for girls, a difference in population averages for boys, and similar differences for mothers and for fathers. The null hypothesis is that these four differences in population averages are all equal. That is, the 1983-1974 difference for girls equals the 1983-1974 difference for boys equals the 1983-1974 difference for mothers equals the 1983-1974 difference for fathers. If this null hypothesis is true, there is no interaction between group membership (girls, boys, etc.) and year (1983 vs. 1974). If the null hypothesis were true, and the results shown in Figure 14.6 were for populations rather than eight samples, the lines that connected the four population means for 1974 would be parallel to the lines that connected the four population means for 1983. The actual data for samples shown in Figure 14.6 do not produce parallel lines (the difference in sample means for girls is very close to zero, and the difference in sample means for mothers is almost nine points), therefore resulting in a statistically significant interaction effect. For the alternative hypothesis to be true, it is not necessary that the 1983-1974 difference in population averages be different for each group, just that two of these differences be unequal.

The row of the ANOVA table labeled "Error" contains statistics that indicate the variation in scores on the ATWS for members of the sample who were in the same group in terms of gender, age, and year. These statistics are based on analyses of sample data for all sampled girls in 1974, all sampled boys in 1974, and so on, concluding with all sampled fathers in 1983. A variance statistic is computed for each of these groups, and these variance statistics are then combined to produce the number in the MS (Mean Square) column. The mean square for error provides a baseline for comparison when we investigate the statistical significance of the other mean squares in the table. To be statistically significant, each of the mean squares for groups, years, and interaction have to be substantially larger than the mean square for error.

Our Interpretation of Results. The authors' statistical interpretations, that there were statistically significant main effects for groups and years, in addition to a statistically significant interaction effect, are absolutely correct. However, the degree to which these results can be generalized beyond the observed samples is questionable, as are the authors' speculations on the social processes underlying their findings.

Although White and Lewis clearly state that they collected data in a single junior high school in a community of 22,000 (in 1974) to 25,000 (in 1983), they provide no information on how they selected that junior high school. Nor do the authors identify the population to which they think their results generalize, although they write about their findings as though they apply to junior high school students and their parents everywhere. In our discussion of the inferences involved in this study, we have assumed that the authors wanted to generalize to all junior high school students, and their parents, in the state of Wyoming. But this assumption was merely a pedagogical device, based on speculation.

Even if the junior high school where data were collected had been sampled randomly from all junior high schools in Wyoming, generalization to the entire population of such schools would have been suspect. No single school is representative of all such schools in a state. Had the authors provided a rich description of the junior high school they used for data collection and the community that housed the school, it would have been possible to imagine a subpopulation of schools to which their results might generalize.

Two classes of error arise in surveys of the sort used in this study: random error and bias error. Random error is controlled by obtaining data from samples that are sufficiently large. Since the authors found statistically significant differences for each of the effects they tested, their samples were sufficient in size to support the analyses they conducted, that is, they controlled random error to a sufficient degree. Bias error arises when the samples that provide usable data are not representative of the population to which results are to be generalized. The possibility of substantial bias error is present in this study for several reasons. First, as we have already noted, the single junior high school where data were collected is not clearly representative of junior high schools in any population of interest. Second, the authors do not make clear how many of the sampled individuals in any group (girls, boys, mothers, and fathers) refused to participate in their study or failed to return usable data. When the participation rate in a survey is low, the risk of bias error must be considered. It cannot be assumed that respondents to a survey are representative of all sampled individuals—respondents and nonrespondents alike—or that respondents will fairly represent the population to which the researchers wish to generalize their findings.

White and Lewis speculated on the processes that gave rise to their findings, and on the meaning of those findings. Although a general shift in social awareness concerning gender roles was certainly present in the decade between their two data collections, it is not clear that the changes in perceptions in the Wyoming community they investigated can be attributed to a national phenomenon. Some local community activities or conditions might well be the principal causal factor underlying their findings. In addition, the significant interaction effect observed in the results of this study might be an artifact of the modification of the ATWS for a junior high school population. Although Lewis and White considered and dismissed the possibility of a "ceiling effect" for girls, detailed analysis of the modified ATWS might reveal a subset of questions that are beyond the comprehension or conceptual ability of junior high school students. Perhaps few junior high school students of either gender endorsed some ATWS questions. Since girls began with a higher average score in 1974 than did boys, this potential artifact of the questionnaire would not evidence itself in the responses of the junior high school boys. The authors report no such detailed item-by-item analysis of students' responses, so the possibility of this rival explanation of their findings cannot be dismissed.

Once again, when conducting or interpreting the results of research, it is important to consider every plausible explanation of the findings that comes to mind. It is also important to spend some time bringing these possibilities to mind.

Assumptions Needed to Generalize. We have discussed the issue of generalizing the findings of this study at some length (you might think, at excessive length) in the previous section. Suffice it to say that trustworthy generalization to another setting would require far more information about the setting in which data were collected, and the characteristics of the sampled junior high school students, than the authors provided. The findings reported in this study might reflect a general, nationwide phenomenon that characterized all junior high school populations and families during the decade that was investigated, but it is impossible to tell, or even to speculate, from the information provided.

Summary

Although this chapter is long, we introduced relatively few new concepts. You've probably realized that the statistical ideas we introduced in Chapter 13 were used heavily in this chapter as well. The basic logic of analysis of variance applies here as it did in the last chapter. Both one-way and two-way ANOVA make use of sums of squares, degrees of freedom, mean squares, F-statistics, and the F distribution to test null hypotheses. The same kinds of statistics are also used in three-way ANOVA.

The most important new idea introduced in this chapter was the notion of an interaction effect. Whenever evaluators and researchers investigate the effects of more than one independent variable at a time, they must be sensitive to the possibility that those variables may interact. Often a single variable will have different effects under different conditions.

The main advantage of two-way and higher-way analysis of variance is that these statistical procedures allow researchers and evaluators to examine more complex relationships than do the techniques we discussed in earlier chapters. Nothing is simple in education or the social and behavioral sciences. Effects rarely have a single cause. Treatments that are effective for one group of students might be ineffective for other groups. In order to discover what works and what doesn't, and to learn how things work, we need statistical procedures that allow us to model nature in its true complexity. Two-way analysis of variance is a small step in the right direction.

Problems — Chapter 14

In 1990, Neymann and Pratt expanded and replicated their study on the relative effectiveness of various methods of teaching beginning statistics at the college level (see Problems for Chapter 13). In this replication they investigated the relative effectiveness of the three methods (Traditional Lecture, Self-Paced Programmed Text, and a Discovery-Laboratory Method) for students at two levels of quantitative aptitude (Low Aptitude and High Aptitude).

The researchers randomly selected 90 students from among those who registered for a beginning statistics course in the Department of Psychology of a major university. They administered a standardized quantitative aptitude test on the 90 sampled students, and divided the group at their median score into a high aptitude group (those who scored above the median) and a low aptitude group (those who scored below the median). Neymann and Pratt then randomly assigned one third of the low aptitude group and one third of the high aptitude group to each of the three instructional methods. At the end of a one-semester instructional period, the researchers administered a common final examination to all 90 students.

The results of the study were reported by Neymann and Pratt in the following analysis of variance table:

Source	Sum of Squares	df	Mean Squares	F
Instructional Method	109.62	2	95.31	5.40**
Aptitude Level	161.85	1	161.85	9.17**
Method x Aptitude	128.84	2	64.42	3.65*
Within Groups	1482.60	84	17.65	
Total	1963.91	89		

*signif. @ 0.05 level
**signif. @ 0.01 level

14.1   The authors tested three null hypotheses in this study; two were concerned with main effects, and one with an interaction effect. Describe these null hypotheses.

14.2   Assuming that the authors acted in accordance with the results reported above, what decisions did they reach on retaining or rejecting the three null hypotheses? Support your conclusions by citing relevant data from the table.

14.3   Interpret the results of this study in your own words. What assumptions are necessary to the interpretation you have made?

14.4   In light of the significant interaction effect noted in the data table, can you safely conclude that one of the instructional methods is more effective than the others for all students, regardless of their quantitative aptitude level? Discuss this point.

15.

Some Advanced Topics

In this chapter we introduce three advanced statistical procedures that are used quite frequently in research and evaluation studies. The first, called the **analysis of covariance**, is an extension of the analysis of variance. The second is **multiple linear regression analysis**. The procedure is particularly useful in studies that involve prediction (such as prediction of students' achievement from their aptitude scores and data on the extensiveness of their instruction). The third procedure is called **factor analysis**. It is often used when constructing attitude scales or tests. Factor analysis allows a researcher to create a few variables (called factors) that do a good job of representing a lot of variables. It is therefore used to make things simpler—an always laudatory goal!

In the balance of this chapter we'll describe each statistical procedure and then discuss one actual research or evaluation study that makes use of each procedure. Discussion of the analysis of covariance often takes up a healthy chunk of an advanced statistics course, so our coverage here will be relatively superficial. Likewise, many universities devote entire graduate courses to regression analysis and factor analysis, so we won't be telling you all there is to know about either of these topics in this relatively brief chapter. Nonetheless, we feel it is important that you gain some sense of the purpose and power of these advanced statistical methods so that they won't be totally foreign when you encounter them in evaluation and research reports.

Analysis of Covariance

The analysis of covariance is conceptually similar to the analysis of variance procedures you've already encountered in Chapters 13 and 14. Its basic purpose is to allow a researcher or evaluator to test the null hypothesis that two or more population averages are equal, against the alternative hypothesis that at least one of the population averages is different from the others. For example, using analysis of covariance procedures you could test the null hypothesis that a population of sixth-grade students would have the same average score on a test of functional writing skills classes whether the students where taught to write in standard English classes (Curriculum A), in creative writing classes (Curriculum B), or in special writing drill-and-practice sessions (Curriculum C). In terms of the fundamental research and evaluation questions it can be used to address, analysis of covariance is just like the analysis of variance.

The analysis of variance and the analysis of covariance differ in two basic ways. First, the analysis of covariance allows a researcher or evaluator to address additional questions that the analysis of variance does not consider. Second, the two procedures differ in their detailed statistical computations. Consider once again the example involving instruction in functional writing. Were you to use the analysis of variance to test the null hypothesis of equal average performances on the functional writing test, you would select a simple random sample of sixth-graders from the population of interest, and then divide that sample randomly into thirds. One third of the students would be assigned to Curriculum A, another third to Curriculum B, and the final third to Curriculum C. At the end of the school year, you would administer the functional writing test to all three samples of students, and use their average posttreatment scores to decide whether or not the null hypothesis of equal population averages was tenable. If the average scores of the three samples of students differed sufficiently, you would reject the null hypothesis that the three population averages were equal.

In using analysis of variance as we have described it, you would assume that the process of randomly dividing the sample of sixth-grade students into three parts had been effective in making the three resulting samples of students equivalent in all ways that were relevant to their writing test performance. In other words, you would assume that the students assigned to each of the three curricula were equally capable at the outset, and that random assignment had ensured this equality. On the average, the assumption is a good one, particularly if the three samples of students are reasonably large. However, even though random sampling and assignment ensures that samples are equivalent on the average, it does not ensure that *every* random sample is equivalent to every other one. Random assignment is particularly vulnerable to the vagaries of Lady Luck when sample sizes are small. It might not be sufficient for you to know that the samples of students assigned to Curricula A, B, and C will be equivalent in their capabilities *on the average*, since you will conduct your experiment only once. It would be far better to have some assurance that the particular randomly assigned samples constructed for your experiment were equivalent, and to correct for differences between the samples, should they exist. This is where the **analysis of covariance** can help.

Suppose you believed that reading skill was an important predictor of a student's functional writing ability, and that you had scores on a standardized reading test that had been administered to all sixth-grade students, just prior to their assignment to the three curricula. Using the analysis of covariance, you could then: (1) examine your belief that performance on the reading achievement test was a predictor of functional writing achievement following instruction; (2) examine the hypothesis that the *relationships* between students' scores on the reading achievement test and their scores on the functional writing test were the same, regardless of the curriculum used to instruct them; and (3) adjust for differences in the average pre-instruction reading achievement of the three samples of students, should such differences be found. In short, the analysis of covariance would allow you to correct for some important differences between the three samples that might still be present, even though the samples had been constituted through a random assignment procedure. By making the samples more "alike" at the outset of the experiment, you would add strength to an assertion that any differences in average functional writing scores at the end of the experiment were due solely to differences in the effectiveness of the three curricula.

Three variables are involved in the hypothetical experiment we just described. Type of curriculum (A, B, or C) is an **independent variable**. It is the treatment variable whose effect is to be ascertained. Reading achievement score prior to instruction is another independent variable that, in this experiment, plays the role of a **covariate**. A covariate is a variable that is correlated with the **dependent variable**. It is measured prior to the administration of a treatment, and might account for some portion of the differences between the average scores of the treatment groups on the dependent variable. Functional writing test score at the end of the experiment is an example of a dependent variable. In the analysis of covariance, we attempt to determine the effect of the independent variable on the average value of the dependent variable, after between-sample differences on the covariate have been eliminated. In the experiment we've just described, we would attempt to determine the effect of type of curriculum on average functional writing scores, after we had eliminated the effect of differences between the average initial reading achievement scores of the experimental samples.

The hypotheses that can be examined using the analysis of covariance are illustrated in Figures 15.1 and 15.2. In each figure, scores on the dependent variable are shown on the vertical axis, and scores on the covariate are shown on the horizontal axis. For the functional writing experiment, students' scores on the writing test would be plotted on the vertical axis, and their scores on the reading test that was administered prior to their writing instruction would be plotted to the horizontal axis. In Figure 15.1, the three diagonal lines represent the relationships between scores on the reading achievement test and scores on the writing test, for the samples of students taught using Curricula A, B, and C. The egg-shaped patterns (ellipses) around the three diagonal lines represent the distributions of scores on the reading test and the functional writing test for the three groups of students. For each group, average scores on the reading test and the functional writing test would fall at the center of the that group's ellipse.

We have drawn Figure 15.1 as though there was a definite relationship between students' scores on the reading test and their scores on the writing test administered after instruction. In fact, the figure suggests that there is an increasing relationship between the two variables (the higher the score on the reading test, the

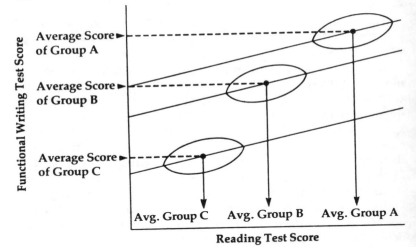

Figure 15.1

higher the score on the functional writing test). If the analysis of covariance is to be effective, there must be some relationship between the covariate and the dependent variable. It need not be a positive relationship, however. If there were no relationship

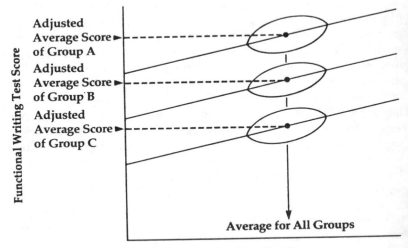

Figure 15.2

between the covariate and the dependent variable, eliminating differences between the groups' average scores on the covariate would not affect their scores on the dependent variable.

We have also drawn Figure 15.1 as though the relationships between the covariate and the dependent variable were the same for all three populations. This is true because the three diagonal lines are parallel to each other. This condition is a basic assumption of the analysis of covariance. If it does not hold, there is no way to eliminate the effect of differences between the groups on the covariate.

Look at the three positions on the vertical axis of Figure 15.1 (score on the functional writing test) marked "Average Score for Group A," "Average Score for Group B," and "Average Score for Group C." Then notice the differences between the average scores of the three groups on the reading test shown on the horizontal axis ("Avg. Group A," "Avg. Group B," and "Avg. Group C"). Part of the reason the three groups differ in their average scores on the functional writing test is because they had different average scores on the reading test, prior to instruction. Imagine what would happen to the groups' average scores on the functional writing test, if they had the same average score on the reading test. This situation is shown in Figure 15.2. You will find that the groups' average scores on the functional writing test would be closer together, had their average score on the reading test been the same prior to instruction. These new average scores on the functional writing test are called **adjusted averages**. In the analysis of covariance, differences between these adjusted averages are tested for statistical significance. The null hypothesis that the analysis of covariance would test in this experiment would be that the populations of students from which the three samples were chosen would have equal adjusted average scores on the functional writing test. That's a long sentence, but there's no shorter way to state it precisely. It means that the analysis of covariance tests the null hypothesis that type of curriculum has no effect on functional writing test score, after differences between the average reading scores of the samples have been eliminated. It is the opportunity to eliminate the groups' differences in average pre-instructional reading score that makes the analysis of covariance more powerful than the analysis of variance.

Research and evaluation studies that make use of the analysis of covariance do not always include tests of the hypothesis that the covariate is related to the dependent variable. Nor do they always include tests of the hypothesis that the relationship between the covariate and the dependent variable is the same in all populations being compared. Regardless of their tenability, these hypotheses are often assumed to be true, and the only hypothesis tested concerns the equivalence of adjusted population averages. This practice is unfortunate, since the appropriateness of analysis of covariance, and the accuracy of its results, depends critically on the correctness of its assumptions.

In the next section we consider an actual evaluation study that used the analysis of covariance, together with other analytic procedures, to examine the effect of computers on posttreatment mathematics achievement scores.

A Study of the Effect of Computers on Middle-School Students' Mathematics Achievement

Purpose of the Study. In the early 1970s, computer-assisted instruction (CAI) was hailed as the coming miracle in elementary and secondary education. Educators expected the availability of microcomputers in the classroom to provide students with an adaptive learning environment that would allow them to progress at their own pace, while freeing teachers to work with students who needed individual assistance. In addition, computers were expected to provide a sufficiently attractive learning environment that they would increase students' motivation, improve students' attitudes toward school, and reduce problems of truancy and disruption.

Although some research on the effects of computers in the classroom has produced encouraging results (Burns & Bozeman, 1981; Fisher, 1983; Kulik, Bangert, & Williams, 1983), Ferrell (1985) reported that most studies of the effects of CAI on students' achievement, attitudes, and behavior have been of short duration, and that positive effects typically diminish as studies increase in duration. These findings suggest that the effects of CAI might be attributable to the novelty of having computers in the classroom, or to the special attention students receive when they are first introduced to computers (the so-called "Hawthorne effect," in which subjects react to the attention they are given rather than the features of the experimental treatment they receive).

The study reported by Ferrell (1985) differed from many previous studies of the effects of CAI on students' performances in that it was conducted over the course of an entire school year, thus diminishing the effects of novelty, and perhaps reducing somewhat the potential "Hawthorne effect." The purposes of the study were described by Ferrell (p. 5) as:

1. [Determining whether] the use of computers as an integral part of instruction would increase mathematics achievement.

2. [Exploring] the impact of computers as an integral part of instruction on other factors, such as student attitude, attendance, discipline, etc.

In our examination of Ferrell's study, we will restrict our attention to analyses and results that are pertinent to the first purpose.

Research Design. Ferrell (1985) conducted her study in a single middle school (grades six through eight) in a large, urban, southwestern school district. A single mathematics teacher presumably volunteered to participate in the study. Two of the teacher's sixth-grade mathematics classes were randomly designated as experimental classes, and two others were designated as control classes. Fifty students were enrolled in the experimental classes, and 41 were enrolled in the control classes. The sample of 91 students was predominantly Hispanic in ethnic composition, but was balanced in gender representation (46 girls and 45 boys).

Students in the experimental classes were taught mathematics via computer for 40 minutes per day in a classroom with 26 Apple II microcomputers. Each student thus had his or her own computer during the entire instructional period. Commercially available instructional materials in mathematics that provided drill and practice on mathematical skills and tutorial assistance in mathematics were used throughout each instructional period (SRA Estimation Tennis and Beano were used 30 to 35 minutes per day, and DLM Dragon Mix, Demolition Division, and Meteor Multiplication were used 5 to 10 minutes per day, at the end of each class period). The teacher provided assistance to individual students or small groups of students when they had problems they could not solve on their own; she worked with the entire class only when a new concept was introduced or when a large number of students encountered the same difficulty. Instruction in the control classes was described by Ferrell (1985, p. 5) as "teacher-directed" and "group-centered." The curriculum materials used in the control classes were not described.

The school district in which the research took place administered the Iowa Tests of Basic Skills to all students in the spring of each school year. Thus, mathematics achievement test scores collected in the spring of the school year prior to the initiation of the study and at the termination of the study were available for all students. Mathematics total scores, as well as scores on the Concepts, Computation, and Problem-Solving subtests were collected at the termination of the study. In addition, students who participated in the study completed two measures of their attitudes toward mathematics, and data were collected from existing school records on the frequency of students' tardiness in their mathematics classes, the number of days each student had been absent from school, and the number of times each student had been cited for a disciplinary infraction during the study. Although all of these data were analyzed in creative and appropriate ways using multivariate procedures, we will restrict our discussion to Ferrell's analysis of achievement test data.

Author's Data Tables. Table 2 of the Ferrell paper (1985, p. 16) contains the results of an analysis of covariance of mathematics total scores on the Iowa Tests of Basic Skills collected at the end of the study, with mathematics total scores collected in the spring of the year preceding the study used as a covariate. Table 6 of the paper (p. 20) contains means and differences between means earned by students in the experimental classes and the control classes for all dependent variables used in the study, including the mathematics achievement test scores. Because Ferrell's interpretation of the results of the analysis of covariance references the data in Table 6, both tables are reproduced here, just as they appeared in her paper, as Tables 15.1 and 15.2.

Author's Interpretation. Ferrell (1985) states that "The analysis of covariance yielded a significant main effect for group mean between the computer immersion students and the control group" (p. 9), and in her later discussion of the results, "The raw score mathematics totals for the computer group and the control group yielded statistically significant differences. . . . When the magnitude of these differences was examined, however, it was found

TABLE 15.1: Analysis of Covariance: 1984 ITBS Math Skills Total Raw Score

Source	Adjusted df	Adjusted MS	F
Between Groups	1	43.184	5.357*
Within	83	8.061	
Total	84		

*$p < .05$

that the mean raw score total for the computer immersion group differed from the control group by just over one item" (p. 10). Finally, Ferrell provides the following trenchant distinction between statistical significance and practical significance, and the implications of this distinction for educational practice:

Interpretations of the data from this study, then, become very much a question of practical significance rather than statistical significance. The mean difference between the math computation raw scores for the two groups was less than two items (1.9). Similarly, a difference of only one time tardy to math class was found between the two groups and no difference was found in the average number of discipline cards filed.

When decisions regarding the implementation of a new program which is as expensive to replicate as the computer immersion project must be made, both statistical and practical significance must be weighed. The evaluation of the computer immersion project did yield statistically significant differences. The practical magnitude of these differences was small, however, and this, coupled with other

TABLE 15.2: Group Means and Mean Differences, All Variables

Overall	Computer N = 48	Control N = 40	Difference	N = 88
ATA	88.3	86.8	1.5	87.6
MATS	43.9	43.9	0.0	43.9
Days Absent	5.7	6.8	1.1	6.2
Tardies	.6	1.6	1.0	1.0
Discipline Cards	.6	.6	0.0	.6
Math Total	67.9	66.6	1.3	67.4
Computation	30.9	29.0	1.9	30.0
Concepts	22.9	21.6	1.3	22.3
Problem Solving	16.1	15.8	0.3	16.0

methodological problems [associated with multivariate statistical analyses that we have not discussed here], resulted in the conclusion that the computer immersion project did not demonstrate an impact of computers even when time is maximized on any of the variables studied. School district officials concurred with this conclusion. The computer immersion model was dropped and the computers were put to other uses. (p. 12)

The Nature of the Inferences. In presenting Table 15.1, we have reproduced results that are pertinent to only one of the inferential statistical analyses Ferrell conducted. The data presented in Table 15.1 provide an abbreviated summary of the results of an analysis of covariance in which students' total mathematics raw scores on the Iowa Tests of Basic Skills (ITBS), collected at the conclusion of the computer immersion experiment, were used as a dependent variable, and students' scores on the same test, collected prior to the beginning of the experiment, were used as a covariate. It is not clear whether students completed the same level or form of the ITBS, or a different form or level, prior to, and at the conclusion of, the experiment.

The important sources of variation in students' ITBS mathematics scores shown in Table 15.1 are "Between Groups," meaning between the sample of students taught sixth-grade mathematics using computers and the sample of students taught sixth-grade mathematics in a conventional classroom without computer assistance; and "Within," meaning within these two samples of students. The "Adjusted MS" column of the table summarizes the magnitudes of these sources of variation.

The value 43.184 for the Between Groups source of variance is the *adjusted mean square* between groups. "Adjusted" means that the effects of the groups' initial average difference in mathematics achievement, measured prior to the initiation of the experiment, have been "removed" statistically, at least to the degree that the assumptions of the analysis of covariance hold for these data. This statistic approximates the groups' posttreatment variation in average mathematics achievement, assuming that the groups had the same average mathematics achievement at the beginning of the experiment. The value 8.061 for the Within source of variance is the adjusted mean square within groups, also computed after the effects of the groups' initial average differences in mathematics achievement have been taken into account. This statistic approximates the variation in mathematics achievement within the two groups, had the groups' average mathematics achievement been the same at the beginning of the experiment. The F value of 5.357 is the adjusted mean square between groups, divided by the adjusted mean square within groups. From the asterisk attached to the F value and the footnote to Table 15.1, we can deduce that the null hypothesis of equal adjusted average mathematics total scores for the population of potential sixth-grade students who could have been taught using the computer curriculum, and the population of potential sixth-grade students who could have been taught using the conventional curriculum, was rejected at the 0.05 level of statistical significance. That is, the adjusted average scores of the two groups differed significantly, when tested with an alpha level of 0.05.

As noted earlier in this chapter, the validity of analysis of covariance depends on several critical assumptions. First, the variability of scores on the dependent variable has to be identical in both populations from which samples have been drawn. In this experiment, the variability of ITBS mathematics total scores would have to be the same for the population of students from which the computer instruction sample was selected, and for the population of students from which the conventional instruction sample was selected. Second, the relationship between the dependent variable and the covariate has to be identical in both populations. In this experiment, the regression lines that resulted from using ITBS mathematics scores collected at the end of the experiment as the dependent variable, and using ITBS mathematics scores collected at the beginning of the experiment as the independent variable, would have to be the same for the population of students from which the computer instruction sample was selected and for the population of students from which the conventional instruction sample was selected. Unfortunately, Ferrell (1985) does not indicate whether the validity of these assumptions was investigated. However, since the pretreatment samples were selected from the same population randomly, it is likely that the variability assumption has been met. Whether the common regression lines assumption has been met would depend on whether the computer instruction treatment and the conventional instruction treatment had different effects on the relationship between students' pre-treatment and posttreatment mathematics achievement.

Our Interpretation of Findings. We agree entirely with Ferrell that her study produced statistically significant results that were of little practical significance. The greatest difference in mathematics achievement between control group students and computer instruction students was 1.9 items correct for the Computation subtest of the ITBS (see Table 15.2). In view of the drill-and-practice emphasis of the computer instruction, it is not surprising that the greatest difference between mathematics performances of control group and experimental group students occurred on the Computation subtest. However, as Ferrell notes, the magnitude of the performance difference was disappointingly small.

Although the Ferrell study incorporated several important design features that strengthened its internal validity—groups of students were randomly assigned to the experimental and control classes; the same teacher taught all classes, thus eliminating potential contamination due to differences in teachers' ability—some potential threats to validity remain. The "John Henry" effect mentioned in Chapter 6 is one potential threat. Since the same teacher taught all classes, she could well have decided to "beat the steam drill" by exerting extra effort in the conventional classes while exerting less instructional effort in the computer instruction classes. Since the ITBS mathematics test was administered in the spring of the school year prior to the study and at the end of the study, the teacher would have been familiar with the content of the test. It would therefore have been easy to provide drill and practice on the specific content of the test in the conventional instruction classes. The author provides no evidence that the John Henry effect occurred, so our comments are highly speculative.

So little information on the content of the conventional curriculum is provided that it is not clear whether the experimental and control classes differed only in mode of instruction, or in curriculum content as well. If both differences existed, it is possible that the content of the conventional instruction was more closely aligned with the content of the ITBS mathematics test than was the computer curriculum. Were this the case, the computer immersion treatment would have been placed at a distinct disadvantage. Again, absence of information makes this argument conjectural at best.

In sum, this study was fundamentally well designed and provided a good illustration of the important distinction between statistical significance and practical significance of findings. With additional description of the content of the curricula used, and information on the motivations of the teacher who participated in the study, several potential threats to the validity of the author's interpretations could have been dispelled.

Regression Analysis

The most elementary form of regression analysis is called **simple linear regression**. One objective of simple linear regression is to predict a person's score on a dependent variable from knowledge of their score on an independent variable. Simple linear regression is also used to examine the degree of linear relationship between an independent variable and a dependent variable. In that application it is an extension of correlation analysis, which was described in Chapter 4.

Let's consider a hypothetical application of simple linear regression for purposes of prediction. Suppose you were the personnel director of a company that built high-technology devices, such as personal computers. One of your tasks was to establish policies for hiring people to work on the company's production line. Management wanted workers hired only if they could produce at least 40 modules per hour, thereby keeping up with the standard speed of the production line. Your job was to determine which prospective employees were likely to be sufficiently productive, and which were not, so that the company could avoid training workers who would later have to be fired.

When applicants for production line jobs sought employment they were given a standardized Test of Assembly Speed (TAS), which had been shown to correlate highly with employee productivity on the line. Your task was to determine the minimum score on the test that would result in an employee who was fast enough on the job. In problems like this, the minimum score on a test that is associated with satisfactory performance on the job is often called a **cutoff score**.

To determine the cutoff score, you might do the following: First, you would administer the test (TAS) to a fairly large group of applicants for production line jobs (about 200 would probably be sufficient), but you wouldn't use their scores as a determiner of whether or not they were hired. In other words, you would hire as many of the 200 as you could, basing your hiring decisions on factors other than their test scores. Next, you would monitor the productivity of these employees as they worked on the production line. You would carefully record the number of modules produced per hour by each employee until you had a good estimate of the productivity of each one. You would use these production data, together with the TAS scores, to determine how well the TAS predicted worker productivity, and the relationship between TAS score and worker productivity. In this problem, TAS score would be an independent variable, and the productivity measure would be a dependent variable.

Instead of just computing the correlation coefficient between the TAS scores and worker productivity, you would plot a scatter diagram of the TAS scores and productivity figures, just as was done in Chapter 4. You would then use simple linear regression analysis to determine the straight line that did the best job of going through the scatter of points. The line that fits a distribution of points in a scatter diagram better than any other line is called a **regression line**. It is determined mathematically, not by a visual estimation. Many computer programs can be used to fit a regression line to the points in a scatter diagram, and some of the more sophisticated hand calculators also calculate a regression line when they are given the values of the points in a scatter diagram.

Once the regression line had been determined from the points in the scatter diagram, it would be a simple matter to find the score on the TAS that was associated with the minimum acceptable production rate of 40 modules per hour. One solution to the personnel manager's problem would then be to hire future applicants who earned scores on the TAS that were at least as high as the one that predicted a 40 module-per-hour production rate, and to refuse future applicants with lower TAS scores. There are other considerations that complicate the hiring problem, but we'll ignore them for the present.

Figure 15.3 illustrates the problem we've just described. Note that TAS score is plotted along the horizontal axis, and production rate (modules produced per hour) is plotted on the vertical axis. The regression line slants upward to the right. This means that, on

Figure 15.3

average, applicants with higher TAS scores turn out to be more productive workers. From the hypothetical data shown in Figure 15.3, you can see that a productivity rate of 40 units per hour has an associated TAS score of 24. So, an applicant who earned a score of 24 on the TAS would be predicted to have a productivity rate of 40 modules per hour. Note that an applicant with a TAS score of 36 would be predicted to have a productivity rate of 50 modules per hour, and that an applicant who earned a TAS score of 12 would be predicted to have a productivity rate of only 30 modules per hour.

We mentioned earlier that there were other considerations that complicated the problem of setting a cutoff score on the TAS. If you look at Figure 15.3 carefully, you may notice that there are some workers with production rates above 40 modules per hour who earned TAS scores that were less than 24. There are also workers with TAS scores above 24 who have productivity rates below 40 modules per hour. This happened because the correlation between TAS score and productivity was less than 1.0. In other words, TAS score does not do a perfect job of predicting worker productivity. In this regard, our hypothetical example is typical of relationships that exist in real life. You will rarely, if ever, find an independent variable that correlates perfectly with a dependent variable. In the problem at hand, the less-than-perfect relationship between TAS score and worker productivity poses a seeming dilemma. If the personnel director recommends that production workers be hired in the future only if their TAS scores are at least 24, some applicants who would be sufficiently productive on the job will not be hired. Other applicants who have TAS scores of 24 or above will be hired, and will later have production rates below the desired 40 modules per hour. If the personnel manager wants to reduce the chances of hiring a worker who would later have a production rate below 40 modules per hour, he or she should recommend that the cutoff score on the TAS be set above 24. Using regression analysis, the personnel director could determine a cutoff score that would reduce the probability of hiring a worker who would have a production rate below 40 modules per hour to 10%, 5%, or any other low probability that was desired. If the probability of hiring a worker who would later turn out to be too slow was reduced, the probability of failing to hire an applicant who would have been sufficiently fast would be increased. The two kinds of errors are interchangeable. When the chances of committing one kind of error are reduced, the chances of committing the other kind are increased.

In most research and evaluation reports that use regression analysis, you will find an equation that expresses the mathematical relationship between the independent variable and the dependent variable. In the case of simple linear regression, this **regression equation** will have two parts on its right-hand side. The first will be a number that will stand by itself, and the second will be a number that multiplies the value of the independent variable. The first number will tell you what the predicted value of the dependent variable would be, if a person had a score of zero on the independent variable. The number that multiplies the value of the independent variable tells you how much the dependent variable would be predicted to change, if the value of the independent variable were to be increased by one unit. In the example we have been discussing, the regression equation would be: Predicted Productivity = 20 + 0.833 (TAS Score). The number 20 shows that an applicant who scored zero on the TAS would be predicted to have a production rate of 20 modules per hour. The number 0.833 shows that for every increase of one point on the TAS, the applicant's predicted production rate would increase by 0.833 modules per hour. How these numbers were determined is not important here, but the interpretation of the numbers is central to this discussion.

Using a regression equation, a researcher or evaluator can find the predicted value of a dependent variable for any value of an independent variable. For example, the predicted productivity rate of an applicant who scored 15 on the TAS would be 20 + (0.833)(15), which equals 20 + 12.5, or 32.5.

Other statistics that can be computed in a regression analysis tell a researcher or evaluator how well an independent variable predicts the value of a dependent variable, and how accurately an individual's score on the dependent variable can be predicted. One statistic that indicates goodness of prediction is called the **coefficient of determination**. In simple linear regression analysis, it is equal to the square of the correlation coefficient between the independent variable and the dependent variable. If in our example TAS score and worker productivity had a correlation of 0.8, the coefficient of determination would be (0.8) squared, which equals 0.64. We would then say that 64% of the variation in workers' production rates could be predicted by knowing their TAS scores. If TAS scores and workers' production rates had a correlation of 1.0, the coefficient of determination would also equal 1.0. We would then say that TAS score predicted 100% of the variation in workers' production rates. This would mean that knowing an applicant's score on the TAS would allow us to make a perfect prediction of that person's production rate as a worker. In practice, perfect prediction is never found. However, knowing a person's score on an independent variable allows a researcher to do a far better job of predicting the person's score on an dependent variable than would otherwise be possible.

Conceptually, **multiple regression analysis** is a simple extension of simple linear regression. In multiple regression analysis, a person's score on a dependent variable is predicted from their scores on more than one independent variable. In fact, any number of independent variables can be used to predict scores on a dependent variable.

We could expand our simple linear regression example to a multiple regression problem merely by administering two tests to applicants, instead of one. In addition to the TAS, we could administer a test of persistence in the face of repetitive work. Let's call the new independent variable the Test of Worker Persistence (TWP). If the TAS and the TWP were both used in selecting applicants for production line work, the scenario would be very similar to the one we've already described. A sample of applicants would be given both tests, but their scores would not be used in determining whether or not they were hired. Their productivity on the job would be measured, just as in the simple linear regression case. Their scores on the two tests, together with their production rates, would be used to compute a regression equation that expressed the relationship between the dependent variable (production rate) and the two independent variables (TAS score and TWP score). The computations necessary to determine the regression equation would be complicated, but they need not be of concern here. In fact, a computer could be used to calculate the regression equation in very little time.

Once the regression equation had been determined, the personnel director could set cutoff scores on both the TAS and the TWP so that future applicants whose predicted production rates were below 40 modules per hour would not be hired. In fact, different combinations of TAS and TWP scores could be used in screening applicants, because someone with a low score on one test could still have a predicted production rate above 40 modules per hour, provided his or her score on the other test was high enough. This conclusion is illustrated by the following hypothetical multiple regression equation:

Predicted Productivity = $15 + 0.8(\text{TAS}) + 0.6(\text{TWP})$

In this equation, an applicant who scored zero on both the TAS and the TWP would have a predicted production rate of 15 modules per hour. For every increase of one point on the TAS, an applicant would have a predicted increase in production rate of 0.8 modules per hour, provided his or her score on the TWP did not change. And for every increase of one point on the TWP, an applicant would have a predicted increase in production rate of 0.6 modules per hour, provided his or her score on the TAS did not change. An applicant who scored 20 on the TAS and 15 on the TWP would have a predicted production rate of 40 modules per hour: 15 + (0.8)(20) + (0.6)(15) equals 15 + 16 + 9, which equals 15 + 25, or 40. A predicted production rate of 40 would also be found for an applicant who scored 12.5 on the TAS and 25 on the TWP, since 15 + (0.8)(12.5) + (0.6)(25) is equal to 15 + 10 + 15, which equals 40.

As was true for simple linear regression, it is possible to compute statistics in a multiple regression analysis that indicate how well scores on a dependent variable can be predicted from scores on the independent variables. Two statistics that often accompany the report of a multiple regression analysis are the **coefficient of multiple correlation** (usually denoted by a capital R), and the **coefficient of multiple determination** (usually denoted by R-squared, or R^2). The multiple correlation coefficient indicates how well the predicted values of a dependent variable correlate with the actual values of the dependent variable. The higher that correlation, the better the prediction. The coefficient of multiple determination is interpreted just like the coefficient of determination in simple linear regression. If the coefficient of multiple determination in our hypothetical example were equal to 0.81, it would mean that 81% of the variation in workers' productivity rates could be predicted by knowing their scores on the TAS *and* their scores on the TWP. As was the case in simple linear regression, perfect prediction (a coefficient of multiple determination equal to 1.0) is desired, but never achieved in practice. In most employment screening applications, a coefficient of multiple determination that was larger than 0.5 would be considered quite good.

We will now consider a research study in which multiple regression analysis was used to determine how well a dependent variable could be predicted from a number of independent variables, and which of the independent variables were the best predictors. In many ways, this study is typical of research that makes use of multiple regression analysis. Its objectives include both prediction of a dependent variable and analysis of the degree of relationship between the dependent variable and a number of potential predictors that should be related to the dependent variable on theoretical grounds.

Prediction of Typing Success in High School

Purpose of the Study. Pante (1980) attempted to identify one or more variables that would predict high school students' typing speed and accuracy at the end of a one-semester typewriting course. As potential predictors, she investigated measures of students' intelligence, motivation, typing experience, rhythmic ability, musical background, and their scores on a specialized test of manual speed and dexterity as potential predictors. The author's objectives were to determine which predictors, individually and collectively, would do the best job of predicting end-of-semester typewriting speed and accuracy, and to determine the strength of the relationship between each potential predictor and both of the dependent variables.

Research Design. Students in six beginning typewriting classes were given three predictor tests at the beginning of their first semester of instruction. The 109 students in these six classes completed the Seashore Rhythm Test, the Digit Recall Test (used here as a measure of intelligence), and the Tapping Test (a measure of manual speed and dexterity that requires subjects to rapidly make a dot inside each of a preprinted series of small circles). The tests were administered in the students' regular classrooms, during a single 55-minute class period, under the supervision of a trained test administrator.

In addition, students participating in the study were asked to complete a questionnaire that indicated whether or not they played a musical instrument, and whether or not they had completed a previous typewriting course of at least six weeks' duration. About 50% of the students responded affirmatively to the latter question.

Teachers' records were used to determine the number of times each student had been absent from the typing class and the number of assignments (out of a total of 18) each student had completed. These variables were used as indicators of student motivation.

The dependent variables used by Pante (1980) were typing accuracy and speed scores obtained on three successive days during the last week of the semester. For purposes of analysis, each student's typing speed score was computed as the average of the speed scores earned in three 3-minute tests administered on successive days. Similarly, an accuracy score for each student was determined by averaging the accuracy scores earned on the three timed tests.

To determine which of her seven independent variables, individually and in combination, did the best job of predicting typing speed and accuracy, Pante conducted a series of multiple regression analyses. She completed separate analyses using the speed and accuracy scores as dependent variables: using the data for all sampled students; using the data for students who had less than six weeks of previous typing instruction; and using the data for students who had at least six weeks of previous typing instruction. Since the method of analysis was identical for all three groups and both dependent variables, we will consider only the prediction of typing speed, using data for all sampled students.

Author's Data Table. Table 1 in the Pante (1980) study contains the results of a multiple regression analysis in which seven independent variables were used to predict the end-of-semester typewriting speeds of 109 high school students. The table is reproduced below, just as it appeared in her report, as Table 15.3.

Table 15.3 actually contains the results of several regression analyses. Pante began with a simple linear regression model, in which typing speed was predicted only from number of student assignments completed. She then used a two-variable multiple regression model, in which the independent variables were number of assignments completed and previous typing experience. Then a third model was used, in which students' scores on the Seashore Rhythm Test were added as a third predictor. Additional models added the independent variables shown in Table 15.3, one at a time, in the order listed in the table. The order in which the variables were added to the model was determined on statistical grounds. Number of assignments completed was found to be the predictor variable that had the highest correlation with typing speed. That is why it was used as the independent variable in a simple linear regression model. Given that number of assignments completed was used as a predictor, previous typing experience was found to be the variable that added most to the prediction of typing speed. That is why it was added to the model next, as the second predictor in a two-variable multiple regression equation. The other variables were added to the prediction equation in the indicated order because they contributed most to the prediction of

TABLE 15.3: Typewriting Speed of Total Students Group (n = 109)

	Order of Variable Entry	Simple R	R-Sq.	R-Sq. Chg.	F Ratio	Degrees Freedom
1.	Assignments Completed	.43*	.18	.1825	23.88*	1,107
2.	Previous Typing Exper.	.42*	.31	.1320	24.31*	1,106
3.	Seashore Rhythm Test	.06	.32	.0093	16.76*	1,105
4.	Tapping Test	.20**	.33	.0036	12.66*	1,104
5.	Digit Recall Test	−.08	.33	.0026	10.14*	1,103
6.	Absences	−.16	.33	.0003	8.38*	1,102
7.	Musical Instrument	.03	.33	.0002	7.12*	1,101

typing speed, given that the variables listed above them had already been added to the model. This type of multiple regression analysis is called **stepwise multiple regression**. Most regression-analysis computer programs allow a researcher to complete a stepwise analysis automatically. The computer determines the order in which the variables will enter the prediction equation, by first using the independent variable that has the highest correlation with the dependent variable, and then adding predictors one at a time, according to their contribution to the multiple correlation coefficient, given the earlier decisions on entry of independent variables. This process allows a researcher to determine how much each independent variable adds to the prediction of the dependent variable, once the preceding variables have been used.

Author's Interpretation. Pante concludes that "the most important variable in predicting speed was assignments completed" (p. 23). She goes on to note that, although "all of the other predictor variables were significant at the .01 level," only previous typing experience added substantially to the prediction of typing speed, once number of the assignments completed had been used as a predictor.

The Nature of the Inferences. As we have noted above, Table 15.3 contains results for seven regression analyses. Because Pante used the stepwise regression procedure, independent variables were added to the regression equation one at a time. Each row of her table therefore contains results for a different regression model.

The column headed "Simple R" is a list of the correlations between each of the independent variables and the dependent variable (typing speed). Notice that Assignments Completed has the highest correlation (.43), and that Previous Typing Experience is next highest (.42). These two variables, and students' scores on the Tapping Test, had statistically significant correlations with typing speed. Although the asterisks in Table 15.3 are not explained in a footnote, the magnitudes of the correlation coefficients suggest that one asterisk denotes statistical significance at an alpha level of 0.01, while two asterisks denote significance at the 0.05 level. This notation is the opposite of tradition, but no other interpretation makes sense.

The "R-Sq." column contains values of the coefficient of determination (or multiple determination) associated with each regression analysis. As we noted above, the coefficient of determination can be interpreted as the proportion of variance of the dependent variable that is predicted by the independent variables in the regression equation. From Table 15.3, we can see that Assignments Completed alone predicted .18 (18%) of the variance of students' typing speed. When Previous Typing Experience was added to the regression equation, the two predictor variables accounted for 31% of the variance of typing speed. The increase in predictability gained by adding Previous Typing Experience to the regression equation is given in the "R-Sq.Chg." column. It is the difference between .31 and .18. Carried to four digits, the increase in variance predicted is .1320 (a bit more than 13%).

Notice that 31% of the variance of typing speed is predicted by the first two independent variables, and that only 33% of the variance of typing speed is predicted by all seven independent variables. The .33 value in the R-Sq. column in the last row of the table indicates that last fact. The regression analysis therefore shows that only the first two independent variables were useful in predicting typing speed. This conclusion is reinforced by the small values in the R-Sq. Chg. column for all independent variables beyond Previous Typing Experience. The R-Sq. Chg. value of .0093 for the Seashore Rhythm Test indicates that it adds less than 1% to the predictable variance of typing speed, once the first two independent variables have been used as predictors. The remaining independent variables add even less, as indicated by their small values in the R-Sq. Chg. column.

The numbers in the "F ratio" column are sample F-statistics that would be used to test the null hypothesis that the independent variables in the regression equation at each step in the analysis contributed *nothing* to the prediction of typing speed. For each of the seven regression models, this null hypothesis was rejected at the 0.01 level of significance (as denoted by the single "*" attached to each F value). The numbers in the "Degrees Freedom" column indicate the appropriate degrees of freedom for determining the significance of the reported F-statistics.

It is important to realize that Pante did not report any of the actual regression equations that resulted from her study. This is because she was interested in determining how well students' typing speed could be predicted using a variety of independent variables, and was not interested in predicting the typing speed of any individual student. One might describe her research purpose as "explanation" rather than "prediction," since the principal objective of her study was determining how much of the variance of the typing skill variables could be "explained" by her seven independent variables.

Our Interpretations and Conclusions. We agree with Pante's interpretation of the results in Table 15.3. Her conclusion that it is possible to predict students' typing speed from an indicator of their motivation (number of assignments completed) is sound. However, you should note that this variable only accounted for 18% of the variance of typing speed, and none of the other independent variables used in the study (other than previous typing experience) contributed in a practical way to the prediction of typing speed. Thus the greater part of the variance of typing speed was not predicted by any of the independent variables Pante (1980) examined.

Pante's study was unusually well documented. It provides a good illustration of the use of multiple regression analysis when explanation of the relationships among a dependent variable and a set of independent variables is of interest. The kinds of statistics reported in this study are typical of those you will find in many reports on multiple regression analyses. When the researcher's objectives include prediction as well as explanation, you will also find the kinds of regression equations we described earlier.

Factor Analysis

Factor analysis is used extensively in research and evaluation studies that involve the development of new measurement instruments. It is particularly useful as a tool for examining the validity of tests or the measurement characteristics of attitude scales.

The principal objective of factor analysis is to construct a small number of variables (called **factors**) that do a good job of conveying the information present in a large number of variables. For example, a 30-item attitude scale might be designed to secure information on students' feelings toward their school, toward their teachers, and toward academic work in general. In the minds of its developers, the attitude scale should measure three attitudinal factors (attitudes toward school, attitudes toward teachers, and attitudes toward academic work) even though it is made up of 30 variables (the individual items in the scale). Using factor analysis, it would be possible to determine whether the 30 items really form three distinct attitude factors, or whether the items measure a larger or smaller number of attitudes. It would also be possible to identify the specific items associated with each factor.

Computationally, factor analysis is a very complex statistical procedure. Most factor analyses would be impractical without the use of a computer. Fortunately, a number of widely available computer programs allow applied researchers and evaluators to complete factor analyses easily and with impressive speed. Although we need not concern ourselves with the computational details of factor analysis, some time spent considering its underlying logic will aid in understanding its purposes and results.

In our example involving a 30-item attitude scale, students' responses to each of the 30 items would define a separate variable. Each student who completed the attitude scale would have 30 scores. Each of these scores would vary across a sample of students. A factor analysis of the attitude scale would begin by calculating the correlation coefficient between every pair of items. From our discussion of correlation in Chapter 4, you might remember that two variables have a correlation of 0 if scores on one have no relationship to scores on the other. If two items on the attitude scale had a correlation of 0, it would mean that students' responses to one of the items would not be linearly related to their responses to the other item. It would be illogical to regard such items as two indicators of the same kind of student attitude; the items would have to represent different attitudes. Conversely, students' responses to another pair of items on the attitude scale might have had a correlation of 1.0. This pair of items would apparently be measuring the same kind of attitude, since higher student responses to one of the items would always correspond to higher responses to the other item. A single variable would convey as much information about students' responses to this pair of items, as would the two original variables. That single variable could be called a *factor*. Its meaning would be determined by the content of the pair of items it represented.

In practice, pairs of items on an attitude scale will rarely have correlations of 0 or 1.0. Most correlations will be somewhere in between. The higher the correlation between students' responses to a pair of items, the more reasonable it would be to think of those items as indicators of a single underlying factor. If the correlation between a pair of items were less than 1.0, no single factor could perfectly represent the items. But if the correlation were high enough, most of the salient information in students' responses could be expressed by their scores on a factor that was constructed from their item scores.

Factor analysis considers the correlations between *every pair* of items on a scale or test. For example, if a scale consisted of only four items numbered 1, 2, 3, and 4, factor analysis would begin with the correlations between Items 1 and 2, Items 1 and 3, Items 1 and 4, Items 2 and 3, Items 2 and 4, and Items 3 and 4. These six correlation coefficients would be analyzed to determine whether the items could be grouped in such a way that all items in a group had fairly high correlations with each other. Each group of items would then be a good candidate for representation by a single factor.

The literature on factor analysis includes a variety of procedures for deriving factors from sets of variables. If you were to read one of the many texts devoted exclusively to factor-analytic methods, you would find such terms as **principal components analysis**, **principal factor analysis**, **image analysis**, **alpha factor analysis**, and **Rao's canonical factoring method**. Each of these factor analysis procedures has the same basic objective—to determine factors that do an adequate job of conveying the essential information in a larger set of variables. The procedures differ in their underlying assumptions and their computational details. In the educational research and evaluation literature, principal components analysis and principal factor analysis appear to be most widely used. Principal components analysis assumes that each of the original variables can be divided into two parts: an error component that reflects the less-than-perfect reliability of all educational measurements, and a **true score** component that is common to all of the variables being factor analyzed. Principal factor analysis assumes that each of the original variables can be divided into three parts: an error component, a true score component that is common to all of the variables being factor analyzed, and a true score component that is unique to each variable. These sets of assumptions will be plausible in different applied problems. Plausibility should be the principal guide in selecting a factor analysis procedure.

After the correlations between every pair of variables have been computed, both principal components analysis and principal factor analysis determine a set of factors called an **original solution** or an **unrotated solution**. In an unrotated solution, an initial factor that does the best job of representing all of the variables is determined first. Then a second factor that does the next best job of representing all of the variables is found. The second factor is required to be uncorrelated with the first. Next a third factor that is uncorrelated with the first two factors is found. This factor must also do the best job possible of representing the information in all the variables, subject to the requirement that it cannot be correlated with the first or second factors. Principal components analysis and principal factor analysis proceed in this way, until the number of factors determined is equal to the number of variables being factor analyzed.

Figure 15.4 is an attempt to illustrate the first two factors that might be found in a principal components analysis or a principal factor analysis. In this figure the short arrows represent the original variables to be analyzed. One group of arrows might represent items that concern students' attitudes toward education. The other group might represent students' attitudes toward their teachers. Any two arrows that are at a right angle to each other represent variables that are uncorrelated. Any two arrows that fall right on top of each other represent variables that have a correlation of 1.0. In general, the smaller the angle between two arrows,

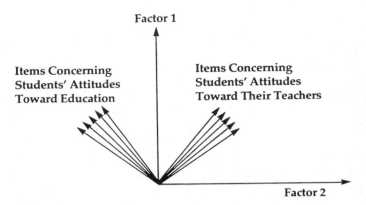

Figure 15.4 The First Two Unrotated Factors Resulting from a Hypothetical Principal Components Analysis of a Student Attitude Scale

the higher the correlation between the variables they represent. The larger arrows labeled "Factor 1" and "Factor 2" represent the first factors that might be derived in a principal components analysis or a principal factor analysis of the variables. Notice that Factor 1 falls roughly midway between the two groups of short arrows, and that Factor 2 is at a right angle to Factor 1. The right angle means that Factors 1 and 2 are uncorrelated, as required by the factor analytic methods.

Several things we have said about the objectives and procedures of factor analysis might appear to be contradictory at this point. First, we stated that the objective of factor analysis is to determine relatively few factors that do a good job of representing a far larger number of variables. But in describing the principal components analysis and principal factor analysis procedures, we said that the methods would produce the same number of factors as original variables. There appears to be a conflict here. In addition, we said that the factors are intended to *represent* the original variables. Yet the factors that are shown in Figure 15.4 do not appear to represent either group of variables. Neither Factor 1 nor Factor 2 is particularly close to the two groups of original variables. The correlations between the variables and the factors would appear to be moderate at best. Additional steps in the factor analysis procedure are needed to resolve these seeming contradictions. The first is called **factor selection**, and the second is called **factor rotation**. We will describe these steps briefly.

Although the number of factors needed to convey *all* of the information in a set of variables is the same as the number of variables, some smaller number of factors can usually do a good job of conveying most of the information. In a principal components analysis or a principal factor analysis it is usually found that relatively few factors (sometimes only two, three, or four) describe or account for most of the information in the original set of variables. The remaining factors often account for very small proportions of the information in the original variables, either by themselves or in combination. One kind of statistic that results from a principal components analysis or a principal factor analysis is a listing of the **proportion of variance** that each factor accounts for. These statistics are regarded as indicators of the relative potency of each factor in conveying the information in the original set of variables. These proportions are reviewed when factors are selected. The only factors that are used in further analyses are those that account for appreciable proportions of the variation in the original variables.

Once factors have been selected for further analysis, they are **rotated** (which we'll explain in a moment), so that they do a better job of representing the original variables. Ideally, after rotation, variables in each group will have high correlations with one of the rotated factors, and low correlations with all of the others. This is the sense in which we say that a factor "represents" a group of variables.

Just as there are many different factor analysis methods, researchers and evaluators can choose from among many different factor rotation procedures. Three procedures that are used quite often in educational research and evaluation are called **Varimax**, **Equimax**, and **Quartimax**. Although these procedures differ in their statistical details, they have identical objectives. All seek to define a set of rotated factors that have high correlations with some of the original variables, and low correlations with all others. All require that the rotated factors be uncorrelated with each other. Factors that are uncorrelated with each other are called **orthogonal factors**. Factors that are correlated with each other are called **oblique**, since if they were graphed as in the figure above, the angles between them would be smaller than right angles. One

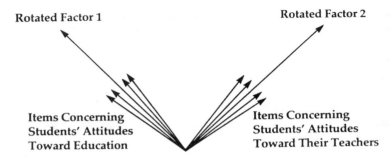

Figure 15.5 The First Two Rotated Factors Resulting from a Hypothetical Principal Components Analysis of a Student Attitude Scale

of the most widely used rotation procedures that results in correlated (oblique) factors is called the **Direct Oblimin** method. Its objectives are similar to those of the orthogonal rotation procedures (Varimax, Equimax, and Quartimax). All rotation procedures seek to determine a set of factors that clearly represent differing subgroups of the original set of variables.

Figure 15.5 illustrates the results of rotating the first two factors shown in Figure 15.4. Notice that rotated Factor 1 goes right through one group of small arrows (representing items that measure students' attitudes toward education in general), and that rotated Factor 2 goes right through the other group (representing items that measure students' attitudes toward their teachers). Because of this, we would call rotated Factor 1 an "attitude toward education factor" and rotated Factor 2 an "attitude toward teacher" factor. In this example, as in all factor analyses, the meaning that is attached to a factor derives from the variables that are highly associated with it.

Because we constructed Figure 15.4 so that two groups of arrows clearly represented distinct sets of variables, and because the groups of variables were centered around arrows that were at right angles to each other, we were able to illustrate two orthogonal factors that do a good job of representing groups of variables. Therefore an orthogonal rotation procedure, such as Varimax, Equimax, or Quartimax, would have been appropriate in this example. Had the two groups of variables not been at right angles to each other, an oblique rotation procedure, such as the Direct

Oblimin method, would have been needed to define factors that did a good job of representing subgroups of variables.

As you read research and evaluation reports that include factor analyses, you will come across additional specialized terms. For example, authors will discuss the **loadings** of the variables on the factors. Although the definition is strictly correct only in the case of orthogonal factor analyses, you can think of factor "loadings" as correlations between the variables and the factors. It will always be the case (whether a factor analysis results in orthogonal factors or oblique factors) that the higher the correlation between a variable and a factor, the higher the loading of that variable on the factor.

Other terms that arise frequently in discussions of factor analysis results are **communality** and **eigenvalue**. Communalities are associated with the original variables that are to be factor analyzed. The communality of a variable is the proportion of its total variance that is shared with (or common to) the other original variables. The higher the correlations among the original variables, the more they have in common, and the higher their communalities. Communalities can range between 0 and 1.0. A variable with a communality of 0.6 would be described as having 60% of its variation in common with the other variables to be factor analyzed. If a variable has a very low communality (close to 0), it is not likely to be associated with any other variables in defining a factor. The second term we highlighted earlier was *eigenvalue*. Eigenvalues are associated with factors. They indicate how much of the variation in the entire set of original variables is "accounted for" by each factor. One rule that is often used to select the factors in an original solution that will be *eliminated* from further analysis is to discard those that have eigenvalues smaller than 1.0. In that way, only factors that convey a nontrivial proportion of the information in the original variables are retained for interpretation. Because of the way factors are defined in a principal components analysis or a principal factor analysis, the first factor will always have the largest eigenvalue; the second factor the next largest eigenvalue, and so forth. Since the eigenvalues associated with succeeding factors will be progressively smaller, a decision to ignore some of the latter factors is often justifiable.

As in earlier portions of this chapter, we will now describe an actual research study that used the statistical procedures we have discussed. In the description that follows, notice that the study is similar in several ways to the hypothetical factor analysis of the 30-item attitude scale we described above. A small number of factors that do a good job of representing the items in a measurement instrument were sought, both in the hypothetical study and in the real one that follows.

A Factor Analysis of an Instructor Rating Scale

Purpose of the Study. Jaeger and Barnes (1981) compared three different methods of factor analyzing a rating scale used by college students to evaluate their instructors. The researchers' objective was to determine whether the three methods would result in the same number of factors, and whether the resulting factors would be defined similarly, regardless of the method used.

Research Design. The rating scale used by Jaeger and Barnes contained 20 items. Its developers thought that it would measure students' perceptions of two related dimensions of instructor quality; they therefore hypothesized two underlying factors. The first ten items in the scale were intended to measure students' perceptions of the overall quality of their instructor. The last ten items were designed to measure students' perceptions of their instructor's conscientiousness.

In one method of analysis, the authors correlated individual students' ratings of instructors on each pair of items on the scale, ignoring the fact that students were rating 13 different instructors in 19 different classes. The correlations were based on ratings provided by 493 students. These correlations were then used to complete a principal factor analysis followed by a direct oblimin rotation of factors with eigenvalues greater than 1.0. Jaeger and Barnes called this procedure an "across students" analysis.

In their second method of analysis, called a "between classes" analysis, Jaeger and Barnes first averaged the ratings of individual students within each of the 19 classes. They then computed correlations between the averaged ratings given the instructor in each class, for all pairs of items on the rating scale. These correlations were used to complete a principal factor analysis, followed by a direct oblimin rotation of the original solution, just as in the across-students analysis.

The final method the authors used was called a "within classes" analysis. In this procedure, Jaeger and Barnes first computed correlations between the ratings provided only by students in a given class, for each pair of items on the rating scale. A separate table of correlations was computed for each of the 15 classes. Corresponding correlations (e.g., between Items 1 and 2, Items 1 and 3, etc.) were then averaged across the 19 classes, to form a final table of correlations. These correlations were then used in a principal factor analysis, followed by an oblique rotation of the factors in the original solution, just as in the other methods.

Authors' Data Table. The three types of analysis constructed by Jaeger and Barnes resulted in three tables of factor loadings, eigenvalues, and correlations among rotated factors. Only the table for the "across students" analysis will be shown here, since all three tables contain the same kinds of statistics. Table 1 in Jaeger and Barnes (1981) is reproduced here, as Table 15.4.

Authors' Interpretation. On pages 7 and 8 of their paper, Jaeger and Barnes stated:

> The four factors resulting from the "across-students" and the "between-class" analyses seemed to represent the same general constructs, although the order of the second, third, and fourth factors in these solutions differed. For example, in the analysis of the across-students correlation matrix, Factor 2 ("Instructor's Effort") was defined by items on the promptness of the instructor's evaluations (Item 11), whether classes were held during regular hours (Item 12), whether the instructor was prepared to teach class (Item 14), and whether the instructor was willing to meet with students outside of class (Item 15).

In their discussion of the correlations among the factors and the percentages of variance accounted for by the first four factors, the authors stated:

> Factor intercorrelations are shown in Tables 1 [Table 15.4 here] and 2 for the across-students and the between-class analyses respectively. Comparison reveals that the correlations resulting from the between-class analysis were consistently lower than corresponding correlations for the across-students analysis. This suggests that the between-class factors were more nearly orthogonal than those resulting from the across-students analysis.

TABLE 15.4: Oblique Factor Pattern Matrix Resulting from Analysis of Students' Ratings of Faculty (Across Students) (Only loadings exceeding 0.45 are shown)

	Factors			
Items	1. Overall Effectiveness	2. Instructors' Effort	3. Students Understand Standards	4. Fair, Equitable Treatment
1. Overall Effectiveness	1.14			
2. Take This Instructor	.78			
3. Take Another Course from This Instructor	.94			
4. Recommend Instructor	.87			
5. Among Best Teachers	1.05			
6. Effect on Learning	1.18			
7. Effectiveness in Stimulating	1.03			
8. Effectiveness, Understanding	.95			
9. Stimulate Interest	1.14			
10. Professional Growth	1.10			
11. Full, Prompt Evaluation		.54		
12. Class Hours Regular		.52		
13. Evaluation Fair, Equitable				
14. Instructor Prepared		1.22		
15. Instructor Willing to Meet		.71		
16. Instructor Ridicules				.82
17. Responsive to Student Concerns				.84
18. Makes Unfair Demands				1.10
19. I Understand Grading			.68	
20. I Understand Course Purposes	.64			
Eigenvalue	10.24	1.86	1.14	1.03
Percent of Explained Variance	51.2	9.3	5.7	5.1
Cumulative Percent of Explained Variance	51.2	60.5	66.2	71.3

Factor Intercorrelations

Factor 2	.80			
Factor 3	.44	.44		
Factor 4	.79	.83	.34	

At least half the variance in the 20-dimensional space of the instructor rating scale was accounted for by the first factor in both the across-students and between-class analyses.... The four rotated factors in the across-students analysis accounted collectively for more than 71 percent of the variance of the 20-dimensional space (pp. 8-9).

The Nature of the Inferences. In contrast to the statistical procedures we have discussed in a number of earlier chapters, it is typically the case that no formal hypothesis tests are conducted in a factor analysis. The kind of statistical inference that takes place in factor analysis is point estimation. In the process of determining factors, a number of population parameters are estimated, including factor loadings, eigenvalues, communalities, and—in the case of oblique factor rotations—the correlation between each pair of factors. One could argue that factor analysis is a descriptive statistical procedure, rather than an inferential one, since the numerical values that result from a factor analysis could be viewed as descriptive statistics that apply only to the original sample. However, researchers are rarely interested in the measurement properties of tests, attitude scales, and other instruments *only* as they apply to a particular sample. It is difficult to imagine a research or evaluation study in which the interpretation of factor analysis would be strictly limited to a given sample of respondents or examinees. They are usually inferring the existence of a factor or factors in a larger population.

The upper portion of Table 15.4 contains the loadings of 20 items on four rotated factors. Because Jaeger and Barnes used an oblique rotation procedure, the factor loadings are *not* correlation coefficients. They can instead be interpreted as the coefficients of the items, were each factor to be used as a dependent variable in a multiple regression analysis, with the items as independent variables. Note that the table title states: "(Only loadings exceeding 0.45 are shown.)." This means that each of the 20 items had a loading on each of the four factors, but that small loadings (those less than 0.45) have been omitted so as to facilitate the interpretation of results.

The labels given the four factors shown in Table 1—Overall Effectiveness; Instructor's Effort; Students Understand Standards; and Fair, Equitable Treatment—are inventions of the authors.

They considered the items that had high loadings on each factor, and attempted to find a concise label that represented the content of each set of items. The process of labeling factors is an art rather than a science. In fact, some who have scoffed at factor analysis consider it to be the only creative part of the procedure. Often, it is necessary to ignore some variables or to do an inadequate job of characterizing the content of others when trying to find a concise name for a factor. It is therefore wise to do a careful review of the content of the original variables when you interpret a research or evaluation study that contains a factor analysis. For example, Jaeger and Barnes' label for their first factor ignores the item "I Understand Course Purposes," even though it has a loading of 0.64 on that factor and does not have a high loading on any other factor. It may well be that students consider their understanding of the purposes of a course when they judge the overall effectiveness of an instructor, but one would not expect such considerations to be paramount. The label given the first factor more obviously reflects items in which students rated the overall effectiveness of their instructor, considered whether or not their instructor was among the best teachers they had experienced in college, and judged their instructor's influence on various aspects of their learning, interest, professional growth, and understanding. Since items involving these content areas had the highest loadings on Factor 1, they are best represented by the factor. The factor label is therefore supportable, even though it is not totally inclusive.

Four variables had moderate to high loadings on the second factor. The variable with the highest loading, Instructor Prepared, reflects one aspect of an instructor's effort in teaching. High ratings on the other variables that loaded on the second factor would also be characteristic of instructors who invested time and effort in their teaching, although one could certainly argue that the content of these items is not altogether clear from the label given Factor 2.

Notice that Factor 3 had only one variable (Item 19) with a moderately high loading on it. Although this often happens in a factor analysis, it is not a desirable outcome, since a factor that is defined by a single variable does not contribute to a reduction in the number of variables necessary to characterize the original set of correlations.

The fourth factor in Table 15.4, labeled "Fair, Equitable Treatment," was defined by three variables. These variables reflect students' perception of the instructor's willingness to meet with them, *absence* of instructor behaviors that would demean or ridicule students, and *absence* of instructor behaviors that would place unfair demands on students. It would seem that these kinds of behaviors do contribute to what many would term "fair and equitable treatment" of students. However, it could be argued that the factor label is too broad, since many other aspects of instructor fairness were not represented in the rating instrument.

The second section of Table 15.4 contains eigenvalues, in addition to rows labeled "Percent of Explained Variance" and "Cumulative Percent of Explained Variance." As we noted above, eigenvalues are proportional to the percentage of the variation in the original set of variables that is "explained" or "accounted for" by the factors. Notice that Factor 1 has an eigenvalue of 10.24, and that its percent of explained variance is 51.2. Since there were 20 variables in the rating instrument, the eigenvalues for all factors (not just the four that were rotated in this analysis) must sum to 20. To determine the percent of variance that Factor 1 explains, one can merely divide its eigenvalue by the sum of the eigenvalues, and then multiply by 100 to convert the proportion to a percentage.

The important information that resulted from this analysis was that the first factor explained over half of the variance in the original set of items. The second through the fourth factors explained relatively small percentages of variance, since their eigenvalues were small. The second factor explained just over 9%, and the third and fourth factors explained just under 6% and just over 5%, respectively. The Cumulative Percent of Explained Variance row in Table 15.4 tells us that, taken together, the four rotated factors explained just over 71% of the variance in the original variables. This means that almost 30% of the variance in the 20 original items was not accounted for by the four rotated factors, and must be presumed to consist either of measurement error or true variance that is unique to individual items. Whether it is sufficient to describe the relationships among a set of variables solely in terms of factors that account for only 70% of their variance is a matter of subjective judgment. Reducing 20 variables to only four representative factors affords great economy of description. Certainly, we cannot expect the representation to be totally accurate.

The final section of Table 15.4 contains correlations among the four factors. It is noteworthy that several pairs of factors have correlations that are quite large. For example, the correlation between Factors 1 and 2 is .80. One might interpret this result by suggesting that Factors 1 and 2 could be replaced by a single factor, consisting of all of the variables with high loadings on both of them. If a single factor were used, the representation of the original variables would be simplified. However, the proportion of explained variance would be smaller, so that the representation of the original variables would be less complete. With a correlation of .80, Factors 1 and 2 have an angle of about 37 degrees between them. Since this angle is far from zero, the use of two factors, rather than one, seems justified.

Conclusions. Our interpretation of the Jaeger and Barnes (1981) study illustrates several important principles that apply to virtually all factor analyses. First, it was possible to "explain" over 70% of the variance of the 20-item rating scale in terms of only four underlying factors. This result illustrates a basic objective of factor analysis—the quest for parsimony. The result also illustrates the less-than-perfect representation of the original variables that one inevitably discovers in a factor analysis. Here, almost 30% of the variance of items in the rating scale was not explained by the four rotated factors. Second, the first factor explained over 50% of the variance in the original rating scale and was defined almost totally by items representing students' perceptions of the overall quality of their instructors. This result was consistent with the intentions of the scale's developers, and confirmed their hypothesis that one underlying dimension of the rating scale would be an "overall effectiveness" construct. However, the remaining items in the scale did not cluster together to define a "conscientiousness" factor, as the developers had intended. Instead, three additional factors with eigenvalues greater than 1.0 were found. Subclusters of the supposed "conscientiousness" items defined the additional factors. Thus the results of the factor analysis were only partially consistent with the developers' expectations about the relationships among their instructor rating items. These results illustrate an important application of factor analysis. The method allows researchers to examine the validity of theories that involve relationships among constructs or the relationships among operational measures and underlying constructs. In response to the partial confirmation of their hypotheses about the two factors underlying their rating scale, the developers of the scale could either revise their instrument or their theory, depending on the importance of having a two-dimensional scale.

In both of the factor analysis procedures we have described and illustrated, the essential outcomes of the analyses were prescribed more by the data than by the researcher. For example, once a researcher decides to retain factors that have eigenvalues greater than one, the relationships among the original variables dictate the number of factors that will be rotated. The data also determine the pattern of loadings of the variables on the factors. Although our interpretation of the results of the Jaeger and Barnes (1981) study was logically confirmatory (since the developers of the rating scale had specific expectations about the number of factors that would be found and which items would define which factors), the method of analysis was essentially exploratory. None of the researchers' expectations about the pattern of factor loadings influenced the analysis. Some factor analysis procedures, called **confirmatory factor analysis methods**, allow a researcher to specify some or all of the outcomes of a factor analysis, in accordance with underlying theory. For example, the researcher can specify the number of factors to be used, the pattern of factor loadings, or the magnitudes of the factor loadings. One outcome of a confirmatory factor analysis is a specific statistical test of the hypothesis that the data fit the hypothesized factor model. Confirmatory factor analyses have not been widely used in educational and social science research to date, but it is likely that they will see increasing application in the near future. If you find a factor-analytic study that has used the **LISREL** computer program (Jöreskog & Sorbom, 1984), you can be sure that the study is confirmatory rather than exploratory.

Summary

In this chapter we have described and illustrated three sophisticated statistical procedures that are used quite frequently in research and evaluation studies. Each of those procedures is often the subject of an entire book, rather than a portion of a single chapter. Our discussion of these procedures is therefore limited and superficial. However, our objective was to introduce you to each procedure, rather than provide complete coverage. Hopefully, when you encounter research and evaluation reports that include these methods, they will appear less mysterious and more understandable. If you can "get the flavor" of the authors' arguments and understand the essence of the studies' outcomes, you've learned what we intended.

The analysis of covariance allows a researcher or evaluator to adjust for pre-existing differences between treatment groups, on one or more continuous variables, when examining the effects of one or more categorical independent variables on a dependent variable. The procedure thus enhances the researcher's control over the outcomes of an experiment, and strengthens the claim that an independent variable "caused" a dependent variable. The procedure is used quite frequently in studies that involve pretreatment and posttreatment measures since it provides a way to adjust for differences between the pretreatment status of experimental groups before examining the effects of various treatments on a posttreatment measure.

Multiple regression analysis is very useful in studies that involve an examination of the relationships between a dependent variable and one or more independent variables. Sometimes the purpose of the examination is prediction, as in situations where candidates must be selected for a limited number of positions. In these situations, the objective of multiple regression analysis is to discover which of a set of potential independent variables is useful in predicting an individual's score on a dependent variable. In other studies, the objective of multiple regression analysis is explanation rather than prediction. In these studies, the researcher wants to know how much of the variation of a dependent variable can be "explained" by one or more independent variables. Another frequent objective of such studies is the determination of the relative potency of several independent variables in predicting a dependent variable.

Factor analysis is a statistical method for determining a relatively small number of variables that "explain" the relationships among a relatively large number of variables. The newly determined variables are called factors. One objective of factor analysis is parsimony—to represent many variables by few variables. Other objectives of factor analysis might be confirmatory (to see whether the factors that result from the analysis are consistent with some underlying theory or hypothesis) or exploratory (to find out what the data "say," without having some *a priori* theoretical expectations). In either case, factor analysis is particularly useful in examining and understanding the composition of measurement instruments used in education or the social sciences.

Conclusion

Although this book does not read like a novel, neither would a definitive manual on the rules of baseball, sailboat racing, or any *serious* sport. If you have read the book carefully and you've worked the problems at the back of each chapter, we hope and fully expect that you will have a firm grasp of the basic rules of most of the sport of applied statistics. We don't expect you to play the game on your own just because you know the rules. However, we *do* expect you to be an informed spectator—understanding many of the plays and tactics, and fully capable of interpreting the results of their application. It is always more fun to be a spectator when you know and understand the rules. We hope your enjoyment of applied research in education and the social and behavioral sciences will be greatly enhanced.

Problems — Chapter 15

15.1 Harbinger and Spring (1988) conducted a study on the effect of "engaged instructional time" on the reading achievement of third-grade students. Their study was a true experiment, in which they randomly assigned 16 third-graders to each of three instructional groups that were identical in every respect, except the length of time during each school day devoted to active instruction in reading. Group A was provided 30 minutes of reading instruction per day; Group B was provided 45 minutes of reading instruction per day; and Group C was provided 60 minutes of reading instruction per day. Teachers were rotated among the three groups, with each of three teachers assigned to each group for a one-week period, prior to moving on to the next group. This design feature helped to separate the effects of length of instruction from teacher effects.

The researchers administered a verbal intelligence test to all participating students at the beginning of the nine-month experiment. After nine months of instruction, they administered the Reading Comprehension subtest of the Iowa Tests of Basic Skills to all participants, as a measure of instructional effectiveness.

The researchers used the analysis of covariance to examine the effect of length of instruction on reading achievement.

   a. Based on this description of Harbinger and Spring's research, identify the following variables:
      Independent variable
      Dependent variable
      Covariate
   b. What null hypothesis were Harbinger and Spring testing in their research study?
   c. Why do you think Harbinger and Spring used the analysis of covariance in their study, instead of an analysis of variance? What advantage could they gain from an analysis of covariance?

15.2 Coleman et al. (1966) conducted a famous study on equality of educational opportunity in the United States. Their results on the relative effectiveness of school factors and home background factors in predicting the academic achievement of elementary and secondary students have been cited by researchers, policy analysts, and politicians for more than two decades. The principal analytic method used by Coleman and his colleagues in investigating the effects of schools and the home on achievement was stepwise multiple regression analysis. Suppose that they reported the following results, with arithmetic achievement for sixth-graders as the dependent variable:

Variables (by order of entry)	Correlation	R-squared	R-squared Change	F
Mother's Education	.42	.18	.18	17.88*
Family Income	.36	.26	.08	16.06*
Hours of Arithmetic Instruction	.16	.28	.02	13.21*
Teacher's Education	.10	.29	.01	11.67*

*significant at 0.05 level

a. Which independent variable contributes most to the prediction of sixth-grade arithmetic achievement? Support your answer by citing data in the table.
b. What percentage of the variance of arithmetic achievement is predicted by the four independent variables?
c. What null hypotheses did the authors test when they reported F-statistics that were "significant at the 0.05 level?"

15.3 In a factor analysis, what does a researcher mean when he or she reports that "Three factors accounted for 76% of the variance of the 10 items"?

References

Alexander, L., & Brown, R. (1978, March). *Evaluating attitudinal change in a multi-cultural setting.* Presented at the Annual Meeting of the American Educational Research Association, Toronto, Canada. ED 169 086.

Borg, W. R., & Gall, M. D. (1989). *Educational Research: An Introduction* (5th ed.). New York: Longman.

Bracht, G. H., & Glass, G. V. (1968). The external validity of experiments. *American Educational Research Journal, 5,* 437-474.

Burns, P. K., & Bozeman, W. C. (1981). Computer-assisted instruction and mathematics achievement: Is there a relationship? *Educational Technology, 21,* 32-39.

Butler, R. P., Wilson, W. L., & Priest, R. F. (1984, November). *Description, evaluation, and validation of a pilot developmental assessment center in a military-educational environment.* Paper presented at the Annual Meeting of the Military Testing Association, Munich, West Germany. ED 251 511.

Campbell, D. T., & Stanley, J. C. (1963). Experimental and quasi-experimental designs for research on teaching. In N. L. Gage (Ed.), *Handbook of Research on Teaching* (pp. 171-246). Chicago: Rand McNally.

Campbell, P. B. (1974, April). *Feminine intellectual decline during adolescence.* Presented at the Annual Meeting of the American Educational Research Association, Chicago. ED 091 620.

Cleland, W. E., & Idstein, P. M. (1980, April). *In-level versus out-of-level testing of sixth grade special education students.* Presented at the Annual Meeting of the National Council on Measurement in Education, Boston, April 8-10. ED 187 725.

Cook, T. D., & Campbell, D. T. (1979). *Quasi-experimentation: Design and Analysis Issues for Field Settings.* Chicago: Rand McNally.

Ferrell, B. G. (1985, March). *Computer immersion project: Evaluating the impact of computers on learning.* Paper presented at the Annual Meeting of the American Educational Research Association, Chicago, IL. ED 276 026.

Fisher, G. (1983). Where CAI is effective: A summary of the research. *Electronic Learning, 3,* 82-84.

Get Set Day Care Program. (1972). Philadelphia, PA: Philadelphia School District. ED 088 561.

Glass, G. V., & Hopkins, K. W. (1984). *Statistical Methods in Education and Psychology* (2nd ed.). Englewood Cliffs, NJ: Prentice-Hall.

Gunter, M. H. (1985). *A Comparative Study of Participants and Nonparticipants in the Florida Beginning Teacher Program.* Ft. Myers: Florida Educational Research and Development Council, Inc. ED 268 097.

Harris, C. (1963). *Problems in Measuring Change.* Madison: University of Wisconsin Press.

Hartigan, J. A., & Wigdor, A. K. (Eds.). (1989). *Fairness in Employment Testing: Validity Generalization, Minority Issues, and the General Aptitude Test Battery*. Washington, DC: National Academy Press.

Hays, W. L. (1981). *Statistics*. (3rd ed.). New York: Holt, Rinehart and Winston.

Hinkle, D. E., Wiersma, W., & Jurs, S. G. (1988). *Applied Statistics for the Behavioral Sciences* (2nd ed.). Boston: Houghton Mifflin.

Jaeger, R. M., & Barnes, E. A. (1981, November). *Methodological influences on the dimensions of instructor performance*. Presented at the Annual Meeting of the North Carolina Association for Research in Education, Greensboro, NC.

Joreskog, K. C., & Sorbom, D. (1984). *LISREL-VI*. Moresville, IN: Scientific Software, Inc.

Kershner, K. M., & Blair, M. W. (1975). *Career education program, 1974-1975*. Final evaluation report, Research for Better Schools, Inc. ED 138 826.

Koffler, S. L. (1977). An analysis of ESEA Title I data in New Jersey. Occasional Papers in Education, New Jersey State Department of Education, Trenton, N.J. ED 146 217.

Kulik, J. A., Bangert, R. L., & Williams, G. W. (1983). Effects of computer-based teaching on secondary school students. *Journal of Educational Psychology, 75* 19-26.

Law, Alexander. (1982). Personal communication.

Lewis, J. L. (1985). *Growth in Academic Performance Project, 1984-85 Evaluation Report*. Cincinnati, OH: Cincinnati Public Schools. ED 269 731.

McConnell, J. W. (1978, March). *Relations between teacher attitudes and teacher behavior in ninth-grade algebra classes*. Presented at the Annual Meeting of the American Educational Research Association, Toronto, Canada, March 27-31. ED 152 751.

Mendenhall, D. R. (1977, March). *Relationship of organizational structure and leadership behavior to staff satisfaction in IGE schools*. Technical Report No. 412. Wisconsin Univ., Research and Development for Cognitive Learning. ED 145 562.

Messick, S. (1981, April). *Evidence and ethics in the evaluation of tests*. Presented at the Annual Meeting of the American Educational Research Association, Los Angeles.

Messick, S. (1989). Validity. In R. L. Linn (Ed.). *Educational measurement* (3rd ed.). New York: ACE/Macmillan.

Pante, C. M. (1980, April). *The relationship between a linear combination of intelligence, musical background, rhythm ability and tapping ability to typewriting speed and accuracy*. Presented at the Annual Meeting of the American Educational Research Association, Los Angeles, April 13-17. ED 201 780.

Porter, A. (1988). Comparative experiments in educational research. In R. M. Jaeger (Ed.), *Complementary Methods for Research in Education* (pp. 391-417). Washington, DC: American Educational Research Association.

Schwer, W. E. (1973, June). *An evaluation of the effects of an open space program on selected seventh grade pupils and their teachers*. Practicum Report, Nova University, National Ed.D. Program for Educational Leaders. ED 088 182.

Shavelson, R. J. (1988). *Statistical Reasoning for the Behavioral Sciences* (2nd. ed.). Boston: Allyn and Bacon.

Spear, M. (1952). *Charting Statistics*. New York: McGraw-Hill.

Tufte, E. R. (1983). *The Visual Display of Quantitative Information*. Chesire, CT: Graphics Press.

Tukey, J. W. (1977). *Exploratory Data Analysis*. Reading, MA: Addison-Wesley.

White, A., & Lewis, J. (1984). *Youth and parent perceptions of female roles one decade apart*. Laramie: University of Wyoming. Technical Report. ED 260 357.

Wrabel, T. J. (1985). *Ego identity, cognitive ability, and academic achievement: Variances, relationships, and gender differences among high school sophomores*. Unpublished doctoral dissertation, International Graduate School. ED 263 185.

Glossary

ABSCISSA: The abscissa is the horizontal axis of a **graph**, often called the "*x*-axis." The abscissa carries the scale of the independent variable in a graph of a simple linear regression line.

ADJUSTED MEAN: Adjusted means are estimates of the values of population means that would be found, were the samples used in an **analysis of covariance**, equivalent in average score on one or more **covariates**, prior to the initiation of experimental and control treatments.

ALPHA LEVEL: In testing a **null hypothesis** the alpha level is the probability of committing a **Type I error**. More explicitly, it is the probability of rejecting a true **null hypothesis**. Also called the **level of significance** of an hypothesis test.

ALTERNATIVE HYPOTHESIS: In **hypothesis testing**, the alternative hypothesis defines one or more values of the population **parameter** of interest. The alternative hypothesis typically includes a range of values of the population parameter, and is the converse of the **null hypothesis**.

ANALYSIS OF COVARIANCE (ANACOVA): An **inferential** statistical procedure used to test the **null hypothesis** that the **means** of two or more **populations** are equal to each other, after random samples selected from the **populations** are adjusted to eliminate differences between their average values on one or more independent variables (called **covariates**).

ANALYSIS OF VARIANCE (ANOVA): An **inferential** statistical procedure used to test the **null hypothesis** that the **means** of two or more **populations** are equal to each other.

BIAS ERROR: A form of error of measurement that is systematic rather than random, in that it occurs consistently for all objects of measurement. A bias error can be constant across objects of measurement or it can differ across objects in a predictable pattern; for example, a scale would incorporate bias error it if consistently measured one pound high or if it consistently measured 20% high.

BIMODAL: A bimodal **frequency distribution** is one that has two score values or two score classes that have higher frequencies than any other score values or score classes. A bimodal **frequency polygon** would thus have two peaks (like a dromedary--or is it a camel?)

BISERIAL CORRELATION: A type of **correlation coefficient** that is used with one variable that is measured on an **interval scale** and another variable that is dichotomously measured (two-valued). The dichotomously measured variable is assumed to represent a **construct** that has an underlying **normal** distribution.

BOX-AND-WHISKER CHART: An **exploratory data analysis** procedure for summarizing and displaying a distribution of scores. A box-and-whisker chart consists of a rectangular box (usually drawn with the long side parallel to the **abscissa**) with horizontal lines (called "whiskers") extending from both ends of the box. The ends of the box are drawn at points on a score scale corresponding to the 25th **percentile** (first **quartile**) and the 75th percentile (third quartile) of a score distribution. The lower whisker extends from the 25th percentile to the 10th percentile of the score distribution, and the upper whisker extends from the 75th percentile to the 90th percentile of the score distribution. A vertical line is drawn inside the box, at the point on the score scale corresponding to the **median** of the score distribution. A box-and-whisker chart thus provides a visual summary of the 10th, 25th, 50th, 75th, and 90th percentiles of a score distribution. In so doing, it portrays the shape of the score distribution.

CHI-SQUARE STATISTIC: This is one of many so-called **test statistics** that are used in **inferential statistics**. The chi-square statistic is used in tests of the statistical independence of two variables, and in tests of the identity of two **frequency distributions**. Depending on the value of a parameter called its **degrees of freedom**, the chi-square statistic is compared to one of a family of known probability distributions, called the chi-square distributions.

CHI-SQUARE TEST: Usually a test of the **null hypothesis** that two variables are **statistically independent**. However, a chi-square test can also be used to examine the null hypothesis that a sample has been selected from a population with a known **frequency distribution**.

COEFFICIENT OF DETERMINATION: A statistic that is used in regression analysis. In simple linear regression, the coefficient of determination is equal to the square of the **correlation** between the independent variable and the dependent variable. In **multiple regression**, the coefficient of determination is equal to the square of the correlation between actual values of the dependent variable and predicted values of the dependent variable. In either case, the coefficient of determination is said to represent the proportion of **variance** of scores on the dependent variable that is "accounted for" by the independent variable(s).

COMMUNALITY: In a **factor analysis**, the communality of a variable is the proportion of the **variance** of that variable that is shared with other variables in the analysis.

CONCURRENT VALIDITY: A type of **validity** evidence that represents the degree of correspondence between a new measurement instrument and a well-established, independently validated measure of the same **construct**. Concurrent validity evidence is usually summarized in terms of a **correlation coefficient** between scores on the new measurement instrument and scores on the well-established measurement instrument.

CONFIDENCE INTERVAL: A confidence interval consists of two values (a lower confidence limit and an upper confidence limit) that provide estimated bounds on a population **parameter**. A confidence interval is the result of interval **estimation**. When a researcher claims to be "95% confident that a population **parameter** is captured by a given confidence interval," that person is stating a level of belief that the confidence interval captures the true value of the population **parameter**. The level of belief is not a probability value.

CONFOUNDING: The inability to separate the potential effects of two or more potential explanations of the results of a research study. The two explanations are thus said to be confounded. Confounding results from flawed research designs.

CONSTANT: A constant is any identical characteristic of all members of a **sample** or **population**. The sex of all members of the population of adult males in the United States is a constant. The converse of a constant is a variable; a characteristic on which members of a **sample** or **population** differ from each other.

CONSTRUCT: A construct is an unobservable, constructed variable that is used to label a consistent set of behaviors or observable variables. Many of the most important variables in education and the social and behavioral sciences are constructs. Examples include intelligence, socioeconomic status, motivation, social class, anxiety, and achievement. Because they are not observable, constructs cannot be measured directly. A major task of social and behavioral research is the development of measures of various constructs.

CONSTRUCT VALIDITY: A type of **validity** evidence that indicates the degree to which an instrument is a measure of the **construct** that it purports to measure. Some researchers assert that construct validation is the essence of all validation. Construct validity is never proved conclusively. To support a claim to construct validity requires a series of empirical demonstrations in the context of a well-defined theory.

CONTENT VALIDITY: A type of **validity** evidence that is concerned with the correspondence between the content of a measurement instrument and the domain of knowledge it purports to represent. Content validity is determined judgmentally, not by using a statistical procedure. To be content valid, a measurement instrument should assess a representative sample of the knowledge or behavior domain which it is claimed to measure.

CONTINGENCY TABLE: A two-dimensional table that is defined by the levels of two categorical variables. The rows of the table are defined by the levels of one variable, and the columns of the table are defined by the levels of another variable. The cells of the table (each cell is formed by the intersection of a row and a column) contain the numbers of observations that are at the respective combinations of levels of each variable. For example, a contingency table would be formed by classifying a sample of adults by sex and political party affiliation (Republican, Democrat, or Independent). The resulting table would have two rows (male and female), and three columns (one for each political party). Each of the six cells of the table would contain the number of adults of that respective sex and party affiliation.

CONTROL PROCEDURES: A variety of methods used to reduce or eliminate the effects of extraneous influences in a research study. Some methods of control are statistical (such as **analysis of covariance**), and some occur during the design of a study, such as selecting random samples and random assignment of subjects to treatments.

CORRELATION COEFFICIENT: This is a **sample statistic** or **population parameter** that indicates the degree of relationship between two variables. There are many kinds of correlation coefficients. The most frequently used are the **Pearson Correlation Coefficient**, a measure of the degree of linear relationship between two variables that are measured on a **interval scale**, and the **Spearman Correlation Coefficient**, a measure of the strength of linear relationship between two variables that are measured on an **ordinal scale**. Correlation coefficients can assume values between +1.0 and –1.0. A value of 0 indicates no linear relationship; a value of +1.0 indicates a perfect direct relationship; and a value of –1.0 indicates a perfect inverse relationship.

COVARIATE: A measure that plays the role of a control variable in an **analysis of covariance**. A covariate is measured or observed prior to the initiation of treatments and is used to control statistically for differences among experimental and control groups that might remain, even though subjects have been randomly assigned to groups.

CRONBACH'S ALPHA: A formula for estimating the **internal consistency reliability** of a measurement instrument. Cronbach's alpha uses data collected during a single administration of a measurement instrument, and can be used with instruments that have items with scores that fall into more than two categories (e.g., five-point scales).

CRITICAL REGION: In **hypothesis testing,** the critical region consists of the range of values of the test statistic that will lead to rejection of the **null hypothesis**. If the test **statistic** computed from **sample** data falls in the critical region, the **null hypothesis** is rejected; if the **test statistic** falls outside the critical region, the **null hypothesis** is retained.

CUMULATIVE FREQUENCY DISTRIBUTION: A cumulative frequency distribution is a two-column table that is used to summarize a set of data. One column contains an ordered list of the distinct score values in the data set. The other column lists the number of scores that are less than or equal to each corresponding score value. For example, if the data set consisted of the scores 1, 1, 2, 2, 2, 3, 4, the cumulative frequency distribution would be as follows:

Score value	Cumulative Frequency
1	2
2	5
3	6
4	7

This is because two scores are less than or equal to 1; five scores are less than or equal to 2; and so forth.

CUMULATIVE PERCENT FREQUENCY DISTRIBUTION: A cumulative percent frequency distribution is a two-column table that is used to summarize a set of data. One column contains an ordered list of the distinct score values in the data set. The other column lists the percentage of scores that are less than or equal to each corresponding score value.

CUTOFF SCORE: In a situation where applicants for admission to an educational institution or applicants for a job are screened by using a selection device (such as a test), a cutoff score is the lowest score on the selection device that contributes to a positive selection decision.

DATA: This term describes the raw material of statistics. Data (plural; singular is "datum") are numbers that provide numerical values for any characteristic of a **sample** or a **population**.

DEGREES OF FREEDOM: A term that distinguishes among members of the family of t-distributions, members of the family of **chi-square** distributions, and members of the family of F-distributions. In a research study, one degree of freedom is gained for every **independent** observation or data point collected, and one degree of freedom is lost for every **population parameter** that is estimated using the data collected.

DEPENDENT VARIABLE: In a research study, the dependent variable defines a principal focus of research interest. It is the consequent variable that is presumably affected by one or more **independent variables** that are either manipulated by the researcher or observed by the researcher and regarded as antecedent conditions that determine the value of the dependent variable. For example, in a study of the relationship between mosquitoes and mosquito bites, the number of mosquito bites per hour would be the dependent variable.

DESCRIPTIVE STATISTICS: The branch of statistics that involves summarizing, tabulating, organizing, and graphing data for the purpose of describing a sample of objects or individuals that have been measured or observed. In descriptive statistics, no attempt is made to infer the characteristics of objects or individuals that have not been measured or observed.

DEVIATION IQ: An IQ-test score that is computed by converting a **raw score** to a **standard score** with a **mean** of 100 and a specified **standard deviation**. For most IQ tests, the standard deviation of the IQ scale is 15 points, but for some it is 16 points.

DIFFUSION OF TREATMENTS: A threat to the **internal validity** of a research study involving two or more groups in the same research setting. The threat derives from the contamination of the respective treatments due to communication among the research subjects or among those who administer the treatments. For example, in a school-based research setting, teachers using different experimental curricula might alter their instruction after talking with their peers about the various curricula.

DIRECTIONAL ALTERNATIVE HYPOTHESIS: In **hypothesis testing**, a directional alternative hypothesis defines one or more values of the population **parameter** of interest that are all larger, or all smaller, than the value specified under the **null hypothesis**. A directional alternative hypothesis typically includes a range of values of the population parameter, and is a converse of the **null hypothesis**.

DOUBLE-BARRED HISTOGRAM: A graph that contains **histograms** for two different variables. The frequencies of the variables that correspond to a given score class are shown in adjacent bars.

ERROR SCORE: In classical measurement theory, error score is the difference between an observed score and the **true score** (the portion of an observed score that represents the average of observed scores, taken over an infinitely large number of measurement occasions in an infinitely large number of equivalent measurement contexts). Error scores are assumed to vary randomly, across examinees.

ESTIMATE: A value computed from sample data that results from use of an **estimator** of a population **parameter**. For example, a sample **mean** of 104.2 is an estimate of the mean IQ score of members of a population.

ESTIMATION: A form of **inferential statistics** in which sample data are used to estimate the value of a population **parameter**. In one form, called "point estimation," the value of a sample **statictic** is used as a "best guess" of the value of a corresponding population **parameter**. In another form, called **interval estimation**, sample statistics are used to form a **confidence interval**, a range of values within which a population **parameter** is thought to fall.

ESTIMATOR: An estimator is a formula that is used to compute an estimate of a population **parameter** from sample **data**. The formula for computing a sample mean is an example of an estimator.

ETA-SQUARED: A sample **statistic** or population **parameter** that represents the proportion of the **variance** of a dependent variable that is predicted by an independent variable. Unlike the **coefficient of determination**, which represents the proportion of variance of a dependent variable that is predicted by an independent variable using a linear regression model, eta-squared represents the "total" predictability of a dependent variable, whether based on a linear model or a nonlinear model.

EXCLUSIVE RANGE: The exclusive range is a measure of the spread of scores in a distribution. It is most often used as a **descriptive statistic**. The exclusive range is equal to the difference between the largest and the smallest observed scores in a distribution.

EXPERIMENTAL DESIGN: A type of research design in which the conditions of treatment are controlled by the researcher and in which experimental subjects are randomly assigned to treatment conditions.

EXPLORATORY DATA ANALYSIS: A class of statistical procedures developed by John W. Tukey in the 1960s that is designed to reveal the nature of a set of data through a process of exploration and description. The procedures are often graphical, are used for description rather than statistical inference, and typically make weak assumptions about **level of measurement** and the shape of the **frequency distribution** of the data.

EXTERNAL VALIDITY: The external validity of a study indicates the extent to which the conclusions of the study can be generalized to populations and contexts other than those sampled and used in the study.

F-DISTRIBUTION: The **frequency distribution** of a **test statistic** that is used in conjunction with a wide variety of **hypothesis tests**, including the **analysis of variance**. In fact, there is an entire family of *F*-distributions that are distinguished by two parameters known as their **degrees of freedom** between groups and their degrees of freedom within groups.

F-TEST: An **hypothesis testing** procedure that is used for a variety of purposes. One application is a test of the **null hypothesis** that two **populations** have equal **variances**. Other applications are in the **analysis of variance** and the **analysis of covariance**.

FACTOR ANALYSIS: A statistical procedure that is used to reduce a large number of variables to a much smaller, representative set of variables, called "factors." The object of factor analysis is to achieve parsimony, and often to discover the essential variables that underlie and summarize the information in a large set of variables.

FREQUENCY POLYGON: A frequency polygon is a picture of a **grouped frequency distribution**. The horizontal axis (bottom) of a frequency polygon is marked off in midpoints of score intervals. The vertical axis (side) of a frequency polygon is marked off in frequencies or percent frequencies. The graph is constructed by plotting points that correspond to the frequencies or percent frequencies associated with the midpoint of each score interval. Adjacent points are then connected to form a graph. The graph consists of many connected straight lines, hence its name.

FREQUENCY DISTRIBUTION: A frequency distribution is a two-column table that is used to summarize a set of data. One column contains an ordered list of the distinct score values in the data set. The other column lists the number of times each score value appears in the original data set. These numbers are termed "frequencies."

GRADE EQUIVALENT SCALE: A score scale that is frequently used to report students' performances on standardized achievement tests. The grade equivalent scale purports to represent the scores on a test that correspond to the **median** performances of examinees in particular grades at particular months during the school year. Thus, a grade equivalent of 4.6 is claimed to represent the median performance of fourth-graders during the sixth month of the school year.

GRAPH: A graph is a pictorial representation of a set of data. Popular graphs include **pie charts, histograms, box-and-whisker charts**, and **frequency polygons**. Just as a "picture is worth a thousand words," a good graph is worth at least 10,000 numbers in a table. Well constructed graphs provide a rapid view of the global features of a set of data, whereas tables often provide more detailed information.

GROUPED FREQUENCY DISTRIBUTION: A grouped frequency distribution is a two-column table that is used to summarize a set of data. The first column lists score intervals, score classes, or score groups (all synonyms). The second column lists the number of scores that fall into each score interval. Construction of grouped frequency distributions follows rules of experience, rather than theory. You will find similar, but not necessarily identical, instructions in any elementary statistics book.

HEISENBERG'S UNCERTAINTY PRINCIPLE: According to Heisenberg's Uncertainty Principle, all measurement is reactive: subjects are changed by the act of measurement. Therefore, it is impossible to measure an object without affecting the quantity that is to be measured.

HINGE SPREAD: An exploratory data analysis term coined by John W. Tukey. The hinge spread is the difference between the 75th **percentile** and the 25th percentile of a score distribution.

HISTOGRAM: A histogram (commonly called a bar chart) is a picture of a **grouped frequency distribution**. The horizontal axis (bottom) of a histogram is marked off in limits of score intervals. The vertical axis (side) of a histogram is marked off in frequencies or percent frequencies. The height of each bar in a histogram indicates the number or percentage of cases in a data set that fall into its corresponding score interval.

HYPOTHESIS TESTING. An application of **inferential statistics** in which a decision is reached concerning the validity of an hypothesis about the value of a population **parameter**. The process proceeds in four steps: (1) A population **parameter** is hypothesized to equal some stated value; (2) **data** are collected on a **sample** of objects or individuals, randomly chosen from the population; (3) a **test statistic** is computed, using sample data; (4) a decision is reached to retain or reject the initial hypothesis, depending on the value of the test statistic.

INCLUSIVE RANGE: The inclusive range is a measure of the spread of scores in a distribution. It is most often used as a **descriptive statistic**. The inclusive range is equal to the difference between the largest and the smallest scores in a distribution, plus the **sensitivity** of measurement.

INDEPENDENT VARIABLE: In a research study, independent variables are antecedent conditions that are presumed to affect a **dependent variable**. They are either manipulated by the researcher or are observed by the researcher so that their values can be related to that of the dependent variable. For example, in a research study on the relationship between mosquitoes and mosquito bites, the number of mosquitoes per acre of ground would be an independent variable.

INFERENTIAL STATISTICS: The branch of statistics that involves making inferences about the value of one or more population **parameters**, on the basis of sample **statistics**. The most common applications of inferential statistical procedures are **estimation** and **hypothesis testing**. Using the data gathered through a sample survey (such as the Gallup Poll) to estimate the proportion of voters who favor a political candidate is an example of statistical inference.

INSTRUMENTATION EFFECTS: A threat to the **internal validity** of a research study that derives from changes in the measurement characteristics of instruments used in a pretest-posttest design from the beginning of the study to the end of the study. The conditions of the study can alter the **construct validity** or the **reliability** of a measurement instrument over the course of the study, rendering pretest and posttest measures incomparable.

INTERACTION: When two **independent variables** interact in their effects on a **dependent variable**, the effect of one independent variable depends on the value of the other independent variable. For example, in an educational experiment, the effect of various curricula on student achievement might depend on the level of motivation of the students. In that case, curriculum and student motivation would be said to interact.

INTERNAL CONSISTENCY METHOD: Procedures for estimating the **reliability** of a test that are based on data collected in a single administration of the test are termed internal consistency methods. These methods assess the degree to which the items on the test are measuring a single variable.

INTERNAL VALIDITY: The internal validity of a research study indicates the trustworthiness of the conclusions of the study, as they apply to the sample observed and the context used in the study.

INTERVAL ESTIMATION: A form of **estimation** in which an interval on the real number line is claimed to capture a **population parameter**. The statement that the interval captures the population parameter is stated with a given level of confidence. See **confidence interval**.

INTERVAL SCALE: This term labels one of four widely referenced sets of assumptions about the relationship between an underlying variable (often called a **construct**) and an observed variable, said to be a measure of the construct. If the construct is measured on an interval scale, a given interval on the scale of measurement corresponds to the same amount of the construct, regardless of where that interval occurs on the scale. The temperature on a thermometer that is calibrated in degrees Fahrenheit is an example of an interval scale, since a five-degree increase on the scale is thought to measure the same temperature increase, whether it occurs between 20 degrees and 25 degrees or between 60 degrees and 65 degrees. The scale value 0 is arbitrary on an interval scale, and does not represent absence of the construct. Note that 0 degrees on the Fahrenheit scale, although a chilling number, does not represent total absence of temperature.

JOHN HENRY EFFECT: Also called compensatory equalization of treatments, this threat to the **internal validity** of a research study derives from the tendency of individuals administering an innovative treatment to regard that treatment as a challenge to their typical mode of behavior (the control treatment). They therefore compensate, by temporarily improving the control treatment.

KUDER-RICHARDSON FORMULAS (20 and 21): These are two formulas used to estimate the **internal consistency reliability** of a test, and use data collected during a single administration of a test. They are typically denoted by KR_{20} and KR_{21}.

KURTOSIS. A statistic used to describe the peakedness of a **frequency distribution**. A distribution that is tall and thin is termed **leptokurtic**; a distribution that is about as peaked as a **normal distribution** is called **mesokurtic**; a distribution that is wide and flat, compared to a **normal distribution**, is termed **platykurtic**.

LEPTOKURTIC: A **frequency distribution** that is leptokurtic is tall and thin in shape. Any distribution that is markedly more peaked than the **normal distribution** is termed leptokurtic.

LEVEL OF CONFIDENCE: The probability associated with a **population** of **confidence intervals** that could be formed by selecting all possible **samples** of a given size from a specified population, and using sample data to construct an **interval estimate** of a population parameter. The probability that a confidence interval drawn at random from this population will capture the population **parameter** is the level of confidence associated with any single confidence interval.

LEVEL OF SIGNIFICANCE: In **hypothesis testing**, the risk of committing a **Type I error** is termed the level of significance of the hypothesis test.

LEVEL OF MEASUREMENT: This term refers to the relationship that is assumed to exist between an underlying variable (often called a **construct**) and an observed variable, thought to be a measure of the construct. The four most widely referenced sets of assumptions about such relationships are termed **nominal**-level measurement, **ordinal**-level measurement, **interval**-level measurement, and **ratio**-level measurement.

LOWER REAL LIMIT: In a **grouped frequency distribution**, the lower real limit of a score class is equal to the smallest scale value of scores in that class, minus half the **sensitivity** of measurement. For example, the lower real limit of a score class containing values 25, 26, 27, and 28 would be 24.5, because the smallest scale value of scores in the class is 25 and the sensitivity of measurement is 1.

MATCHING DESIGN: A research design in which the subjects assigned to various treatments are first matched on one or more variables that might cause or explain differences in their posttreatment performances. For example, subjects assigned to different dietary treatments might be matched on initial weight, gender, height, and so forth.

MEAN: This sample **statistic** or population **parameter** is the most frequently used indicator of the middle of a score distribution. Its other names are the "average" and the "arithmetic average." For a collection of **raw scores**, it is found simply by summing the scores and dividing by the number of scores.

MEAN SQUARES: A statistic that is central to the **analysis of variance**, mean squares represent average **variation** in a set of data. The mean square within groups is equal to the average of the squared deviations of scores from their respective group means. The mean square between groups reflects variation among the means of different samples.

MEASURES OF ASSOCIATION: This generic term includes all **sample statistics** and **population parameters** that indicate the degree of relationship between two **variables**. Examples include the **Pearson Correlation Coefficient**, the **Spearman Correlation Coefficient**, and the **chi-square statistics**.

MEASURES OF CENTRAL TENDENCY: This generic term includes all **sample statistics** and **population parameters** that indicate where the middle of a score distribution falls. The most common measures of central tendency are the **mean** (or arithmetic average), the **median**, and the **mode**. These **statistics** and **parameters** tell us where the center of a distribution "tends to be." In modern statistical parlance, the term **measures of location** is sometimes used.

MEASURES OF LOCATION: A modern term for **measures of central tendency**. Measures of location are sample statistics and population parameters that indicate the location of the center of a score distribution or frequency distribution.

MEASURES OF VARIABILITY: This generic term includes all **sample statistics** and **population parameters** that indicate the spread of a score distribution. Examples include the **range**, the **standard deviation**, the **variance**, and the **semi-interquartile range**.

MEDIAN: This **sample statistic** or **population parameter** is an indicator of the middle of a score distribution. It is equal to the point on a score scale that divides a distribution exactly in half, in the sense that half the scores fall above the median and half the scores fall below. Other names for the median are the **50th percentile** and the **second quartile**.

MESOKURTIC: A **frequency distribution** that is mesokurtic is neither tall and skinny nor wide and flat, it is about as peaked as a **normal distribution**. In fact, the **normal distribution** is used as a standard for describing **kurtosis** which means "peakedness."

MIDPOINT. In a **grouped frequency distribution**, a midpoint is the score value that is halfway between the **lower real limit** and the **upper real limit** of a score class.

MODE: The mode is sometimes named an indicator of the middle of a score distribution, and is therefore classified as a **measure of central tendency**. For a group of scores, the mode is defined as the score value that occurs more often than any other score value. However, all scores in a group might occur with the same frequency (in which case there would be no mode), or a group of scores might have two score values that occur with the same highest frequency (e.g., there might be ten 5's and ten 8's in the **sample** of scores where there are no more than five occurrences of any other score value). In this case, there would be two modes. Finally, even though a score distribution has only one score that occurs more frequently than any other, that score value might not fall in the middle of the distribution (think of the distribution of heights of a group composed of five basketball players and fifty typical 20-year-old males). The principal advantage of the mode is that it requires only **nominal**-level measurement.

MORTALITY: A threat to the **internal validity** of a research study that derives from subjects in different groups dropping out of the study at different rates because of the treatments they receive. The subjects remaining at the end of the study might therefore differ systematically from subjects who were assigned to treatments at the beginning of the study, even if random assignment was used.

MULTIPLE CORRELATION COEFFICIENT: This sample **statistic** or population **parameter** summarizes the degree of linear relationship between a criterion variable (a variable that is predicted or dependent) and a linear combination of independent variables (used as predictors). The multiple correlation coefficient tells a researcher how well a given variable can be predicted using a number of other variables as predictors. It is used in conjunction with **multiple regression** analysis.

MULTIPLE REGRESSION: A statistical procedure that is used to predict the value of one variable (called a **dependent variable**) from the values of at least two other variables (called **independent variables**). A procedure called the "least square method" is used to find the linear combination of independent variables that does the best job of predicting the dependent variable.

NEGATIVELY SKEWED: A **frequency distribution** that is negatively skewed is shaped so that the majority of its scores fall above its **mean**. The distribution of heights of professional basketball players is negatively skewed, since most professional basketball players are quite tall, but a few of them are relatively short.

NOMINAL SCALE: This term labels one of four widely referenced sets of assumptions about the relationship between an underlying variable (often called a **construct**) and an observed variable, said to be a measure of the construct. If the observed variable measures the construct on a nominal scale, it is not assumed that a larger scale value corresponds to a larger amount of the construct. Nominal scale values merely serve as labels for different categories of the construct, and have no other meaning in terms of amount or quantity. The following numerical scale could be adopted to distinguish between people with different eye color: 1, if brown eyes; 2, if blue eyes; 3, if black eyes; and 4, if green eyes. A person categorized as a "1" would have a different eye color than a person categorized as a "2", but would not have *more* eye color.

NORMAL DISTRIBUTION: The normal distribution is a theoretical contrivance that is the backbone of **inferential statistics**. Without it, statisticians would be lost. A graph of a normal distribution is shaped like a bell. In fact, the normal distribution is often called the "bell-shaped curve." The normal distribution is often a good approximation to many actual **frequency distributions**. Statisticians have proven that **frequency distributions** of **sample means** almost always look like normal distributions.

NORMATIVE INTERPRETATION: When the results of measurement are interpreted normatively, the score earned by an individual is evaluated by comparing it to the scores earned by other examinees. Converting an individual's score to a **percentile rank** provides a basis for interpreting it normatively. Tests that are designed to facilitate normative interpretations of examinees' performances are termed "norm-referenced" tests.

NULL HYPOTHESIS: In **hypothesis testing**, the null hypothesis is an initial statement of belief about the value of a population **parameter**. The object of hypothesis testing is to reach a decision on the truth or falsity of the null hypothesis that the population **parameter** of interest is equal to a specified value.

ORDINAL SCALE: This term labels one of four widely referenced sets of assumptions about the relationship between an underlying variable (often called a **construct**) and an observed variable, said to be a measure of the construct. If the observed variable measures the construct on an ordinal scale, a larger scale value is assumed to represent a larger amount of the construct. Data that are in **ranks** are usually assumed to be ordinally scaled, since a higher rank (smaller number) represents more of the construct than does a lower rank (larger number). If students are ranked in terms of their standing in a high school class, the student ranked 1 is thought to have a higher academic standing than the student ranked 2, and so forth. However, it is not assumed that the difference in academic standing between the student ranked 1 and the student ranked 2 is the same as the difference between the student ranked 2 and the student ranked 3.

ORDINATE: The ordinate is the vertical axis of a **graph**, often called the "*y*-axis." The ordinate carries the scale of dependent variable in a graph of a simple linear regression line.

PAIRED-DIFFERENCE *t*-TEST: A procedure for testing the null hypothesis that two population means are equal that makes use of data collected from two pairwise-related samples--such as sibling pairs, husbands and wives, or pretreatment and posttreatment observations on the same sampled individuals. Elements of the populations to which generalizations are made are also related in a pairwise manner.

PARALLEL FORMS: The forms of a test that have near-identical statistical properties and similar content are said to be parallel forms. Strictly observed, distributions of scores for parallel test forms must have the same **mean**, the same **standard deviations**, and the same **standard error of measurement**. Scores on parallel test forms must also have the same **correlation** coefficient with any other variable.

PARAMETER: A parameter is a summary value that describes some characteristic of a **population**. Examples of parameters include **means**, **standard deviations**, **proportions**, and **correlation coefficients**. The correlation between height and weight for the population of adult women in the United States is a parameter.

PEARSON CORRELATION COEFFICIENT: A sample **statistic** or population **parameter** that indicates the degree of linear relationship between two **variables** that are measured on an **interval scale**. The Pearson correlation coefficient can assume values between +1.0 and −1.0. A value of +1.0 indicates a perfect direct linear relationship; a value of −1.0 indicates a perfect inverse linear relationship.

PERCENTILE: A percentile is a point on a score scale that divides a score distribution into two parts. There are 99 different percentiles--the 1st percentile, the 2nd percentile, and so on, up to the 99th percentile. Together the percentiles divide a score distribution into 100 parts. For example, the 25th percentile is the point on the score scale where exactly 25% of the scores in a distribution either equal it or fall below it.

PERCENTILE RANK: The percentile rank associated with a given **raw score** is the percentage of scores in a distribution that are less than or equal to that raw score. Percentile ranks are used to interpret an individual's raw score by comparing it with the performances of others. For example, if a raw score of 68 on a nationally normed test had a corresponding percentile rank of 55, one could conclude that 55% of the individuals in the norms sample earned **raw scores** of 68 or less.

PHI COEFFICIENT: A type of **correlation coefficient** that is used with two variables that are dichotomous (two-valued), such as gender or voting behavior (did vote / did not vote).

PIE CHART: A pie chart is a type of **graph** used to display the percentage of cases in a data set that fall into various categories. The graph is called a pie chart because it is circular in shape, with a wedge of the circle identified with each category. The width of each wedge is proportional to the percentage of cases that fall into its corresponding category. Thus a category that contained 10% of all cases would have a wedge that was twice as wide as the wedge of a category that contained only 5% of all cases.

PLATYKURTIC: A **frequency distribution** that is platykurtic is wide and flat in shape. Any distribution that is markedly less peaked than the **normal distribution** is termed platykurtic.

POINT BISERIAL CORRELATION: A type of **correlation coefficient** that is used with one variable that is measured on an **interval scale** and another variable that is dichotomous (two-valued).

POPULATION: Formally, a population is any collection of objects or individuals that have at least one characteristic in common. In **inferential statistics** one usually wishes to determine the value of some characteristic of a population, called a population **parameter**. Populations are the objects of generalization in **inferential statistics**.

POSITIVELY SKEWED: In a positively skewed **frequency distribution**, a majority of the scores fall below the **mean**. The distribution of scores of sixth-grade students on a beginning calculus test would be positively skewed, since most sixth-graders would earn low scores, but a few (who learned some calculus from older siblings, from their parents, or on their own) would quite well.

POWER: In **hypothesis testing**, the power of a test is the probability that a false **null hypothesis** will be rejected, in favor of a true **alternative hypothesis**. Power is equal to the converse of the probability of committing a **Type II error**.

PREDICTIVE VALIDITY: A type of **validity** evidence that is represented by the effectiveness with which a measurement instrument can be used to predict future performance on some criterion variable. Predictive validity evidence is usually summarized in terms of a **correlation coefficient** between scores on the measurement instrument and scores on a measurement of the criterion variable. For example, the predictive validity of a test of reading readiness administered to beginning first-graders might be measured in terms of its **correlation** with those students' second-grade reading achievement scores.

PRETEST-POSTTEST DESIGN: A type of research design in which the same subjects are measured prior to the initiation of treatment and following the completion of treatment.

PRINCIPAL COMPONENTS ANALYSIS: A statistical procedure that has the same objectives as **factor analysis**. In a principal components analysis, all of the variables being analyzed are assumed to be derived from a set of common factors and none of the variables is presumed to be dependent on underlying factors that are unique.

PROBABILITY SAMPLE: A sample of observations collected from a well-defined **population** through a procedure that assures potential selection of any member of the population and permits calculation of the probability of selecting any sample, prior to selection.

QUARTILE: The quartiles of a score distribution are the points on a score scale that divide the distribution into fourths. The most frequently used quartiles are the first, corresponding to the 25th **percentile**; the second, corresponding to the **median**; and the third, corresponding to the 75th percentile.

QUASI-EXPERIMENTAL DESIGN: A type of research design in which the conditions of treatment are controlled by the researcher. A quasi-experimental design is distinguished from an experimental design in that experimental subjects are randomly assigned to treatment conditions.

RANDOM ERROR. A form of error of measurement that is unpredictable and inconsistent across objects of measurement, rather than systematic.

RANDOM SAMPLING FLUCTUATION: The tendency of **estimates** of a population **parameter** to vary across **samples** of the same size selected from a common **population**.

RANGE: The range is a measure of the spread of scores in a distribution. It is most often used as a **descriptive statistic**. The range is equal to the difference between the largest and the smallest scores in a distribution.

RANKS: Ranks are used to convert a set of data to an **ordinal scale**. The original data are first listed from largest to smallest. The largest score is assigned a rank of 1; the next largest a rank of 2; and so forth. If two scores have the same value, they are given the average of the ranks they would have been assigned, had their values been different. For example, if the data set consisted of the scores 10, 9, 9, and 8, the corresponding ranks would be 1, 2.5, 2.5, and 4.

RATIO SCALE: This term labels one of four widely referenced sets of assumptions about the relationship between an underlying variable (often a called a **construct**) and an observed variable said to be a measure of the construct. If the observed variable measures of the construct on a ratio scale, a given interval on the scale of measurement corresponds to the same amount of the construct, regardless of where that interval occurs on the scale. In addition, zero on the scale of measurement corresponds to complete absence of the construct. Height measured in inches is an example of measurement on a ratio scale. The four inches between 18 inches and 22 inches represent the same difference in height as does the four inches between 58 inches and 62 inches. Also, a person who measured zero inches from the bottom of his or her feet to the top of his or her head would have no height at all. (We've never seen a person who was that short.)

RAW SCORE: A piece of data that has not yet been cooked is called a raw score. To be raw, a score cannot be transformed to a derived scale, such as a **percentile rank** or a **standard score**.

RELIABILITY: A measurement concept that represents the consistency with which an instrument measures a given performance or behavior. A measurement instrument that is reliable will provide consistent results when a given individual is measured repeatedly under near-identical conditions. For example, a reliable bathroom scale would produce very similar weight measurements if a given individual were to step on the scale, then off, then on, then off, and so forth. Reliability is usually represented by a **correlation coefficient**, and can assume values between 0 and 1.0. In practice, perfectly reliable measurement instruments are never found, but some standardized achievement tests have reliabilities as high as 0.95.

REPLICATE: To repeat a research study under conditions that are essentially identical to those used in the original study, using an independent **sample** of subjects.

RESENTFUL DEMORALIZATION OF THE COMPARISON GROUP: A threat to the **internal validity** of a research study that results from members of the comparison group reducing their typical performance because they have been denied access to a desirable experiment treatment.

RESIDUAL: The difference between the value of a **dependent variable** and the value predicted by a statistical model, such as a **multiple regression** model.

SAMPLE: A sample is any subset of a **population**. In **inferential statistics**, one usually attempts to select a sample that represents a **population**, and then collect data on all members of the sample. Sample **statistics** are then computed, in order to infer the value of population **parameters**.

SAMPLING DISTRIBUTION: A sampling distribution is the frequency distribution that a sample **statistic** or **estimator** would follow, if a researcher were to select repeated, independent samples, and compute a value of the **statistic or estimator** for each sample. Sampling distributions are essential to **inferential statistics**, since they allow a researcher to determine the likelihood that **statistics or estimators** of a given magnitude will be observed.

SCATTER DIAGRAM: A scatter diagram is a type of **graph** that is used in conjunction with **correlation coefficients**. Each plotted point in a scatter diagram represents the values of an individual observation of the two **variables** being correlated. Values of one variable are shown on the horizontal axis (bottom) and values of the other are shown on the vertical axis (side of the graph).

SELECTION: A threat to the **internal validity** of a research study that derives from nonrandom assignment of subjects to experimental and control treatments.

SELECTION-HISTORY: A threat to the **internal validity** of a research study that derives nonrandom assignment of subjects to experimental and control treatments and resulting differences in the experiences of these subjects, apart from the experimental and control treatments, during the course of the research study.

SELECTION-MATURATION: A threat to the **internal validity** of a research study that derives from nonrandom assignment of subjects to experimental and control treatments and resulting differences in the maturation of these subjects during the course of the research study.

SEMI-INTERQUARTILE RANGE: This **sample statistic** or **population parameter** is a measure of the spread of scores in a distribution. The more spread out the scores, the larger the semi-interquartile range. The semi-interquartile range is not used as often as the **standard deviation**, but has the advantage that it only requires **ordinal-level** measurement. It is equal to half the distance on the score scale, between the 75th percentile and the 25th percentile.

SENSITIVITY: The smallest interval on a score scale represented by the scores that result from a **measurement** process. A typical teacher-made test has a sensitivity of 1.0, because students' scores are usually represented to the nearest whole number of items correct.

SIMPLE RANDOM SAMPLING: A **probability sampling procedure** in which every member of the **population** has the same chance of being sampled and each person or object is sampled independently.

SKEWED: A skewed **frequency distribution** is not **symmetric** in shape. That is, the shape of its distribution below the **mean** is not the mirror image of its distribution's shape above the mean. If more than half the scores in a distribution fall below its **mean**, the distribution is called **positively skewed**; if more than half the scores in a distribution fall above its mean, the distribution is called **negatively** skewed.

SOLOMON FOUR-GROUP DESIGN: A research design that involves four groups of subjects. Two of the groups receive an experimental treatment, and two receive a control treatment. One of the groups that receive the experimental treatment is pretested, and one is not. One of the groups that receive the control treatment is pretested and one is not. The design permits estimation of a treatment effect and a **testing effect**, and--of greater importance--control of the testing effect, should it exist.

SPEARMAN CORRELATION COEFFICIENT: The Spearman correlation coefficient is a sample statistic or population **parameter** that indicates the degree of linear relationship between two **variables** that are measured on an **ordinal scale**. The Spearman coefficient provides the correlation between the ranks of two variables. It can assume values between +1.0 and −1.0.

SPEARMAN-BROWN PROPHECY FORMULA: A procedure that is used to adjust test **reliability** estimates that are computed using the **split-half method**. Since longer tests are generally more reliable than shorter tests, and the split-half method correlates examinees' scores on halves of a test, the split-half method underestimates the reliability of the entire test. The Spearman-Brown Prophecy Formula compensates for this underestimation.

SPLIT-HALF METHOD: A procedure for estimating the **internal consistency reliability** of a test in which examinees' scores on one half of the test (usually the odd-numbered items) are correlated with their scores on the other half of the test (usually the even-numbered items).

STABILITY: Stability of performance is one form of measurement **reliability**. It indicates consistency of performance across time. The stability of a measurement procedure is typically represented by the **correlation** coefficient between measurements taken on two occasions that are separated by a time interval short enough to prevent changes in an individual's true performance.

STANDARD DEVIATION: This **sample statistic** or **population parameter** is the most popular measure of the spread of scores in a distribution. The more spread out the scores, the larger the standard deviation. The standard deviation requires **interval-level** measurement, and is equal to the square root of the **variance**; a distribution with a **variance** of 16 would thus have a standard deviation of 4.

STANDARD ERROR OF MEASUREMENT: In classical measurement theory, the standard error of measurement is the **standard deviation** of the distribution of **error scores** for an individual examinee. The larger the standard error of measurement, the lower the **reliability** of the measurement procedure.

STANDARD SCORE: A standard score is a type of derived score that is the result of transforming a variable to a scale having a specified **mean** and **standard deviation**. Widely used standard-score scales include the z-score, which has a **mean** of 0 and a **standard deviation** of 1.0; the Z-score, which has a **mean** of 50 and a **standard deviation** of 10; and the T-score, which is scaled exactly like the Z-score, but is often transformed to produce a **normal distribution** of scores.

STATISTIC: A statistic is a number that provides a summary of some characteristic of a set of data. Statistics are usually associated with **samples**, rather than **populations**. Examples of statistics include **means, ranges, correlation coefficients**, and **standard deviations**. The average height of a group of fourth-grade students is a statistic. So is the proportion of Fortune 500 executives having lunch at the Ritz on Monday who put on their pants one leg at a time.

STATISTICAL REGRESSION EFFECT: A threat to the **internal validity** of a **pretest-posttest research** study that derives from use of a less-than-perfectly reliable pretest. Subjects who score above the **mean** of their distribution on pretest will tend to score lower on posttest, because of errors of measurement. Likewise, subjects who score below the mean of their distribution on pretest will tend to score higher on posttest.

STATISTICALLY INDEPENDENT VARIABLES: Two variables are statistically independent if knowledge of the value of one of them provides no information for predicting the value of the other one. For example, gender and voting behavior would be statistically independent, if knowing the gender of a potential voter provided no information that would help determine whether or not the potential voter would actually vote. This would be the case if the proportion of the population of men who voted were exactly the same as the proportion of the population of women who voted.

STEM-AND-LEAF DISPLAY: An **exploratory data analysis** procedure for summarizing and displaying a distribution of scores. A stem-and-leaf display preserves all of the scores in a data set while displaying the frequency distribution in a form that conveys a clear visual image of the shape of the distribution. The "stem" in a stem-and-leaf display consists of the numbers in the left-most column of a set of data (e.g., the numbers in the hundreds column of a set of values that range from 100 to 999), while the "leaves" consist of the numbers in the rest of the columns. Stem-and-leaf displays are akin to raw oysters; you have to try one to know what they're about, since no amount of verbal description is adequate.

STEPWISE MULTIPLE REGRESSION: A **multiple regression** procedure in which the regression equation is constructed by alternately adding and deleting **independent variables**, one variable at a time, until all independent variables in the equation satisfy prespecified statistical criteria.

SUM OF SQUARES: A statistic that is central to the **analysis of variance,** sum of squares represents **variation** in a set of data. The sum of squares within groups is equal to the sum of the squared deviations of scores from their respective group means. The sum of squares between groups reflects variation among the means of different samples.

SYMMETRIC: A **frequency distribution** that is symmetric has the same shape, both above and below its **mean**. In fact, if you were to fold a symmetric **frequency polygon** in half, around its **mean**, its lower half would fall right on top of its upper half. In a symmetric **frequency distribution**, half the scores fall below the mean and half the scores fall above it.

SYNERGISTIC EFFECT: Synonymous with an **interaction** effect. Two **independent variables** operate synergistically if the effect of one on a **dependent variable** is determined, in part, by the value of the other.

TABLE OF SPECIFICATIONS: Synonymous with a **test blueprint**--a table that specifies the content organization and measurement objects of a **test**.

t-TEST: Several widely used **hypothesis testing** procedures are termed *t*-tests. One such procedure is used to test the **null hypothesis** that a **population mean** is equal to a specified value. Another *t*-test is used to examine the null hypothesis that the **means** of two **populations** are equal to each other.

TEST BLUEPRINT: A table that specifies the content organization and measurement objectives of a **test**. A test blueprint indicates how many test items are to be used to assess each category of test content and each category of examinee skill or behavior. For example, a blueprint for an arithmetic test might specify the number of items that were to assess application of addition rules, the number that were to assess comprehension of multiplication rules, and so forth.

TEST-RETEST METHOD: A procedure of estimating the **reliability** of a test in which the same test is administered to a group of examinees on two occasions, and the scores the examinees earn are correlated. The test-retest method is used to test the **stability** of a measurement procedure.

TEST STATISTIC: A statistic that is used in conjunction with an **hypothesis test**. A useful test statistic has a known **frequency distribution** when the **null hypothesis** is true. The null hypothesis is rejected when the observed value of the test statistic is deemed to be very unlikely, assuming the null hypothesis were true.

TESTING EFFECT: A threat to the **internal validity** of a research study that derives from the measurement of subjects prior to the initiation of treatment. According to Hiesenberg's Uncertainty Principle, all measurement is reactive: subjects are changed by the act of measurement. Therefore, pretreatment measurement becomes a part of the treatment.

TESTS and MEASUREMENTS: Instruments used to collect information on a characteristic of an individual or a group of individuals. Tests and measurements used in education and the social sciences are often standardized (meaning that their administration procedures are specified in detail), and scores on tests and measurements are typically assumed to measure individuals' standings on a **construct**.

TETRACHORIC CORRELATION COEFFICIENT: A type of **correlation coefficient** that is used with two variables that are dichotomously measured (two-valued). The dichotomously measured variables are assumed to represent **constructs** that have an underlying **normal** distribution. Tetrachoric correlation coefficients are often used to represent the degree of relationship between students' scores on two test items.

THREE-WAY INTERACTION: A type of **interaction effect** that can be present in a three-factor analysis of variance. In a three-way interaction, the effect of one **independent variable** on a **dependent variable** is determined, in part, by the values of two other independent variables. For example, the effect of gasoline on explosive force is dependent on the presence of an oxidant and a source of combustion (such as a match).

TRUE SCORE: In classical measurement theory, true score is the portion of an observed score that represents the average of observed scores, taken over an infinitely large number of measurement occasions in an infinitely large number of equivalent measurement contexts. True score is that which we wish to measure, in contrast to that which we can measure on a single measurement occasion.

TWO-WAY ANALYSIS OF VARIANCE: An inferential statistical procedure that can be used to investigate the effect of two categorical **independent variables** on a continuous **dependent variable**. An example would be an analysis of the effect of type of curriculum and students' gender on students' achievement. Type of curriculum and gender are the two independent variables and students' achievement is the dependent variable.

TYPE I ERROR: In **hypothesis testing,** a Type I error is committed when a true **null hypothesis** is erroneously retained. The probability of committing a Type I error is usually denoted by the Greek letter alpha.

TYPE II ERROR: In **hypothesis testing,** a Type II error is committed when a false **null hypothesis** is erroneously retained. The probability of committing a Type II error is usually denoted by the Greek letter beta.

UNIMODAL: A unimodal **frequency distribution** is one that has a single score value or a single score class that has a higher frequency than any other score value or score class. A unimodal **frequency polygon** would thus have a single peak.

UPPER REAL LIMIT: In a **grouped frequency distribution,** the upper real limit of a score class is equal to the largest scale value of scores in that class, plus half the **sensitivity** of measurement. For example, the upper real limit of a score class containing values 25, 26, 27, and 28 would be 28.5, because the largest scale value of scores in the class is 28 and the sensitivity of measurement is 1. (In fact, the upper real limit would be 28.4999999. . . . , but it is conventional to round the limit to 28.5).

VALIDITY: A measurement concept that is concerned with the degree to which a measurement instrument actually measures what it purports to measure. Validity is not absolute, but depends on the context in which a measurement instrument is used and the inferences that are based on the results of measurement. It has been noted that no measurement instrument has inherent validity. One can make both valid and invalid inferences from the results of measurement. A number of categories of validity evidence have been identified in the measurement literature. They include **content validity** evidence, **construct validity** evidence, **concurrent validity** evidence and **predictive validity** evidence.

VARIABLE: A variable is any characteristic on which the elements of a **sample** or **population** differ from each other. Height and weight are variables, as are sex and national origin group. The converse of a variable is a **constant,** which is identical for all members of a **sample** or **population.**

VARIANCE: This **sample statistic** or **population parameter** is an indicator of the spread of scores in a distribution. The more spread out the scores, the larger the variance. The variance is used quite frequently in **inferential statistics,** but less often in **descriptive statistics.** The variance is the square of the **standard deviation;** a distribution that had a **standard deviation** of 4 would thus have a variance of 16.

WECHSLER SCALE: A **standard-score** scale with a **mean** of 10 and a **standard deviation** of 3. This scale is used with the Wechsler intelligence tests.

Answers to Problems

Chapter 1

1.1 The correct answer is b., since 75 out of 100 students scored below 36. Four students scored between 46 and 50, so a. is not correct. Since the majority of students scored below 36, c. is not correct. Two students scored at or below 10, so d. is not correct.

1.2 The correct answer is c., since the distribution has two "humps" and the majority of the distribution falls in the low end of the score scale. The distribution is not symmetric and, having more than one peak, it is not unimodal.

1.3 The category "6-10" has the tallest bar, and therefore has the highest frequency of schools associated with it. The frequency of that category can be read from the vertical scale of the histogram as 8.

1.4 Response a. is true, since there were 1,882 third-grade participants and 1,117 first-grade participants. Response b. is false, since there were 1,707 second-grade participants. Response c. is true, since a standard score of 50 is the national average, and 52.6 is the average standard score on the posttest for first-graders. This is higher than the average posttest standard score for second-graders or third-graders. Response d. is true, since the average gain for first-graders was five points (from 47.6 to 52.6), and this is higher than the corresponding gains in other grades.

Chapter 2

2.1 The correct answer is d. The average wouldn't be good for projection purposes, because the $210,000 spent in one year would inflate the projection too much. The mode wouldn't be useful for several reasons: First, there might not be one. Second, the mode ignores most of the data and is therefore not a good predictor of future performance. The smallest of the annual expenditures would undoubtedly underpredict future expenditures.

2.2 Response a. is correct. Whenever a distribution is unimodal, and the mean is smallest, the median is between the mean and the mode, and the mode is largest, the distribution is negatively skewed. The problem did not state that the distribution was unimodal, but it's a safe bet since we're considering a distribution of test scores for 40,000 students.

2.3 Response a. is true, because in a positively skewed distribution, more than half of the distribution falls below the mean. In this case, you know that is true, because the median is given as $2.10. Response b. is true, because the median of

$2.10 divides the payoff distribution exactly in half. Response c. is false, because the median is $2.10, not $2.00. Response d. is false, because the mode is $2.00, not $3.75.

2.4 a. In all likelihood, the average is not an appropriate statistic to use in summarizing the morale data because the scale probably measures morale at the ordinal level of measurement, and not at the interval level.

b. You should not accept the conclusion that morale in Department B is more than twice as high as that of employees in Department A. To support that conclusion, you would have to believe that the scale measured employee morale at the ratio level of measurement, which is very unlikely. If ratio-level measurement held, an employee who scored zero on the measurement scale would have no morale at all.

c. If you believe that the scale measured employee morale at least at the ordinal level of measurement, you should accept the conclusion that employees in Department B had a higher morale level than did employees in Department A.

Chapter 3

3.1 Response a. is false, because the polygon for girls is far wider than the polygon for boys. Response b. is true because the polygon for girls has far larger spread than the polygon for boys. Response c. is false, because Response b. is true.

3.2 In a symmetric distribution, the middle 50% of the scores fall between the median plus the semi-interquartile range and the median minus the semi-interquartile range. In this case, the lower value is $28 - 4 = 24$ and the upper value is $28 + 4 = 32$.

3.3 Response a. is true, because five years is four standard deviations above the mean, and most of a normal distribution is no more than three standard deviations above the mean. Response b. is true, because one year is four standard deviations below the mean and most of a normal distribution is no more than three standard deviations below the mean. Response c. is true because about 95% of a normal distribution falls between points that are two standard deviations below the mean (as is two years in this case) and two standard deviations above the mean (as is four years in this case). Response d. is false, because the median and the mean are equal (three years in this case) in a normal distribution.

3.4 a. The mean and standard deviation are not appropriate measures of central tendency and variability (respectively) in this case, because they both assume at least interval-level measurement. Rank-in-class is an ordinal-level variable.

b. Ordinal-level measurement is assumed when data are reported as ranks.

c. The median would be a more appropriate measure of central tendency, and the semi-interquartile range would be a more appropriate measure of variability.

Chapter 4

4.1 The correct response is d. because, in a general population that includes both children and adults, older people would tend to weigh more. Therefore the correlation between age and weight would be positive. However, it would not always be the case that an older person weighed more than a younger person, so the correlation would be less than 1.00.

4.2 Response a. is true, because a higher correlation, regardless of its sign, indicates a better predictor, and -0.85 is larger in magnitude than 0.60. Response b. is false, because it is the converse of Response a., and Response a. is true. Response c. is false, because Response a. is true. Response d. is true, because there is a negative correlation between number of absences and arithmetic achievement scores.

4.3 Response a. is the appropriate conclusion, because correlation coefficients are always in the range −1.0 to +1.0. The other responses are not true, for a variety of reasons. Responses b. and d. are causal statements, which can never be supported solely on the basis of a correlation coefficient. Response c. ignores the obvious error in the reported correlation coefficient and is therefore false.

4.4 Response b. is true, because the scatter of points is upward and to the right (indicating a positive correlation) and the points do not fall right on a straight line (indicating a correlation coefficient that is less than 1.0).

Chapter 5

5.1 Response a. is correct because the test-retest method of estimating reliability indicates stability of measurement, whereas the KR-20 method indicates only the degree to which the items on the test tend to measure the same thing.

5.2 Response b. is correct because criterion-referenced tests are often designed to assess mastery of specific objectives, and a percentile rank is, inherently, a norm-referenced report of performance. A percentile rank specifies the performance of an individual examinee in terms of the performance of other examinees.

5.3 Response c. is correct because your objective is to use the test to select those who will do best in honors physics. Predictive validity is an indicator of the value of a measure in predicting future performance. Response a. is not correct because reliability is a necessary, but not a sufficient, component of high predictive validity. Response b. indicates high concurrent validity, which is not relevant for purposes of prediction. Response d. indicates high content validity, which is not relevant for purposes of prediction.

5.4 Response a. is correct, since a T-score of 70 is two standard deviations above the mean of the norm group, which corresponds to a percentile rank of about 97 in a norm distribution of scores; a percentile rank of 87 is well above average (which would be the 50th percentile in a symmetric distribution of scores); and a z-score of 0.25 is only one quarter of a standard deviation above the mean, which is pretty close to average performance. Based on this discussion, Responses b. and c. are clearly wrong. Relative to each other, Bob did best, Mary was next, and Joe did least well, so Response d. is wrong.

Chapter 6

6.1 Responses c. and d. are true, and Responses a. and b. are false. Response a. is false because the single-group research design does not rule out a variety of plausible rival explanations, including the influence of other events that took place while the program was being conducted. For example, a major U.S. Supreme Court ruling on the future of Roe vs. Wade might have caused respondents' attitudes to change. Response b. is false because we have no way of knowing whether the public information program was, or was not, the sole causal agent. Response c. is true, because of reasons stated earlier, and Response d. is true because the effects of "history" might have been the true cause of the observed change.

6.2 Response a. is correct. Those initially classified as the slowest runners on the basis of a single quarter-mile run would likely be faster when they ran a second time, and those initially classified as the fastest runners would likely be slower when they ran a second time, due to any number of factors other than their "true" speed, such as the way they felt on the day of the first run, or the way the wind was blowing when they ran. Therefore, statistical regression effect would operate in the same direction as the reported experimental results for both classes of runners.

Those in the "average" group would be close to the mean of the overall distribution of running times, so that regression effect would not change their posttest scores in a consistent manner. Since there is no comparison group in this "study," the last three threats to validity would not affect the internal validity of the findings.

6.3 Response b. is correct. By using random assignment, the researchers would ensure, at least at the outset of the experiment, that no variable other than the provision of vouchers could explain the differences in dropout rate they observed. As the research was designed, better educated parents were more likely to be aware of the opportunity to obtain vouchers, and of the procedures necessary to enroll their children in nonpublic schools. Since dropout rates are strongly associated with parental education--the better the education of the parent, the less likely the child will drop out of school--parental education alone could explain the results observed. Responses a. and c., administering a standardized achievement test to ninth-graders and collecting data on parental socioeconomic status, are good ideas; they would provide information on the plausibility of rival explanations that the children of "voucher" parents were higher achievers (and thus less likely to drop out of school) or that the "voucher" parents were richer and therefore more supportive of the educational pursuits of their children. Response d., recording the ages of school leavers, would be least helpful. Although those data might be interesting, they would not help to explain the differences in dropout rate observed for the two groups.

6.4 Response d. is the best answer. Just because the experimental treatment appeared to be successful for clients in general, it was not necessarily successful for older clients. The external generalizability of the study's results was thus limited to a client population that was heterogeneous in age. Response a. is not correct for the same reason that Response d. is the best. Although it is true that older adults generally have more health problems (and therefore require more medical care than do younger adults), preventive physical examinations might substantially reduce older clients' needs for medical services. Since the study did not provide information on the effects of the experimental treatment for clients at any specific age, we cannot rule out the possibility that it would be effective for older adults. Response b. is therefore irrelevant. Random selection of clients will increase support for the generalization of findings from an observed sample to the sampled population. However, it does not strengthen the generalization of results to clients in any specific age group. Random assignment of clients strengthens the internal validity, but not the external validity, of the study. Thus Response c. is not the best of the four.

Chapter 7

7.1 Response c. is correct; the correlation coefficient would be a population parameter, since it was the object of estimation.

7.2 Response d. is correct. The 1500 voters constituted a sample selected from the population of potential voters.

7.3 Response b. is correct. The percentages are computed on the basis of sample data, and are therefore sample statistics. They could also be termed estimates of the population percentages that would be found were all voters in the population to be polled.

7.4 Response a. is correct. A formula that is used to compute an estimate of a population parameter is called an estimator.

Chapter 8

8.1 Response b. is correct, because the 95% confidence interval is based on sample data. In fact, Response b. practically defines a 95% confidence interval. Response a. is not correct because, for a given randomly selected school system, the percentage of funding from state foundation programs is either between 43.2 and 67.8 (in which case the probability is 1.0) or it is not between those values (in which case the probability is zero). Responses c. and d. are not correct, because a confidence interval provides estimates of the value of a population parameter, not the true value of a parameter.

8.2 Response a. is correct, since 19.4 days is a sample statistic that provides a point estimate of the true population mean. Responses b., c., and d. are incorrect for a variety of reasons. The value 19.4 is not based on data from an entire population. Since 19.4 is a sample mean, it cannot be a lower confidence limit. Since the sample of classrooms was randomly selected, it is not the case that 19.4 has nothing to do with the true population mean; it is a good estimate.

8.3 a. This study is an example of inferential research. Undoubtedly, the meteorologists are interested in the relationship between sunspot activity and rainfall in future years, not just for the year that they sampled.
  b. The population would be all weeks--past, present, and future.
  c. The sample would be the 52 weeks in the year that was observed.
  d. The +0.42 is a sample statistic, based on a sample of 52 weeks.

8.4 Response d. is correct, and is self-explanatory. Responses a., b., and c. are incorrect for a variety of reasons. No sample data can predict the future with certainty. Even if the Yankees had won all games in the past, one could not be sure that the Dodgers wouldn't make a comeback. Confidence intervals cannot be used to specify probability values. Response c. is pure nonsense. Even if the upper confidence limit had been 1.00, the Dodgers would have some chance of winning in the future.

Chapter 9

9.1 Response a. is false for several reasons. First, because the data were not collected in a true experiment, one cannot form causal conclusions. Second, testing a null hypothesis at a significance level of 0.05 does not provide "95% certainty." Response b. is false because the reported value is the outcome of a hypothesis test, and cannot be used to infer the width of a confidence interval. Response c. is true because the null hypothesis of no difference in population means was rejected with an alpha level of 0.05. Response d. is true, and is self-explanatory.

9.2 a. The authors might be generalizing to a nationwide population of elementary schools, or perhaps to a statewide population of such schools.
  b. The authors are testing the null hypothesis that, in the specified population of elementary schools, the correlation between age of school building and dropout rate equals zero.
  c. The alternative hypothesis implied by the authors' statement is that, in the specified population of elementary schools, there is a correlation between age of school building and dropout rate that is different from zero.
  d. No, you cannot be certain that a correlation of +0.21 would be significant at the 0.05 level just because it is significant at the 0.10 level.

9.3 a. The alternative hypothesis in this study was that the percentage of moviegoers in the younger population was different from the percentage of moviegoers in the older population.

b. The null hypothesis would be rejected, because the test statistic fell into the critical region.

c. The test statistic was surely significant at the 0.05 level, because it was reported to be significant at the 0.01 level.

9.4 a. Null Hypothesis: For all students in the school system, the average motivation would be the same, regardless of which curriculum were to be used.

b. Alternative Hypothesis: The average motivation of students in the school system would be different, depending on which curriculum were to be used.

c. A Type I error would be committed if the null hypothesis of no difference in average motivation were to be rejected, even though both curricula were to produce the same average motivation.

d. A Type II error would be committed if the null hypothesis of no difference in average motivation were to be retained, even though one curriculum were to produce a higher average than the other.

Chapter 10

10.1 a. The null hypothesis was that the average sales produced by the population of radio advertising campaigns is equal to the average sales produced by the population of newspaper advertising campaigns.

b. The alternative hypothesis was that radio advertising campaigns and newspaper advertising campaigns are not equally effective, in terms of average sales produced.

c. The two asterisks attached to the t-statistic of 4.62 indicate, according to the footnote to the table, that the statistic was significant at an alpha level of 0.01. This means that the author tested a null hypothesis that the mean sales produced by radio advertising campaigns and newspaper advertising campaigns were equal, using a Type I error probability of 0.01, and that this null hypothesis was rejected.

10.2 A t-test for independent samples and a paired-difference t-test should be used with data collected in accordance with different research designs. The t-test for independent samples should be used when two statistically independent samples have been selected from a given population and then have been subjected, independently, to different treatments. It should also be used when independent samples have been selected from two different populations, and then have been subjected, independently, to the same or different treatments. The paired-difference t-test should be used when pairs of objects or persons have been randomly sampled from a single population, after which elements of the pairs have been subjected to two different treatments or have been measured independently. For example, the paired-difference t-test would be appropriate to test the null hypothesis that the mean IQ-test score of pairs of siblings is the same, even though the siblings have been raised in different environments.

Serious statistical errors can result when the paired-difference t-test is used inappropriately, when the t-test for independent samples should have been used instead. Likewise, use of the t-test for independent samples, when the paired-difference t-test should have been used, can result in serious statistical errors.

10.3 A nondirectional alternative hypothesis is usually of the form: A population parameter is *not equal* to a specified value. In contrast, a directional alternative hypothesis is usually of the form: A population parameter is *greater than* a specified value, or, a population parameter is *less than* a specified value. The distinction has implications for the mechanics of a hypothesis test. When a nondirectional alternative hypothesis is used (e.g., the population mean is not equal to 100), critical regions typically exist in both tails of the sampling distribution (e.g., reject the null hypothesis if the sample mean is either greater than 110 or less than 90). When a directional alternative hypothesis is used, a single critical region typically is defined in one tail of the sampling distribution (e.g., reject the null hypothesis if the sample mean is less than 95).

Chapter 11

11.1 a. The population to which the results of this study apply is presumably all adults in New York state. To support this generalization, it is necessary to assume that the 436 sampled adults were randomly sampled from all adults in New York state, and that some formal definition of an "adult" was used to determine who was and who was not a member of the population.

b. No, you cannot conclude on the basis of these data that additional formal education results in adults reading more books. This would be a causal interpretation, which cannot be supported solely on the basis of a correlation. It could be that adults complete more formal education and read more books because of some third variable that was not measured in the study.

c. A 95% confidence interval, computed using the same data, would have been wider than the 90% confidence interval reported in the study. If no additional data are collected, the effect of raising the level of confidence will always be to make the confidence interval wider.

d. Yes, the author could have used the same data to test the null hypothesis that years of formal schooling and number of books read per year were not correlated. The null hypothesis would have been that, in the population of adults in New York state, the correlation between years of formal schooling and number of books read per year equaled zero. Since the hypothesized value (zero) did not fall within the confidence interval, you can conclude that the null hypothesis would have been rejected at an alpha level of 0.10 (note that this alpha level is 1.0 minus the level of confidence of the confidence interval).

11.2 a. The authors were testing the null hypothesis that teacher salaries and average student reading achievement were uncorrelated in the population of elementary school classes (grades one through five) in North Carolina.

b. The authors retained their null hypothesis, since they reported that the correlation was "not significant at the 0.10 level." One can therefore infer that the null hypothesis was tested using an alpha level of 0.10, and that the test statistic did not fall into a critical region.

c. These results might generalize to the population of all elementary school classes in grades one through five in the state of North Carolina. Such generalization would be based on the assumption that the researchers selected their 120 classes randomly, from a list of all such classes in the state.

d. The critical assumption that would be necessary to generalize these results to a larger population is that the sample is representative of the population. This would require the use of some probability sampling procedure (such as simple random sampling) in selecting the 120 classrooms used in the study.

11.3 a. The null hypotheses to which the footnote with one asterisk refers are identical, except that one applies to a population of fourth-grade boys and the other applies to a population of fourth-grade girls. For each population, the null hypothesis states that the correlation between mathematics aptitude test score and mathematics achievement test score equals zero.

b. The null hypothesis to which the footnote with two asterisks refers is that, for a population of fourth-grade boys and a population of fourth-grade girls, the correlations between mathematics aptitude test score and mathematics achievement test score are equal to each other.

c. It is difficult to say, based on the information given in the problem, what population might be appropriate for generalization of these results. If it were the case that the 88 fourth-grade girls and 85 fourth-grade boys had been randomly sampled from lists of fourth-graders in a single school system, then generalization to the populations of fourth-graders in the school system would appear to be warranted. The appropriate populations for generalization depend on how the fourth-graders were sampled for this study.

11.4 a. The research question you define should certainly involve the degree of linear relationship between two variables. If you intend to use a Pearson correlation coefficient in examining your research question, the variables used in your study should be measurable at least at the interval level of measurement.

b. The population parameter that is central to your study should be a correlation coefficient. The population you identify should be defined very carefully, so that you can clearly identify who or what is a member of your population, and who or what is not a member.

c. The null hypothesis that is relevant to your study might state that a population correlation coefficient is equal to zero, or that two population correlation coefficients are equal to each other. In the first case, the alternative hypothesis would be that the population correlation coefficient is not equal to zero. In the second case, the alternative hypothesis would be that the two population correlation coefficients were not equal to each other.

d. If you were to reject the null hypothesis, in the first case (see answer to part c.), you would conclude that the variables being correlated did have some degree of linear relationship in the population from which you had sampled. In the second case, you would conclude that the variables being correlated did not have the same degree of linear relationship in the populations from which you had sampled.

Chapter 12

12.1 Jefferson and Jackson were testing the null hypothesis that, in the population of voters of 1842, the two variables, political party affiliation and position on extension of the Voting Rights Act of 1834, were statistically independent.

12.2 Jefferson and Jackson were attempting to generalize their results to the population of voters of 1842 who were declared or registered as Republicans, Democrats, or Independents.

12.3 If they acted in accordance with their findings, Jefferson and Jackson rejected their null hypothesis. This conclusion is supported by the footnote to their table, that indicates the statistical significance of the chi-square statistic of 93.0, using an alpha level of 0.05.

12.4 a. The authors were testing the null hypothesis that scores on their standardized attitude scale and academic major were statistically independent variables, for some populations of students with majors in sociology, psychology, education, and political science.

b. The authors reached the decision to retain their null hypothesis, since they reported that the chi-square statistic was "not significant at the 0.10 level." Apparently, 0.10 was the alpha level they used in testing their null hypothesis, and the chi-square statistic of 7.04 did not exceed the critical value associated with this alpha level.

c. Interpretation of the results of this study depends on the assumptions you are willing to make about how the authors sampled the 50 students of each major they used in the study. Another assumption that is critical concerns the validity of the standardized attitude scale the authors used. Unless the scale is a valid measure of attitude toward education, any conclusion about the authors' results, either for their sample or for some larger population, would be suspect.

Chapter 13

13.1 The authors were testing the null hypothesis that, for the population of students registering for beginning statistics courses at the major university, the mean score on the final examination would be the same, regardless of the method used to teach statistics. The null hypothesis is therefore that all three teaching methods examined in the study are equally effective. The alternative hypothesis is that the three methods of teaching statistics are not equally effective; at least two of the methods would result in different mean scores on the final examination, were each method to be used with the entire population of students.

13.2 The authors rejected the null hypothesis, since the reported F-statistic (5.67) was larger than the reported critical value of 3.13. Also, the F-statistic was reported to be "significant at the 0.05 level" in the footnote of the table.

13.3 This study suggests that method of teaching beginning statistics makes a difference, in terms of average performance on a statistics final examination, and that this conclusion applies to a population of beginning students in a major university. Whether the results of this study have implications beyond the university where the research was conducted depends on several factors, including the characteristics of the sampled students, the precise nature of the instructional methods used, and the composition of the final examination used to measure the dependent variable.

13.4 a. Your research questions should involve a comparison of three or more population averages.

b. The population parameters that are central to your research study should include three or more population averages.

c. Your null hypothesis should involve the equality of at least three population averages. Your alternative hypothesis should state that at least one pair of these population averages is different from each other.

d. If you were to reject the null hypothesis, you would have to conclude that at least one population had an average that was different from the average of at least one other population. Depending on the nature of your research, this conclusion might support the contention that at least one of a number of treatments was more effective than at least one other treatment.

Chapter 14

14.1 One null hypothesis was that the three methods of instruction were equally effective; that is, that the population of beginning statistics students would have the same average score on the final examination, regardless of the method used. Another null hypothesis was that populations of low-aptitude and high-aptitude students would have the same average score on the statistics final examination. The third null hypothesis was that there were no interaction effects between instructional method and student aptitude; that is, that the relative effectiveness of the three instructional methods was the same, regardless of student aptitude.

14.2 The researchers rejected all three null hypotheses, because all three F-statistics were described as being "significant" at either the 0.01 alpha level or the 0.05 alpha level (in the case of the interaction null hypothesis). The footnote to the table supports this conclusion.

14.3 Assuming that the results of this study generalize at least to the population of beginning statistics students at the major university, one can conclude that instructional method has an effect on performance on a statistics final examination, as does quantitative aptitude level. Furthermore, the relative effectiveness of the three methods of instruction examined in the study depends on the quantitative aptitude level of the students.

14.4 No, you cannot conclude that one of the instructional methods is more effective than the others for all students. Because the interaction effect was found to be significant, it might be the case that one instructional method is most effective for low-aptitude students, whereas another is most effective for high-aptitude students.

Chapter 15

15.1 a. The independent variable in this study was length of instruction per day or "engaged instructional time." The dependent variable was score on the Reading Comprehension subtest of the Iowa Tests of Basic Skills. The covariate was score on the verbal intelligence test administered at the beginning of the study.

b. The researchers were testing the null hypothesis that the population of third-graders would have the same average score on the Reading Comprehension sub-test of the Iowa Tests of Basic Skills, regardless of the length of instruction in reading each day.

c. By using the analysis of covariance instead of the analysis of variance, Harbinger and Spring were able to eliminate possible differences in the achievement of the three samples attributable solely to differences in their average verbal intelligence at the beginning of the study. The researchers were thus able to eliminate one potentially contaminating variable from their study, and gain statistical precision in their investigation of the effects of length of instruction on reading achievement.

15.2 a. Mother's education contributes most to the prediction of sixth-grade arithmetic achievement. This assertion is supported by two facts. First, mother's education was entered first in the stepwise multiple regression analysis. Second, the correlation of mother's education with the dependent variable is higher than the correlation of any other predictor with the dependent variable.

b. Twenty-nine percent of the variance of arithmetic achievement is predicted by the four independent variables. This assertion is supported by the "R-squared" value of .29 noted in the last line of the table. When .29 is multiplied by 100 to yield a percentage, the result is 29%.

c. The null hypotheses the authors tested when they reported that their F-statistics were "significant at the 0.05 level" were all similar. At each step of the regression analysis, the authors were testing the null hypothesis that the variables when used as predictors (the independent variables in the regression equation) did not contribute to the prediction of arithmetic achievement. Statistically, they were testing the null hypothesis that the coefficient of determination (R-squared) was equal to zero at each step of the analysis.

15.3 In a factor analysis, a report that "three factors accounted for 76% of the variance of the 10 items" means that the three underlying variables (called factors) do a relatively good job of representing the relationships among 10 original variables (items). Just over three fourths of the variation among scores on the 10 items is explainable by variation among scores on the three underlying factors. It must therefore be the case that the 10 items cluster together, to a considerable degree, around three factors.

Index

About the Author

RICHARD M. JAEGER (B.A., Mathematics, 1962, Pepperdine College; M.S., Mathematical Statistics, 1964, Stanford University; Ph.D., Educational Research Methodology, 1970, Stanford University) is Professor of Educational Research Methodology and Director of the Center for Educational Research and Evaluation at the University of North Carolina, Greensboro. He is a Past President of the National Council on Measurement in Education and of the North Carolina and the Florida Educational Research Associations. He is former Editor of the *Journal of Educational Measurement (JEM)*, and serves on the editorial boards of *JEM, Applied Measurement in Education, Quantitative Applications in the Social Sciences*, and as Series Editor of *Measurement Methods for the Social Sciences*. His books include *Sampling in Education and the Social Sciences* (Longman, 1984), *Statistics: A Spectator Sport* (Sage, 1983), and (with Carol Kehr Tittle) *Minimum Competency Achievement Testing* (McCutchan, 1980). He has served as Chair of the American Educational Research Association Committee on Professional Development and Research Training, is Editor of *Complementary Methods for Research in Education* (AERA, 1988), and was a member of the Editorial Board of the *Educational Researcher*. He has authored over 100 journal articles, book chapters, and research reports, principally on topics related to educational measurement.

Dr. Jaeger was Chair of the Defense Advisory Committee on Military Personnel Testing and was a member of the National Academy of Sciences Committee on the General Aptitude Test Battery. He has served as a consultant to the United States Geological Survey, U.S. Departments of Education, Agriculture, and Defense, the Law School Admissions Council, the Association of American Medical Colleges, and numerous colleges, universities, and state government agencies. He specializes in educational measurement and applied statistics.